Spirits in Rebellion

The Rise and Development of New Thought

By Charles S. Braden

RELIGIOUS ASPECTS OF THE CONQUEST OF MEXICO

MODERN TENDENCIES IN WORLD RELIGIONS

VARIETIES OF AMERICAN RELIGION, *Editor*

PROCESSION OF THE GODS, *with Gaius G. Atkins*

THE WORLD'S RELIGIONS

MAN'S QUEST FOR SALVATION

THESE ALSO BELIEVE

THE SCRIPTURES OF MANKIND

WAR, COMMUNISM AND WORLD RELIGIONS

JESUS COMPARED

CHRISTIAN SCIENCE TODAY

Spirits in Rebellion

The Rise and Development of New Thought

Charles S. Braden

SOUTHERN METHODIST UNIVERSITY PRESS • DALLAS

*Published with the assistance of a grant
from the Ford Foundation
under its program for the support of publication
in the humanities and social sciences*

Library of Congress Cataloguing-in-Publication Data

Braden, Charles Samuel, 1887-1970
    Spirits in rebellion; the rise and development of new thought.
Dallas, Southern Methodist University Press, 1963.

    571 p. 23 cm.

    Includes bibliography.

    1. New Thought—Hist. 2. International New Thought Alliance.
I. Title.

BF639.B576   289.9   63-13245
ISBN 0-87074-025-3

To

The memory of my son

GEORGE WILLIAM BRADEN

1914-1963

Preface

WRITING ABOUT the rise and development of any of the minority religious groups is not an easy task. Concerning their basic ideas and practices there is not so much difficulty, but when one seeks to go back and discover their beginnings and the stages through which they have evolved, it is another story.

In general the libraries have paid little attention to them. Many libraries will not even accept their publications as gifts. And, if they do, they frequently discard them as required by the limitations of shelf-room for what they regard as more important books. This is especially true with respect to periodicals. One must travel far and consult many of the great libraries to find even the more outstanding sources necessary to a comprehensive study. This is time-consuming, expensive, and at times frustrating.

Nor, in general, have the various movements themselves been history-conscious. The Mormons are a notable exception, and Unity has also developed something in the nature of a small research library, dealing chiefly with Unity itself, but to some extent also with other related movements.

Oddly enough even theological libraries have not been interested in such movements, and have only scattered items bearing on one or another of them. For years the writer has sought to interest some seminary library in specializing in this field—if not in all such movements, then in one or more selected ones. At the same time he has urged some of the minority groups to make a definite effort to preserve materials which are of historic interest, if not today, then certainly tomorrow: for the story of these groups is genuine religious Americana—most of them were born on American soil and are the expression of the American mind and spirit at some level.

Happily, Bridwell Library of Southern Methodist University's Perkins School of Theology has now agreed to develop special collections of material on movements of this sort. Already it has received as a gift one of the finest and most nearly complete collections of Christian Science material in America. The International New Thought Alliance (INTA) voted in 1960 to deposit its older archives at Bridwell, and to provide eventually an entire file of its important magazine, as well as to encourage its leaders to furnish copies of their books as they appear. Bridwell will welcome correspondence with anyone having relevant historical materials—books, pamphlets, periodicals, manuscripts, letters— which he is willing to place in the library.

Religious Science has contributed a long, if not complete, run of its periodical *Science in Mind,* as well as books written by its founder and by some of its most outstanding leaders. Unity has provided copies of most of its publications. Brother Mandus of England, founder of the World Healing Crusade, has sent most of his publications; the Society for the Spread of the Knowledge of True Prayer (SSKTP), founded by Frank L. Rawson, has contributed an almost entire run of its magazine *Active Service,* besides some of its books; Nicol Campbell of South Africa has sent his books and some issues of his magazine. All these materials and more already in hand and surely to be contributed will be available to accredited scholars interested in the field. The Pacific School of Religion Library at Berkeley, California, has also become interested in this area.

The writer desires to express his sincere gratitude to many librarians from Boston to Berkeley, from Chicago to Dallas, who have been helpful in one way or another in his quest for material. To the leaders of the various New Thought movements who have given freely of their time and interest he is greatly indebted. Particularly is he in debt to Dr. Robert H. Bitzer, president for many years of INTA, and his staff for many hours of counsel, as well as access to both the earlier and later files of the overall organization of New Thought. To Dr. Raymond Charles Barker, who for more than ten years had urged the author to make this study, and has kept up a steady stream of correspondence and fed into the New Thought Collection at Bridwell materials new and old, especial indebtedness is gladly acknowledged. Other New Thought leaders too numerous to mention by name have been most generous in their help given through personal conference or correspondence.

The author is grateful to all the publishers and individual owners of copyright who have so generously given permission to quote the passage or passages from the books or articles named in each case where used. They include: Abingdon Press, New York-Nashville; Bobbs-Merrill Co., Inc., Indianapolis; Dodd, Mead and Co., New York; Mrs. Harry Gaze; Harper and Row, Publishers, New York; Macalester Publishing Co., St. Paul, Minn.; Little, Brown and Co., Boston; Macmillan Co., New York; Dr. Virgil Markham, owner of certain poems of his father, Edwin Markham; the *New England Quarterly*, Brunswick, Maine; Prentice-Hall, Inc., Englewood Cliffs, New Jersey; Dr. Robert Russell, Denver, Episcopal Church of the Epiphany.

And to authors of other books and articles, either not copyrighted, or otherwise now in the public domain, he also expresses his appreciation (many of the books in the field were privately published and never copyrighted).

And finally, to the American Council of Learned Societies which provided a grant to help defray the considerable expense of travel in the quest for materials, without which the completion of the book would have been impossible, the author expresses his thanks.

It is his sincere hope that this study of a great movement will be a welcome help to followers of one or another of the various branches of the movement in seeing themselves as a part of a movement greater than their own particular branch of it. And to those who stand outside the movement, may it serve as an aid to the understanding of a vital phase of religion that while differing from the usual orthodox expressions in many ways, nevertheless represents essential insights and practices which, once present in historic Christianity, have largely fallen into disuse.

CHARLES S. BRADEN

Dallas, Texas
May 15, 1963

Contents

Spirits in Rebellion

The Rise and Development of New Thought

Introduction

NINETEENTH-CENTURY AMERICA was notable for many things. It saw the original thirteen colonies along the Atlantic seaboard expand into a continent-wide nation, the frontier pushing steadily westward to the Pacific; and just at the turn of the century the nation reached out into the Pacific to claim as its own, in trust at least, the far distant Philippine Islands, and was on the way to becoming a world power.

It was a century of industrial expansion, the exploitation of the vast resources of timber, minerals, and oil, as well as agricultural and other riches. Great cities grew up, bringing with their rapid growth its inevitable problems. Churches followed wherever the frontiersmen went, and schools and colleges came soon after. The freedom and challenge of the frontier days, along with what some have called the peculiar "bumptiousness" of young growing America, gave rise to a great variety of new social experiments, and naturally enough to new forms of religion.

Few periods in world history have been more prolific in the production of new sects, breaking away from the established denominations, adding some new element to distinguish them from the old, or centering pre-eminent emphasis on some one or other element of their religious heritage; or what is of greater significance, creating peculiarly new forms of genuine American religious faith. Many of these were of only passing importance, never became widely held, and finally disappeared; but several of them became national and finally international in character, and have been spread widely over the world.

3

Where else in the world could a poorly educated farm boy from upper New York announce himself as a prophet of God, produce a scripture, create a new faith, and attract a following from all over America and Europe which, after his death, would found a veritable theocratic empire in the western desert, and finally make itself at home in every state in the union, with missionaries all over the world, carrying the Mormon faith to men everywhere?

Where else in the world could concern for communication with the departed become a popular religion? Psychic experiences have occurred among people of every race, but it was in America that Spiritualism arose as a distinctive religious faith.

Oriental thought, finally brought to the West, reached America and made a significant impact, as it had in western Europe; but it was in America that it became blended with Western thought and Christian idealism, mixed with at least an initial interest in Spiritualism, and finally became the Theosophical Society, ostensibly a philosophy, but certainly, for many persons, effectively a religious faith.

And it was in America where first a definitely religious faith developed around the healing of disease. Healings had occurred in Europe without benefit of physical medicine. Mesmerism had developed as a therapeutic method; but it was in America that it was invested with religious significance and gave rise to a complex of religious faiths varying from one another in significant ways, but all agreeing upon the central fact that healing and for that matter every good thing is possible through a right relationship with the ultimate power in the Universe, Creative Mind—called God, Principle, Life, Wisdom, and a dozen other names by one group or another—since man in his real nature is essentially divine.

This broad complex of religions is sometimes described by the rather general term "metaphysical," because its major reliance is not on the physical, but on that which is beyond the physical.

It was the Portland healer, P. P. Quimby, who seems to have started it all, around the middle of the nineteenth century. It was a woman, Mary Baker Eddy, who, healed of a serious ailment by Quimby, first made a religion of it, produced a scripture, *Science and Health,* and is regarded by her followers as the final revelator of Truth. Where but in America could such a movement have arisen?

The general movement has proliferated in many directions. Two main streams seem most vigorous: one is called Christian Science; the other, which no single name adequately describes, has come rather generally to be known as New Thought.

Just what is this New Thought?

PART I

The Nature and Sources of New Thought

PART I

The Nature and Sources of New Thought

1

What Is New Thought?

FEW TERMS can be defined adequately in only a few words or sentences, because they mean something different to different people at different times. Especially is this true of terms employed to represent historic movements that have been in existence long enough to have undergone considerable development either in thought content or in organization. Such a term is *New Thought*, one loosely used to cover a wide range of philosophical, theological, psychological, and practical approaches to God, to the world, to life and its problems, that had its development within the last hundred years, chiefly in America, though under one name or another it has extended itself over much of the Western world.

A concise definition is the statement of purpose adopted by one of the earliest recognizably New Thought groups, the Metaphysical Club of Boston, founded in 1895: "To promote interest in and the practice of a true philosophy of life and happiness; to show that through right thinking, one's loftiest ideals may be brought into present realization; and to advance intelligent and systematic treatment of disease by spiritual and mental methods."

Somewhat later, this same club issued a rather careful statement of the meaning of the metaphysical movement which came to be called New Thought, characterizing in detail its main features. (The numbers employed here were no part of the original statement, but were inserted by the writer to facilitate comparison later in this chapter with certain Christian Science parallels.)

(1) First and most important, the belief that "ideals are

realities and that all primary causes are internal forces. [2] Mind is primary, and causative, while matter is secondary and result-ant." (3) "The children of men are living souls now, Children of God . . . Spiritual citizens of a divine universe." (4) As a method of healing bodily disease, and as a cure for social ills and a philosophy of life, "it stands squarely on the belief that the remedy for all defect and disorder is metaphysical, beyond the physical, in the realm of causes which are mental and spiritual. . . . It neither denies sickness nor pain . . . but holds that they are not positive realities . . . rather negative conditions, the lack of ease, of harmony, of health."

(5) As a philosophy of life,

it takes for its fundamental reality the idea of God as immanent, indwelling Spirit, All-wisdom, All-goodness, ever-present in the uni-verse as a warm and tender Father, and not as a cold abstraction. . . . [6] Evil then can have no place in the world of permanent reality and power. It is not denied that it exists now, but only as an accompani-ment of incompleteness . . . a negative quantity, the absence of good. . . . Sin, and moral evil are largely an ignorant selfishness, ignorant of an Almighty Love under whose divine providence all things work together for good to those who obey its law.

(7) It believes in a divine humanity, a "human brotherhood with a divine Fatherhood." (8) It is profoundly religious, it is non-sectarian. "It teaches the universality of religion." (9) It believes in present and progressive revelation of truth, but rev-erently acknowledges our debt to the prophets of God in all ages; especially in the Christian scriptures are found "clear and com-prehensive statements of the truth that has power to bless, to liberate and to heal." . . . (10) "It would proclaim to man his freedom from the necessity of belief in disease, poverty and all evil as a part of God's plan."

(11) Without a formal creed,

[12] it stands for the practice of the presence of God, reduced to a scientific method, of living a selfless life through union with a power that is Love in action; . . . [13] a power which can bring sweetness and

light and peace to people; [14] rob death of its sting, and pain of its poignancy; [15] takes the terror out of disease . . . and [16] crowns life with the joy and health and abundance which are the rightful inheritance of every child of God. (Horatio W. Dresser, *Spirit of New Thought*, pp. 215-24, *passim*)

Charles Brodie Patterson, one of the truly great early leaders of New Thought, editor of *Mind* and of the widely circulated *Library of Health*, discusses these same points in his book, *What Is New Thought?*

The religion and philosophy of New Thought, he says, "has for its foundation Eternal Law." It rests on "the Oneness of Life-God-Universal Life-Love-Intelligence in all, through all and above all." As opposed to the "old thought," New Thought insists that "the truth regarding life and its laws is to be found in man's inner consciousness rather than in the study of phenomena." "Man's real search is the discovery of his own soul," for there God lives and moves and breathes, even though man may be unconscious of it. We know God or ourselves as we are directed by Love and Wisdom in all our ways, for such knowledge causes us to yield personal will and to desire to live consciously in the universal life. It teaches that evil, as understood generally, has no place in the plan of God. It holds that fear is the root of all so-called evil, all sin, sorrow, disease, and death having their origin in it. But perfect love casteth out fear. It teaches that we have the God-given right to be perfect even as our Father in Heaven is perfect.

New Thought is neither church, cult, nor sect; it asks no allegiance to creeds, forms, or personality, and is quite nonracial. It stands for Universal Brotherhood, teaches that the Son of Man has power to forgive sins, including the healing of the sick; that health, happiness, and success are the birthright of every child of God. There is no future punishment. The individual rewards and punishes himself as he conforms to or opposes the Eternal Law of life. New Thought believes that the great need is not so much a theoretical Christianity as an applied one; that living the Christ life does not so much imply uniformity of creed or form, as being activated by the same inward Spirit, demonstrated by loving helpfulness to one's fellows.

It holds that all religions and all peoples are at different stages of growth. It makes war on none, but recognizes the right of individuals and groups to work out their faith according to their stage of development. Every man has a right to live his own life in accordance with the highest dictates of his own conscience, for where truth is there must be freedom.

A succinct statement of the central features of New Thought was given in the first Constitution and By-laws of the International New Thought Alliance, as the purpose of the Alliance, which represents broadly the whole range of New Thought. Its purpose was: "To teach the Infinitude of the Supreme One; the Divinity of man and his infinite possibilities through the creative power of constructive thinking and obedience to the voice of the indwelling Presence, which is our source of Inspiration, Power, Health and Prosperity."

An article published in the INTA *Bulletin* of December 15, 1916, attempts to answer the question, "What is New Thought?" First, as to what it is not: it is not a name of any fixed system of thought, philosophy, or religion, for when molded into a system, it ceases to be *New* thought. But some things can be said of it. "It practices in the twentieth century what Jesus taught in the first." He taught healing; "it practices healing." He said, "Judge not"; it sees the good in others. He said, "take no anxious thought for to-morrow"; it "practices divine supply." He taught love and brotherhood; "it is demonstrating unity and cooperation." "The New Thought is the Christ thought made new by being applied and proved in every day affairs." New Thought is positive, constructive, a philosophy of optimism, "the recognition, realization and manifestation of God in Man."

A pamphlet published by a prominent New Thought minister, Elmer Gifford, under the title, *New Thought Defined* (Pasadena, n.d.) may be taken as fairly representative of what its contemporary exponents consider its nature to be. It is, he writes, "a theory and a method of mental life with special reference to

healing and the quickening attitudes and mood which make for
the improvement of conditions generally." But it is more than a
theory and a method, it is a "life," for "it has literally meant life
to millions of people." It stands squarely, he asserts, on the faith
that

the correction of all defect and disorder is metaphysical and spiritual,
boldly claims that we are spiritual beings and that we car̄e forth from
God sound and whole. . . . It does not deny the body but would honor
and glorify it as the instrument of an immortal spirit. . . . It in no way
regiments the thinking of its adherents nor prescribes what they shall
or not read or study. It stands for the principle of liberal tolerant
worship.

The term New Thought is used to convey the idea of an ever-
growing thought . . . man is an expanding idea in the Mind of God,
and is held forever in the Mind of God, functioning under and operating through the law of Mind in Action.

New Thought as now taught is the creation of a perpetually advancing mind. It is not satisfied with any system originating in
other ages, because systems do not grow, while Mind does. Mind
is always expanding and reaching out for a better definition of
itself. "As Mind advances, the old forms die, because they no
longer serve or satisfy men's needs. . . . New Thought can never
therefore be a finished product and if it remains truly New
Thought, it will never be completed enough to creedalize it. . . ."
Change is the changeless law of the universe. Indeed change and
growth are the "silent mandates of Divinity . . . thought can never
be final and still remain thought." New Thought, he says, "we
think of as a science because Science is demonstrable and the
knowledge of Truth is demonstrable. New Thought is definitely
committed to finding and revealing the good and the beautiful in
life. It is dedicated to the development of latent possibilities in
man." New Thought is constructive, never destructive; "it teaches
men to live not to die. . . . The adherents of New Thought worship
God Omnipotent in whom 'we live and move and have our
being,' " and of which we are perfect individualizations. Our God
is not an absentee God, but "a Universal Mind and Spirit that

permeates all nature and finds its highest expression through and as the mind of man," revealing himself to man continually "through the reasoning mind and the whispering inward voice of intuition. We teach men the unity of themselves and God, so that in the exaltation of their own spirit they may say as the Master, 'I and my Father are one.'"

Elsewhere, in the sections on the various groups which are or have been a part of the International New Thought Alliance (hereafter written INTA), it will be seen how similar they are, while differing at points both in belief and practice. Christian Science has chosen to dissociate itself rather sharply from the New Thought Movement, and to claim a unique revelation of truth given to it through the Founder, Mrs. Eddy. But in order to see how close Christian Science is to New Thought, it will suffice to quote a few statements taken from *Science and Health* or Mrs. Eddy's other writings paralleling statements given in summary of the nature of New Thought. This is not of course to argue that New Thought and Christian Science are identical, for they differ significantly at a number of points; but only to show that they are both facets of the same general thought movement, sometimes described as the Metaphysical Movement.

Here then are certain statements taken from the Boston Metaphysical Club's summary of New Thought in parallel with others taken from the writings of Mrs. Eddy, with an occasional word of comment:

NEW THOUGHT	CHRISTIAN SCIENCE
	The references here are to page and line of *Science and Health* and Mrs. Eddy's *Miscellany, Miscellaneous Writings, Retrospection and Introspection,* and *No and Yes.*
1. All primary causes are internal forces.	"... divine Science declares that they [forces] belong wholly to divine Mind, are inherent in this Mind ..." (*S&H*, 124:28-30)

NEW THOUGHT	CHRISTIAN SCIENCE
2. Mind is primary and causative.	"From the infinite elements of the one Mind emanate all form, color, quality, and quantity, and these are mental, both primarily and secondarily." (*S&H*, 512:21-24)
3. Man is a living soul now, a child of God, a spiritual citizen in a divine universe.	"The universe of Spirit is peopled with spiritual beings, and its government is divine Science." *S&H*, 264:32-265:1. Man is the "blessed child of God." (*S&H*, 573:18)
4. The remedy for all defect and all disorder is metaphysical, beyond the physical, in the realm of causes which are mental and spiritual.	"The Christian Scientist, understanding scientifically that all is Mind, commences with mental causation, the truth of being, to destroy the error." (*S&H*, 423:8-10)
5. God is immanent, indwelling Spirit, All-Wisdom, All-Goodness, ever-present in the universe.	"The only logical conclusion is that all is Mind and its manifestation, from the rolling of worlds, in the most subtle ether, to a potato-patch." (*MW*, 26) "God is . . . Spirit. . . ." (*S&H*, 465:9-10) "The attributes of God are justice, mercy, wisdom, goodness, and so on." (*S&H*, 465:14-15) "1. God is All-in-all. 2. God is good. Good is Mind." (*S&H*, 113:16-17)
6. Therefore evil can have no place in the world as a permanent reality; it is the absence of good.	". . . evil has in reality neither place nor power in the human or the divine economy." (*S&H*, 327:20-21) "It is unreal, because it presupposes the absence of God . . ." (*S&H*, 186:12-14)
7. It believes in a divine human-	"One infinite God, good, unifies

NEW THOUGHT

ity, a human brotherhood, and a divine Fatherhood.

men and nations; constitutes the brotherhood of man . . ." (S&H, 340:23-24) "In Science we are children of God . . ." (S&H, 572: 8-9) "The divinity of the Christ was made manifest in the humanity of Jesus." (S&H, 25:31-32).

8. It is profoundly religious.

"This Science is the essence of religion . . ." (My., 178)

9. It believes in present and progressive revelation.

(This is the greatest point of difference between the two groups. Accepting Mrs. Eddy as final Revelator is the first requisite of Christian Scientists today, the thought and statements of her followers being strictly limited to her private vocabulary.)

"Truth cannot be stereotyped; it unfoldeth forever." (No, 45) But Mrs. Eddy's writings show that she increasingly regarded her doctrine as a terminal revelation of all Truth. ". . . this final revelation of the absolute divine Principle of scientific mental healing." (S&H, 107:5-6) "Christian Science is absolute; it is neither behind the point of perfection nor advancing towards it; it is at this point and must be practised therefrom." (My., 242)

10. It would proclaim to man his freedom from the necessity of belief in disease, poverty, and all evil as a part of God's plan.

"Through discernment of the spiritual . . . , man will . . . find himself unfallen, upright, pure, and free . . ." (S&H, 171:4-8, passim) "To fear them [sickness and death] is impossible, when you fully apprehend God and know that they are no part of His creation." (S&H, 231:27-29) ". . . can Life, or God, dwell in evil and create it?" (S&H, 357:30-31)

11. Without a formal creed.
(This ideal has been largely

Mrs. Eddy declared hers "a church to commemorate the words

NEW THOUGHT	CHRISTIAN SCIENCE
realized in New Thought, though a tendency may be noted in some groups toward a type of orthodoxy of belief and practice.)	and works of our Master, a Mind-healing church, without a creed, to be called the Church of Christ, Scientist, the first such church ever organized" (*Ret.* 44), asserting that "practical manifestations of Christianity constitute the only evangelism, and they need no creed." (*Ret.* 65) However, there is a set of twelve Tenets, printed in the *Church Manual*, which every member of the Mother Church must accept in writing, and the teachings of Mrs. Eddy are asserted with a dogmatic rigidity the equal of that found in most Fundamentalist orthodox churches.
12. It stands for the practice of the presence of God reduced to a scientific method; of living a selfless life through union in thought with a power that is Love in action.	"Christian Science is demonstrable." (*S&H*, 112:4) ... "demonstration is Immanuel, or *God with us* ..." (*S&H*, 34:7-8) "Where the spirit of God is, and there is no place where God is not, evil becomes nothing ..." (*S&H* 480:2-4) "... let us labor to dissolve with the universal solvent of Love the adamant of error, —self-will, self-justification, and self-love,—which wars against spirituality and is the law of sin and death." (*S&H*, 242:16-20)
13. Bringing sweetness and light and peace to people:	"Teach ... that they find health, peace, and harmony in God, divine Love." (*S&H*, 416:32-417:2)
14. Robs death of its sting, though not specifically denying its reality;	"The forever fact remains paramount that Life, Truth, and Love save from sin, disease, and death

NEW THOUGHT

CHRISTIAN SCIENCE

... 'Death is swallowed up in victory.' " (S&H, 164:23-29, *passim*)

15. takes the terror out of disease;

"The only reality of sin, sickness, or death is the awful fact that unrealities seem real to human, erring belief, until God strips off their disguise." (S&H, 472:27-29)

16. crowns life with the joy and health and abundance that are the rightful inheritance of every child of God.

"Divine Love blesses its own ideas, and causes them to multiply,—to manifest His power. Man is not made to till the soil. His birthright is dominion, not subjection. He is lord of the belief in earth and heaven,—himself subordinate alone to his Maker." (S&H, 517:30-518:4) "... to all mankind and in every hour, divine Love supplies all good." (S&H, 494:13-14)

But if there are similarities there are also very real differences.

I once asked a man who was for years a well-known Christian Science leader, though he has since withdrawn from the Christian Science organization, what he thought of as the differences between New Thought and Christian Science.

There are three, said he, which are clear and unmistakable: (1) The authoritarianism which has grown out of Christian Scientists' conviction that Mrs. Eddy's teachings constitute a final revelation has been no part of New Thought and its outlook. Truth continues to reveal itself, nor has any human organization the authority to declare what the Truth is. (2) Negativism has always dominated and still does dominate the Christian Science Movement. Mrs. Gestefeld, once an ardent follower of Mrs. Eddy, could charge that "Christian Scientists are the most fear ridden people on earth." *(Jesuitism in Christian Science)* On the other hand, the New Thought groups have "accentuated the positive," and enjoyed a pervadingly intuitive optimism impossible to the Christian Scientist, preoccupied as he obviously is with mortal mind's Malicious Animal Magnetism (M.A.M.). (3) Christian Science is utterly opposed to materia medica. Most New Thought followers take no such absolute position in regard to co-operation with doctors in the treatment of disease, though obviously preferring nonmedical means. Most will say, with some unorthodox Christian Scientists, that they see no fundamental reason why effective co-operation may not occur without sacrifice of principle.

A corollary of these, he adds, is that New Thought groups are therefore likely to be less dogmatic, more tolerant, and more open to the progressive development of their thought.

In all this it should probably be indicated that there are various levels of thought and practice within both New Thought and Christian Science—even in the writings of Mrs. Eddy herself. Some Christian Scientists are less dogmatic than others and tend in the direction of New Thought, while some New Thought followers approach much more closely to Christian Science than others.

But perhaps in general, the Christian Scientist who made the distinctions above noted was right in indicating that a predominant emphasis in New Thought in general is on the creative power of thought. You visualize what you desire and bring it into manifestation. There is in some sayings of Mrs. Eddy support for such a view. She once made the remark that sufficiently intense thought could produce anything from a rose to a cancer. But, he avers, this was but a passing assertion buried in a mass of contrary material. While the emphasis of New Thought, he says, is on creative thinking, in Christian Science it is on "ascertaining the already established truth of reality, or the perceiving, realizing or demonstrating of what is already true, however obscured by belief," an assertion with which some leading New Thought writers would readily agree. The differences in this area are not so clearly and sharply distinguishable as in those noted above.

Christian Science, with its acceptance of Mary Baker Eddy

as more than a mere teacher, healer, or organizer, though she
was all of these, but rather as revelator of Divine Truth, early
developed under her guidance and close personal direction a
tight centrally controlled institutional form quite different from
that of the more centrifugally inclined New Thought Movement.
Although, along with New Thought, Christian Science has generally, at least in theory, exalted Principle above personality—and
solid support for this can be found in Mrs. Eddy's own writings—
actually, in Christian Science Mrs. Eddy has provided a personal
center around which loyalties could develop and have developed
to a degree which has caused many outside the movement to
declare that she has been deified (a charge categorically denied
officially by the Christian Science church).

But it was she who produced by inspiration the textbook of
Christian Science, *Science and Health*. It was she who dictated
the form of organization the movement assumed. It was she who
by directives handed down from time to time as need arose, and
adopted by the growing organization, provided the *Church
Manual* under which the church today operates, and which by
specific declaration of the Founder can never be amended, since
there is written into it the declaration that only with her written
approval can this be done; and now of course her hand has been
stilled by death. And the Board of Directors, first named and then
their powers fixed by her directives, can operate only within the
framework of this book of discipline, regarded, just as *Science
and Health* is, as a divinely inspired book.

All this was lacking in New Thought. To be sure, P. P. Quimby
was regarded as the founder of the movement, but there was no
sense of personal attachment to him or to Warren F. Evans or the
Dressers that was in any way comparable to that of Christian
Scientists toward Mrs. Eddy. Of New Thought it could be said
that it was like the famous general who mounted his horse
and rode off in all directions. Not even after well over a half-
century has it been able to effect more than a rather loose
International Alliance to which the loyalties of many are but
weak and sometimes shifting.

As a result of Mrs. Eddy's attempt at complete control of her movement and of its ideas, some very able persons were alienated, and in the case of a few, such as Mrs. Emma Curtis Hopkins and Ursula Gestefeld, they became outstanding leaders in the development of New Thought. But this happened oftener in the earlier than the later years. A few have attempted to set up rival organizations, but none have achieved permanence. Annie Bill organized the only one that had any considerable degree of success, and it has not survived in any recognizable form. A loosely organized group of persons who followed John Doorly, a leading English Christian Science leader, who was expelled from the church because of alleged deviation from the official interpretation of Christian Science, carry on in England chiefly the healing and teaching of Christian Science as he taught it and they think of it. They maintain a publishing house, the Foundational Book Company, for the printing and circulation of Mr. Doorly's writings and their own, but they regard themselves still as quite definitely Christian Scientists. And there are other similar groups in Switzerland and Germany, as well as in America.

In America, the Great Litigation of 1919-21 settled for all time the legality of the control of the Mother Church by the Board of Directors and forced a number of able leaders either to resign or be expelled from the Church. Herbert Eustace, who led the opposition and forced the matter into the courts for settlement, never ceased to practice and to teach Christian Science after being excommunicated by the church, and he had a considerable following. One of his books bore the title, *Christian Science; its Clear, Correct Teaching*. But his work was never organized as other than the Herbert Eustace Association, just as in the case of most teachers. There has been a general reluctance on the part of those who have been expelled or have withdrawn from the church to effect any kind of organization. The general distrust of organization, expressed in Studdert-Kennedy's *Christian Science and Organized Religion,* is clearly seen and illustrated in the case of Arthur B. Corey, who has probably a larger following than any other Christian Science leader outside the church.

Mr. Corey was a very successful practitioner in Chicago and First Reader in one of the larger churches in that city. Class-taught by Bicknell Young, he was an intensive student of Edward Kimball and other prominent teachers of Christian Science through possession of an unparalleled collection of full transcriptions of their Primary and Normal Class teachings. Thus, though he had never himself taken the Normal Class Instruction, which is little more than a repetition of what has already been given in the Primary class, he was thoroughly familiar with the content of instruction in it as given by some of the greatest of the teachers. It serves mainly the purpose of certification of those who can be chosen as members of the very limited class given to only thirty persons once every three years, by the Christian Science authorities. It is thus a part of the very system to which Mr. Corey had come to object. During the six years when he was listed in the *Christian Science Journal* registry he had become convinced that if Christian Science were indeed a science and "the Truth which shall make men free," it belonged to all mankind and should not be limited in its access to the people through the closed system of Class Instruction imposed by the church.

To bring the inner teachings out into the light for public scrutiny, he eventually wrote a book, *Christian Science Class Instruction*, resigning from the church with its publication in 1945. Since that time his treatise has gone into some twenty printings, is circulated in the thousands today all over the world, and is studied by many Christian Scientist and New Thought leaders. Not only did he publish this book, but he proceeded to teach frequent and very large classes not limited to the thirty pupils annually allowed each church-franchised teacher, and he continued in the general practice of Christian Science for another dozen years. In 1957 he withdrew his name from all public listings as practitioner, in order to devote fuller attention to writing and to the worldwide promotion of interest in and exploration of genuinely scientific disciplines in the approach to God.

Mr. Corey became immensely popular and was besought to set up an organization. This he has steadfastly refused to do, because of the basic conviction that organization involves containment and control incompatible with any genuinely scientific thought. He has declined to align himself with any group. Ernest Holmes, founder of Religious Science, at one time sent representatives to talk with Arthur Corey and later came himself to confer with Mr. Corey, with the apparent view of bringing him into leadership in Religious Science. But to no avail.

A person of deeply inquiring mind, Mr. Corey feels that he is finished with "organization," and he goes his independent way. He heads the nonprofit Farallon Foundation at Los Gatos, California, a federally recognized religious-educational facility which publishes the Corey writings, as well as the above mentioned *Christian Science and Organized Religion* by Studdert-Kennedy and the works of a number of other authors. He is a deeply committed Christian Scientist who believes that *Christian* science is truly a science and therefore not to be taught as fixed dogma, but allowed to progress and disseminate itself like mathematics, independently of institutional sponsorship. He has tried to bring it to the man in the street in his *Personal Introduction to God,* and maintains a worldwide association with persons who read his works and seek his counsel.

Joel Goldsmith is another who was once a Christian Scientist, but is no longer within the church. Some have thought of him as a "New Thoughter," and it is true that his books are found everywhere on the book tables of New Thought groups and he lectures sometimes for New Thought groups—or if he is not lecturing under their direct auspices, he draws New Thought followers to his talks in considerable numbers. His movement, which is little if anything more than a personal following, he calls the Infinite Way. His ideas seem to be in thorough agreement in most essentials with Christian Science, yet he is independent. Whether his movement will take a more definite organized form it is too early to say.

In contrast to highly organized and institutionalized Christian Science, New Thought may thus appear to be more a point of view than a movement, or a movement rather than a closely organized institution. But New Thought institutions have developed, a number of them, each with some difference from the others in thought or in emphasis, and considerable difference in techniques and methods of operation. Some of these have chosen to maintain themselves apart from the attempted grouping into the overall organization, the International New Thought Alliance (INTA). Some individual leaders and their groups have remained outside any of the limited or regional groups which have arisen around some dynamic leader or some particular emphasis, essentially independent of any connection beyond their local center. Yet they are exponents of the general New Thought point of view.

One of the great difficulties in building a nationwide or international organization has been the strong individualistic element in New Thought. Since knowledge of God—aided, to be sure, by scriptures and the recorded insights of others—is ultimately a highly personal, intuitive, experiential matter, how can it submit to any limitation upon its freedom of expression? Even when New Thought adherents enter into organization, they are likely to be extremely watchful that there be no encroachment upon that spiritual freedom. They wear lightly, therefore, their institutional loyalties. And this hardly makes for organizational strength.

There is usually a deeper loyalty to the particular group which best represents the thought of a given individual, than to the overall organization through which the various New Thought groups co-operate. One is likely to be more closely linked to Unity, for example, than to the International New Thought Alliance if one belongs to both. This is natural, and may be roughly paralleled with the greater felt loyalty of a member of a local Methodist church to the Methodist church in general than to the National or World Council of Churches, to which of course the Methodist church belongs. Thus the International New Thought Alliance is under constant scrutiny, and in some cases judgment, at the hands of the members of the constituent bodies, just as the National and World Council of Churches are at the hands of Methodists and the other denominations which adhere to them.

There is here, however, one difference, namely, that individuals as well as organizations may be members of the International New Thought Alliance, while neither local churches nor individuals, but only denominations, may belong to the overall National and World Councils of Churches.

Whence came this New Thought Movement? What are its sources? Who were the pioneers that first gave it form? Who were its early leaders? How was it organized, and how did it develop? What are its constituent bodies? How has the idea spread? How has it penetrated into the general culture of which it is a part, through prominent leaders, through literature, art, drama? How far has it reached beyond the limits of the land of its origin, and how? These are the subjects of our inquiry. Let us first look at the possible sources.

2

The Sources of New Thought

THE TERM New Thought as descriptive of a movement which had its rise near the middle of the nineteenth century is not a happy one to be employed in the mid-twentieth century. For "new" is a relative term, and has relevance only to those who know what the "old" was, over against which it stands out as "new." As a matter of fact, much of what was included in New Thought in the earlier day was not new at all. Almost all of its major ideas had appeared at some period in the history of the Christian faith, or, if not there, certainly in some of the other religions of the world. As an expression of philosophic idealism, its basic belief could be traced certainly as far back as Plato; and did not P. P. Quimby, the founder of the movement, claim only to have rediscovered Jesus' method of healing, and in this claim find the support of Mrs. Eddy in her earlier career?

New Thought embraces a wide range of thought and practice. Teachers and practitioners of New Thought healing are in considerable disagreement at a number of points; but always there are discernible in the variants two distinctive emphases: a practical concern about healing humanity's ills, and an ideology or theology which explains to the practitioner's satisfaction the sources of the healing power—basically an idealistic philosophy, with definite religious overtones.

Perhaps the thing that is really important about New Thought —or, more broadly, the whole "metaphysical" movement, which includes Christian Science as well as New Thought and other developments also—is that it represents a merging of the two emphases. The idealistic philosophers never carried out what New Thought sees as the logical implications of their thought, namely the healing of disease, and many who were working practically toward the cure of disease by mental means found no support in religion or philosophy for the methods they sought to employ. It was in New Thought that these two were combined, and it was in the person of P. P. Quimby that they were first linked together in ways which ultimately produced what is known today as New Thought.

That Quimby consciously took his ideas from any one particular thinker, or indeed any particular school of thought, it is quite impossible to prove at this remove in time, since he nowhere makes specific reference to any outside source from which his ideas came. But we do know what the major intellectual currents of the time were, and there is no doubt that whether consciously dependent upon them or not, he does express the central ideas of one of the three important thought emphases of his time in New England.

In general there were three widely divergent outlooks upon the world current in the New England of the first half of the nineteenth century. First of all, there was orthodox Christianity, chiefly in its Calvinistic interpretation, which had successfully held the field in New England until near the beginnings of the nineteenth century, and was still in the middle of that century largely the popular form of the Christian faith.

But there had come a strong liberal reaction against this rigid tradition which had given rise to the Unitarian-Trinitarian controversy and had split the Congregational church, the strongest of the New England denominations. The liberal wing had established itself as the new Unitarian church, and this was the prevailing faith of the intellectuals of the period. Most of the outstanding preachers of the period were Unitarians.

Reacting strongly against the thoroughly Protestant view of the authority of the scriptures upheld by a more or less mechanical concept of revelation, which made the Bible an infallible book, equally inspired in all of its parts, the Unitarians were

themselves thoroughly Protestant in insisting on the Bible as
a primary source of the Christian faith, but a book to be used
with discretion—a discretion imposed upon man by reason of
his possession of the power of reason which he was obliged to
use in the area of religion as in other areas of thought.

The dominant philosophical influence underlying their revolt
was that of John Locke, and his theory of knowledge. It was
simply that the only avenue of certain knowledge was through
the senses. His system had been characterized as sensationalism as
over against idealism, which holds that knowledge may also
come by way of intuition. It was really a phase of the struggle
between science and religion, at a time when scientific advance
had not yet reached its full stride in the direction which ultimately led to the widely held logical positivism of our own time.

It was in reaction against this sensationalism of the Unitarians
that the third group to be distinguished in New England arose
and flourished for a time—the comparatively small but extremely
vocal group known as the Transcendentalists. And it is in New
Thought that is to be found the continuing emphasis on the
peculiar Transcendentalist concept of intuition as a basic source
of the knowledge of reality; its teaching concerning the nature
of man as essentially divine or possessing divine qualities; and
its fundamentally idealistic view of reality and the universe. The
dependence on Transcendentalism of the earliest figures in New
Thought may not have been conscious, but it was real.

Transcendentalism has been variously defined. Perry Miller,
who edits an anthology of Transcendentalist writings (*The Transcendentalists: An Anthology* [Cambridge: Harvard University
Press, 1950]), calls the Transcendentalist Movement "fundamentally an expression of a religious radicalism in revolt against a
rational conservatism," "a protest of the human spirit," he says,
"even in its more fatuous reaches, against emotional starvation."
(p. 8)

George Ripley, one of the more illustrious of the group, calls
the Transcendentalists persons who "believe in an order of truths
which transcend the sphere of external sense," whose leading

idea is "the supremacy of the mind over matter"; who maintain that "the truth of religion does not depend on tradition nor historical facts, but has an unerring witness in the human soul." They believe, he says, "that there is a light that lighteth every man that cometh into the world; that there is a faculty in all—the most degraded, the most ignorant, the most obscure—to perceive spiritual truth when distinctly presented" and they also believe that the ultimate appeal in all moral questions "is not to a jury of scholars, a hierarchy of divines, or the prescriptions of a creed, but to the common sense of the human race." (From a letter to his congregation, *The Transcendentalists*, p. 225)

Orestes A. Brownson, in reviewing a book on the gospels by Andrew Norton, chief critic of Emerson's Divinity School address, reveals a Transcendentalist mind at work, not alone in the field of religion, but also in the political world. He insists that Norton rests all the value of the gospels on the fact that they can be proved to have been historical. To the Transcendentalists, he says, the question of the genuineness of the four gospels is a matter of comparative indifference, for they have in themselves the witness for God, and may know the things whereof they affirm. With these, Christianity is not a mere matter of opinion but of experience, and they can speak of it as something "they know, which they have seen, felt, handled." That is, knowledge does not come solely through the senses or even reason, but intuitively, experientially. He then goes on to say that the philosophy underlying Norton's position is equally fatal to democracy. "This philosophy," he writes,

disinherits the masses. It denies to man all inherent power of attaining to truth in religion. . . . In politics it does the same. It destroys all free action of the mind, all independent thought, all progress, all living faith. It cannot found the state on the inherent rights of man; the most it can do is organize the state for the preservation of such conditions, privileges and prescriptions, as it can historically justify. (p. 208)

"The doctrine that Truth comes to us from abroad," he continues, cannot coexist with true liberty. . . . The democrat is not he who only believes in the people's capacity for being taught, but . . . he who believes that reason, the light which shines out from God's throne, shined into the heart of every man, and that truth may indeed . . . kindle her torch in the inner temple of every man's soul whether patrician or plebeian. It is only on the reality of this inner light, and on the fact that it is universal in all men and in every man, that you can found a democracy which shall have a firm basis and which shall be able to survive the storms of human passions. (p. 208)

The little group which came to be called by others (not by its own members) "Transcendentalists" was quite local in its makeup. But it had a far-reaching influence out of proportion to its numbers, because of the men and women who belonged to it. It was apparently formed at the suggestion of Dr. William Ellery Channing, the great Unitarian preacher, who after talking with George Ripley invited several persons to a meeting for serious discussion. The first meeting was disappointing. A second was held, but, Emerson recalls, with no permanent effect. But gradually a small number of young Unitarians, who were in revolt against Unitarianism, drew together and met from time to time for an afternoon of serious conversation in each other's homes. Among them were George Ripley, Margaret Fuller, Ralph Waldo Emerson, greatest of them all, Bronson Alcott, Orestes A. Brownson, Dr. Hodges, Theodore Parker, James Freeman Clarke, William H. Channing, and others. There was no concerted action among them other than the founding of a magazine, the *Dial*, edited by Margaret Fuller, which lasted through but four years, serving chiefly to publicize the thought of the various individuals of the group. It never enjoyed a wide circulation, being as Perry Miller suggests rather "the work of friendship among a narrow circle of students than the organ of any party. Perhaps the writers were its chief readers." (p. 502) By whom the group was first called Transcendentalist, no one knows.

The account of the Transcendentalist movement given by Octavius Brooks Frothingham, a distinguished New England preacher who was himself a Transcendentalist, makes it clear that it was by no means an isolated phenomenon, but part of a wide movement of thought with European as well as oriental connections.

According to Frothingham's *Transcendentalism in New England* (long out of print but recently republished in paperback edition by Harper and Brothers), the Transcendentalist philosophy had its origin in Immanuel Kant's *Critique of Pure Reason*. From Jacobi, he says, it received an impulse toward mysticism, and from Fichte an impulse toward heroism. It was through the literature of Germany that the transcendental philosophy chiefly communicated itself; Goethe, Richter, Novalis, Frothingham states, were more persuasive teachers than Kant, Fichte, or Jacobi. And these authors were mediated to the English world largely through Thomas Carlyle. Goethe was enormously influential in New England. Among French sources were principally Theodore Jouffroy and Victor Cousin. The latter was frankly an eclectic who held that the whole truth is found in no single system, but that each has something to contribute. "The true philosophy would be reached by a process of distillation by which the essential truth would be extracted." In England it was chiefly Coleridge who was the prophet of the new philosophy, and he had drawn largely upon German sources, especially Schelling. Frothingham calls Coleridge a "pure Transcendentalist of the Schelling school." Carlyle was for a time inclined to Transcendentalism, but changed. But Wordsworth the poet, for example in "Tintern Abbey" and "Intimations of Immortality," was clearly Transcendentalist.

In England, Frothingham feels this type of thought influenced poetry and art greatly, but left largely untouched the daily experiences of men and women. In New England, on the other hand, the ideas found rootage in native soil and "blossomed out in every form of social life." New England furnished the only plot of ground on the planet where the Transcendentalist philosophy really had a chance to show what it was and what it proposed. (p. 105)

The New World democratic faith in man's capacity to make states, laws, religions for himself and society furnished a favorable soil for the new philosophy. A philosophy that laid its foundations in human nature and placed stress on the organic capacities and endowments of the mind was as congenial as the opposite system was foreign. Whether he knew it or not, says Frothingham, "every New Englander was radically and instinctively a disciple of Fichte or Schelling or Cousin, or Jouffroy." (pp. 106-7) Protestant Christianity had always claimed the possibility of knowledge through revelation or by intuition, at least for favored individuals, as in the Bible or for the elect. Transcendentalism simply claimed for all men what Protestant Christianity claimed for the elect. (p. 143)

The Unitarians, as a whole, belonged to the Lockean school which had abandoned the doctrine of innate ideas and like beliefs, distrusted mysticism, and were distinguished by "practical wisdom, sober judgment and balanced thoughtfulness that weighed opinions in the scale of evidence and argument." This was true even of the great Channing, though the sentiment of Channing, thinks Frothingham, went beyond his philosophy. He is quoted as saying, "In human nature there is an element truly divine and worthy of all reverence." The Unitarians had fixed upon no specific creed and no universally accepted system of philosophy upon which they could build one. Rather, they insisted upon the right to sit in judgment on all creeds.

Against the Lockean rationalism or sensationalism which characterized Unitarianism, Transcendentalism was a reaction. Though it took the form of a reaction against formalism and tradition, it went beyond that. "Practically," says Frothingham, "it was an assertion of the inalienable worth of man; theoretically it was an assertion of the immanence of divinity in instinct, the transference of supernatural attributes to the natural constitution of mankind." (p. 136)

This would be given expression according to their peculiar cast of genius by philosopher, critic, moralist, poet. Every phase of idealism would be presented, and the outside spectator might well consider it a mass of wild opinions; but running through all, Frothingham points out, was "the belief of the Living God in the Soul, faith in immediate inspiration, in boundless possibility and in unimaginable good." (p. 137)

But Transcendentalism was also highly practical in its tendencies. Self-culture was a primary duty, "the perfect unfolding of one's individual nature," to use the phrase of Emerson; but by self-culture, says Frothingham, the Transcendentalists meant

the culture of that nobler self which includes heart and conscience, sympathy and spirituality, not as incidental ingredients, but as essential qualities. They never identified selfhood with selfishness, nor did they ever confound or associate its attainment with the acquisition of place, power, wealth or eminent repute.

They were, many of them, practical reformers. Among their reforms was vegetarianism. The new philosophy gave man a new and better reason for doing some of the things that men who regard man as a body were already doing. The materialist who prescribed temperance, continence, sobriety, did it in order that life might be long and comfortable, free from disease. The idealist prescribed the same in order that life might be intellectual, serene, pacific, beneficent. (pp. 150-51)

The Transcendentalist could never be satisfied with men as they were, for he was by nature a reformer. The doctrine of the inherent capacities of men, even moderately stated, kindled an enthusiastic hope of change. Emerson, in his "Man the Reformer" lecture, declares that "there is an infinite worthiness in man, which will appear at the call of worth, and that all particular reforms are the removing of some impediment." The principle determined the method. Generally it was the method of the awakening of the individual and his regeneration, which was to be effected "through the simplest ministries of family and neighborhood fraternity, quite wide of associations and institutions." (Quoted by Frothingham, p. 155)

Note that this squares well with today's practices of both

New Thought and Christian Science, which put much emphasis
on personal culture but have little or no interest in the larger
society. The Transcendentalist was more a regenerator of the
human spirit than a reformer of human circumstances. No
reform would interest him that did not assume his first principle—
"the supreme dignity of the individual man." (p. 156) The one
most conspicuous reform of a social character was the famous
Brook Farm experiment, which flourished briefly, but ultimately
failed.

The Transcendentalists championed the enfranchisement of
women. The beginnings of this reform can be traced to them
more definitely than to any other source. It was a logical result
of the Transcendental belief that souls were of no one particular
sex. Men and women were alike human beings, with all their
human capacities, longings, and destinies, and should enjoy
equal rights.

The Transcendentalists believed likewise in man's ability to
apprehend absolute ideas of Truth, Justice, Rectitude, Goodness;
he could speak the right, the true, the beautiful as eternal verities
which he perceived, while the whole sensational philosophy was
"shut up in the relative and the conditioned." Man could be
satisfied with nothing short of "the absolute right, the eternally
true, the unconditioned excellence." (p. 182)

Politically Transcendentalism represented a reaction against
"the moral and political scepticism which results directly from
the prevailing philosophy of sensationalism." (p. 185) It
believed in man's spiritual nature,

in virtue of which he had an intuitive knowledge of God as being
infinite in power, wisdom and goodness; a direct perception like that
which the senses have of material objects. . . . To the human mind, by
its original constitution belongs the firm assurance of God's existence
as a half latent fact of consciousness, and with it a dim sense of his
moral attributes. (p. 190)

The Transcendental view of Christianity is summed up by
Frothingham as "an illustrious form of natural religion—Jesus

was a noble type of human nature; revelation was the disclosure of the soul; mystery; inspiration was the filling of the soul's lungs, salvation was spiritual vitality." (p. 204) All of which runs very close to what may be seen clearly in later New Thought's delineation of the Christian faith, though Transcendentalists in general never saw the logical implications for healing that Quimby and later New Thought saw and practically demonstrated.

In an article in a periodical now long since discontinued, a writer asserted that New Thought and other kindred movements believing in and practicing mental healing were followers of Emerson, the greatest of the Transcendentalists, in this as well as in their acceptance of his idealism. He declared that Emerson in many of his lectures spoke of sickness as the result of mental imperfection and a failure to think soundly and give the mind control over the body. He says that not even Mrs. Eddy was more emphatic in her utterances as to the cause of disease as spiritual, not physical, though Emerson never followed theory with practice. Unfortunately the writer does not cite the sayings which support his statement. (George W. Cook, *Current Literature*, XXXIV, 90)

But of all the Transcendentalists, it was undoubtedly Emerson who seems most to have influenced New Thought, at least in its development after the passing of Quimby and Evans. It is quite customary for New Thought leaders to claim Emerson as the Father of New Thought. Articles appear with frequency in New Thought periodicals representing detailed studies as well as casual reading of Emerson, and he is often quoted by New Thought speakers. While it has usually been recognized that Emerson never saw, or at least never followed, the theological implications of his philosophy for healing, a contemporary New Thought leader recently claimed that Emerson himself experienced healing from the dread disease of consumption or tuberculosis.

Dr. Frederic Bailes, in an article appearing in *New Thought*, asserts that Emerson's father and brothers had died of tuberculosis, and that in his young manhood Ralph Waldo had also

been tubercular, so that his relatives did not expect him to out-
live the disease. Yet he was healed completely and lived until
he was almost eighty years old. That his healing was not consciously effected, Bailes admits. Emerson certainly never inti-
mates that he treated himself mentally; but, says Bailes, in keeping with a metaphysical maxim "that we are healed by what
we turn *to* rather than by what we turn *from*," Emerson unconsciously used the true method. Instead of seeking to overcome
his illness, "he dwelt deep in the sense of oneness with the Over-
Soul" and gradually, without knowing it, was healed, "as an
effect of his dominant inward thought patterns."

Emerson, so far as is certainly known, never professed to be
able to heal sickness by mental means, but certain statements
are frequently quoted by New Thought writers as having a
practical bearing on health. For example, in "The Natural History of Intellect" Emerson writes: "The measure of mental health
is the disposition to find good every where." Again in "Resources,"
in *Letters and Social Aims,* he says, in contrast to the philosopher
Schopenhauer,

If instead of these negatives you give me affirmatives; if you tell me
there is always life for the living; that what man has done man can
do; that this world belongs to the energetic; that there is always a way
to everything desirable . . . I am invigorated, put in genial working
temper; the horizon opens, and we are full of good will and gratitude
to the Cause of Causes.

He urged upon his listeners an active attitude in the face
of unpleasant realities: "The causes of malignity and despair
are important criticism which must be heeded until he can
explain and rightly silence them. . . . Man was made for conflict
not rest. In action is his power, not in his goals, but in his transi-
tions man is great."

Once more, in "Society and Solitude" he wrote: "Don't have
a dismal picture on the wall, and do not daub with sables and
glooms in your conversation. Don't be a cynic and a disconsolate
preacher. Don't bewail and bemoan. Omit the negative propo-

sitions. Nerve us with incessant affirmations. Don't waste yourself in rejection, nor bark against the bad, but chant the beauty of the good."

Frothingham quotes Emerson as saying also, "Shun the negative side. Never wrong people with your contritions nor with dismal views on politics or society. Never name sickness, even if you could trust yourself on that perilous topic; beware unmuzzling a valetudinarian who will soon give you your fill of it." He seems to be perpetually saying, "Good morning," Frothingham goes on to remark.

It is certain that in its conceptions of God and man New Thought follows closely the ideas of Emerson expressed in various of his essays, and in particular in "The Over-Soul," in which is abundantly apparent the influence of oriental thought. In that famous essay, Emerson wrote: "There is no bar or wall in the soul, where man, the effect, ceases, and God, the cause, begins. The walls are taken away. We lie open on one side to the deeps of spiritual nature, to the attributes of God." And again: "The heart which abandons itself to the Supreme Mind finds itself related to all its works, and will travel a royal road to particular knowledge and powers."

Bailes thinks that the majority of students miss the real Emerson, approaching him chiefly from an intellectual angle, whereas he must really be approached from the standpoint of the heart, with "spiritual intuition," particularly in such essays as "The Over-Soul," "Circles," "Spiritual Laws," and "Fate."

"We live in succession," writes Emerson, "in division, in parts, in particles. Meantime within man is the soul of the whole; the wise silence; the universal beauty, to which every part and particle is equally related; the Eternal ONE ... the act of seeing and the thing seen, the seer and the spectacle, the subject and object are one." He points out, says Bailes, that "consciousness is the only reality ... the only God there is." That, says Bailes, "is the whole secret of Emerson's philosophy. Learn to place yourself in the midst of that great stream of power and wisdom ... every desire you have is the desire of the Over-Soul through you." (*New Thought,* Vol. XXXVIII, No. 3, pp. 13, 14, 41 ff., *passim*)

According to Emerson, man is "by his nature as unconditioned, as pure, as perfect and alone as the infinite. But he doesn't know it and the smoke screen of his own conditioning forever fogs him." (p. 36)

Arthur Christy, in an article on Emerson's debt to the Orient (*Monist,* XXXVIII, 56), sums up what he conceives to be Emerson's ideas concerning man and matter. He writes:

Emerson regarded matter as the negative manifestation of the Universal Spirit. It has its life and development through the direct immanence of the Absolute. And in like manner, Mind is an expression of the Universal Spirit in its positive power. Man himself is nothing but the Universal Spirit present in a material organism. Man is Divine, lives in the Divine, and in every power he manifests he shows the Divine life within. The soul is not a separate individuality, but part and parcel of God.

This is basically the New Thought position today. As is this:

The height, the deity of man is to be self-sustained. . . . Everything real is self-existent. Everything divine shares the self-existence of Deity. All that you call the world is the shadow of that substance which you are, the perpetual creation of the powers of thought . . . you think me a child of my circumstance. Let any thought or motive of mine be different from that they are, the difference will transform my condition and economy.

In the beginning of the essay on "History," Emerson writes: "There is one mind common to all individual men. Every man is an inlet to the same and to all of the same. He that is once admitted to the right of reason is made a freeman of the whole estate. . . . Of the universal mind, each individual is one more incarnation." The late Ernest Holmes interpreted this to mean, "I am that mind in which everything is and because that Mind in which everything is is the Mind I use, I can perceive and understand the nature of things that are akin to me in that mind in whom we live and move and have our being." (Ernest Holmes, "The Heart of Emerson," in the *International Bulletin of New Thought*, Vol. XXXVI, No. 1, p. 15)

As early as 1839 Emerson, who had been reading translations of oriental scriptures from his sixteenth year, included within the term "Bible" the sacred writings of the other great religions, as sharing with the Hebrew-Christian Scriptures "ethical revelation." That is, accepting revelation as a source of religious knowledge, he did not restrict that revelation to the Hebrew-Christian tradition. Nor did he think that it was derogatory to Christianity to recognize the achievements of other religions. In this New Thought has generally agreed with him.

Mental healing, which formed the basis of New Thought, and which became so popular around the end of the nineteenth century, proliferating into a variety of sectarian healing groups, was by no means a modern discovery. Long before medicine became scientific, healings were being effected through mental means, as for example in the sleeping chambers of the ancient Temples of Health. A renowned physician in Rome, Aesclepiades of Bythynia, is said to have made systematic use of the "induced trance" in the cure of some diseases.

In one of Plato's *Dialogues*, Socrates, centuries before the Christian era, quotes a Thracian physician as saying: "You ought not to attempt ... to cure the body without the soul. ... This is the reason why the cure of many diseases is unknown to the physicians of Hellas, because they are ignorant of the whole which ought to be studied also; for the part can never be well unless the whole is well." For, adds Socrates, "all good and evil, whether in the body or in human nature, originates, as he declared, in the soul. ... Therefore, if the head and body are to be well, you must begin by curing the soul; that is the first thing." "Let no one," his Thracian friend had said, "persuade you to cure the head, until he has first given you his soul to be cured. ... For this ... is the great error of our day in the treatment of the human body, that physicians separate the soul from the body." ("Charmides, or Temperance," *Dialogues of Plato*, trans.

Benjamin Jowett [New York: Charles Scribner's Sons, 1907],
I, 11)

Solon, the statesman-poet of early Greece, sang of something
which sounds very much like some form of hypnotic cure:

> The smallest hurts sometimes increase and rage
> More than all art of physic can assuage;
> Sometimes the fury of the worst disease
> The hand by gentle stroking will appease.

But if mental means were employed, there was little or no
attempt at an explanation of how they effected healings until
near the beginning of the modern period. A sixteenth-century
philosopher, Petrus Pomponatius, tried to prove that disease could
be cured without the use of drugs through the medium of "magnetism," which gifted persons seemed to possess. "By employing
the force of the imagination and the will," he wrote, "this force
affects their blood and their spirits which produce the intended
effects by means of an evaporation thrown outward." (Bruce,
Outlook, XCII, 1040). John Baptist Von Helmut also proclaimed
the curative power of imagination, which he described "as an
invisible fluid called forth and directed by the power of the
human will." Sir Kenneth Digby published in 1658 an interesting
book of cases of cure by nonmedical means, laying stress on the
power of the imagination not only to heal, but also to cause
disease, an idea which was to recur over and over again in the
teachings of P. P. Quimby two centuries later in New England.

But the ideas of these men failed to gain recognition among
scientists and physicians, for one reason, because they seemed
so foreign to the dominant modes of philosophic and scientific
thought of the day. Also, it has been suggested that the development of the science of chemistry and its obvious relationship to
the healing of disease may have contributed to the failure. Some
practitioners of these principles continued to exist, but they were
usually considered as crackbrained visionaries in the same class
with astrologers and alchemists.

It was a century or more later that a student of medicine in

Vienna, Anton Mesmer, who gave his name to the developing science of mesmerism, became interested in the work of Von Helmut and earlier users of what later came to be called hypnotism, and carried out a series of experiments to establish or disprove the existence of the unusual force which these men had claimed to have employed in healing. Mesmer called it, for want of a better name, "animal magnetism," a term not unknown to Christian Scientists of today who find in Malicious Animal Magnetism, or M.A.M., the possibility of untold harm to those against whom it is directed by irresponsible or unscrupulous persons. In a number of editions of *Science and Health*, Mrs. Eddy included a chapter on Animal Magnetism. The present chapter heading is "Animal Magnetism Unmasked." True, she gave the term a meaning somewhat different from that Mesmer attached to it. (For a vivid account of the experiments of Mesmer see Stefan Zweig, *Mental Healers*. A somewhat briefer and perhaps more scientifically accurate story of his work is told by Walter Bromberg, *Man Above Humanity*.)

By Mesmer and others who followed him this strange phenomenon was explained theoretically as a mysterious fluid—but others began to suspect that the actual explanation lay in what is now called "suggestion." A learned Portuguese cleric demonstrated in 1815 that the notion of a fluid was quite unnecessary to explain it. All that was necessary was to "provoke a high state of expectancy in the patient." The cause of the trance lay not outside of but within the patient. It was purely a subjective matter. But physicians and scientists still held themselves largely aloof from the practice, in part because it was so often tied up with some sort of occult beliefs or supernatural influence.

In 1841 an English physician, James Braid, witnessed the use of this strange method by a French mesmerist. He was himself completely incredulous and thought it a work of cunning and deception, but he felt obliged to investigate it and expose it. To his surprise, he found that the phenomena, however they were to be explained, were without question genuine. Experimenting with the effect, he came to the conclusion that Faria had reached a half-century earlier, that no fluidic theory was necessary to account for it; that it was really only the result of suggestion. To get away from the crude theorizing of the mesmerists and to distinguish his system from theirs, he employed to describe the phenomenon the word "hypnosis," the term usually employed in our day. And he continued to use hypnosis as a therapeutic agent in the healing of disease. This may well be said to be the beginning of scientific psychotherapy. But he came to be thought of by his fellow-physicians as little better than the mesmerists.

It was a country physician, Dr. A. A. Liebault of Nancy, France, who in 1860, the year of Dr. Braid's death, was to gain wide and respectful attention from scientific workers in the healing art. He experimented long and carefully before he opened his clinic in Nancy and announced that he would treat gratis all who would submit to hypnosis. Few accepted at first, but the undoubted benefits of the method won for it an increasing response and his name became widely known. Other doctors wanted to learn about it. Soon inquirers were coming from distant parts of France, from England, and from most of the more advanced European countries. They were impressed and carried away with them the conviction that here was a new and wholly respectable method for the treatment of disease without benefit of drugs or of chemistry.

Meanwhile other workers were also experimenting independently, particularly at the Salpêtrière in Paris, under the eminent Dr. Charcot. It soon became apparent that scientific psychotherapy was laid on solid foundations, and the method began quickly to find acceptance over the world.

Walter Bromberg, writing on the development of mental healing and particularly of psychotherapy, finds that by a curious twist of medical fate, dynamic phychotherapy had its rootage in a "mixture of Paracelsian common sense, rudimentary chemistry, and mystical astrology." For Mesmer, two centuries after Paracelsus, revived his theories in discovering animal magnetism, which he thought of as the result of the influence of the stars

and planets, from which a "magnetic fluid passed to man." Half
a century later, he says, magnetism became mesmerism, and
this gave way to hypnosis, which half a century later gave way
in its turn to analytical psychology, upon which dynamic psychotherapy is based. (*Man Above Humanity*, p. 169)

Bromberg describes psychotherapy as a method which
"strengthened the will through suggestion, moved naturally along
the lines of intellectualism, of rationally explaining away dis-
turbing bodily ailments and distressing mental states." But,
though this was written of psychotherapy as it had developed
by the turn of the present century, is it not exactly what P. P.
Quimby was practicing in the late 1850's and early '60's? Compare
the work of the psychotherapist Dubois, who used both explanation and persuasion along with suggestion. As we shall see,
Quimby definitely used suggestion.

Perhaps the most important result of the investigations carried
on by the continental scientists working with hypnosis was the
discovery of the "unconscious" or the "subconscious," in which
at a level below the threshold of consciousness were stored
memories and impressions of events and experiences long since
forgotten, but still influential in determining the mental and
even the physical health of the individual. When persons without
any conscious memory of suggestions made while in trance carried out these suggestions hours or even days after the suggestions were made, thoughtful investigators began to wonder where
and how these suggestions had registered and been retained
to produce the appropriate action at the predetermined time. The
hypothesis of a mental life somehow carried on at a subconscious
level has long been regarded as valid, and on it is based much
of the work of the psychoanalysts, the psychiatrists, and the
dynamic-psychotherapists. The discovery of these early investigators that through hypnosis and powerful suggestion physical
organs could be affected—for example, bleeding caused, blisters
raised, hearing and sight affected, the processes of circulation,
nutrition, and digestion modified—led to the conclusion that
many so-called physical disorders were mental, and could there-

fore be cured by nonphysical, nonchemical, nonmedicinal means.
They labored long to discover just what diseases could be, or
probably were, caused by some mental disturbance; and where
this could be determined, the mental method either of psychotherapy and later of psychoanalysis, or of psychiatry—that is,
psychological means of treatment—was employed.

It was at this point that these investigators differed from the
religio-mental healers, and from Christian Science completely,
for to the latter diagnosis is quite unnecessary. If all disease is
unreal or nonexistent, it doesn't really matter which one of the
unreal diseases the practitioner is called upon to treat. And with
New Thought healers it really didn't matter too much. Disease
was real enough, pain was a present fact to be dealt with, but
it was all a matter of wrong thinking. There was, perhaps from
the Swedenborgian influence, a kind of table of correspondence
between the physical and the mental realm. Evans illustrates
this, as will be seen later. Theoretically, it is not apparent that
Quimby excepted any disease from the list of those mentally
caused. Practically, New Thought has been less absolute in its
rejection of physical aids in healing. Even Quimby, as we shall
see later, did not hesitate to use some such aids, and in his
earlier period he co-operated with medical practitioners. Christian Science makes no exception, so far as is evident, in respect
to diseases that may be cured. Practically, Christian Scientists
recognize in specific cases that either the patient or the practitioner or both have not been able completely to "demonstrate" a cure, but that is not taken as a failure of theory, but
rather as a weakness and ineffectiveness in its practical application. They ordinarily do accept the work of the dentist and the
oculist, and sometimes of the bone surgeon in cases of fracture,
but always with some sense of guilt at not having the requisite
faith to accomplish the cures in these cases. New Thought practitioners differ, but certainly many of them do not hesitate to
work along with medical practitioners in a given case, and referral
of cases to orthodox surgeons and specialists by New Thought
practitioners is by no means rare.

Did Quimby and Evans and the other early New Thought pioneers know anything about the "unconscious" or the "subconscious"? Evans, yes, because he was a diligent student and an omnivorous reader in his field, and he had access to the reports of the scientific investigators in this area. Quimby, in a few instances, uses language which Horatio Dresser interprets as "levels of consciousness," which might suggest some adumbration on Quimby's part of what later became clear to the scientific investigators. But it needs to be recalled that Dresser did know these things, and with that knowledge it would be quite easy to interpret Quimby's language thus. It would be truer to the facts to suggest that Quimby may have worked practically on the basis of a belief which he never clearly formulated for himself. That is, just as there were people who used the most effective psychological methods in some cases long before there was any recognized science of psychology, so Quimby practically achieved results that, from the vantage point of those who know the theories of the unconscious or subconscious, seem to be based upon some such understanding of the nature of consciousness. But Quimby appears never to have stated such a hypothesis.

At least partly as a result of the success and rapid growth of the mental healing movements, both New Thought and Christian Science, churchmen rightly began to be concerned about the health of their people. It was no accident, therefore, that two Boston clergymen, Dr. Elwood Worcester and Samuel McComb, men of both scientific and theological training, in 1906 opened a clinic in their church in which, working hand in hand with the best medical skill available in the city, they sought to bring the healing values of religion to the service of health. That is, they sought to make use of nonphysical, nonchemical means to health —in other words, the known principles of psychotherapy—joined with religious faith in all cases in which careful diagnosis by competent medical men caused them to believe that it would be of benefit, and thus to supplement the employment of the usual methods of materia medica by mental and spiritual therapy. This came to be known as the Emmanuel Movement. It had

enormous popular acceptance for a time, and has left a permanent
impress upon the church's attitudes toward healing. More recently
the interest of the church in healing, particularly in the area of
mental disturbances, has taken the direction of a growth of
emphasis upon what may in general be called pastoral psychology.

3

Phineas P. Quimby, Founder

PHINEAS P. QUIMBY was born in Lebanon, New Hampshire, February 16, 1802, one of seven children of the village blacksmith. When he was about two years of age his parents moved to Belfast, Maine, where he spent the greater part of his life. From here as a base, he went out to lecture, to give exhibitions, and later to engage in the practice of healing in other towns and cities of New England. Even after 1859, when he opened his office in Portland, Maine, where he became widely and favorably known for his healing without medicine, he kept his Belfast home to which he returned at intervals to rest for a little while from his exacting practice. And finally, almost completely spent physically, he returned once more in late 1865, only shortly before his passing on January 16, 1866.

He was born into a family of modest means, and his formal education did not go beyond that of the common school of his day. He was apprenticed to and himself became a clockmaker. He was skilful in mechanical matters and of an inventive turn of mind, having to his credit various inventions, though none of great importance. He was reported by his son, George, to have been interested in scientific subjects, mechanics, and philosophy, but there is little to indicate what he read on these subjects. Unlike Warren Felt Evans (discussed later), who quoted extensively from many sources and carefully footnoted all his borrowings, Quimby placed very little reference in his writings to indicate what were the sources of his thinking. I do not recall even half a dozen references to any published authority in all

47

the material from his pen to which access is afforded in Dresser's
Quimby Manuscripts.

In his early thirties he apparently was afflicted with tuberculosis—he called it consumption. He was being treated by a
physician whose major dependence was, it seems, calomel, for
he says he had taken so much of it that it had thoroughly poisoned
his system. He became so weak, he relates, that he had to give
up his business and all hope of recovery.

But he had a friend who, he writes, had cured himself by
horseback riding. Unable to mount a horse, Quimby thought
riding in a carriage might serve as well. But on a carriage trip
once his horse balked and refused to move. He had to get out,
weak as he was, and lead it up a long hill. Later an obliging
farmer started the horse, and quite unaccountably Quimby
became excited and drove the animal at top speed up hill and
down until he reached home. On arriving, he found to his amaze-
ment that he felt as strong as ever. What had happened? To a
mind as active as Quimby's, it must have caused a great deal of
reflection. Nothing further is told concerning this event, but
apparently healed, or at least relieved temporarily, Quimby
resumed his work and continued it for some years without
incident.

Then a man appeared in Belfast who was to change the whole
outlook of clockmaker Quimby. In 1838 a Dr. Collyer gave a
lecture and demonstration of a curious phenomenon, mesmerism,
which had been introduced into America some two years before
by the Frenchman, Charles Poyan. This amazing new force,
now known as hypnotism, had created a great furor in New
England, and was being lectured about, studied, and practiced
all over that part of America and beyond. It at once attracted
the inquisitive mind of P. P. Quimby. He began to investigate it,
reading what he could find on the subject, and soon began to
practice it whenever he could find anyone willing to submit to
the experience. It was thus that he discovered Lucius Burkmar,
with whom he experimented over a period of months. Through
the results of these experiments and his reflection upon them he

finally arrived at the basis of his theory of mental healing, which was the real beginning of the New Thought Movement.

Quimby became a very successful mesmerist or hypnotist. He was described by a writer in the local paper as

a gentleman, small in stature, rather smaller than the medium of men, with well balanced phrenological head, and with the power of concentration surpassing anything we have ever witnessed. His eyes were black and very piercing, with rather a pleasant expression, and he possesses the power of looking at an object even without winking, for a length of time. (Quoted in Q. MSS, p. 30)

A prominent physician of Belfast writes to a fellow-physician describing an operation which he performed without the use of any anesthetic save the hypnotic sleep into which Quimby had thrown the patient, who exhibited not the slightest indication of any pain during the period of the operation. He was convinced, he wrote, that he could have amputated her arm and that she would not have felt it. (Q. MSS, pp. 32-33)

Under magnetic influence, that is under hypnotism, Lucius proved to have extraordinary clairvoyant powers, which, interesting in themselves and provocative of not a little reflection on Quimby's part, led into the field of healing, and so pointed the direction of Quimby's great interest, which made him the pioneer mental healer in America. For in the "magnetic state" Lucius seemed to have an uncanny ability to diagnose disease or clairvoyantly to perceive what was apparently the internal condition of the ailing folk, and further, to prescribe a remedy. Thus Quimby quite naturally became for a time a "mesmerist" healer, and so gave a basis for a later rival claimant in the field of mental healing to dub him a "mere mesmerist," thus effectually damning him as somehow inferior and unworthy of being followed. In all frankness, even the most devoted followers of Quimby are forced to recognize a stage in his career in which he did use the hypnotic or "animal magnetism" method of healing. But this was in his earlier period of development. To characterize him thus at the height of his career is a gross injustice which deliberately overlooks the gradual growth of his whole theory of disease and its cure which, in the end, completely rejected the use of mesmerism, in the sense of hypnotic sleep. Of course he never abandoned, nor have any of the so-called metaphysical healers, including of course Christian Science, the use of the power of suggestion in the cure of disease.

It is clear that in the earlier employment of Lucius Burkmar in the diagnosis and prescription of cure, Quimby had not abandoned faith in physicians and their remedies, for he was sometimes called in by physicians to diagnose a case with Lucius' aid, and prescribe a remedy. Cures sometimes followed this treatment, and certainly the physicians thought them due to the prescribed remedy. At first probably Quimby did too. But doubt soon entered his mind—indeed, two doubts: (1) as to whether Lucius' clairvoyant report of the patient's condition was really true to the facts, or the result of his perception through thought transference of what either the physician or himself thought was the patient's condition; and (2) whether it was the prescribed remedy which really effected the cure. Enough had been written and heard in New England at this period about thought transference, in connection with the interest in spiritualism, to awaken such a suspicion, for Quimby was now reading, apparently, such literature as was available touching mesmerism and mind control. Furthermore, his own experience of at least temporary improvement in his physical condition when there had been no introduction of any physical remedy must have caused him to think seriously of the subject. The chronological sequence of events in his development as recorded in the *Manuscripts* is unfortunately not clear.

In a letter to a Portland paper in 1862, Quimby writes that sometimes when Lucius prescribed a simple herb that could do no harm or good in itself, the patient recovered. He added that any medicine would have the same effect. It seemed to him, therefore, that the cure could not be attributed to the medicine, but rather to the patient's confidence in the doctor or the medium through whom the prescription was made.

Then, Lucius left him and went with another mesmerist who taught him to prescribe a remedy of the mesmerist's own manufacture, under a learned-sounding Latin name. When, later, Lucius returned to Quimby, and was again employed in a healing case, he diagnosed the disease and prescribed the Latin-named remedy. On taking the prescription to the druggist, it was discovered that it would cost some twenty dollars, a sum the patient could ill afford. Quimby once more put Lucius under hypnosis, whereupon he prescribed a harmless and quite economical remedy —and the patient got well! What must one conclude from this?

But of perhaps more influence was the condition of Quimby's own health. Curiously enough, he never reverts to the case of his own temporary relief from "consumption," as narrated above, but does tell quite in detail of his experience of healing at a later time. He states that he was not really well when he began to mesmerize. He still believed in the current concepts of disease and physical remedies. His physical condition troubled him, but while he used Lucius to look inside other patients, he apparently shrank from seeking his aid in his own case.

But one day, when entranced, Lucius described the pain which Quimby himself felt in his back. He says that he had never before dared to ask Lucius to examine himself, for he felt sure that one of his kidneys was nearly gone. His subject put his hands on the very spot where he felt the pains, and informed him that his kidneys were in a very bad condition, that indeed one of them was half gone, that a piece of it was separated from the rest, held only by a slender thread. This agreed wholly with what he himself believed to be his condition, and with what the doctors had told him, the basis undoubtedly of his own belief.

"Is there any remedy?" he asked Lucius, for he had come to think, he says, that he must continue to the end of his days to suffer from a condition which no medicine had power to cure.

Lucius, to his surprise, assured him that there was indeed hope of a cure. "I can put the piece on so it will grow, and you will get well," he said. So saying, Lucius placed his hands on Quimby and said that the pieces he had joined would grow together.

A day or two later Lucius announced, apparently again in a trance, that they had actually grown together. "And," writes Quimby, "from that day I have never experienced the least pain from them." (Based on a description of the case, *Q. MSS*, pp. 27-28)

An ordinary patient might only have thankfully acknowledged the healing and gone about his business. Not so Quimby. His was a mind that inquired, and at once questions arose within him. "How could such a cure come about?"

If his condition had been as bad as described, how could a remedy so simple have been effective? He had entertained no doubt of the condition, and if Lucius had said there was no cure, he would, he says, surely have died within a year or so. Now, maybe the condition was not what Lucius described. Did not Lucius tell him really only what he himself was thinking, and had he himself not gotten the idea in turn from the doctors? Maybe Lucius was not really seeing clairvoyantly the actual internal condition, but only reading his own mind concerning it. In so many words, he wrote, "the absurdity of the remedy made me doubt the fact that the kidneys were diseased." Was it therefore only a mistaken belief as to their condition that was the real cause for his suffering? If they were not really so diseased, then the cure in the form of an absurdly simple statement that the sundered parts would be joined, and that after a day or two they had been so united, seemed to indicate that his trouble was essentially mental, something of his own making. And this conclusion was corroborated in his mind through further investigation, both in his own personal health and that of others.

In a case similar to his own, Lucius described the patient's lungs as looking like a honeycomb, and his liver as covered with ulcers. Yet a simple herb tea prescription effected a cure. The doctor, he says, believed that the remedy effected the cure, but Quimby says that he himself "believed that the doctor made the disease, and his faith in the boy made a change in the mind, and the cure followed." (*Q. MSS*, p. 29) Thus he was led to a lack of confidence in doctors and a "belief that their science was false."

"Man," he writes in the same place, "is made up of truth and belief; and if he is deceived into a belief that he has, or is liable to have a disease, the belief is catching and the effect follows it."

Clearly, he was well on the way to the discovery of the basis of all mental healing. But he was still a mesmerist. Even if he had discovered that the secret of the cure of disease was, as would logically follow from what has just been stated about disease as a wrong belief, the substitution of the truth, the mesmeric spell still might serve as a very effective, or perhaps the most effective, method of changing the mental condition. For the use of hypnosis, not upon a third party but upon the patient himself, offers a means of immensely heightening his suggestibility, thus rendering him receptive to a change of mind concerning his condition. But Quimby still continued for a time to employ Lucius in his healing, meanwhile experimenting to discover how it really is that mind is affected by mind.

In the course of these experiments he discovered that it was not necessary for him to direct Lucius by means of his voice, while entranced. He found that he could concentrate mentally on what he desired him to do and the subject responded. Thus, he could be made to laugh by thinking of an amusing situation; to express fear by imagining vividly the figure of a ferocious wild animal.

Here was the revelation of a strange power of mind to affect mind. In a sense the mind was able to create. There was of course no wild animal where Lucius thought he saw one. It was purely the creation of Quimby's own mind, but it became real to his subject. He tried all sorts of experiments. He found that anything which he could visualize or to which he could give form in his own mind could be reproduced in the mind of the subject, though when he thought in abstract terms of that which could not be reduced to tangible form, Lucius could not see them and could not, therefore, apparently grasp them; at least, he could not describe them. In his own words, Quimby came to believe "that man has the power to create ideas and make them so dense that they can be seen by a subject who is mesmerized." (*Q. MSS*, p. 46)

This eventually had considerable influence on Quimby's estimate of Spiritualism, the phenomenon of which, it seemed to
him, might well be explained on the basis of the effect of mind
on mind, quite as well as by supposing that spirits were real.
Whatever credence he had ever given to the claims of Spiritualism
he seems to have abandoned, and he denied specifically the
charge sometimes leveled at him that he was a Spiritualist.
Mrs. Eddy, then Mrs. Patterson, also absolved him from such
a charge in a letter to the *Portland Evening Courier* of June, 1862.
(The letter is reproduced in *Q. MSS*, p. 23.)

Further experiments with Lucius and others made it certain
that mind could affect mind not only in the "magnetic state,"
but in a normal state of consciousness. He found that merely by
thought he could cause a person to stop walking. If this were
possible, then why use mesmerism? By this time he had come
to reject as a theory in explanation of mesmerism that there was
some mysterious fluid involved, even electricity. It was a question
of the influence of mind upon mind. Attention was the clue to
its explanation. In modern terms, by narrowing the field of attention, it rendered the subject more highly suggestible and less able
to criticize or evaluate ideas than in the normal conscious state.
But there was nothing essentially mysterious about it.

But what was the relation of all this to the cure of disease,
which had become increasingly the concern of Quimby? On
the basis of his own personal healing he had already come to
believe that the disease from which he suffered was really due
to a mistaken belief in what the physicians had told him concerning his condition. Accepting on faith their suggestions, he
had felt ill. Acting on the suggestion of Lucius, his subject, that
the condition had been changed, he was healed. That is, by the
correction of a wrong or mistaken belief a cure had been effected.
The faith of patients in the remedies offered them by doctors
was curative in its effect. But if the same effect could be secured
by a change of mind through suggestion and without medicine,
as in his own case, why employ medicine? It appeared to him
more and more that that which was most deeply involved in

healing was mind. If only the mind of the patient could be effectively changed, cure would result. He therefore eventually abandoned completely the use of mesmerism.

If Quimby became convinced that at least some of what Lucius reported in his diagnoses of disease by clairvoyance was really only the result of mind reading or thought transference, Lucius did in some experiments display what appeared to him to be real clairvoyant ability. It seemed to him important, if possible, that he himself should become clairvoyant, but without mesmerism. How this was accomplished does not appear in anything I noted in reading the *Manuscripts* as published by Dresser, though Dresser makes the statement, unsupported by any evidence, that the clairvoyant or intuitive powers of Lucius were not generated in him by Quimby, for "these are latent powers of the human soul, and all minds have access to things, persons, events at a distance." (*Q. MSS*, p. 52) But that Quimby did eventually develop clairvoyant powers is abundantly evident in many of his writings, seen both in his quiet diagnosis of his patients' ills and in their treatment.

The basis was now laid for mental healing. As Julius A. Dresser, a patient and a major figure in the early development of New Thought, has pointed out, Quimby had come to his conclusions not from the Bible or from any religious considerations, though he later identified his method as like that of Jesus. Thus far they had been based upon observation, experiment, and reflection. One might conceivably operate as a healer in entire disregard of religion or religious faith. Indeed, this has often been done. There is a distinct secular mental healing movement which has worked upon the basis of Quimby's theory of disease and cure. Scientific psychotherapy operates on substantially this basis. As we have seen, it possibly stems directly from other sources than Quimby; but that it received great impetus from the burgeoning of the vigorous young New Thought Movement there can be no doubt. And increasingly in our own day, what may be generally described as secular mental healing practitioners tend to take the dynamic of religious faith into account in dealing with their patients. If this is quite lacking, they will still believe that cure can be effected through the mind. But when it is present it may be a powerful ally of the healer.

Nevertheless, the movement as a whole has a definitely religious basis. Was this the result of Quimby's thought and practice, or was it something added on by those who came after? Mrs. Eddy's basis is proclaimed as a rediscovery of not only the healing but the religion of Jesus the Christ, and a sharp distinction is made officially between mere mental healing and Christian Science healing. A recent writer in this area has made the interesting and suggestive remark that for all the supposed differences between New Thought and Christian Science as it has developed, it shows evidence of being more under the influence of Mrs. Eddy than of P. P. Quimby. (Israel Regardie, *The Romance of Metaphysics* [Chicago: Aries Press, 1946])

Is this the case? Was there no religious element in Quimby's teaching and practice? Horatio Dresser unquestionably thought there was. He writes:

It was a long road for Quimby to travel from where he started out, as a believer in medical practice and a student of mesmerism, to faith in an inner or higher self immediately open to the Divine presence with its guiding Wisdom, quickening the "mind of Christ." The guide throughout was love of truth, leading the way to inductions from actual experience. (*Q. MSS*, p. 53)

But before looking into his religious beliefs, let us see what it was he taught about disease and its cure, and how he went about curing the sick. Fortunately, we have in carefully written form a mass of manuscripts which set forth his beliefs and to some extent how he came by them, and how he went about his all-important task of healing.

He had begun his healing work in Belfast, his home. Many patients had sought him out there, and he had also done some practicing in other cities or villages in Maine. In 1859 he had set up an office in Portland, Maine. Here for nearly seven years he carried on his work, which included personal contact with numerous patients in his office; healing through correspondence and occasional visits to persons in other towns; and conversations with interested persons who were awaiting their turn to see him, or with persons in the process of treatment in which he did a good deal of informal teaching concerning his system. Also, at the suggestion of some of his patients he began to write down his ideas. He would then permit patients to read what he had written and discuss it with them. Two sisters, daughters of the well-known Judge Ashur Ware, of the United States Supreme Court, undertook to make copies of them, which his patients were permitted to borrow. Some of them still extant show corrections made at his suggestion when they were read back to him.

Among those who were healed by him and admitted to the inner circle of his patients and admirers were the Dressers, Warren F. Evans, and a Mrs. Patterson, later to be known as Mrs. Eddy, the founder and discoverer of Christian Science. She too had access to some of his manuscripts, for she was a very warm friend who delighted to recognize in him one who healed by the method of Jesus. The often noted similarities between the Quimby teachings and her own led later to the assumption that she had borrowed extensively from him. This she stoutly denied, and intimated that if anyone had borrowed it might well have been Quimby rather than herself, for she had corrected some of his manuscripts, inserting in them ideas that were really her own. At the time of this statement the Quimby Manuscripts had not yet been published, though they were frequently referred to. She threw doubt upon the very existence of such manuscripts, but in 1921 they were issued under the editorship of Horatio W. Dresser. Carefully dated, they revealed beyond question to any but the most convinced Eddy disciples that Quimby had held the basic ideas of mental healing years before Mrs. Eddy sought healing at his hands in 1862.

In October, 1859, three years before Mrs. Eddy sought his help, he wrote (and I quote verbatim, lest it be charged that a possible bias of the writer had caused him to impute to Quimby what was not really there): "Disease is what follows the disturbance of the mind or spiritual matter. . . . Disease is what follows an opinion, it is made up of mind diverted by error, and Truth is the destruction of this opinion." (*Q. MSS*, pp. 180-81)

The important thing here is that disease is mental. Note too that Quimby was using the terms "error" and "Truth," capitalizing the latter, just as is regularly done in *Science and Health*.

Writing in 1859, he asks the question that had undoubtedly been raised by someone, "Is the curing of disease a Science?" His answer is a categorical "Yes." Who then was the founder of that Science, he was asked. Note that the word science is also capitalized as it normally is in Christian Science. Again his answer is, "Jesus Christ." Dresser remarks in a footnote (*Q. MSS*, p. 185) that this was the first article in which Quimby identified Science with Christ, adding that he later used the term "Christian Science." Incidentally, a book had been published by a prominent minister, the Rev. William Adams, in 1850, with the title, *The Elements of Christian Science*. So the term had already been used well in advance of the time when Mrs. Eddy gave it to the system which she developed later.

In the same month he wrote an article answering the question "Is Disease a belief?" He replies:

I answer that it is, for an individual is to himself just what he thinks he is, and he is in his belief sick. If I believe I am sick, I am sick, for my feelings are my sickness, and my sickness is my belief in my mind. Therefore all sickness is in the mind or belief. . . . To cure the disease is to correct the error, destroy the cause, and the effect will cease. (*Q. MSS*, p. 186)

Over and over he reaffirms the mental basis of disease. In an article dated December, 1859, he put it this way:

The trouble is in the mind, for the body is only the house for the mind to dwell in. . . . Therefore, if your mind has been deceived by some invisible enemy into a belief, you have put into it the form of a disease, with or without your knowledge. By my theory or truth, I come in contact with your enemy, and restore you to health and happiness. This I do partly mentally, and partly by talking till I correct the wrong impression and establish the Truth, and the Truth is the cure. (p. 194)

Certain questions were asked frequently of Quimby. One questioner made out a list of fifteen questions, and he wrote out his answers. Copies of this "Questions and Answers" were passed out freely to thoughtful patients who came to him for healing, in order that they might study them. Thus it was that they came into the possession of Mrs. Patterson, later Mrs. Eddy. In the Quimby-Eddy controversy it was alleged by Georgine Milmine that "Questions and Answers" constituted the basis of Mrs. Eddy's "The Science of Man," and ultimately of the important chapter in *Science and Health* entitled "Recapitulation." This is vigorously denied by defenders of Mrs. Eddy's originality in her discovery and development of Christian Science. Those who desire to consult the evidence upon which the charge of such dependence is based may consult *The Life of Mary Baker Eddy,* by Georgine Milmine (New York, 1909). The book, long out of print, is still to be found in the larger libraries. An article appeared in the *New York Times* of July 10, 1904, in which parallels between "Questions and Answers" and Mrs. Eddy's writings were included.

In this famous article, Quimby defined disease thus: "Disease is something made by belief or forced upon us by our parents or public opinion.... Now if you can face the error and argue it down then you can cure the sick." (pp. 173-74). What is disease? "It is false reasoning," he writes (p. 295), or again, "The cause of man's misery and trouble lies in our false reasoning." (p. 268) "If I find [in a patient] no opinion, I find no disease, but if I find a disease I find an opinion." (p. 380) "Diseases are in the mind, as much as ghosts, witchcraft, or evil spirits and the fruits of this belief are seen in almost every person." (p. 211)

Statements of this, his conception of the mental basis of disease, could be quoted by the dozens, but this will suffice. Whence come these erroneous beliefs which entail so much illness and suffering and misery?

Quimby's two pet peeves were priests and doctors. "The two

most dangerous to the happiness of man," he writes, "are priests and doctors. These two classes are the foundation of more misery than all other evils, for they have a strong hold on the minds of the people by their deception and cant. They claim all the virtue and wisdom of the nation, and have so deceived the people that their claims are acknowledged in war and peace." (p. 328) "Religion was what crucified Christ. Pilate's wisdom found no fault in him, but religion and the priests cried 'crucify him.' " (p. 329)

Quimby frequently associates priest and doctor. In "Questions and Answers" he links them inextricably as major threats to humanity, offering some explanation of the cumulative effects of their inventions:

The priests and doctors conspire together to humbug the people, and they have invented all sorts of stories to frighten man and keep him under their power. These stories are handed down from generation to generation until at last both priests and doctors all believe they are God's laws and when a person disobeys one he is liable to be cast into prison [i.e., suffer disease]. . . .

No one knows the mischief or the misery that physicians of all kinds make by their opinions, and this never will be known until man learns that his belief makes his trouble. . . . No, when people are educated to understand that *what they believe they will create,* they will cease believing what the medical men say, and try to account for their feelings in a more rational way. (pp. 262-63)

Disease, he alleges,

was conceived in priestcraft and brought forth in the iniquity of the medical faculty. The priests prophesied falsely and the doctors flourished by their lies, and people love to have it so. Then the question arises, what can you do to prevent it, I say, repent and be baptized in the Science that will wash away your sins and diseases with your belief. (p. 267)

But Quimby did not talk simply of disease in general. He often named specific ills. In the scope of about a hundred pages of the *Manuscripts* ailments mentioned, most of them as having been cured by him, include cancer, hip lameness, vertebral pain, consumption, heart disease, smallpox, fever, spiritual affection, cold, brain fever, lung fever, tumor, neuralgia, general debility of the nervous system, and diphtheria. Particularly interesting is his handling of smallpox, a disease already recognized by the more advanced physicians of his day as definitely an infection which could be avoided by vaccination.

Of smallpox Quimby says that, "according to the world, there is indeed such a disease. It is like a tree whose fruits are scattered abroad, infecting those who eat of them. It is a superstitious idea and like all such it has a religious cast. It deceived the world so that every person was liable." (p. 260) Not just a specific doctor suggests the false belief to a specific patient. There is rather a cumulative effect of doctors in general which creates the belief which is held by the masses of men, quite sincere it may be on the part both of the doctors and of the individual persons. Thus children, he avers, "suffer if they are in the vicinity of the disease [smallpox] for their parents' sins [i.e., their false beliefs]. Their diseases are the effect of the community." (p. 278)

Since all were thus liable to smallpox, the idea of kine-pox was sent into the world that all might be saved, or vaccinated. As many as received the virus or were baptized with the belief were saved." Here he is clearly parodying Scripture in satiric vein. "Here is introduced another world which is deliverance from small-pox. To all who have passed from their old belief into the world of vaccination, there is no fear of death from small-pox, but a fear lest they have not been vaccinated with genuine virus." (p. 269) They do not know it or recognize it, but if there is any escape through vaccination it is not because of any inherent creative or preventive power in that which through vaccination is introduced into the body, but rather it is the patient's belief in its efficacy which gives it whatever value it may seem to have as a preventive of disease. For, he asks, upon what does their salvation rest? "It rests upon no principle outside the mind. In ignorance of causes, people are satisfied with someone's belief that there is virtue in this savior. Thus their minds are quiet and the fruits are a milder disease, if the graft is put into a healthy tree (or child).￼" That is, he means, if it "takes." (p. 260) And the same, he declares, applies to all diseases. "Every disease is an invention of man, and has no identity in Wisdom, but to those who believe it, it is a truth." Smallpox, he continues, "is a reality to all mankind," but "Small-pox is a lie, and so is kine-pox . . . both are the invention of superstition." (p. 270)

Together with his definition of disease as an erroneous belief, he has suggested with great simplicity the cure, namely the exchanging of false beliefs for the truth. In so many words, he declares in a circular which he had prepared and printed years before coming to Portland, "THE TRUTH IS THE CURE." The circular had been prepared for use in various communities in which, previous to his Portland period, he had carried on his practice. It began:

"Dr. P. P. Quimby would respectfully announce to the citizens of ————— and vicinity, that he will be at the ————— where he will attend those wishing to consult him." He puts his cards on the table, announcing clearly that his practice is unique in that he "*gives no medicine,* and makes no outward applications." Rather, he sits down with his patients, "tells them their feelings and what they think is their disease." Note that he does not ask them, he tells them. If they recognize that what he tells them is true to their feelings, "then his explanation is the cure; if he succeeds in correcting their error, he changes the fluids of their system and establishes the truth or health." Then in italics he declares, "*The truth is the cure.*"

There is much more to the circular. He has a few things to say uncomplimentary to the doctors who from mercenary motives "impress their patients with a wrong idea—namely that they have a disease. This makes them nervous and creates in their mind a disease that otherwise would never have been thought of." He himself "makes no charge if no explanation is given, for no effect is produced." (pp. 144-45)

From other sources we know that his fees were very modest. Once in a letter he returns a fee of $2.00, sent him apparently in advance. He gives an explanation and directions. If after following these the patient feels he is entitled to anything "in the shape of a gift," it will be received, "if ever so trifling." (p. 131) Again, he returned a fee of $5.00, "until the cure is performed." (p. 133) That the fees, which seem to have been variable and quite elastic, did not prevent patients from seeking his help, may be judged from the fact that, as he notes, he sat with some twelve thousand different persons during his seven years in Portland. Many of them he saw many times.

Nor did he take all who came to him. On one occasion he wrote concerning a case of blindness: "I should not recommend anyone like your description to come to see me, for I have no faith that I could cure him." (p. 121) To another he wrote, "Your belief would probably prevent me from helping you." (p. 143)

Writing of himself in the third person, as he did rather frequently, in an article dated January, 1860, and entitled "How Dr. Quimby Cures," he gave this explanation: "Dr. Quimby, with his clairvoyant faculty, gets knowledge in regard to the phenomena, which does not come through his natural senses, and by explaining it to the patient gives another direction to the mind and the explanation is the science or cure." (p. 191)

He goes on to illustrate, saying in substance that the patient comes in for an examination. Together they sit down quietly, no questions asked by either. He becomes perfectly passive. The patient's mind being troubled, this is felt by him clairvoyantly, and he knows the patient's thoughts and feelings. Thus informed of the history of the trouble, together with the name of the disease, he relates it to the patient.

In his articles Quimby frequently says, "Now I will explain to you," or "show you," or "prove to you." Quite frequently the reader on finishing the explanation or proof does not feel that he has at all adequately fulfilled his promise. And Quimby himself sometimes appears to be conscious that his explanation has not made sense to the reader. After one account of how he clairvoyantly determines the root of a disease and goes about effecting its cure, he exclaims, "I cannot find language to explain this so you will understand it." (p. 342)

On another occasion, he says:

When the enemies of Science and progress are mustering the thought of the scientific world and casting every one into prison for their belief, I enter the land of darkness with the light of liberty, search out the dungeons where the lives of the sick are bound, enter them and set the prisoners free.

How does he know the location of dungeons and their prisoners? Because they can be detected by their atmosphere, he says, for all diseases are but "opinions condensed into an idea of matter that can be seen by the eye of Wisdom," which he claims to possess. He can detect equally well the errors taught by priests. Like Moses, "he enters the land and leads them out, going before them in the wilderness, and all who listen to him and his explanations are healed from the bite of the creeds [the reference here is to Moses lifting up the serpent in the wilderness, that those bitten by serpents might be healed]. So, he is hated by some, laughed at by others, spit upon by doctors, sneered at by priests, but received into the arms of the sick who know him." (p. 334)

Dr. Quimby used a variety of methods in his work of healing. He does not spend much time or effort in explaining how he works or how his effects are achieved, but in one instance he does draw back the curtain and let us see how he thinks at least that the silent method operated. Most frequently he talked with and explained audibly the error which was causing the misery. In this case there was apparently no exchange of words. He describes it, as so frequently, in the third person. Here, in sub-stance, is his explanation. The patient came in. Quimby at once shut everything out of his mind but the patient's feelings. These he says were daguerreotyped on him. In more modern language, they were photographed on his consciousness, producing a reflec-tion of themselves—that which the patient interpreted as disease. In turn Quimby, laughing at the false idea, impresses upon the sensitive plate of the patient's consciousness his own feeling concerning disease—that is, health or strength. The patient, seeing the shadow of his disease in a new light, gains confidence. This change is photographed on his own sensitive plate, which in turn he continues to treat. So, he says, "The patient's feelings sympathize with his, the shadows grow dim and finally the light takes its place and there is nothing left of the disease."

Sometimes Quimby employed physical means, such as rubbing the afflicted part, i.e., manipulation, but purely as a means of intensifying the suggestion of which he was making use in his verbal communication with his patients. It gave the patient a feeling that something tangible was happening. George Quimby, his son, wrote that his father always insisted that "his manipulation conferred no beneficial effects upon his patients, although it was often the case that the patient thought that it did." (*New England Magazine*, March, 1888)

In a letter to a patient he writes: "As you seem to want your head cured I will rub the top of it [clearly *in absentia*, and therefore undoubtedly by power of suggestion] and while doing this I will tell you what makes you feel so giddy." His explanation of her illness was that she thought too much on religion. "This makes you nervous for it contains a belief which contains opinions etc." Giving some of his own religious ideas, he closes, "Hoping this will settle your head and make you easy on the subject of another world." (p. 116)

Mrs. Eddy, following her mentor in this as in so many other ways, in her earlier period manipulated her patients and taught her students to do so, but later repudiated the practice. It was in part Quimby's use of this technique that caused people to rate him as a mesmerist long after he had ceased entirely to believe in mesmerism or practice it in his healing.

In absent treatment, which consisted partly of detailed explanation in letters of the cause of the patient's condition, definitely practical steps were sometimes encouraged as part of the cure. In a letter only part of which is published, Quimby writes to a man who seems to be suffering. Explaining how this came about, he tells the patient to "stand upright, put hands on hips and bend

forward and back." This, he declares, "relaxes the muscles around
the waist at the pit of the stomach ... takes away the pressure
from the nerves of the stomach, and allays irritation." Then the
patient is to sit down, and Quimby would "work upon his stomach
two or three times in three or four days." This, he said, would
affect the patient's bowels and help him keep color. He is to
take a little water while sitting, about nine o'clock in the evening.
How would Quimby work upon his stomach at a distance of many
miles? In another case he offers something of an explanation.

He seems to have carried on his absent treatments by letter
very much as he did those given in person. "I will now sit by you,"
he writes,

as I used to, for I see I am with you and talk to you a little about
your weak back. You forgot to sit upright as I used to tell you. Perhaps
you cannot see how I can be sitting by you in your house and at the
same time be in Portland. I hear you think and speak. . . . If you
understood you would not doubt that I am talking to you. I have
faith to believe that I can make you believe in my Wisdom. So I shall
try to convince you that although I may be absent in the idea or
body, yet I am present with you in the mind. (pp. 123-25, *passim*)

Quimby had learned through his experiments with mesmerism
that mind is apparently not subject to the limitations of time or
space. Lucius' clairvoyant powers seemed to prove this, and he
had himself become clairvoyant. He was acquainted too with
the idea of thought transference, which likewise disregards time
and space. There was therefore a basis for absent treatment.
Indeed in a letter to a patient, he characterized distance as but
a form of error. He writes: "For distance is nothing but error
that truth will some time explode. If my faith and your hope
mingle, the cure will be the result, so I will give my attention
to you as far as my faith goes, and shall like to hear how I
succeed." He also promises to send her a circular which will tell
of his treatment, and adds, "It is easier to cure than to explain
to a patient at a distance." (p. 131)

But in a number of his absent treatments direct suggestion

is very artfully used. An interesting case is one in which the woman is suffering from a stomach ailment. Writing her, he says he will do his best, while sitting by her as he writes the letter, to produce an effect upon her stomach. He asks that she take a tumbler full of water and drink a little now and then. He is with her, seeing her.

Don't hurry when you read this, but be calm and in a short time you will feel the heat start from your left side and run down like water; then your head will be relieved. Be slow in your movements. . . . I will take you by the hand at first . . . I am in this letter, and as often as you read this and listen to it you listen to me. . . . Take about one-half hour to devote to reading and listening to my counsel, and I am sure you will be better. (pp. 133-34)

In a letter to the editor of the *Portland Courier* (date not given), published in the *Quimby Manuscripts*, a Mr. Whitney tells of a case of healing by Dr. Quimby. The gentleman had written the good doctor requesting that he visit his wife, living in another Maine city, Wayne. She had been confined to her bed for more than a year, unable to lie on her left side or raise herself in bed. Unable to visit her in person, Quimby said he would try an experiment and asked to be informed of the results. He would, he said, begin absent treatment, continuing until the next Sunday, when between eleven and twelve o'clock he would make her walk.

The letter was received Wednesday. That night the wife was nervous and uneasy, but on Thursday was more comfortable, turning on her left side for the first time in almost a year. On Sunday her husband attended church between eleven and twelve, and on his return found her up and dressed. She had arisen and walked across the room and into the drawing room. Next day she had breakfasted with the family and continued to improve.

The editor was much impressed by the fact that a woman in Lancaster, New Hampshire, where Quimby was at the time, related that at the hour when he promised to visit Mrs. Whitney, Quimby had said that he must go to Wayne to visit a patient; that he had retired to the parlor for an hour, then returned and said that he had gotten the lady up, that she walked, and that three persons had witnessed it. This was corroborated by Mr. Whitney, the writer of the letter. (pp. 98-99)

The examples we have given thus far have left religion quite out of account, leaving healing on an apparently purely mental level. And it may justly be said that this was Quimby's great contribution. If he did not originate the notion of the inter-dependence of body and mind in matters of health, he was certainly the pioneer in America of the theory of the mental basis of all disease, and so the founder of New Thought. But he did also have religious ideas. They were not orthodox ideas according to the theological standards of his day, but that he held profound religious convictions none can deny who has read the *Manuscripts*. Religion in its traditional form, particularly the Calvinist version of it, was exceedingly distasteful to him and was the cause, he thought, of not a few of the insistent fears that lay at the basis of many of the maladies from which people suffered.

It was a wrong belief, an error, which brought as its result physical disorders; and part of the process of cure was the dis-illusioning of the patient's mind concerning the truth of those particular religious beliefs. Naturally this brought upon Quimby the enmity of many of the confirmed religionists of the day, who thought he was undermining all religion and attempting to destroy the Christian faith.

But in an introduction he wrote for one of his collections of writings which he evidently thought he might some day publish, is to be found a statement of purpose which certainly indicates a deep religious interest:

My object is to correct the false ideas and strengthen the truth. I make war with what comes in contact with health and happiness, believing that God made everything good, and if there is anything wrong it is the effect of ourselves, and that man is responsible for his acts and even his thoughts. Therefore, it is necessary that man should know himself so that he shall not communicate sin and error. (p. 280)

Note that God made everything good.

The religious overtone is definitely present also in a later declaration of the purpose of his work—not orthodox, of course, but clearly religious:

If I can show that man's happiness is in his belief, and his misery is the effect of his belief, then I have have done what never has been done before. Establish this and man rises to a higher state of wisdom, not of this world, but of that world of Science which sees that all the human misery can be corrected by this principle, as well as the evil effects of error. Then the Science of Life will take the place with other Sciences. Then in truth it can be said, "Oh, death, where is thy sting? Oh, grave, where is thy victory?" The sting of ignorance is death. But the Wisdom of Science is Life eternal. (p. 243)

In a rather more formal statement of the basis of his thinking, he approaches much more closely the metaphysical thought usually associated with New Thought as expressed by its later leaders. This statement not only links Quimby with the purely mental healing stage of New Thought, but at least anticipates some of its later more religious emphases.

The basis of his theory, he writes,

is that there is no intelligence, no power or action in matter itself, that the spiritual world to which our eyes are closed by ignorance or unbelief is the real world, that in it lie all the causes for every effect visible in the natural world, and that if this spiritual life can be revealed to us, in other words, if we can understand ourselves, we shall then have our happiness or misery in our own hands; and of course much of the suffering of the world will be done away with. (p. 319)

What precisely was Quimby's religion, and what views did he hold concerning the major theological ideas of the Christian faith? H. W. Dresser notes, in *Health and the Inner Life,* that at least half of Quimby's *Manuscripts* is filled with references to religious problems and the Bible. And he finds this logical since Quimby had observed that so many of his patients' fears, beliefs, and feelings which he thought were the basis of disease, were bound up with the religious creeds and experiences. How could he avoid concerning himself with religion? His observations set him to studying it. He shows great familiarity with the Bible, and his study of Jesus and his cures of disease led to "new conclusions concerning the mission of Jesus, the nature of sin, and the significance of the atonement." It became clear to Quimby that the "truth which shall set men free must explain both disease and sin . . . that the method of cure must apply both to the problems of disease and the problem of sin." Both, he saw, were the products of ignorance, and if this were true, "the cure of both was Wisdom, which relates not alone to the life of the flesh, but also to the life within." (p. 226 *passim*) And Wisdom, as we shall see later, he identifies with God.

He seems sometimes to ride roughshod over the commonly accepted religious beliefs and practices of the time.

Until the world is shaken by investigation so that the rocks and mountains of religious error are removed and the medical Babylon destroyed, sickness and sorrow will prevail. Feeling as I do and seeing so many young people go the broad road to destruction, I can say from the bottom of my heart, Oh, priestcraft! fill up the measure of your cups of iniquity, for on your head will come sooner or later the sneers and taunts of the people. Your theory will be overthrown by the voice of Wisdom that will rouse the men of Science, who will battle your error and drive you utterly from the face of the earth. (p. 270)

Again: "A great many make their disease out of the world's religions." Once more:

Religious creeds have made a large class of persons miserable, but religion like all creeds based on superstition must give away to Science. So superstition in regard to religion will die out as men grow wise, for wisdom is all the religion that can stand, and this is to know ourselves not as man, but as a part of Wisdom. (p. 277)

He was often accused of interfering with the religion of his patients, but he always defended himself against the charge by saying that if a particular biblical passage or some religious belief —for example, the nervousness resulting from the conviction that one has committed the "unpardonable sin"—affects his patient he attacks it. The patient's belief is what Quimby believes is a false "opinion" or interpretation of the biblical passage and the cause of the disturbance. It becomes necessary, therefore, "to destroy the false opinion in order to relieve the patient."

What he is really saying is that he is attacking not religion itself, but a false idea of religious truth, replacing the error with the truth, which is his declared method of cure. And a careful reading of his *Manuscripts* quite bears this out. Though he uses other terminology than the traditional orthodox religious leaders do, it is difficult to avoid the conviction that Quimby was really a deeply religious person, who merely found himself unable to accept religion in its traditional forms. He never worked out— I think most students of his writings will agree—a thoroughly self-consistent system of belief, but he acted in a prophetic fashion in his attitude toward the traditional religious beliefs of his period, as the Hebrew prophets and Jesus had done each in his own day. And he certainly pointed in the direction in which New Thought in general has moved as it has evolved in the late nineteenth and twentieth centuries.

"All the religion I acknowledge is God, or Wisdom," he writes. "I will not take man's belief to guide my barque. I would rather stand at the helm myself"; but priests and doctors have intervened and between them nearly destroyed body and soul. In all these systems "intelligence and goodness are not included." That is, religion as he saw it currently was deficient both intellectually and morally and he could have none of it—nothing, that is, but God. One who has God at the center of his thought and life could hardly be called nonreligious or antireligious, though he might well be *other-religious*, and that is about what Quimby was religiously.

Specifically now, what did he teach concerning the great central religious themes? First, his idea of God.

Negatively, God is not an identity such as man is, else he would be matter, and matter is surely not God. (p. 365) God is God of the living. (p. 366) God is equated with Science and

Truth. Science is represented as leading men to "that happy state where there is no sickness, sorrow, or grief, where all tears are wiped away from our eyes, and there we shall be in the presence of this great Truth that will watch us and hold us in the hollow of its [not his] hand, and will be to us the light that will open our eyes." (p. 366) All of which sounds almost as though it were taken from the book of Revelation. (See Rev. 7:17 and 21:4). And he affirms, "The true God never changes." (p. 324)

Quimby's idea of God expressed in the chapter "God and Man" in the *Manuscripts* (chapter xvii) "stands in sharp contrast to the opinions of men." Man has invented a God, he says, so God is the embodiment of man's belief, so as man changes, God changes. Such a God is, he says, the most convenient God he knows of. Writing in 1861, he says God listens to the prayers of the North as well as of the South; he leads men to battle and "from the prayers of His followers is as much interested in the victory as the winning party. The God of the North and the God of the South are as much at war as the Christian worshipers," and all this cant, he says, is "kept up with a certain solemnity of form as though there were real truth in it." (p. 324) But, "they worship they know not what. This false idea is the foundation on which the Christian world stands and the waters that flow from this fountain are corrupt, for where the foundation is corrupt the stream is also." (p. 325) To be an infidel, he says, "is to question the God of man's opinions." The true God "is not acknowledged . . . is in the hearts of the people working like leaven till it leavens the whole lump." (p. 324)

Now all nations have some idea of God, but a belief contains no wisdom, but is rather "a shadow of something that cannot be seen, worshipped by a man who knows not what it is." (p. 326) Even to the wise it is an unexplained mystery. "It stands at the door knocking, but is not recognized as having an identity . . . yet it is always the same, calm, and unmoved . . ." What is it? "It is invisible. Wisdom can never be seen by the eye of opinion any more than truth can be seen by error. It is what has never been acknowledged to have an identity . . . it is God." (p. 326) It is invisible wisdom, which fills all space, and whose attributes are all light, all wisdom, all goodness and love, which is free from all selfishness and hypocrisy, which makes or breaks no laws, but lets man work out his own salvation; which has no laws and restrictions, and sanctions men's acts according to their belief, and holds them responsible for their beliefs right or wrong without respect to persons. (p. 327)

It is worth noting that these are all attributes of God as conceived certainly within the Christian faith by important groups, if not by all. While seemingly at times of an impersonal nature, "mysterious, strange, invisible," God yet possesses the attributes normally associated with personality—goodness, love, freedom from selfishness and hypocrisy, etc. In a later passage Quimby becomes more specific in attributing personality to God. Where, he asks, "is the God in whose Wisdom I believe?" His answer is: "In the hearts of the people. He is not a man," clearly reacting against the crude physical anthropomorphism of much of the popular religion which made God just a *big man*. "Neither has he form. He is neither male nor female." But he is not *it* to Quimby, as he becomes later to New Thought writers, at least some if not all of the time.

Quimby's somewhat rambling articles demonstrate strikingly that he is attempting to clarify his own ideas by expressing them; that he was clearly unhappy with religion as he found it, but not yet clear in his own mind as to what he did think; that he was probably either consciously or unconsciously being affected by the religious ferment of his time represented by the Transcendentalist thinkers—though so far as I have discovered he never mentions even one of them, not even Emerson, perhaps the best known of them all. This seems a little strange, but is in keeping with his almost complete failure to refer to any of his sources in his writings. Dresser remarks that he was not a reader of philosophy or theology and that those who think that he borrowed from Berkeley or Swedenborg are quite mistaken. (p. 12)

His genius lay in another direction. He was perhaps as much of an original thinker as one is likely ever to find. Though he might have refined his ideas if he had read what others had thought, he apparently did not do so, probably being too much engrossed in the practical application of his new method of healing to the many who sought him out. I get the impression that he was weary when he tried to write some of his articles. Or is it that his was just an untrained mind clearly aware that all was not well with religion and religious ideas as he found them in his environment, but not equipped or trained to think through the difficult problems to clearly consistent conclusions? His originality lay rather in the elaboration of his theory and practice of healing than in the philosophical or theological realm.

Concerning Jesus, Quimby declared that he "was as any other man"; but he distinguished sharply between Jesus and the Christ, of whom he said: "he [Christ] was the Science which Jesus tried to teach." (p. 272) In another connection he put it this way: "Christ is the God in us all"; and "this Christ or God in us is the same that was in Jesus, only in greater degree in Him." (p. 303) That is, Jesus was "the natural man of flesh and blood, and Christ was the God manifested in the man Jesus."

This is an old distinction, dating from perhaps even the first century of the Christian era among the Gnostics, and reappearing at intervals throughout Christian history.

The moment it began to be believed that Jesus was an incarnation of God, serious problems arose. Was Jesus really God? If so, what of his human nature? Or was he only a human figure through whom God appeared at a historical moment in history? If so, at what point in his life did this take place? Was it from birth, or at the baptism and the beginning of his ministry? As God manifested himself in Jesus, did he then lose his human character? Or in what way were the human and the divine intermingled? The doctrine of the two natures, human and divine, in Jesus has been the generally accepted doctrine of the church. While a distinction between Jesus and the Christ has often enough been made, it has rather been the orthodox custom to do so with the emphasis on the perfect union of the two in Jesus Christ, rather than upon their separateness, as has been the emphasis of some more modern groups, which have uniformly held to a lower Christology than that which is expressed in the great historic creeds.

"Jesus was a man of flesh and blood," Quimby writes, "like anyone else. The difference between him and other men was called Christ. Now what did the difference consist in? In his life." Notice, he says "in his life," not his death, as appears so often in the more orthodox formulation of doctrine concerning Jesus. (p. 350)

Jesus, the human figure, Quimby regarded as a person who taught very much what he himself believed and taught about religion. He says:

I believe there was now one person who had the same ideas [those he had just been expounding] and to that person I give all the credit of introducing this truth into the world, and that was Jesus. I have no doubt of his being the only true prophet that ever lived who had ideas entirely superior to the rest of the world. Not that he was any better, but he was the embodiment of a higher Wisdom, more so than any man who has ever lived. (p. 283)

Again and again Quimby exposed what he considered some of the more harmful beliefs taught in Christianity, which incidentally read a little like some of the characterizations of the then current popular teaching to be found in the writings of the great liberal Unitarian preacher, Theodore Parker, who was in his prime during the period of Quimby's development of his ideas. There is no direct evidence that Quimby ever read Parker, but many of the same ideas expressed by Parker are reflected in Quimby's criticism of the doctrines held in the churches of his day. Once, after an exposition of erroneous Christian teaching, he wrote:

Jesus never taught one single idea of all the above, but condemned the whole as superstition and ignorance. He not only condemned the idea of a world independent of man, but proved there was none by all his sayings and doings. He looks upon all the above theories or beliefs as false and tending to make man unhappy. (p. 193)

Jesus, he continues, "came to destroy these beliefs and establish the Kingdom of God or Truth in this world."

The term Christ, he thinks, was never intended to be applied to the man Jesus, but to a "Truth superior to the natural man Jesus, and this Truth is what the prophets foretold." (p. 201)

The remarkable things attributed to Jesus which men regard as miracles were no miracles at all to the Christ, of which Jesus was the embodiment. These were really acts which were true to the Science with which Quimby frequently equates the Christ. Christ is called Wisdom, Truth, the intelligence of Jesus. It was the Christ in Jesus who did the mighty mysterious things difficult to explain on a human basis, but not at all on the basis of the Christ as the Truth, or Science.

Even the resurrection of Jesus from the dead was quite misunderstood by the people. They thought it was the man Jesus who arose. Jesus had foretold his resurrection and the people believed it was his intention to prove that his body of flesh and blood would arise. But this was not what Jesus meant at all. Had they known the facts they would not have concerned themselves about the human body, but would have left it in the tomb. Actually Quimby thinks they took the body away from the tomb to "establish their belief that it arose from the dead." But Jesus never had reference to a natural body. All he meant to say was that not his body, composed of matter which he believed was "nothing but a medium for the sense to use and control," but "his senses should arise from the dead," or from the "error of the people who believed that the senses are a part of the idea called body."

It all seems a bit complicated and unclear, but actually it is bound up with Quimby's concept of death—in which he says categorically that he does not believe. (p. 283) If there is really no death, then arising from the dead can have no meaning. At best death is only a change, but never, according to Dresser, a fundamental change. (p. 136) He thinks of death as "the name of something error wants to destroy and that is life."

Quimby never becomes specific concerning his ideas of the life after the crisis men call death. He clearly repudiated the then current ideas of heaven and hell, declaring that "Man's belief is his heaven and hell." But he does believe that Christ came "to destroy death or belief and bring light and immortality to light." (p. 186) Clues to his belief may be found scattered through his *Manuscripts*. He says in one place that the idea that we get rid of all sickness and sorrow when we shuffle off this mortal coil is mistaken. (p. 406) Again, he asserts, "The time will come when such words as death will be obsolete. They will not be used where there is knowledge. . . . Our next world is here where we are and must always be. This teaches us to do to others as we would that they should do unto us, because we are all a part of each other. When we injure one part, the whole feels it." (p. 407)

Jesus was of course the great healer, indeed the very founder of the science of healing which Quimby was practicing. Replying to a question which was evidently frequently asked of him, he wrote: "You ask if my practice belongs to any known Science. My answer is No, it belongs to Wisdom that is above man as man. The Science I try to practice is the Science that was taught eighteen hundred years ago, and has never had a place in the hearts of man since; but is in the world and the world knows it not." (p. 144)

Quimby often speaks of Christ as Science, and definitely employs the term Christian Science in an article written in February, 1863. Jesus' Science is never heard in the churches, he complains, "for it would drive aristocracy out of the pulpit and scatter freedom among the people. Nevertheless, the religion of Christ is shown in the progress of Christian Science while the religion of society decays as the liberal principles are developed." (p. 388)

Though this is the first appearance of the term Christian Science in the *Quimby Manuscripts*, and is dated some four months after Mary Baker Patterson, later Mary Baker Eddy, came to Portland to be healed by him, he may well have made frequent use of the term in conversation with his patients, only writing it down here for the first time. While it cannot be proved that Mrs. Eddy saw or heard the term used by Quimby, it is believed by Dresser that it is the origin of the term which has been given such wide currency by Mrs. Eddy in *Science and Health* and in the organization popularly known as the Christian Science church. (p. 389)

Little is said about the work of Christ beyond that of healing. Quimby had discarded most of the current ideas of Jesus as Savior, or Redeemer. There is in the *Quimby Manuscripts* no word of his mediatorial function, or his vicarious atonement other than in its repudiation. Quimby recites at one point the typical belief of the time of a humanity that had wandered from God and was lost; that God, seeing no other way whereby man might be saved, sent his Son as a ransom, etc. Then categorically he declares that he will show that Jesus never taught this at all. (pp. 192-93)

Because Quimby claimed he was using the method of Jesus in healing, it was asserted by some, apparently, that he was making himself equal with Christ—a charge which he completely repudiated. (pp. 350-51)

When he once stated Jesus' healing method in simple fashion it indeed seemed exactly like his own—the method of changing the minds of the sick. "If a person was well," he wrote, "it made no difference to Jesus what he believed, but he came to those who had been deceived. Well, how did he cure them? By changing their minds. For if he could not change their minds he could not cure them." (p. 379)

From what has been said thus far it may well enough be inferred that Quimby was not, in his teaching concerning God and Christ, within the Trinitarian tradition. Yet he does have a belief of a kind in a Trinity, as appears in what he calls "P. P. Quimby's Trinity": P. P. Quimby, he says, "believes in one living and true Wisdom called God, in Jesus (flesh and blood) a medium of this truth, and in the Holy Ghost, or explanation of God to man. . . . The Holy Ghost is the Science which will lead you into all truth; it will break the bond of error and triumph over the opinion of the world." (p. 304)

The Bible—or rather false beliefs about the Bible—gives rise,

Quimby thinks, to half the diseases from which his patients suffer. The fear implanted in men by the Bible concerning what will happen to them after death is the cause of the trouble of many. (p. 352) To counteract these fears and free men from the anxieties from which they suffer, Quimby is forced at times to attack some portion of the sacred book. (p. 287) And he does not hesitate to do it. Sometimes it is only a question of wrong interpretation and he finds it necessary to correct this to effect a cure. "So to cure," he writes, "I have to show by the Bible that they have been made to believe a wrong construction. My arguments change their minds and the cure comes. This is my excuse for what I have said upon the scriptures." (p. 231)

Quimby was quite familiar with the Bible but had his own way of interpreting it, in this following the fundamental Protestant principle of freedom of interpretation. It need hardly be said that his method was not that of modern technical scholarship. There is no evidence that he knew anything about such an approach to the Bible, though, had he known it, it is likely that he would have been influenced by it. Instead, he usually uses the allegorical method, seeing in the simple factual narratives hidden meanings. Thus, for example, in the story of the calling of the disciples by Jesus, he finds Andrew and Peter "fishing in the old Mosaic laws or sea." At Jesus' call they followed him to become "teachers of this truth to man." They abandoned their nets, or "old beliefs," and went with him. Going on, they saw others mending their nets, or "creeds," for the nets "like the priesthood were worn out." "These also left their fathers (old beliefs) in their ships (error) and followed him." (p. 344)

Mrs. Eddy, who exercised much the same freedom that Quimby did, called her method the "Scientific Interpretation." It was this method she employed in what is known as the "Key to the Scriptures," which forms chapters xv and xvi of *Science and Health*. In these two chapters she applies her method, a highly subjective one, to the books of Genesis and the Apocalypse. Charles Fillmore, founder of Unity School of Christianity, does much the same thing but with quite different results in his

Mysteries of Genesis, and New Thought writings are full of like interpretations. Emma Curtis Hopkins, from whom Charles Fillmore learned much as a student, contributed for several years to a Chicago newspaper a weekly "Metaphysical Interpretation of the International Sunday School Lessons." All of them have followed the essential method of Quimby, who was himself, whether consciously or not, following a method as old as the New Testament itself and even older.

Of the church and its dogmas he has a very low opinion. He was an individualist, not an organization man. As already observed concerning his criticism of orthodox Christian doctrine, he followed the pattern of Theodore Parker, whether consciously or not. So with reference to the church. Whether he would have been happy over the organizational forms New Thought has taken is not altogether clear.

His idea of man was not quickly or easily arrived at. In 1865 he wrote that for twenty-five years he had been trying to find out what he was—and had at last found out what he was not. He found that "what we call man is not man, but a shadow of error. Wisdom is the true man, and error the counterfeit." (p. 276) That which we call man, really a straw man, does not think of himself as a part of God, or as being with Him. He belongs to this world and expects at death to go to God. He lives in fear of death and brings misery on himself, inventing all sorts of diseases to torment himself.

But, Quimby declares positively, "Every man is a part of God, just so far as he is wisdom." (p. 396) Is this an assertion of the divinity of man, or only of his potentiality of achieving divinity? Actually Quimby distinguishes between the natural man and scientific man. Of natural man he has a low opinion. He says he is naturally "indolent, brutish and wilfully stupid, content to live like a brute." (p. 237) The scientific man he characterizes as "man outside of matter." (p. 236) "Natural man cannot see beyond matter, is in matter, but thinks he is outside it." Just as the moon's light is only a reflection of the light of the sun, so the "light of the body, or natural man is but the reflection of the scientific man." (p. 236) So long as the natural man does not know this he is in darkness, which is man's misery, his prison, until the "light of Wisdom bursts his bonds and sets the captive free." It was the mission of the Christ to preach to the prisoners bound by error and set them free. Here Quimby seems to be making the distinction that is made in later New Thought between man as he is and the *real* man. At least once he uses the term "real" to characterize man, saying, "Jesus taught that the real man is of wisdom." (p. 235)

One looks in vain in Quimby's writings for an explanation of good or evil. "There is to be found nowhere in the earlier writings," states the editor of the *Manuscripts,* "a clear idea of the nature and origin of evil." And again, "He never says explicitly 'there is no evil.'" (p. 390) Practically, Quimby seems to attribute such evil as exists to ignorance. Here again it seems evident that we are dealing with a practical man concerned with the practical task of meeting evil and disease rather than with working out a consistent theory of a philosophical nature concerning them.

What did Quimby think concerning mind and matter? Did he deny the reality of matter, as it is usually thought that Christian Science does, the idea being based on such statements of Mrs. Eddy's as "Matter and death are mortal illusions"? (*Science and Health,* 289:29)

It is extremely difficult to get a thoroughly consistent idea of what he did think, perhaps just because he himself was not clear in his own thought. In Warren Felt Evans there does appear a well-thought-out definition of mind and matter. Quimby, who lacked the philosophical background of Evans and later New Thought leaders, seems to have been groping for a consistent theory, but never quite to have achieved it.

At times he calls mind "spiritual matter," which seems to be a strange and incongruous use of terms (e.g., pp. 235, 334) The nearest he comes to a straightforward idealistic definition of matter is in his statement, "I have shown that there is no matter independent of mind or life." The addition of the term "life," which he seems to equate with mind, somewhat complicates matters. God, equated elsewhere with Wisdom, and Wisdom with mind, "made matter and condensed it into certain forms and elements that were necessary for man." (p. 392) Therefore matter is a derivative of mind, mind being primary, matter secondary. Perhaps that is what Quimby means by his use of the term "mind" as spiritual matter: mind as matter in its spiritual state before being "condensed" into forms which are recognizable as matter. Is matter therefore just mind or spirit which has been given form, form being the characteristic of matter as we ordinarily think of it, that is, as capable of being recognized by the senses, as being limited in space and also in time?

At another point he speaks of matter as "held in solution called mind." (p. 234) "What is there that is not matter that can be changed?" he asks. "It cannot be Wisdom," he replies. "It is matter held in solution called mind, which the power of Wisdom can condense into a solid so dense as to become a substance called matter." (p. 234) This furnished him a basis for an explanation of how man can get sick and be healed through a change of mind. Elsewhere he says that after he had found that mind was spiritual matter, he found that "ideas were matter condensed into a solid substance called disease." (p. 334)

It must be clearly recognized that here Quimby is writing not as a trained thinker working with carefully defined concepts, but as a practical man working to relieve the illnesses and sufferings of men and women, completely convinced of the wrongness of current ideas of medicine in relation to health, trying to explain in intelligible terms the theoretical basis of what he was actually doing, but lacking the dialectical skill and the necessary acquaintance with the thought of the past in which Evans was later to find support for the theory they both followed. Quimby undoubtedly laid the basis for the later thought developed by New Thought and Christian Science, even though he never stated it with complete clarity or consistency.

He can and does say in "Questions and Answers," "There is no Wisdom in matter." (p. 167) Mrs. Eddy, whether consciously building upon that or not, could go on to elaborate from it what she calls "The Scientific Statement of Being": "There is no life, truth, intelligence, nor substance in matter...." (*Science and Health*, 468:9-10) as it appears under her heading "Recapitulation" which, it is supposed by many, represents the development in Mrs. Eddy's mind which began with Quimby's "Questions and Answers."

P. P. Quimby died in 1866. A healer of many thousands of people, himself healed of a serious malady in the beginning of his career, he died at a comparatively early age—worn out in body by the incessant labor during his Portland years in bringing healing to others. His son George writes that "the last five years of his life were exceptionally hard." Overcrowded with patients and overworked, he could or would not take opportunity for relaxation. Nature at last rebelled, and he could no longer bear up under the strain. He had always been able when strong to ward off disease, but tired and weakened by overwork, he had neither the strength of will nor the reasoning powers to fend off the illness which brought his life to a close. "Physician, heal thyself" has often enough been the taunt of the unconvinced when a healer himself falls victim to disease. Had Quimby been willing to give up or even to limit himself sharply in his healing ministry, he might well have been able to heal himself. His loyal son, who worked closely with his father during the Portland years, attributes his death to "too close application to his profession and overwork." He proposed as a fitting epitaph the scriptural verse, "Greater love hath no man than this, that he lay down his life for his friends," and added, "if ever a man did lay down his life for others, that man was Phineas P. Quimby." (*New England Magazine*, March, 1888)

It is nearly a century now since Quimby passed off the scene. How has history dealt with the man?

The New Thought Movement, though not organized in any way by himself, is Quimby's living monument, and in a sense its far-reaching influence, in all its varied manifestations, is but "the lengthening shadow of the man," not always recognized, of course, even by those most devoted to it. Much of his thought and

method have been modified, even outgrown, but one who attempts
to trace New Thought back to its original source is likely to agree
that the real source of it was unquestionably the doughty little
Portland healer.

What were some of the judgments upon Quimby and his
thought and practice—first from those who were close to him,
indeed were healed by him?

Mrs. Julius A. Dresser—Annetta Seabury—wrote of him:

> He was one of the few profoundly original men. Working alone and
> without aid from books and according to methods of his own, he not
> only regained his own health . . . but saved the lives of thousands of
> others . . . and produced a philosophy . . . which has wrought trans-
> formation in a vast number of lives. It is no exaggeration to say that
> few men ever lived who, working single-handed in a new field, have
> accomplished as much as he. (*The Philosophy of P. P. Quimby*, pp.
> 10-11)

Mary Baker Patterson (Mrs. Eddy) published a poem in a
Lynn, Massachusetts, newspaper entitled, "On the Death of P. P.
Quimby, Who Healed with the Christ Truth taught in Opposition
to all Isms." (Feb. 22, 1866) A score or more of letters and
articles published in various newspapers of the time leave no
doubt of the very great admiration which she felt for him, her
healer from a long endured physical malady, and the gratitude
she felt for his teaching her a method of which she felt herself
a very humble and grateful learner, who had only thus far par-
tially glimpsed, like the blind man who at first "saw men as trees
walking" (Mark 8:24), the possibilities that lay in it. (These
writings are to be found in the original edition of H. W. Dresser,
The Quimby Manuscripts [New York: Thomas Y. Crowell, 1921],
chapter xii. This chapter is lacking in later editions. Her later
statements, written after her organization was already making its
way against heavy opposition, are quite different in tone.)

As time passed, and the movement grew and developed in
many respects far beyond what Quimby had taught, at least
explicitly, it is not surprising that he was not often mentioned

even by the leading exponents of New Thought. This is partly the result of the general tendency within the organization not to magnify personality, but to emphasize Truth. This characteristic has made it rather difficult for the historian to find much factual information even concerning the greater leaders of the movement. A New Thought writer in one of the movement's publications entitled his article—a very brief one, and one that communicated little concerning the man—"Quimby, the Forgotten Man." And but comparatively few articles have appeared in New Thought journals about him.

Dr. Ervin Seale wrote one in the *Bulletin of the International New Thought Alliance* (XXXVIII, 17, 18, 48 ff.) in which he represents Quimby as anticipating by many decades some of the pronouncements of modern psychology. Quimby taught, he says, that "all our actions are really reactions. All that you and I say and do and engage ourselves in, are not direct actions of our conscious will; they are really reactions of our subjective conditioning. Modern psychology has just come to that point. But it was Quimbyism." (p. 17)

Considering the kinship of much that Quimby taught with New England Transcendentalism, there is special relevance in any article or book which relates the two. An article in the *New England Quarterly*, Volume XVII, does just that. Under the title "P. P. Quimby Scientist of Transcendentalism," the author, Stewart W. Holmes (not, like Ernest Holmes, a member of the New Thought following, but a Methodist or of Methodist background), writes of Quimby as one who anticipated a number of extremely important discoveries which are today regarded as very modern. Says Holmes:

There lived in the "province" of New England, contemporary with Emerson a man who in some measure anticipated our modern neuropsychiatrists and in himself made a fusion of their therapeutic practice and the theories of Transcendentalism. This man, almost forgotten today, was P. P. Quimby, called Dr. Quimby, because of the thousands of cures he effected on his New England neighbors. Dr. Quimby may be called the scientist of Transcendentalism because he demonstrated visibly on human organisms the operational validity of Emerson's hypotheses.

In a footnote (p. 357), he adds: "Although Quimby's name was writ in water, owing to his modesty and the time consuming devotion to his patients, elements of the therapeutic technique survive in the New Thought and Christian Science Movements which stem from him and preserve his ideas in somewhat bastardized form."

While Emerson, whom Holmes regards as the most representative of the Transcendentalists, arrived deductively at his theories, never submitting them to anything like laboratory proof, Quimby forged his theories and thence his metaphysic from "years of patient experiment with individual persons." And "something lawful and orderly occurred when he applied his technique." He carefully checked himself as observer, a thing which, Holmes notes, few scientists did before Einstein, and "his untutored and unprejudiced approach enabled him to anticipate modern colloidal and physical researches, and some of the theories and practices of our present-day neuro-semantic, neuro-linguistic therapy."

Quoting almost the exact words of the Cambridge *History of American Literature* (New York, 1933, I, 347), Holmes speaks of the weakness of the Transcendentalists as a group, "their tendency to neglect proximate for primal causes, their attempt to attain the spiritual, not by subduing but by turning their backs on the material, their proneness to substitute passivity and receptiveness for alert and creative force, their ineffectualness and atrophy of the will." In contrast, he says, Quimby, holding the same metaphysics but like his model, Jesus, putting it into action, helped thousands of people to regain health and happiness by working with the proximate and the material.

Proving his effectiveness daily, he was continually stimulated to alertness; working in the world where man is destined to live, willy nilly, rather than meditating apart from it, his reaction to life had survival value. Realizing the danger of living predominantly on the verbal level

like a philosopher, rather than predominantly on the object level, like
a scientist, he adjusted his reactions to the inevitable condition of
human existence — that human beings are primarily social beings.
(p. 368)

Holmes asserts that Quimby anticipated some of the discoveries of psychiatry and general semantics when he reduced to a
system having a fair amount of predictability "the healing of
people by semantic means—that is by influencing their beliefs."
(p. 369) His discovery that certain physiological conditions had a
psychical cause runs close to much that is found in case books
of abnormal psychology, though his technique of discovery,
i.e., by clairvoyance, differed. Second, his method of healing
by explaining "how each effect has resulted from a certain remote
semantic cause" is similar to much in psychiatric practice today.
And third, Jung, like Quimby, "urged on his patients the values
of a faith in God (that is eternal, lawful life) saying that in
every human being past middle life, the essential problem is a
religious one." He notes that with Quimby religion and health
are not two different things, and his patients "almost always have
received a spiritual regeneration when he healed them."

Holmes insists on the close connection between semantics
and health. Quimby, he thinks, states, as does Korzybski, that the
power which words have over the mind keeps man in bondage to
primitive beliefs. His method was partly to undo the false reasoning and teach the patient what should be the correct interpretation of his first sensations, that is, to retain his semantic reactions. (p. 371) Thus, "when a physician tells a person he has
consumption, the healer, instead of giving the disease a name
should explain how it came, and this the physician does not do,"
but Quimby did. Disease is due, according to Quimby, "to a wrong
direction of the mind." Hence it is not an evil but an error. That is,
says Holmes, it is a semantic disturbance. (p. 372)

Holmes finds Quimby's clairvoyance also not out of line with
modern parapsychology's demonstrated theories of ESP. And in
his estimation, Quimby proves himself to have been far ahead
of most of us in the present day.

Finally, in Quimby's conclusions as to the nature of things, Holmes asserts that his empirical researches led him to postulate general premises about the nature of things very similar to what some modern physicists hold today, e.g., Eddington, Jeans, Einstein. (see pp. 375-77) He concludes his article with this remarkable tribute to the Portland "doctor": "This self-taught, hard headed imaginative Yankee, formulated certain premises and conclusions, certain techniques, among which we find ideas current before the dawn of history and ideas that are only now coming into acceptance and use by some of the more rigorously trained scientists." (p. 379)

It may well be that Stewart Holmes has overstated his case. Certainly it is possible to demonstrate that healers such as Coué, psychologists like Jung, and semanticists like Korzybski did not arrive at their ideas via the study of Quimby—they may even not have heard of his name. But it is undoubtedly a vast tribute to a man living largely in the first half of the nineteenth century to say that he caught glimpses at least of what great figures in these areas in the first half of the twentieth century have asserted to be scientifically demonstrable fact.

4

Warren Felt Evans, Pioneer Writer

WHILE PHINEAS P. QUIMBY may without cavil be regarded as the founder not only of the New Thought Movement but of the whole so-called Metaphysical Movement in America, credit for the spread of his ideas and methods, as well as for the organization of movements that have made these a force in American life, must go to four others. These were four sick people who sought healing at his hands within a period of less than two years, in 1862-63: Annetta G. Seabury, Julius A. Dresser, Mary Baker Glover Patterson (later Mary Baker Eddy), and Warren Felt Evans.

Julius A. Dresser and Annetta Seabury, who were husband and wife, were the first effectively to organize what has since been called New Thought; Mary Baker Eddy became the founder of Christian Science; and Warren Felt Evans became the first to give literary form to the new ideas and methods of cure, though he never seems to have concerned himself with any institutional expression of either—save that he established a kind of mind-cure sanitarium at Salisbury, Massachusetts, to which people came for rest and healing.

Biographical details concerning the life of Warren Felt Evans are extremely meager. It seems rather strange that a man whose influence was so considerable should not at some time have been the subject, if not of a full-length biography—and many men of lesser stature have been so honored—at least of some magazine articles. But only one series of four articles is to be found. These articles, by William J. Leonard, appeared in *Practical Ideals*, published in Boston (Vol. X [1905], No. 2, pp. 1-15; No. 3, pp.

1-23, No. 4, pp. 9-26; and Vol XI [1906], No. 1, pp. 10-26). The articles in the *Dictionary of American Biography* and in such other encyclopedias as have included him as a subject rely on one small pamphlet, now hardly to be found, as their major source. And even this (W. J. Leonard's *The Pioneer Apostle of Mental Science: A Sketch of the Life and Work of Rev. Warren F. Evans, M.D.*, undated, but said to have been published in 1903), is rather an appreciation than a factual biography of the man.

He was a farmer's son, a descendant of John Evans of Roxbury, Massachusetts, born to Eli and Sarah Edson Evans at Rockingham, Vermont, on December 23, 1817, the sixth of their seven children. He studied at Chester Academy and in 1837 entered Middlebury College. In 1838 he transferred to Dartmouth College at Hanover, New Hampshire, as a sophomore, but left in the middle of his junior year to become a Methodist minister. He served eleven different charges in that denomination. He married M. Charlotte Tinker on June 21, 1840, and continued his Methodist ministry until 1863, when he left that church and joined the Church of the New Jerusalem (Swedenborgian), having somewhere along the way begun to read the works of the great Swedish seer, Emanuel Swedenborg, and been converted to the truth of his doctrines.

But before this he had contracted a serious illness, "a nervous affection, complicated by a chronic disorder." He got no help from physicians or their medicines. How he first heard of P. P. Quimby is not disclosed, but the fame of the good Portland healer had spread throughout New England through patients he had healed and through articles in the public press concerning his amazing healing powers without benefit of any physical remedy. At all events, Evans appeared in Portland in 1863. Mary Baker Eddy, then Mrs. Patterson, had come there, as had the Dressers in 1862. Evans, like them, found healing in the philosophy and methods which Quimby employed and taught, and became a devoted disciple, as did the others. He visited Quimby a second time, felt that he understood the philosophy and method and told the Doctor that he thought he, too, could heal. Quimby encouraged him to do so, with the result that he began the practice of mental medicine at Claremont, New Hampshire.

In 1867 he opened an office in Boston and for more than twenty years, with his wife, practiced and taught informally the principles of mental healing. For years they received patients in their own home, in Salisbury, where they had moved in 1869. No charge was made for their services or instruction beyond free will offerings, and no one, however poor, was ever turned away. But he created no institution to perpetuate his teaching. He died in 1889.

Horatio W. Dresser says in *Health and the Inner Life* that Evans had already been well prepared for the experience with Quimby through his reading of the idealistic philosophies, particularly of Bishop Berkeley, and books such as *Love and Wisdom* by Swedenborg. (p. 119) That he had read Swedenborg there can be no doubt, but I am not sure of his acquaintance at this time with Berkeley and the other great idealistic philosophers. Among all his references to thinkers and writers of the past, in his first book, *The Mental Cure*—and he referred to a considerable number—there was none at all to Berkeley, Fichte, Schelling, Hegel, and others who are so frequently quoted or mentioned in later books in connection with his discussion of mind, matter, the spiritual nature of the universe, and kindred topics. It was enough that he had read Swedenborg, in whose writings, as Dresser observed justly, there are teachings "which directly lead to the practical method for which Dr. Quimby stood." Evans needed only "to find a man who was actually proving what he had theoretically anticipated in order to accept the entire therapeutic doctrine." (p. 119)

It may strike one as strange that in all his six volumes on various phases of mental healing, Evans should have mentioned Quimby but once, and that in a book written seven years after Quimby's passing. He wrote in *Mental Medicine:*

Disease being at its root a wrong belief . . . change that belief and we cure the disease. By faith we are thus made whole. . . . The late

Dr. Quimby of Portland, one of the most successful healers of this or any age, embraced this view of the nature of disease and by a long succession of most remarkable cures effected by psychopathic remedies, at the same time proved the truth of the theory and the efficiency of that mode of treatment. . . . He seemed to reproduce the wonders of Gospel history. (p. 210)

But Dresser notes, "There is nothing he wrote in the six volumes that does not relate directly to Quimby's teaching." (*Health and the Inner Life,* p. 119)

W. F. Evans not only healed, but wrote a great deal. He published three small books on phases of Swedenborg's teachings —"none of enduring significance," says the *Dictionary of American Biography.* But his great distinction lies in the fact that he was the first to write of the new healing and its basis as taught and practiced by Quimby. His first book, *The Mental Cure, Illustrating the Influence of the Mind on the Body, Both in Health and Disease, and the Psychological Method of Treatment,* was published in 1869, only three years after Quimby's death and six years before the appearance of *Science and Health* by Mrs. Eddy. Quimby had, of course, long taught and practiced, even before Mrs. Eddy appeared as a patient in his office, the fundamental bases of healing through the mind; but his "Manuscripts" had not been published—indeed, they were not published until just fifty years after Evans' first book which set forth the basic philosophy underlying his healing and his method of practice.

Thus Evans becomes the first of a long line of exponents of the basis of New Thought ideas and methods to set them forth in published book form. Although the books were never mentioned by Mrs. Eddy in any of her writings, she might well have read not only *The Mental Cure,* published in 1869, but also *Mental Medicine,* published in 1872, three years before *Science and Health.* Evans' third book, *Soul and Body,* saw the light the same year *Science and Health* did, 1875, and Dresser asserts that it came out earlier than the latter, though not early enough to have been read by Mrs. Eddy before the appearance of her own book.

Even if Mrs. Eddy had never heard of or met Dr. Quimby,

whose influence upon her thought or her system both she (in her later years) and her followers so insistently disavowed, she could thus have found publicly expressed the fundamental doctrine of the Portland healer concerning the primacy of Mind in the universe and its power over matter—or, as she saw it, over that which to the senses seems to be matter—particularly in questions of healing. She could have found this: "A man is really sick in mind, when he believes himself sick." (*The Mental Cure,* p. 82) Or this: "All disease being an outward visible effect, its cause must be sought within. . . . It has its origin in some disordered state of the inner man, for there is a pathology of the mind as well as of the body." (p. 67) Or, once more: "All disease is in its cause an insanity . . . its secret spring is some abnormality, unsoundness of the mind." (p. 98)

Evans continued to write during his whole active career. His most widely used book, *The Divine Law of Cure,* appeared in 1881 and went through many editions. Down to the end of the century it was still being advertised in New Thought publications and sold. *The Primitive Mind Cure* was issued in 1885, and a year later, in 1886, Evans' last book, *Esoteric Christianity and Mental Therapeutics,* was given to the public. This too had a wide sale.

None of these is currently published. They are to be found only in libraries or occasionally in secondhand bookstores, but they are basic to an understanding of the development of the whole metaphysical movement in America. In them, within the active mind of a profound believer one can find reflected almost every phase of that movement as Evans met the practical and theoretical problems in his practice and in his wide reading in the fields of philosophy, psychology, science, and medicine. For he was a wide reader, in this contrasting sharply with Quimby (in so far as we have been able to discover his reading habits) and with Mary Baker Eddy.

Of persons or their books referred to in *The Mental Cure,* by far the most frequently mentioned is Emanuel Swedenborg. There are at least seventeen such references—sometimes only casual, but in a number of cases citing specific teachings or ideas. Among other important philosophers or scientists, ancient or modern, referred to in this book are Aristotle, Plato, Descartes, Leibnitz, Thales, Bacon, John Locke, Auguste Comte, Coleridge, Bichat, Schelling, Herbert Spencer, Immanuel Kant, Condillac, Sir Humphry Davy, Euler, Dr. Justus Kerner, Samuel K. Wells, William Hazlitt, Madame Guyon, and Friedrich von Schlegel. And of course there were Jesus and Paul. No reference appears to Emerson, Quimby, or any other American thinker.

In general, it appears that at this stage Evans was more specifically the mental healer than in his later books. To be sure, he did couple religion with healing, but by no means so insistently as at a later time. He was very little under the influence of occult beliefs other than those of Swedenborg. He did not refer to oriental thought, the Kabbala, or the Hermetic philosophy, as he did in later books.

There are numerous indications in his various books that Evans' was an active mind. He speaks once of studying for a year the questions and principles involved in absent treatment, which he very definitely practiced. He mentions a case in which he was examining a patient hundreds of miles away, evidently clairvoyantly, and was affected sensibly with his diseased state of both mind and body. Once when the patient was suffering from nausea, it occasioned vomiting in himself. This confirmed him in his belief in the power of the mind over the body, and in the possibility of the healer's availing himself of this mental force in healing another. He found this more effective even than "magnetic manipulation." He says that he devoted a year to the study of laws governing the transmission of vital force to a distance, and experimented with it. As a result, "many quite desperate cases of chronic disease were cured in a few days." (p. 262) Jesus clearly was able to do this, (p. 263) and so can others who attain to the state exhibited by him. (p. 264)

Warren Evans speaks also in *The Mental Cure* of experiments with medicine. For example: "A cloth wet with a solution of sulphate of magnesia to cause a movement of the lower intestine in a costive state of the bowels, and that without inflaming the whole alimentary tube, as when administered through the stomach," the organ seeming to attract to itself an element for which it has a hungry affinity when applied to the skin over it. Also an application of plain salt to the lumbar plexus will relieve the inflammation of the kidneys caused by an excess of sugar in the urine. But, he adds, "an intelligent application of spiritual or mental force, may produce all the effect that can be produced by medicines." (pp. 166-67) He has, he says, thrown persons into a gentle perspiration in five minutes though they were miles away. (p. 167) For, he continues, "a psychological influence can effect a physiological action of any organ of the body." (p. 167)

Evans seems to have read widely in the medical, and especially the medical-psychological, literature of the day. He pays a great deal of attention to diagnosis. It is his theory that almost all diseases can be diagnosed from the brain. He claims to know just what part of the brain is involved in specific kinds of illness. Evidently he has the brain charted phrenologically. In a rather amusing paragraph in *Mental Medicine*, he writes: "The liver receives its peculiar cerebral or nerve stimulus from a part of the brain situated between combativeness and cautiousness; the kidneys from a point on each side of causality; the bowels from the brain between hope and veneration etc." (p. 147)

In *The Mental Cure* he also expresses belief in the efficacy of the laying on of hands on the affected portion of the body, since "the spiritual emanation or those that proceed from our affectional and intellectual states are continually flowing from our bodies, and from the palms of our hands more copiously than from any other part of the body," because there are more pores in this part of the anatomy. Hence, he says, "the imposition of hands was not once an unmeaning ceremony nor a mere symbol," but an actual "communication of spiritual life." (pp. 73-74) It was therefore logical that he should make constant use of physical manipulation in his treatments, e.g., "Place the left hand on the right side, just under the right shoulder and as far down as the ribs extend. Place the right hand on the left side of the patient just under the ribs near the end of the stomach and spleen etc." (*Mental Medicine*, p. 114) In this he followed Quimby's practice, as did Mrs. Eddy also in her earlier career, though later she forbade it categorically and urged her followers to avoid it as a plague.

Evans also frequently speaks of the use of magnetic force, by which he means the hypnotic method, as a cure of disease. He says that he has known the whole disorder of body and mind to be removed in a very short time through the "judicious use of the magnetic treatment." Whether this was his own method is not stated. He may only have observed it as practiced by another. Certainly "the shortest way to a cure of the body is by relieving the mind of the patient from this morbid state," indeed a necessary step before any remedial agent in the form of medicine can be effective. It matters not if this be done through a doctor's own psychological influence or through the prayers of the devout, "if it only be well and effectively done." (p. 154)

Evans also was evidently aware of and to some extent influenced by the current beliefs in Spiritualism. This is shown in his declaration that the manipulation of medicines by the physician and his mental state while compounding them, "produce psychometric effects upon a sensitive patient." (p. 169)

In his earliest book Evans again and again gives expression to his belief, undoubtedly reflecting the influence of Swedenborg, that there is an angel world from which there may flow into our earthly minds that which may be of great help.

Our angel guardians know or may learn what we need and will communicate it to us if we will open the inner ear to receive it. . . . We may rely on such impressional intelligence and intuitive flashes of a higher light, far more than upon the prescriptions of a well meaning but imperfectly enlightened physician. (pp. 292-93)

Throughout the whole first book—much more than in his later books—there is also a constant emphasis upon the correspondence between the spiritual and physical worlds. He states the doctrine thus: "Every part of the body has some correspondence with the spiritual nature of man, and is the ultimate expression of some mental faculty from which it exists and derives stimulus or the force that enables it to accomplish its appropriate use in the animal economy." (p. 120)

This obviously stems from Evans' Swedenborgian predilection, for the chapter headings in *The Mental Cure* follow rather closely the correspondences of the Swedish seer. Some of Evans' headings are: "The Relation of Intellect to Love"; "The Correspondence of the Brain and the Mind"; "The Heart and Lungs and Their Relation to Love and Intellect"; "Correspondence of the Stomach and the Mind"; "The Excretions of the Body and the Mind and Their Relation"; "The Skin, Its Connection with the Internal Organs and Correspondence with the Mind"; "The Senses, Their Correspondence and Independent or Spiritual Action," etc. Compare section headings in Swedenborg's *The Divine Love and Wisdom*, 1947 edition, pp. x-xi, "All things of the created universe viewed in reference to uses, represent man in an image and this testifies that God is man." (N. 319) and especially "Will and understanding which are the receptacles of love and wisdom are in the brains, in the whole and every part of them, and therefore in the body, in the whole and in every part of it." (N. 362) "There is a correspondence of the will and the heart and of the understanding with the lungs." (N. 371; cf. Evans, *The Mental Cure*, ch. xii) This influence of Swedenborg is found running all through the New Thought Movement and in Christian Science as well.

In his *Mental Medicine*, published in 1872, to which he gives the subtitle *A Theoretical and Practical Treatise on Medical Psychology*, Evans quotes a number of writers from the medical-psychological field on the effect of the mind on the physical organism. These writers sound surprisingly like contemporary psychiatrists. In chapter iv, Evans speaks of how unimportant somnambulistic sleep is in comparison with what is later called "suggestibility"; i.e., that the patient be thrown only into the "impressible conscious state." But as he goes on to describe this it seems that he is really speaking of a hypnoidal state, though not that of deep hypnotic sleep. Perhaps countering the charge that this is harmful to the patient, he claims that it is wholly voluntary both in its commencement and in its continuance, and insists that so far from rendering the patient potentially, at least, the object of evil intent, it magnifies and refines his moral and spiritual sensibilities.

Evans differs from Christian Science, and in general from New Thought also, in the importance he attributes to diagnosis. "The first step toward a cure," he asserts, "is a correct diagnosis of the disease." (*Mental Medicine,* p. 85) The gaining of an accurate knowledge of the morbid state is half the problem, he maintains. How is this knowledge to be had? He mentions "clairvoyant diagnosis" or intuitive perception of the sensitives—but some have no knowledge of anatomy, a lack which he evidently thinks a serious defect. Some doctors depend on "intuitive perception" or clairvoyant means while criticizing it in others, he says. This power of intuitive perception, which is innate in human nature, is unfolded and stimulated to activity by spiritual influences. (p. 187)

In *The Divine Law of Cure* (1881), without for a moment disavowing the religious—indeed, the Christian—basis of mental healing, he is at pains to demonstrate that it has at the same time quite a rational basis. It is, he affirms, but the logical, practical application of what the great idealistic philosophers of the past have always taught, though they themselves seem never to have grasped the meaning of their thought in relation to mankind's health.

Nowhere does Evans intimate that his own interest in or practice of healing derives from these philosophers or their philosophies. He apparently got his practical interest from an experience of personal healing at the hands of Phineas P. Quimby, just as Mrs. Eddy did; and from his background of Christian training and experience he recognized in Quimby's healing work a rediscovery of the method of Jesus, just as did Mrs. Eddy. In all his writings he continues to emphasize that mental healing is an integral part of the Christian gospel, and that purely mental healing, while possible, is still greatly facilitated by Christian faith. In *The Divine Law of Cure,* he seems to be trying deliberately to broaden the base of the mental healing ministry by asserting that it is but the practical application of ideas widely held in New England in his day by persons who had become dissatisfied with the current faith of orthodoxy and who felt themselves alienated from Christianity. "All right," he seems to be saying, "maybe the miraculous element in the New Testament seems to you to be an obstacle to your belief. But quite apart from the New Testament, or indeed any religious basis, mental healing squares with the best thought of the great idealistic philosophers of the centuries, and particularly those to whom many of the transcendentalists looked as their philosophical guides." And he names them and quotes from them—Hegel, Schelling, Berkeley, Fichte, Jacobi, Cousin, Coleridge.

As an example of his method, he quotes Berkeley as saying: "There is not any other *substance* than spirit." (p. 147) Leibnitz, he says, taught "that all force is spirit"; Schelling wrote that "Nature is spirit visible, and spirit is invisible nature." Hegel affirms that all the objects of creation are in their inmost reality thoughts of God. (p. 151)

All the objects of nature are *phenomena* or *appearances,* as Hegel, Fichte, Berkeley, Swedenborg, and all the idealists affirm. By this we do not mean that they are an empty show, but that the appearance does not stand on its own feet, and has its being, not in itself, but in something else of which it is a form or manifestation. . . . The same is true of the human body. It is the phenomenon of spirit, an appearance of which the soul is the underlying reality. (p. 152)

He goes on to say that "it was the doctrine of Fichte, Schelling, Hegel and Cousin that matter and mind, in their underlying reality, or substance, are one and the same. Matter is only a phenomenal manifestation of mind or spirit." (p. 153) He even finds Huxley admitting "that matter may be properly considered as a *mode of thought*," (p. 157) and Faraday declaring his "belief in the immateriality of physical objects." (p. 157) Whereupon, Evans asks, "If they are not material, in the popular sense of that term, what are they but modifications of the mind, or phenomena of spirit? If on this admission they have any reality at all, they must be ideas or sensations in a perceiving mind." (p. 157) He affirms with "Bishop Berkeley, the English Plato," and with Swedenborg, the Scandinavian Seer and spiritual philosopher, that mind is the only *substance*. Without it nothing material could exist. The body has no independent being or life itself. The soul, which he equates with mind, "is the real *man* and the body is its *ex*-istence or outward manifestation, to itself and others." (p. 163) He does not in the least deny the real existence of the body, "but only that it has an independent being. It perpetually lives and from the mind." (p. 164) The idealists, he declares,

do not deny the *reality* of external things. They only deny that they have any reality independent of mind. . . . When men attribute to objects a real existence, they do not err; they only err when they suppose that these objects can or do exist independently of a perceiving mind. . . . The world of matter with all it contains is bound up in an indissoluble unity with the world of mind, and in fact exists in it. So it is with regard to the body. All the properties of our bodies are only modifications of our minds. They are reducible to feelings or sensations in the soul. (p. 168)

He invokes the renowned Jonathan Edwards in support of this when he writes, "The human body and brain itself exist, only mentally in the same sense that other things do." (p. 169) He calls Edwards, whom he identifies as the greatest American metaphysician, a Berkeleyan follower in respect to his ideas of the external world.

That "the body with all its varying states of health and disease, pleasure and pain, strength and weakness, is only the externalization or ultimation or projecting outward in appearance to ourselves, of our inward condition," he finds clearly held and stated by Fichte (p. 172), whom he quotes at some length. From this it seems to him clearly to follow that the condition of the body is an effect of which the state of the mind is the cause. Underneath and back of disease there is a fixed and chronic mode or habit of thinking and feeling that must be changed, and when this is effected, by whatever means we employ, the abnormal condition is remedied at the root, and the body adjusts itself to the new order of things in the spiritual organism as surely as an effect is connected with its producing cause. (p. 173)

So, he continues, "our bodily condition is the result of our thinking." If we wish to change it for the better, "let us *imagine*, or *think* and *believe*, that the desired change is being effected, and it will do more than all other remedial agencies to bring about the wished for result." (p. 174)

Medicine has proceeded upon the basis of sensualistic and materialistic philosophy, which Hegel had called the "dirt philosophy." It was Evans' purpose to show "that idealism is capable of furnishing a more efficient means of the cure of disease." And this, he contends, was the basis of Jesus' healing. (p. 176)

Evans has a full chapter which he entitles "The creative power of thought, or Hegel's philosophy as a medicine," in which he seems to argue that Hegel's philosophy, as he knew it through Sterling's *Secret of Hegel* and Hegel's *Logic,* furnished a basis for what he calls phrenopathy, or mental healing, and is quite in line with the teaching of the New Testament. He asks directly the question: "Is the philosophy of Hegel of any practical value? Can it be made available in constructing an efficient system of phrenopathy or mental cure?" (p. 251) And though he seems never to give a direct answer to the question, one gets the impression that he thinks it can, since Hegel's concept of the world is a thoroughly idealistic one "in which the universe is an expression, a manifestation of the ideas in the Divine Mind." Thought, he says,

is the ground of reality. . . . Take away the thought of a thing and it becomes as nothing . . . but that which is out of thought is to us out of existence. . . . Pain which is not thought of is not felt. . . . When we think of it, it passes from nothing to something, for it is only by this that it comes to have any reality for us. Disease without this would be as nothing, for it is only a wrong way of thinking, or . . . a false belief. Banish it from thought and it no longer exists. . . . Here is the grand remedy, the long sought panacea. It is the fundamental principle in the phrenopathic cure. (pp. 250-52, *passim*)

The Primitive Mind Cure was published in 1884. A fifth edition bears the date 1885. The subtitle of the book is *The Nature and Power of Faith, or Elementary Lessons in Christian Philosophy and Transcendental Medicine.* In the Preface, he calls it "lessons in transcendental philosophy." Did he mean thereby to ally himself consciously with the Transcendentalists?

He begins with a discussion of the nature of ideas and idealism, then turns to an application of the idealistic philosophy to the cure of mental and bodily maladies. "That which we most need," he says,

is to develop into consciousness our inner and higher life and to give to it what rightfully belongs to it, an absolute sovereignty over all below it. It should be our aim to elevate the principle of thought above the plane of the senses and free it from their distorting influence. (p. 14)

To achieve this state we must first discover our true self, which, he finds, the ancient Vedas of India hold as the highest knowledge. The frequent references in this book to oriental sources show that Evans was, along with others in New England of the time, either studying oriental ideas directly or getting them from others who had studied them. This highest self or *atman* he identifies with the Over-Soul of Emerson, showing that he was acquainted with what Emerson was teaching at the time. In a succeeding paragraph he quotes the great Muslim mystic Al-Ghazali as saying: "O seeker after the divine mysteries, know that the door of knowledge of God will be opened first of all to man, when he knows his own soul and understands the truth about his own spirit, according as it had been revealed." He quotes also from a book by the great oriental scholar Max Muller, thus demonstrating that he had read at least some of his works.

In his *Esoteric Christianity and Mental Therapeutics* (Boston, 1886), written three years before his death, and his last publication, Evans goes farther than in his earlier writings in identifying the essential teaching and ideas of Christianity with oriental thought, both Hinduism and Buddhism, as well as with Platonism, the Hermetic philosophy, and the Kabbala. This he calls Esoteric Christianity, and it is on this that he bases the mental cure or therapeutics. In the description of his practice he does not differ essentially from what he had written earlier.

Here as in all his books he refers repeatedly to Swedenborg. In *The Divine Law of Cure* there are some thirty such references, some merely in passing, some at length, showing a definite dependence on Swedenborg as a major influence. Indeed, in *Esoteric Christianity* Evans declares,

In the present mental cure system, I know no principle which is true that is not found in the New Testament and in the true spiritual philosophy of all ages and nations. He who carefully studies that development of Christianity which we have in the writings of Swedenborg, will find all the truth there is in the various schools of mental cure. And his spiritual philosophy is nothing but a reproduction and amplification of the ancient Hermetic and Kabbalistic science. (p. 134)

What precisely did Evans teach concerning the major central ideas that have been characteristic of the New Thought Movement? If he did not develop anything strikingly new in this area of thought, he did in his numerous writings define and give wide currency to these central ideas; and he consciously, as we have seen, sought to buttress them by finding support for them among the great recognized thinkers of the past, both remote and more recent. He is at one with New Thought in general and with Christian Science in declaring that "God is All and in All." And he uses practically all the capitalized synonyms current in Christian Science to characterize God (Love, Wisdom, Good, Life, etc.), though he does not always capitalize the words. But he is quick to assert that "all things are not God," for all things, both singly and

collectively, are finite and the finite is always limited, while
God, by definition, is infinite and therefore unlimited. Thus he
escapes the charge of being pantheistic in his thinking. The universe and God are not identical. He seems rather to express a
belief in God as transcendent Being which nevertheless is immanent in all that is. I do not recall his ever using the neuter "It"
as descriptive of God. In this he differs from both Quimby and
later New Thought writers.

Conscious of the prevailing beliefs of orthodox Christianity
as to God as a personal being, he asks, "But is God personal
or as infinitely diffused Principle?" His answer is that he is both
one and the other. "He is," he declares, "love and wisdom" and
these are "essential properties of personality ... an impersonal
affection or intelligence is an impossible conception." (*The Mental Cure*, p. 24) This was his first book, but he returns to the
question again and again. In his last book, written in 1886, reacting perhaps from the idea of the impersonality of God as taught
by Quimby and Mrs. Eddy, Evans declares that it is not necessary in the successful practice of mental healing "to deny the
personality of God as some have done, and reduce him to an
inconceivable sea of being, an ocean of spirit without bottom
or shore." (*Esoteric Christianity*, p. 155) This, he claims, is to
apply to deity that which can only be predicated of matter, its
quality or property of extension. Such a God, he holds, "would
be to us no God," for "personality consists in love and wisdom,
and there is no abstract impersonal love or understanding." "The
infinity and immensity of God are not boundless space, but the
negation of space—absolute freedom from limitations of space.
So the eternity of God is not endless time, but the denial of
time." (p. 155)

In his thought concerning Jesus and Christ, Evans does not
differ significantly from the typical New Thought conception,
unless it be, particularly in his earlier books, in a disposition to
express it in a way less likely to be objectionable to the Christian
thought—at least the liberal Christian thought—of his day. In his
first book, *The Mental Cure*, he writes that without entering into

a prolonged theological discussion regarding Jesus, he could not avoid confession of faith in him

as the only God made flesh and dwelling among us ... that he had complete human nature which passed through a perfectly human development from its birth to its glorification and ascension. And what the divine nature did for him, it is willing to do for us, in a degree, and we may be glorified and spiritualized with him. This is certainly the teaching of the New Testament. (pp. 264-65)

Here he was unquestionably closer than in his later writings to the conception he had held as a Methodist preacher.

In *The Divine Law of Cure,* written twelve years later, there are still lingering elements of his older conceptions, though they are clearly modified. He now is willing to define his position as a Christian pantheism. Indeed, he asserts:

A Christian pantheism which does not destroy the individuality of man, nor separate God from the universe which he continually creates out of Himself, nor sunder Him from the activities of the human soul by the intervention of second causes, is the highest development of religious thought. An intuitive perception of the unity of the human with the Divine existence is the highest attainable spiritual intelligence, and one which raises man above disease and the possibility of death. Before Jesus this knowledge had nowhere existed; and through the dreary dismal centuries of the history of the church, it has been covered with a deep layer of externalism, and well nigh lost sight of. (pp. 42-43)

But Jesus was being rediscovered, Evans claimed, and his significance duly understood. Using the familiar terms even of orthodox belief, he declared:

Jesus in his glorified humanity, is a mediator. He bridges the chasm which our ignorance and sensualism have opened between the human soul and God, and in him the finite spirit may meet and mingle with the Infinite Life. A genuine faith ... is one of the greatest moral forces in the universe. It summons into activity all there is of life and power in man, and develops all that is good in germ in human nature. Faith in Jesus, not as a theological myth, a mere theoretical and unsubstantial, divine *apparition,* but as a personal human, living and ascended, but still present Christ, places the soul, through the overflowing fullness of his spiritual being, in communication with the unfathomed depth of the One life. (p. 77)

But the historic Jesus and the Christ are not to be regarded as identical. Jesus was not born the Christ any more than Lincoln was born President of his country. "He gradually became the Christ, the anointed or knowing one," just as Gautama, who was born son of Queen Maia, became the Buddha, or enlightened one. Evans looked upon Jesus the Christ, he said, "as the highest illustration in the history of mankind, of a fully and harmoniously developed humanity." And in such a blending of the purely human and the divine "it is difficult to tell where the boundary is that separates one from the other." (pp. 79-80, *passim*)

But he felt constrained to believe

that the Christ Principle, the living Word, the Divine Logos, the reception of which in full measure made the son of Mary the Anointed One, or the Christ, is of far more importance than the mere historical Jesus. The Word that lighteth every man that cometh into the world, and the unsealed fountain of all inspiration, was personified and incarnated in him and this light is still the light of men. (pp. 133-34)

In a later book, *The Primitive Mind Cure,* Evans speaks specifically of the incarnation, and attempts some explanation of it:

As all human minds are connected though a universal mind, through Jesus Christ as an inlet, the Christ entered into humanity and deposited in it the germ of a newer higher life. In a pre-eminent degree, he was an incarnation of the Christ—not that no one else ever was, for all spiritually enlightened mind is a manifestation of the Christ and the Word. But owing to the unexampled spiritual evolution of the man Jesus, his individual life became merged and blended into a unity with the "only Begotten of the Father," the universal Christ. . . . In Jesus we witness a complete humanized expression of the Christ, the Word, and the Spirit. His personality is an inlet and an outlet of those universal principles, and a medium through which they may enter into each one of us, and through which the human race may have access to them. (p. 175)

In his last book, Evans has obviously gone far beyond what was expressed in his earliest. The influence of his reading of the literature of the oriental religions and of Hermetic and Kabbalistic philosophy is to be seen in his thought of the Christ and Jesus. "The whole," he writes,

the All, that from which individual life springs, is the Christ, who is called Father also, as being the parent source of all existences in earth and heaven. Jesus as an incarnate expression and manifestation of the Christ, came from the supreme realm of spiritual being, and in him was focused the life of the whole world. . . . Without this mediation and conjunction with the unbroken wholeness of life, we are like a branch severed from the vine that withers and dies. (*Esoteric Christianity*, p. 29)

"The Collective Man, the universal Divine Humanity," he continues, "is the Christ of whom Jesus is the incarnation. All men as to their real humanity, the essentially human principle in them, are included in the Christ, and are the finite limitations of him." (p. 31)

"Jesus came to do for the world at large," he writes,

by revealing the sublime wisdom of the ancient mystical sects and brotherhoods, what had been done only to the chosen few in the sacred privacy of the inner recesses of the temples. . . . He is the Jehovah of the Old Testament, the third emanation from the Unknown, the perfect union of pure intelligence with pure love; and as such is the saviour or the health-giver of the souls and bodies of men. . . . In Jesus, Jehovah becomes once more to men not a deity to be feared, but the Bon Dieu, the Good God, to be loved and trusted with the whole heart. (p. 80)

Concerning the nature of man, Evans asserts that "in all men the Divinity becomes finitely human." (*The Mental Cure*, p. 32) That is, he believed in the essential divinity of man. "All men of every clime and color," he continues, are sons of God and "are incarnations of the Divinity. All conception is an operation of the central living Force, whether in the womb of Mary or any of the daughters of Eve. . . . The consciousness of this grand verity would be a living moral force to elevate the debased populations of the globe." (p. 32)

Man as he appears to the human senses is really a soul that had an existence prior to its embodiment in visible form. What the nature of this prior existence may have been Evans does not affirm. Indeed, he suggests that "it may lie beyond the limits of human understanding for the present, if it is not to be classed among things *unknowable*." (*The Divine Law of Cure*, p. 179) But whatever its nature, he confidently affirms that "it preceded the bodily organism and forms the body according to its nature and for its use in the external world." (p. 179) It is what constitutes *myself*. (p. 163) It is the real *man*, the body only its *ex*-istence or external manifestation both to itself and to the world, as Evans had declared earlier in *The Mental Cure* (p. 93), calling it there the evolution of the mind. This he elaborates at greater length in *The Divine Law of Cure*, where he says that just as the soul is continually formed of God, so the soul forms the body of itself, as the perpetual creation of mind. The universe is the projection outward of the thought of God; so also is the little world of the body a projection of soul. The body is not a mere something added to the mind but a representation of the mind to itself and, when rightly interpreted, to others also. Thus the dualism of man as made up of soul and body is reduced to an indivisible and inseparable unity. He is thus "not a living personality divisible into two distinct and separate halves, but they are one, and the soul is that one." (pp. 164-65)

Here he says nothing of a third element of the total being of man which in *The Mental Cure* he calls "the spiritual body." His idea is that between the interior soul of man and the outer material body there is an intermediate and spiritual form which Paul and Swedenborg call the spiritual body. It "spans the discrete chasm between mind and matter, connects the two links in the chain of our being, conjoins the soul and body into a unity and through it they mutually act and react upon each other." (p. 59) This inner form, he thinks, is the prior seat of all diseased disturbances of the body. "Any abnormal mental states that immediately affect the inner principle, and impede its free circulation through the external organs, so as to weaken and loosen its connection with them, is the primary cause of disease. When this correspondence ceases the body dies." (p. 63) He returns to this concept in slightly different language in *The Primitive Mind Cure,* using the imagery of the temple, calling the spiritual body the "inner sanctuary of the soul."

"There is," he writes,

first the outer court of sense, next the inner sanctuary of the intellectual soul; and lastly, in the East, the most holy place, the spirit where like the high priest, we may commune with God. This is the inmost region of our being, and our *real* self. It is included *in* the Christ, or the Universal Spirit. . . . This summit of our being which is the real and divine man, is never contaminated by evil, nor invaded by disease. The recognition of this truth, and the separation in thought of sin and disease from our inmost and only true self is the Platonic [and also Pauline] idea of redemption. (p. 187)

Evans has little to say about evil. He appears to have regarded it as only the negation of good. A clue to his view may be seen in his definition of pain as "pleasure misunderstood." Man, he says, falsely views it as an evil, and by thinking so makes it so. "But pain is always a good, and all good is in its nature and essence pleasant and delightful. . . . A thing is to us what we *think* and *believe* it to be." In the same vein he continues, "Loss is gain, sorrow is joy, and death is life." He even extends the principle to filth, which he says is "only so to a superficial gaze and shallow way of thinking. "What we call filth is in its inner essence, its divine chemistry as pure as the diamond or precious stone. . . . As filth is not filth except to the stupid gaze of ignorance . . . so disease has existence only as a misbelief." (p. 63 *passim*) From this, it would seem, one might infer that evil is only unrecognized good.

He did not, to be sure, positively deny at any time the reality of evil, or affirm, as Christian Science does, its illusory character. He did have something to say about specific evils which were of a very real quality, something definitely to be met and overcome. That is, they were practical realities, if not theoretical ones, and must of necessity be dealt with.

Coming from a background of the Methodist ministry, Evans could hardly have avoided thinking of the great evangelical doctrines of sin, salvation, immortality, heaven, so though these are not stressed greatly by either New Thought or Christian Science, he does express his thought on each.

Sin, he says, is fundamentally, in most if not all languages, "error, mistake, and aberration from truth." It is born of ignorance. Any other meaning attached to it is a sort of "theological veneering" put upon the word which does not belong to it. He finds that the scriptural sense of the term is "a want of knowledge . . . the result of ignorance," the remedy for which is "the truth or knowledge in its reality." (*The Divine Law of Cure,* pp. 239-40) He recognizes sin as "a moral or evil disorder." He has much more to say about sin as the cause of disease than otherwise. "Sin as the cause of disease," he says,

is an error, a wrong way of thinking, feeling and acting. It is a great aberration from the truth to suppose that the body has life in itself, that disease, properly so called, is in the physical organism or that the condition of the body is ever anything but an effect of which the mind is the cause. Christ came to convince the world of this sin—this grave mistake. (John 16:8,9)

He cites Jesus' sayings after the cure of certain diseases, "Go in peace and sin no more," or "Son, thy sins are all forgiven thee," as evidence that Jesus also equated sin and disease. And he thinks he is following Jesus' thought in insisting that "a sick man ought not to be punished either here or hereafter, but rather cleansed and made whole or holy—the two words having the same radical or etymological meaning." (p. 236) And Jesus did seek to do precisely this. He was sent into the world, declares Evans, "to save his followers from sin and thus redeem them from the spiritual seeds of disease." (p. 237) But how?

Evans regards love as "the inmost essence of our being and the fountain in us of all vitality and activity." A man's character, he thinks, is shaped by his prevailing affectional states. Instead of a genuine faith's producing love or charity, it is rather generated by it. No man is saved by faith alone, Evans declares, but "by a predominant holy love." No faith that is not grounded in love can save a man. He regards the doctrine of salvation by faith alone, therefore, as a great error of the religious world. It is clear that salvation, to Evans, is rather a process than something that occurs once and for all. It is not something to be attained only in a hereafter. He clearly did not believe in the then current views of heaven and hell.

"Let us ever keep in mind," he writes,

that all there is or can be in what men call heaven is already in us, like the miniature plantlet in the seed of the sacred lotus. It is there as a celestial germ. The kingdom of God is within. This narrows down our search for it to a small compass, and heaven is at hand or within our reach. And surely, where heaven is there must be health and happiness. . . . Happiness, health, and heaven, which in their very essence are one, are always within us, and can never by any possibility be external to the mind. To *believe* this is to find them. (*The Primitive Mind Cure*, p. 40)

But he does not therefore disbelieve in immortality. On the contrary, from his earliest to his latest books he continues to affirm it. In *The Mental Cure*, he writes:

Ancient philosophers thought that mind in its own nature was indissoluble and indestructible. But this is not true of any finite thing in the universe. Nothing has life in itself, but all live from God. He alone has their immortality in himself, eternally springing from the depth of his own being. Immortality depends upon the will of God. The immutability of that will is the ground of its certainty . . . because he lives, we live also . . . by virtue of our being finite receptacles of the one and only life. (pp. 30-31)

In his last book, reacting probably against the oriental idea of the loss of individuality in the totality of Being, Evans declares that it is quite unnecessary to deny the personality and persistent individuality of the human spirit. To be sure, "personality is not predicable of the body," since the body is not man, but

The feeling that I am I is as immortal as the Deity ... and we cannot divest ourselves of that consciousness without annihilation. ... Heaven is not a countless number of beings reduced in a crucible to a molten sea of being. ... The self-hood is not *lost* in Godhood, but the true self, the undiseased and undying spiritual entity is found included in the Christ, who is the manifest God. To believe this of myself will save me, for it is the highest state and act of faith. ... The cessation of our distinct (not separate) individuality would be equivalent to our annihilation. (*Esoteric Christianity*, pp. 155-56)

To the evidence of the senses, the individual human being disappears at what men call death. But "there is no death," says Evans. "All is boundless, endless, omnipresent and omniactive life. Death is an illusion, or deceptive appearance, viewed from the lofty altitude of an assured faith." For, he declares, "it is a law as universal as the presence of God in nature, that out of what the world falsely calls death, there is always evolved a higher form or order of life." That is, the real man never dies, but only the external *ex*-istence ceases. The real man lives on. (p. 77)

Evans does not furnish any blueprint as to what happens after this present life span. He is conscious that others, particularly in the Orient, believe in re-embodiment in other forms. But he never pronounces either for or against such a belief in reincarnation. His primary concern seems to be with the discovery in this present existence of the true nature of the real man, which seems to him to be the clue to a life of health, happiness, and peace.

Evans' views concerning Mind or Spirit and matter were typically idealistic. He frequently quotes the great idealistic philosophers from Plato to Berkeley in support of the primacy of Mind or Spirit. And he places Swedenborg, under whose influence he operates at many points, among the great idealists.

In the earliest of his books he addresses himself to the question of the relationship between matter and mind or spirit. It is his view that there are two substances in the universe, mind or spirit and matter, both to be thought of as "real being," but discrete, having no properties in common. To say that mind or spirit is immaterial is not to detract from its reality, but only to mean "that its essence is invested with properties entirely unlike those by which matter is manifested to our senses," yet it is "the most vitally real thing in the universe."

We know matter because of its possession of properties cognizable to our senses, but mind or spirit by other distinct properties or powers "known only to our consciousness or inner perceptions." Yet our knowledge of one is as certain as our knowledge of the other. Matter is commonly thought of as something solid. But even at the time when he wrote, long antedating our modern conception, Evans declared that what we call solidity is only a measure of force, resistance, "more a sensation in us than a property of matter." But if all we know of matter is force and its properties are only modifications of force, "its inmost essence may be spiritual, and what we call matter may be only the outward clothing or ... external manifestation of some spiritual reality." (*The Mental Cure,* pp. 27-29, *passim*)

Mind or spirit he declares to be a "higher and diviner force" much nearer to "the Central Life." It is a "manifestation of force entirely distinct from what we call matter." Time and space are the essential conditions of material existence, while mind or spirit is not limited by either space or time, but quite as independent of one as of the other. (p. 30)

Evans' use of the term *substance* to describe both mind or spirit and matter is apt to be confusing to the casual reader. Ordinarily it is equated with that which is observable by means of the senses. Evans follows Swedenborg, he reveals in *The Divine Law of Cure,* in using the term substance in its etymological sense (from *sub,* under, and *sto,* to stand) as "that which is the spiritual basis, the underlying reality of things." He regards "substantial things" as the "primitives of material things," differing from them as "the prior from the posterior, or in other words, as cause and effect." Thus matter is spirit made visible and tangible, or the externalization of mind. (p. 148) "Mind and matter," he continues, "sustain the necessary relation of substance and form. . . . Matter is the form of spirit, or that which gives it a definite limitation in space." The mind or spirit is thus "the substance or underlying reality of the body." This Evans feels to be confirmed by the fact that a "change of mental state is followed by a corresponding alteration of the bodily condition, either in the direction of health or disease."

In his final book, *Esoteric Christianity* (1886), Evans seems to fall at least verbally into the pattern of Christian Science in his view of matter, though perhaps he is influenced in this by his reading of oriental philosophy. He declares there that "the natural world, including the human body is not the real world. It is in itself vanity and emptiness. It is *maia* or illusion. Matter as a deceptive appearance is the prison of the immortal spirit, the real man and son of God." He goes on to apply this principle to the treatment of disease, saying that "to terminate this unnatural bondage and convince the patient of the unreality of the body and its diseases is to cure him." (p. 129)

But in *The Divine Law of Cure* (1881) he had more than once taken occasion to assert that neither he nor the idealists generally denied the reality of matter. Rather, he had only affirmed "that it had no separate existence, but is bound up in an eternal unity with mind, and if the realm of spirit should cease to be, the material world would instantly perish with it and in it." (p. 150) The idealists, he wrote, did not deny the reality of external things but only that "they have any reality independent of mind." Men do not err in attributing a real existence to objects, but do err when they think that these objects can or do exist 'independent of a perceiving mind," for "there can be no external world without a world of spirit in which it exists." (p. 168)

In the practice of mental healing, he thinks, it is certainly not

> necessary to deny the existence of matter, but only to affirm the sovereignty of mind over it. Matter exists as a mode of consciousness in us and is as real as that mode of thought. So disease exists as a wrong way of thinking, and to change that way of thinking for the belief in the truth is to cure the disease, of whatever nature it is. (p. 156)

We come now to a consideration of Evans' thought and practice of healing. It was his own need of healing that brought him first to Quimby, and he continued to practice and expound the gospel of healing to the end of his life. It was his constant preoccupation, his main drive. His one reference to Quimby asserted that in his healing and teaching he seemed to "reproduce the wonders of Gospel history." Ever thereafter healing was at the center of his own preaching, writing, and practice.

We have already quoted a simple statement embodying his basic belief concerning disease and its cure. In *Mental Medicine*, written in 1872, he had said: "Disease, being at its root a wrong belief, change that belief and we cure the disease." No better or more easily understood statement is to be found anywhere in his writings, though the general principle is stated over and over again in all his books. The very titles of four of his six books carry the implication of the mental basis of illness and its cure: *The Mental Cure, Mental Medicine, The Primitive Mind Cure*, and *Esoteric Christianity and Mental Therapeutics*. In his last book, he expressed the idea in very nearly the same words: "Disease is a wrong way of thinking, and to change that way of thinking for the belief of truth is to cure the disease." (p. 156)

In this same book, a somewhat more detailed expression of the idea is given thus:

> Disease must be considered as the translation into a bodily expression of a prior inharmony of thought and feeling. All disease resolves itself into this in the last analysis. We shall not go far from the mark in our

diagnosis of any malady when we pronounce it a case of the *divergence of thought from a divine rectitude*, a deflection of the mind from the real truth. . . . It is only our way of thinking which makes them [our feelings] mean disease or health. On that pivot our destiny turns. . . . Hence disease, which is an abnormal mode of existence, in its radical significance, is a wrong way of thinking, or if you prefer so to call it, a mistaken belief. . . . As I think, so I am. (*Esoteric Christianity*, pp. 37-38)

Evans by no means condemns the use of materia medica as did Mrs. Eddy, nor does he refuse to co-operate with physicians. He declares,

We find medical science an auxiliary to the mental system of cure. And we would take occasion to remark that no intelligent practitioner of the mind-cure will ignore wholly all medical science. Mind is the only active principle in the universe. The mind of a skillful surgeon performs marvels in saving the lives of people.

But he does find simultaneous treatment by both mental medicine and materia medica unwise. In the practice of medical psychology, he says,

I have made it a general rule to require the patient to suspend the use of all other remedies except those of hygienic nature, knowing that it is sometimes more difficult to neutralize the effect of drugs than to cure the disease for which they are administered. Those of a poisonous nature operate to cure disease by creating another morbid condition inconsistent with the first. (*Mental Medicine*, p. 85)

Evans regards all things as only the outward expression or correspondence of some spiritual reality or essence, which represents it to the senses. In the case of medicines he thinks that it is spiritual essence which gives the drug its curative power over the dynamic disturbance which constitutes the disease. This, he thinks, makes it of the nature of a sacrament. Lacking this the drug has no healing power. It also gives to the one who administers the medicine a sacred character, thus lifting the physician to the dignity of a priest, even a vicar of God. As a matter of fact, the medical and ministerial professions ought never to have been separated in function, but should have remained as one, and as in older civilizations the priest should have continued to be physician of both body and soul. (pp. 55-56)

While it is not altogether certain that Evans is here talking of the ordinary doctor, he does pay the good physician a very high tribute. The first inquiry of a good physician ought to be not as to what ails the body, but what are the needs of the soul, the real needs. Working at the body alone he is working only at the circumference of our being, but by giving attention to the mental or spiritual state he begins his cure at the center of our existence. Like the divine law of divine order, he works from without inward. "The divinest and most Christlike man in human society is," he says, "the good physician—he who from the overflowing stores of his spiritual intelligence and goodness is governed by an irrepressible impulse to impart life, health and peace to others." (p. 233)

Much more than many of the later New Thought leaders, Evans seems to have read widely in the medical literature of the time. Numerous references to books in the fields of physiology, anatomy, and medicine are to be found in his writings, and of course also in psychology, especially in respect to hypnotism and the power of suggestion. Psychotherapy is a term frequently found in his later books. In all his works there is to be found but one reference to germs or bacteria. In *The Primitive Mind Cure* (1886), he writes:

The general current of the world life is crowded with the soul-germs of disease, which in their essence are morbid ideas and fallacious beliefs. These are the latent causes, a sort of spiritual bacteria, they may under certain conditions, find lodgement in men's souls, and germinate, as it were, in the *prima materia* of the brain, and thus be fruitful seeds of disease and develop into actuality in the physical body. These morbid ideas are to be taken up . . . and borne away from the patient. So when the evil, the morbid idea, the *sin* that lies at the root of the malady is removed, a vacuum is, as it were, formed, which God and nature are said to abhor, and the opposite good and truth, from a fixed divine law flow in. A living, life-giving truth cannot be received until the error, the illusion, the *sin* which occupies the mind is removed. Healing, saving truth does not crowd out error, or a false belief . . . but when the error or sin is removed truth spontaneously flows in. (pp. 158-59)

Evans knows the power of thought over the physical functioning of the body. To direct attention to the part, he knows, increases its sensitiveness and vital action. Thus it contains within itself, when its spiritual forces are intelligently directed to a given aim, "more potential virtues that can be found in a drug shop." *(The Mental Cure,* p. 115) As long as the medical profession ignores the spiritual organism of man, it is bound to be ineffective. (p. 118)

Psychological influence is potent in healing. It acts, Evans says, upon the spiritual body and through this on the material organism. And the direct action of mind on mind which goes to the root of all diseased conditions "carries a remedial agency into the realm of causation." It may operate, he says, through mesmerism, psychology, biology, animal magnetism, pathetism, hypnosis, and even psychometry, for all these are in the last analysis "reducible to one general principle—the influence or action of mind on mind and the communication of spiritual life from one person to another, who is negatively receptive of it." (p. 212)

He knows also the value and power of suggestion. The greater part of the first half of *Mental Medicine* is devoted to a discussion of healing by this means, with little or no mention of any religious element in it. Evans discusses the relative merits of suggestion at various levels, from a simple suggestion conveyed in ordinary conversation all the way to one given in the complete hypnotic state. He distrusts the use of the latter method, preferring a hypnoidal state which falls short of complete hypnosis but in which the degree of suggestibility of the subject is scarcely less. Cure may come through autosuggestion or from without. In case of a simple headache, he advises:

Suggest to yourself that it is gone or is leaving you, and it will be instantly relieved.... Whatever you suggest and will and *believe* is at once done. The body obeys the slightest hint of the sovereign mind.... If you will any change to be effected, and *believe* it, it is certain to be so, for the whole system now comes under the law of faith; for ... it is one of the laws of our being that while in the susceptible state the body is subject to the mind.... You are not called upon to exercise a blind faith, but an intelligent confidence in the operation of the divine laws of nature. (*Mental Medicine,* pp. 67-68, *passim*)

Health, declared Evans, is the normal thing, disease the abnormal. There is a mysterious healing power always at work in the human body whenever there is an injury or malfunctioning of any kind. This will often effect a cure unaided. But the healing process can be greatly accelerated by the conscious and voluntary action of the mind, assisted, if necessary, by some other person. This sanative power which God has given to the physical organism can be quickened by some volitional effort of the mind, whether fancy, imagination, or faith, and intensified in its action on the body. Herein, Evans thinks, lay the "secret philosophy of the cures effected by Jesus the Christ." If we understand the laws involved and the mental processes by which they are accomplished, "they may be repeated upon ourselves or others in like conditions." (*The Divine Law of Cure,* p. 129)

Jesus seemed to have "a divinely clear conception of the spiritual origin of disease, and of the efficacy of spiritual remedies in its cure," for Jesus did not regard sickness of the body as the *real* disease, rather as the effect of a prior spiritual malady. Naturally when the cause ceased to operate, the evil effect would also come to an end. Finding the cause of disease essentially a mental or spiritual disturbance, he used a means consistent with that cause to effect the cure. He applied his power to heal to the mental cause of the ill. He viewed matter as an unsubstantial appearance, and mind as the only reality. "Through the restored and redeemed soul, he healed the body of its diseases, both functional and organic." (p. 122)

In his last book Evans tended more to identify sin and disease. Speaking of the cures of Jesus, he calls them a "radical change in the mental status of the patient, and no half-way affairs. The body was saved from disease by redeeming the soul from the dominion of sin, or the illusion of the senses, and the life of iniquity to which it led." This system of eighteen hundred years before, he thought, was returning to the world of his day. The mental history of the race, he believed, repeats itself in regular recurring cycles, and the revolving wheel of life was bringing the early Christian method of healing by faith once again into operation under the name of phrenopathy or mind cure. Thus he identified his own system of mind cure, as Mrs. Eddy did hers, as a rediscovery of the method of Jesus.

If the things he has been saying are true, then obviously cure of disease is possible to the individual without the help of another. If to think and to be are one and the same thing, if "I think" and "I am" are identical expressions, then one needs only to think rightly to be well and happy. In order to cure himself by this ideal method, he needs first of all to separate in thought his inner conscious self, "the immortal divine Ego," from the disease. Disease must be viewed as no part of the self, but something foreign to it. Disease is made a part of the self only when one thinks of it as such, thus giving it a certain vitality and a hold upon him. But this is, says Evans, "a falsity, a phantasy, an error, an illusion, and a *sin* in the New Testament and proper sense of the word." (*The Primitive Mind Cure,* p. 117)

Over and over again he asserts that it is the idea which creates an organic expression. "If we form the true idea of man and apply it to ourselves, and hold it steadfastly in the mind and *believe in its realization,* by one of the deepest and most certain laws of our nature, it will tend to recreate the body after the pattern of that mental type." (p. 125)

We can never get well until we stop thinking that we are ill, declares Evans. If we can just leave off thinking that we are diseased and dwelling upon our unhappy condition, we may be sure that the spiritual cause of our ills "will disappear like darkness before the rising sun." And the patient must learn the importance of controlling the morbid tendency to talk of his troubles and his diseased condition, for it is a law of our nature "that to express a feeling in words intensifies it." (*Mental Medicine*, p. 35)

Evans sounds a healthy note in urging, "Get well by curing others." The good you intend for others will come to you in divine measure, more than you give. Impart life, he exhorts; "Communicate from your own stock of vital force to others, and life from God, its sempiternal source, and from the angel world will flow in to replenish your store." (p. 220)

Most of what has been said thus far has related to self-treatment by the afflicted individual. Much of Evans' writing seems to have been designed to help sufferers from illness to help themselves. But he himself was a healer, and he frequently alludes to his own method of healing and also directs his words to others who would heal.

Two things, says Evans, are necessary if a patient would receive a spiritual sanative influence, whether through self-treatment or at the hands of another. One is the desire to get well. The other is a faith in the efficiency of the remedial agent. Without these two things the cure of disease by any mode of treatment is to say the least, if not impossible, exceedingly difficult. (p. 244) After reiterating the influence of the mind on the body, he says:

But faith is the most intense form of mental action . . . when the mind rises from the pre-conscious to the conscious range of action its activity separates itself into two distinct phases, the intellectual and the emotional; but at the summit of our being in a genuine act of faith they unite in one intense focus.

The way to the cure of another is to forget that the patient has a physical body and "speak as a spirit to his spirit." Doing this, he declares, "the better mental state, which is always stronger will prevail over and suppress the other and weaker. . . . The patient is renewed in mind, the inner man. He is spiritually healed." The body then becomes quickly adjusted to the new interior state, and thus is whole or well. (*The Mental Cure,* p. 269)

Referring to an oft-repeated story of the student's making a person ill by causing him to think that he was ill, he says that the phrenopathic method of cure represents simply the reversal of the process and makes the man well by inducing him to think of himself as well. This does not mean denial of the fact of the disease as a state of consciousness, but asserts simply that the immortal Ego, the spiritual entity and real man, is neither diseased nor unhappy, for the disease is in a region of our existence that is below or external to the man, the essentially human nature and principle. But how shall this be done? Simply by the power of thought, uttered in appropriate words or symbolic signs, or unexpressed, for there is a living energy in thought. As Evans states it:

In treating a patient by the mental method, with a kindly, positive, affirmative attitude of mind, we are to think steadfastly the truth in regard to his inner self, and maintain in our minds the correct *idea* of ourselves and him; and the silent sphere of our minds, according to the law of thought transference, will influence him in a degree proportioned to his susceptibility. (*Esoteric Christianity,* p. 149)

In order to modify a patient's thinking in regard to himself and his disease, Evans was accustomed to employ the principle of suggestion or positive *affirmation*—not mental argument, for argument, he thinks, creates doubt and reaction. No sick man was ever cured by reasoning with him mentally or verbally. Compare this with the Christian Science admonition to argue either audibly or silently (*Science and Health,* 376:21-24), and also Quimby's habit of reasoned explanation to his patients. It is rather the business of the man who knows the truth not to argue, but to *affirm.* "But," he continues,

the effect of the suggestion is the result of the faith of the subject, for it is always proportioned to the degree in which the patient *believes* what you say. If the patient is predisposed to believe you, the magnetic state [hypnosis] is not necessary to the influence of your affirmations upon him. If he is not thus disposed we employ silent or mental suggestion, and ofttimes with marvelous effect. (pp. 152-53, *passim*)

Thus, affirmation, which has come to be so much used in New Thought practice, finds a support in Warren Felt Evans, even though it is by no means so constantly used as at present. Indeed, he provides at least one affirmation which he suggests may well be used in the healing of the self or others.

Since disease is but the translation of a false idea of man into corporeal expression, its cure must begin with the obliteration of that false view and its replacement by a true idea. Once the true idea of man is formed, a tacit verbal expression of it may be given by using the following formula (or "any form of words that will ultimate the conception"):

In our inmost and true existence and real self, we are and cannot be diseased, for we are included in the being of the Father of Spirits. Our real life and true being are hid with Christ in God, and our spirit as a manifestation and personal limitation of the Universal Spirit is already immortal in its nature and essence, and disease and pain and sorrow are impossible to it. And this disease (naming it if we desire to do so) is outside of our unchanging and undying personality, and we view it as non-existent. We pray the Father in the name of Jesus Christ to make us whole. In the silence and stillness of our own soul and will, we pray Jesus, who represents the only saving healing principle in the universe, will speak the vivifying inner Word, the Word of life to the soul of this person; and cause the light of that supreme and eternal truth which can alone make us free, to illumine the darkness of his mind, and liberate the inner man from the fetters of sense and the dominion of sin. (*Esoteric Christianity*, pp. 53-54)

In this, his latest book, it should be noted that Evans has become much more "metaphysical" in his healing thought and practice, in contrast to his more specifically mental method of healing in the earlier books. This sounds more like later metaphysical healers, and may well have been that which influenced them in their thought and practice.

In giving treatment to another, he declares, it is necessary to form in our minds a distinct conception or idea of the change to be effected in him, then "commit this to the Universal Life Principle, the Demiurgic Intellect, the Living Intelligence, that forms the world and all that is in it, and even the human body after the pattern of pre-existing ideas." When our idea has been transferred to the soul of the patient, it will result in a physiological impulse which will move in the direction of the desired change. (p. 51)

Treatment may be given in the presence of the sufferer or at a distance. Absent treatment may be just as effective as that which is given directly to the individual. This follows from the underlying concept of mind or spirit being the ultimate basis of all that is. It is in no wise subject to the limitations of either time or space.

Following Quimby in his belief and apparently also his practice of clairvoyant diagnosis and in his insistence that the action of mind on mind is not dependent on proximity of the patient to the healer, Evans frequently gave absent treatment to a patient. We have already alluded to his experimentation with it for the period of a year or more, and related instances in which he found himself able to induce physiological effects at a distance, solely by mental means.

The divine principle of love is, he asserts, the real source of the cure of disease by spiritual means. Love is the most divine and powerful thing in the world. "One who has developed this within himself exercises a sanative influence whether he is aware of it or not. We cannot escape from the operation of this principle, and every time we *think* of an absent person we affect him for good or evil." (*The Mental Cure,* pp. 266-68) This opens up, of course, the possibilities of Malicious Animal Magnetism which so plagued Mrs. Eddy, but there is no indication of any such conclusion's having been drawn by Warren F. Evans.

In a later book he speaks of the psychic and magnetic force which goes forth from a person as a part of his own living self, but always under control of his own volition, obeying the silent or expressed command of that volition. Like a disembodied spirit it can pass through all known substances. A person may be made to feel the influence of the hand when it is is not in direct contact with him but several feet away. The ordinary clothing worn by a person constitutes no obstacle to its effective application, and it can be communicated from one person to another independent of the spatial distance between them. Evans had made experiments with it at a distance of as much as four hundred miles, and at lesser distances hundreds of times. Like spirit, this force seems to be quite free from all material limitations. (*Mental Medicine*, pp. 129-30)

Like others, including P. P. Quimby and Mrs. Eddy, Evans often seems to have taken on himself the diseased feeling of his patients. Jesus likewise did so, he asserts, citing Matt. 8:17, "Himself took our infirmities and bore our sicknesses." But the effect upon the healer is transient, he says, though the benefit to the patient is permanent. The feelings taken on can, he says in *Mental Medicine*, be thrown off quickly by a few minutes of tranquil sleep. (p. 152)

Mr. Evans has a good deal to say at one time or another concerning the qualifications necessary in what in *Mental Medicine* he calls "the psychopathic practitioner." In the second chapter of that book he sets forth specifically his ideas. The practitioner should be "one of high mental and moral character, and actuated solely or mainly by the love of doing good." (p. 21) The nearer he approaches the character of Jesus, the greater will be his power to heal. He should also have "an adequate knowledge of anatomy and physiology of man, especially of the nervous system." (p. 22) He should understand the nature and symptoms of disease, know the relation of the mind and body and their mutual interaction, and have a profound knowledge of human nature. It is easy to see that later healers have not always followed Evans in his insistence that the practitioner should have a knowledge of physiology and anatomy.

Also, he must have faith in God and confidence in his own ability (p. 23); "be in sympathetic conjunction with Christ and the realm of life above, and endued with power from on high" (p. 25); and "be in sympathy with the fountain of life and light, not as an occasional transport by which a soul is carried out of its natural element, but as an habitual and confirmed state." (p. 26)

Later in the same volume Evans discusses at greater length sympathy as an element in healing. The physician who best meets the inner want of the touch of a sympathetic hand of kindness and of a pure heartfelt love that will understand, will be the most successful in relieving the patient of his diseased condition. (p. 144) Such a person "connects the sundered link between them and the universal life." And of course sympathy is not conditioned by space, so that persons may be treated successfully at a distance. (p. 147)

It is best, he thinks, for a practitioner not to attempt to cure a disease by the mental method when himself suffering from excessive fatigue or exhaustion. (p. 154) He believes that much may be accomplished in mental healing by the ordinary unaided individual, but actually there is spiritual help to be had from Christ and the angels, or angelic beings which lift this power to vastly greater heights. In this one may perceive the influence of Swedenborg.

It is difficult to measure the influence of Evans at this distance in time. If one were to consider only the relative paucity of material concerning him to be found in New Thought literature (only two articles, both published in *Practical Ideals*, deal with him at any length), it might be deduced that his influence was small. But one must keep in mind the fact that there is a dearth of biographical material about most New Thought leaders, due in all probability to the general tendency among them to emphasize ideas rather than personality.

A better and more tangible evidence of his importance is found in the wide circulation of his books during the formative years of the movement. Of his first book, *The Mental Cure*, published originally in 1869, a seventh edition was issued in 1885; a ninth edition is cited in the literature, but with no indication of the date of its issue. Nothing is known about the size of the editions, but continuing success is indicated by the fact that a new edition of the book was called for more than sixteen years after it was first issued.

The Library of Congress copy of *Mental Medicine,* his second book, is the fifteenth edition, issued in 1885. That is, it went through fifteen editions in twelve years, having appeared first in 1873.

Mrs. Eddy's *Science and Health,* published for the first time in 1875, had reached only its thirteenth edition in 1885, and she had the advantage of a rapidly expanding organization to aid in its circulation during a part of this period, while Evans had at most only a small sanitarium where he carried on his healing work.

Evans' *The Divine Law of Cure* was first published in 1881; a later edition is dated 1884, with no indication of what edition it is. The New York Public Library has a copy of the fifth edition of *The Primitive Mind Cure.* The literature refers to no edition other than the first of either *Soul and Body* or *Esoteric Christianity and Mental Therapeutics,* though it is quite possible that various editions of either or both appeared.

Organizationally, of course, his influence was not felt. Evans was clearly not an organization man. Though the Dressers and a few others were carrying on in organized fashion before his passing in 1889, there had been but little or no effort made to go beyond purely local organizations in which each leader worked very much alone. Whether he would have participated in the regional and wider group organizations that began to take form in the nineties, there is no way of knowing.

But the one certain fact is that he was the first and indeed the only important figure, aside from Mrs. Eddy, who attempted to work out a consistent and philosophically supported system of what may be called mental or metaphysical healing, during the first two decades after the death of P. P. Quimby. The New Thought periodicals which began to appear in the late eighties continued to carry advertisements of his books at least to the end of the century; and copies of the books were to be found in the major public libraries and the libraries of most New Thought leaders and centers. Also, though he was but infrequently quoted directly by the early New Thought writers, there is no lack of evidence that they had read him.

5

The Developing Movement

WE HAVE WRITTEN of the sources of New Thought, the New England background out of which it sprang; the interest in Spiritualism, which had certain healing accompaniments also; the great and original discoveries of P. P. Quimby; the wide circulation of the writings of the first articulate writer on New Thought, Warren F. Evans, who was part product also of the Swedenborgian faith. But how did it become an organized movement? What road led from Quimby to the world-wide International New Thought Alliance and its many constituent groups?

Quimby, like many of the founders of movements, either religious or nonreligious, had no organization at all. Nor did he seem concerned with having one formed. It was only at the urgent solicitation of some of his followers that he began to write down his reflections, prompted by his own personal experience of healing and that of others whom he was instrumental in healing. And a part of what he wrote was circulated only in manuscript form among a few of his more trusted patients, among them Mary Baker Patterson—later Mrs. Eddy. That he thought of publishing these reflections sometime seems clear from the fact that he wrote an introduction which would properly accompany their publication. (See H. W. Dresser, *The Quimby Manuscripts*, p. 270) But he did not live to carry out such a project. The manuscript lay in the possession of his son and secretary George Quimby until his death, seen and read in part by only a few persons. At last, in 1921, it was published by Horatio W. Dresser under the title *The Quimby Manuscripts*.

129

It was natural that some of Quimby's patients and students, for he did do some informal teaching of a few persons who sought him out in the hope of being healed, should have desired to impart to others something of what they had received. Shortly after having herself been healed by Quimby, Mary Baker Patterson gave some public lectures on his healing system in Warren, Maine, advertising her subject as, "P. P. Quimby's spiritual science healing disease as opposed to deism or Rochester-Rapping Spiritualism." Warren F. Evans told Quimby that he thought he too could heal, and was encouraged to try. Beyond the sanitarium he maintained for a time, in which the Quimby system, supplemented by his own ideas, and also influenced in part by Emanuel Swedenborg, was employed in healing, Evans had no organization. He must have done a good deal of lecturing on the subject, but the means chosen by him to spread the knowledge so acquired was the writing of books. And in this he was not only the first, but one of the most effective of a long line of New Thought writers. Though he promoted no organization himself, his books were widely read and influential among the followers who did form organizations a little later.

The first really to organize a healing ministry was Mary Baker Eddy, and it must be recognized that it was her organizing activity which produced, either directly or indirectly, both Christian Science and what may be termed the whole "Metaphysical Movement," of which both Christian Science and New Thought are component parts.

Would New Thought have emerged as a distinct movement if Christian Science had not appeared? Who can know? What is definitely known is that at Quimby's passing there was no movement. He had no successor. When Mary Patterson, who had published not a few letters acclaiming Quimby as the discoverer and practicer of the method of Jesus in healing human ailments, fell one day on the ice and suffered a serious injury, she felt lost without his sustaining healing power and wrote Julius A. Dresser urging that he take up the work and try to heal her.

Two weeks earlier, she wrote, she had fallen and now found

herself "the helpless cripple" she had been before she saw Dr. Quimby. She was, she confessed, frightened. "Now can't you help me?" She believed he could. She had placed no intelligence in matter, and she believed that she could help another in her condition. "Won't you write me," she urged, "if you will undertake for me?" (This entire letter has been frequently published. It can be found in *The Quimby Manuscripts* [hereafter indicated by *Q MSS*], in the original edition published in New York in 1921, p. 163).

Who was Julius A. Dresser and what was his role in the history of New Thought? Born February 12, 1838, in Portland, Maine, he had intended entering the ministry in the Calvinistic Baptist church, and was studying in Waterville College, Maine, when his health failed. Hearing of P. P. Quimby as a healer, and thinking he had not long to live, he went to him and in a short time was healed. This was in 1860. At Dr. Quimby's office he met Annetta Seabury, who also came seeking health, and in 1863 the two were married. Dresser became an enthusiastic advocate of Quimby's system and devoted himself to explaining it to others. He had become editor of a Portland newspaper in 1866, but moved to Webster, Massachusetts, where he became editor and publisher of the *Webster Times*. He was thus engaged when Mrs. Eddy wrote him. He refused to take up the responsibility, and a little later moved West and lived there several years. Returning to Massachusetts, he and his wife took up the practice of mental healing in Boston in 1882.

Meanwhile Mrs. Eddy had recovered from her accident. Later she dated her discovery of Christian Science from that event, in 1866. Here the story becomes confused. Up until this time she had been a warm admirer of Dr. Quimby, paying him the highest tributes as a spiritual healer, definitely employing the method of Jesus in his successful practice. On the occasion of his death she composed a poem published in a Lynn newspaper, under the title "Lines on the Death of Dr. P. P. Quimby, Who Healed with the Truth that Christ Taught in Contradistinction to all Isms." (February 22, 1866)

During the years following this she was a lonely figure, going from place to place talking about a new system of healing without benefit of medicine, reading from a manuscript she was working on, teaching an occasional pupil, and finally conducting classes in the principles underlying the healings. In 1875 she published a book which she called *Science and Health,* in which was set forth a philosophy of healing of which she claimed to be the discoverer. A small group had been organized in Lynn, Massachusetts, of which she was the minister, and in 1881 this group was moved into Boston and the foundations of the Christian Science organization were laid. In that year the Massachusetts Metaphysical College was chartered. For a number of years it was Mrs. Eddy's principal teaching base. In 1883 the *Christian Science Journal* was launched. Christian Science was now a going concern. Its meetings, first at Hawthorne Hall, then at Chickering Hall, were drawing large crowds of interested persons. There was as yet no New Thought organization.

The Dressers, who as we have seen had set up as mental healers in Boston in 1882, had no public meetings at first, but only personal contact with individuals seeking to be healed. They operated strictly on the basis of the Quimby principles.

When in 1883 they began teaching classes, it was the Quimby system they taught, encouraged to do so by seeing pupils of Mrs. Eddy and some she had rejected practicing and doing what the Dressers considered to be work inferior to that of Quimby. They made use of the Quimby manuscripts in their teaching. Thus the teachings of Quimby and Mary Baker Eddy were set in contrast and the so-called Quimby controversy began.

The Dressers, who had known Mrs. Eddy when she was at Portland with Dr. Quimby, knew how much she had admired him and praised him as the one discoverer of the method of Jesus. They were irked by her claims and those made for her as the discoverer of Christian Science, and rose to the defense of the good Dr. Quimby, thus provoking a still more radical disclaimer on the part of Mrs. Eddy that she owed anything to this "mesmerist," and causing her to push farther and farther back her first intimations of the truth only vaguely suggested by the Portland healer.

In 1884 the Dressers issued a circular setting forth their theories and methods, which closely followed Dr. Quimby's ideas and method. Answering various questions concerning their method they assert that it is not that of any of the "isms" of the day, but rather "a purely mental treatment, and its results are a triumph of mind over the ills of suffering humanity, and of the real truth of a sick person's case over the opinions that assume to know when they do not know." (Quoted in H. W. Dresser, *Health and the Inner Life*, p. 122)

They make no use of medicines or other material means. It is, they assert, "natural and right to be well, and the simple truth understood and applied destroys the error of disease." Their examinations are by mental perceptions (intuition) which reveal the nature of the disease. In this and the method of cure they are following out specifically "the principles of truth discovered and reduced to a science by Mr. P. P. Quimby of Maine." (p. 22) They had learned it from him personally, and knew no other name for it than "The Quimby System of Mental Treatment of Diseases." The system might properly be called a Spiritual Science, and must be judged only by its fruits.

There is a great lack, they say, of "man's understanding of himself," and it is this lack which they seek to supply through their teaching and practice. They ask only that those who are sick or suffering, and have failed to get help, put their system to an actual test. "There is," they claim, "a truth not generally known, the understanding of which tends to avoid sickness and leads to health and happiness. It is no man's belief; it is an eternal truth." They ask only that if the reader is interested the truth be tested, and that "their words be proved." (p. 123)

They were successful in their healing practice. People who were healed wanted to know by what means the healing was wrought. Instead of writing it down and letting patients read it as Dr. Quimby had done, the Dressers held classes, giving instruction through lectures. Generally there was a series of twelve for each class (note the similarity here to Christian Science). Horatio W. Dresser has given in *Health and the Inner Life* a general summary of their course. It began with a lecture on the analysis of experiences of mental influences, showing how powerful mind is in its effects upon man's life, its fears, anxieties, emotional excitement, anticipations, hopes—in general, the power of thought. Next came a discussion of the divine immanence of God in the world and in man. Fortunately his son has conserved his thought concerning this, which he calls The Omnipresent Wisdom, at least some small portion of which is found in every man, of however lowly a nature. Following this was a lecture on the nature of matter, in which not only were Quimby's words quoted at length and explained, but (as in the writings of Evans, from whom they no doubt drew) additional evidence from the great idealistic philosophies was adduced in support of Dr. Quimby's theories. Thus was provided a basis for the powerful influence of mind on mind as well as of mind on body, which they considered in great detail, drawing from their own experiences with the ill as well as the experiences of others. In the course of this much emphasis was placed on the "mental atmosphere" and the subtler phases of the mental life discovered by the healer, especially of the fact that "we are members one of another," in a very intimate sense.

The subconscious aftereffects of man's dynamic opinions and beliefs were explained as leading logically to their statement of the general mental theory of disease, for which they found ample support in Dr. Quimby's manuscripts. Also there was constant reference to the teachings of the New Testament concerning the healing of disease. Man's spiritual nature was discussed at length, and here the Dressers followed Quimby in distinguishing between the historic Jesus and the Christ, "the universal ideal or consciousness" (p. 125), a distinction which seemed to them, as it had to Dr. Quimby and has to most New Thought leaders since, to be very important because it "made clear the possibilities open before everyone who is faithful to the guidance of the omnipresent wisdom," and served to encourage the beginner to undertake the work of spiritual healing. (p. 125) They were careful to insist that this in no way was to be construed as a denial of the divinity of Christ. Rather, "to the love of Christ as the elder brother was added the practical conception of the Christ ideal as the highest standard of service among the sick," something in the nature of a new revelation to many minds of the day. (p. 125)

The spiritual life, it was pointed out, is continuous — we already live in eternity. Man is really spiritual by nature, the possessor of powers linking him to the higher realm of being, and death is therefore relatively "an external incident, of which man need not stand in fear. Rather, once having accepted the thought of 'eternity now,'" man might remain calm, poised, free, and overcome the "illusion of sense experience with its manifold bondages." (p. 125)

Of all the fears of which man has to rid himself, fears which constitute the "backbone of disease," that of death is most persistent of all. And only by being able to show that men are already sons of God, "members of an eternal order," could it be displaced. Thus, says H. W. Dresser, from a discussion of the power of thought in its effect on practical present ills, they were led finally to "the fundamental principles of a comprehensive spiritual philosophy of life." The healing of disease was thus only "preparatory to the larger ideals of Christian living." (p. 126)

Horatio Dresser pays a high tribute to the effective influence upon his own life of the ideals and teachings by which his parents were guided.

To be told in one's youth about the Christ within, to be taught to seek the guidance of the inner world in every moment of need, is an inestimable privilege in more senses than one. One then grows up not only with the thought of health rather than the fear of disease, the thought of life in the place of the dread of death, but with an empirical basis free from the encumbrances of dogmatic theology. The philosophy of the immanent God then appeals to the mind in later life, as a natural consequence of what has already been an experience. (p. 127)

In most respects it is clear that the Dressers follow closely the thought and practice of Quimby, though one gets the impression of a kind of religious warmth in them that goes beyond anything in Quimby's teachings. God is omnipresent wisdom, immanent in all the universe and man. Every man possesses in some degree God within; indeed, man has no good quality or power that is wholly his own, rather all that he possesses is God within. All the qualities of love, mercy, justice, truth that reside in man, though they are but a spark of the infinite love, or mercy, or justice, or wisdom, "yet they must be of the same kind else they would not be true love, or mercy, or justice, or wisdom." If this be true, that God is man's life, strength, wisdom, then man's true attitude should be one of receptivity to God and a willingness to follow whatever comes from that source, and this becomes "the perfect key to health, happiness and success." Quimby would have agreed that it was the key to health, but one does not find him speaking of either happiness or success. If he believed, as later New Thought leaders teach, that either happiness or success as well as health is the inherent right of every man, he does not so declare. A little later on in the article from which the above is taken (*Journal of Practical Metaphysics,* December, 1896), in discussing Christ in relation to man, he does state that "Christ's love is the economy of life, the open door for the powers of the infinite to flow through to us, to secure our prosperity, and to do mighty works." Note he brings in "prosperity," to which Quimby gives no importance, but which later New Thought leaders have emphasized greatly. (See, for one example, Charles Fillmore, *Prosperity.*) But if Julius Dresser used the term he certainly gave it no such emphasis as did later leaders. Horatio Dresser accounts for the development of this emphasis as a result of a tendency on the part of some devotees of the popular mind cure toward a shallow individualism. Taking their cue from the emphasis upon the creative power of thought, they asserted that man might attain his rightful estate by claiming as his own every good thing. From claims of health they passed to affirmation concerning wealth, success, and many other things. This application of Dr.

Quimby's proposition, "Whatever we believe, that we create," should not, he declares, "be attributed to the parent teachers." (*Health and the Inner Life*, p. 94)

The controversy as to Mrs. Eddy's dependence upon Quimby has been so frequently discussed by persons on both sides that there is nothing new that can be said about it. Whether she was or was not influenced by Quimby is largely an academic question at present. Violent partisans, pro and con, have presented the evidence alleged for and against such influence. Perhaps the best summary of the stages through which the controversy has passed was furnished by H. W. Dresser in his *The Quimby Manuscripts*, Appendix I, where the various stages are presented in chronological order and the sources clearly indicated, so that interested students who desire to go into the matter may easily satisfy themselves as to the facts. The most cogent feature is the confronting of the clear statement of the early Mrs. Eddy with the Mrs. Eddy of a later date, when the defense of a going organization very much under fire was a major concern, and when it had become a matter of necessity, as it seemed to her, to assure her following of her originality as revealer of the new truth which Christian Science purportedly brought to the world. It is exceedingly difficult for an objective student of the movements to accept at face value the later statements in the face of the earlier ones, made spontaneously and out of a profound sense of gratitude to her great benefactor. There was certainly no practical purpose to be served by her quite gratuitous and eloquent early tributes to the importance of P. P. Quimby other than the enhancement of the reputation of the man who cured without medicine, who healed by mental or spiritual means, the first, in America at least, to do so.

Thus in a sense New Thought owes its development in the first place, in part at least, to the feeling of loyalty of the Dressers to P. P. Quimby. They thought he was being betrayed by Mrs. Eddy in her denial of any dependence upon him, and were convinced that Mrs. Eddy and those who accepted her as revelator of the Truth and as the Founder and organizer of what she was calling Christian Science, were misrepresenting what he had taught and practiced.

A second way in which New Thought was debtor to Christian Science was that certain persons, once in high favor with Mrs. Eddy and her trusted lieutenants, reacting against her authoritarian possessiveness, broke with her and became the teachers of men and women who later founded movements of considerable extent and influence that have collectively been considered as New Thought groups. Two of the most important of these were Ursula Gestefeld and Emma Curtis Hopkins.

Mrs. Gestefeld, born April 22, 1845, in Augusta, Maine, of an invalid mother, was a sickly child, and friends thought she would never live to maturity. But she did, married, and bore four children. She was already middle-aged before she heard of Christian Science, when a friend loaned her a copy of *Science and Health*. Something of a radical by nature and training, according to C. B. Patterson, who wrote a sketch of her life in *Mind* (IX, 251-54) as one of the New Thought leaders, she was out of sympathy with the traditional religious thought of the day, but in *Science and Health* she saw, "despite its contradictions and inconsistencies," "a truth that if applied to the problems of individual and social life would make all things new." Applying its principles to her own case she had in a period of three months, without the help of any practitioner, achieved a state of health beyond any previously enjoyed. When Mrs. Eddy appeared in Chicago and offered class instruction, she became a member and was taught by Mrs. Eddy in her class of May, 1884, held in Chicago. Mrs. Eddy early recognized in her a person of outstanding ability and welcomed her as an exponent of the new faith. Mrs. Gestefeld was a very able individual, and she gave herself unreservedly to the practice and teaching of Christian Science. A very effective teacher, she soon won a substantial following. In her zeal to communicate her faith to others she turned to writing. But when in 1888 she published a book under the title, *Ursula N. Gestefeld's Statement of Christian Science*, though she gave full credit to

Mrs. Eddy as its founder, she got into trouble. Christian Science had already been stated by Mrs. Eddy in *Science and Health* and her other writings, and apparently she felt that was sufficient. She denounced Mrs. Gestefeld in the *Journal* and practically cut her off from her movement. But far from ending Mrs. Gestefeld's career as teacher and practitioner, this launched her upon an independent career of healing and teaching. One of the most articulate of the early Eddy converts, she eventually became recognized as a leader in the metaphysical movement which came to be called New Thought. A great deal of her work was done in Chicago where she established herself and regularly taught classes, maintained a center and a church, and published a magazine, *The Exodus*, as a means of disseminating her ideas. She reacted vigorously to Mrs. Eddy's attack upon her and wrote a caustic pamphlet under the title *Jesuitism in Christian Science*. To the system which she eventually evolved, she gave the name "Science of Being." She formed a club, the Exodus Club, a nonsectarian group which had for its purpose the imparting and receiving of instruction in the Science of Being. Mrs. Gestefeld's instruction was obtainable through the club at a rate not otherwise available. The annual payment was $25.00. The club maintained rooms and offered certain social and cultural advantages to its membership beyond that of mere instruction. Out of the Exodus Club seems to have grown the church to which Mrs. Gestefeld gave the name of the Church of the New Thought. No member was required to make any profession of faith or to subscribe to anything which his reason rejected. Through the club Mrs. Gestefeld readily threw in her fortunes with the nascent metaphysical movement, was a frequent speaker on the platform of its congresses, served as member of the Executive Committee of the Metaphysical League, and was present at the formation of the INTA in London in 1914.

Her other books, widely used by New Thought groups, were: *The Breath of Life: A Series of Self-treatments, Reincarnation or Immortality, How We Master Our Fate, The Builder and the Plan,* and *A Chicago Bible Class.*

Emma Curtis Hopkins, more than any other single teacher, influenced New Thought. Little is known of her private life. What led her first to an interest in Christian Science is not known, but in the list of Mrs. Eddy's students in the class of December, 1883, her name appears. Though four of the members of her class later took Normal Class Instruction also, Mrs. Hopkins apparently did not.

That she was an apt pupil was quickly recognized by Mrs. Eddy, who had but recently begun the publication of the important *Christian Science Journal*. For the first year Mrs. Eddy edited the *Journal* herself, assisted apparently by Mrs. Hopkins. But beginning with No. 9, September, 1884, in the second volume, Emma Curtis Hopkins' name was at the masthead, not as assistant editor as has sometimes been stated, but as editor, introduced to the readers by Mrs. Eddy as "its new and able editor." (August, 1884, p. 4). This continued through the remainder of Volume II to No. 16, March, 1885. Beginning with Volume III, April, 1885, the *Journal* assumed a smaller format and carried no masthead at all indicating who was editor. Editorials were signed with initials, a number of them E. H., presumably Emma Hopkins, though there were also some by A.J.S. An article in the "Editor's Table" department in the July issue, signed E. Hopkins, discusses "What is Plagiarism," an attack upon the editor of *Mind Cure*, a "Metaphysical magazine published in Chicago." She assumed full responsibility for what had been written against A. J. Swartz, since from September, 1884, to April, 1885, she said, Mrs. Eddy had nothing to do with the magazine, she herself being "editor pro tem of the *Journal*." (p. 81)

In an article in the *Journal* (September, 1885, pp. 112-13) on "Teachers of Metaphysics," Mrs. Hopkins pays high tribute to Mrs. Eddy:

No student (I speak from knowledge of facts) has ever yet been qualified to teach Christian Science except rudimentarily. . . . But she whose life of cleansing sorrow left her the fit transparency for revelations straight from the Infinite Source, teaches the science of God and His creation in all its divine completeness. No member of a class at the college ever left till he had ascended the full height of his understanding, borne thither by the strong pinions of our leader's inspiration.

Taught in the class of December, 1883, Mrs. Hopkins was listed as practitioner in the February, 1884, issue of the *Journal* and in successive issues until August, when her name is missing. Apparently she became fully engrossed in the editorial work and gave up her private practice, for her name does not appear again among the "professional cards." As late as October, 1885, she was listed as the one who could furnish names and addresses of practitioners and patients mentioned in the department, "Letters and Cases of Healing." (III, 134) In the November issue such information might be gotten from Mrs. S. H. Crosse. No clearly identifiable article by Mrs. Hopkins or reference to her is found in the *Journal* beyond this date. Just what happened is not altogether clear, but she was dismissed as editor in October, 1885, and succeeded by Mrs. Crosse. Why? Bates and Dittemore say that it was because she began to read other metaphysical books besides Mrs. Eddy's writings. *(Mary Baker Eddy,* p. 265)

Her independence and her indisposition to bend to the will of her superior probably lay at the bottom of it, though I have seen nothing from Mrs. Hopkins herself in reply to Mrs. Eddy's attack upon her. From the direction of her subsequent activities it is clear that she was an extremely able individual, with ideas very much her own, and with the ability to communicate them to others. She could not accept the role assigned to her by Mrs. Eddy, and so became an independent teacher.

Mrs. Hopkins made Chicago her headquarters. Just when she went there is not certain; but Mrs. Bingham, who taught Nona Brooks in Pueblo, Colorado, probably in 1886, had sought out Mrs. Hopkins, had been healed by her, and had taken instruction from her before that time. Bates and Dittemore, discussing Mrs. Eddy's activities in 1886, say she was worried when Mrs. Plunkett and Mrs. Hopkins opened offices in Chicago. (p. 276)

In the *Christian Science Journal* for April, 1887 (p. 25), under

"Questions Answered," Mrs. Eddy comments on the following: "Emma Hopkins tells her students Mrs. Eddy teaches mesmerism. Is that true?" Her reply was:

If one half of what I hear of Mrs. Hopkins teaching on the subject of Christian Science is correct she is deluding the minds she claims to instruct. She took a Primary Course at my College but was not permitted to go farther. She never entered my Normal Class, is not qualified to teach Christian Science and is incapable of teaching it.

A want ad in the *Chicago Inter-Ocean* of May 18, 1888, stated that Mrs. Hopkins had arranged to receive patients for mental cure at her residence, 2019 Indiana Avenue, and all would come under her direct attention. A limited number could be received into her home for board and treatment. In the same issue it was announced on the church page that she would speak at Kimball Hall on the subject, "There Is No Matter." She was at this point clearly still a loyal follower of Mrs. Eddy. Incidentally, this was the only Christian Science service listed, though the following week Joseph Adams advertised a theater meeting.

In the *Christian Science Journal* for March, 1888 (p. 595), Mrs. Eddy declares that Christian Science is hampered by "immature demonstrations . . . incorrect teachings . . . unprincipled claimants," who appropriate her ideas—specifically naming her former favorite:

This dishonesty—yea, fraud—is conspicuous in the verbose lectures of Mrs. Emma Hopkins. She adopts my ethics, or talks them freely, while departing from them. Her injustice to her Teacher and benefactor to one who tenderly rescued her from unnamable conditions, and then to spare vanity a blow, receipted her in full for her tuition, without ever receiving a cent—this ingratitude is startling to those who know it all.

She had earlier bracketed Mrs. Hopkins with Julius A. Dresser, A. J. Swartz, and Mary Plunkett as "spreading abroad patch work books, false compendiums of my system, crediting some ignoramus or infidel with teachings they have stolen from me." She called them Mind Quacks. (Quoted by Bates and Dittemore in *Mary Baker Eddy*, p. 272)

Mrs. Hopkins has well been called the teacher's teacher. The list of persons who sat under her teaching, either in Chicago where she settled and founded the Christian Science Theological Seminary, or in some of the other cities where she taught classes from time to time, reads like a *Who's Who* among New Thought leaders. To name only a few, there were Frances Lord; Annie Rix Militz and Harriet Rix; Malinda E. Cramer, co-founder of Divine Science; Mrs. Bingham, teacher of Nona L. Brooks; Helen Wilmans; Charles and Myrtle Fillmore, founders of Unity School of Christianity; Charles A. and Josephine Barton, editor of *The Life,* Kansas City, Missouri; Dr. H. Emilie Cady, writer of the Unity textbook *Lessons in Truth;* Ella Wheeler Wilcox, New Thought poetess; Elizabeth Towne; and considerably later Ernest Holmes, founder of the Church of Religious Science.

It would not do to say, of course, that hers was the sole, or even the determining, influence upon the thought and future plans of any of these; but that she did exercise an influence upon them and upon a great number of other persons there can be no doubt. At just what point this influence was exerted cannot always be pointed out, but perhaps it was more than anything else her mysticism. Fenwicke Holmes says that this was a very potent influence upon Ernest Holmes and has been passed on to his following, who in an earlier day were perhaps primarily intellectual in their approach. It contributed a factor which has been important in enhancing the mystical element within that movement. It may indeed be one of its major appeals. Yielding to none in the vigor of its emphasis upon the necessity of using the mind in religion as well as in science, the movement has nevertheless included in the more recent years a wholesome element of mysticism as well.

Another student on whom she made a profound impression was Charles Fillmore. An article in *Modern Thought,* Volume I, No. 7, announces a class to be given in Kansas City January 6, 1890. Of Mrs. Hopkins the article says, and it undoubtedly represents the opinion of Charles Fillmore, even if he did not himself write it:

She is undoubtedly the most successful teacher in the world, her instruction not only gives understanding to the student by which he can cure the ills of himself and others, but in many instances those who enter her classes confirmed invalids come out at the end of the course perfectly well. She dwells so continually in the spirit that her very presence heals and those who listen to her are filled with new life.

After the class, he writes (No. 9, January, 1890, p. 8) a most enthusiastic note of appreciation. In praising her personally, he says that he is doing violence to her expressed desire that she should not be credited with the wonderful success of the lectures in which she was merely an "instrument of the spirit of truth." He doubts "if ever before on this planet were such words of burning truth so eloquently spoken through woman." He reports a listener as saying that he had heard many great orators, Wendell Phillips, Henry Ward Beecher, T. De Witt Talmadge, Neal Dow, and others, but she had surpassed them all. Yet the chief claim of the lectures lay not in their eloquence, but in the sweet spirit of charity which pervaded them, with never a word of criticism of any sect or school.

An article by Mrs. Hopkins taken from *International Christian Science* is published in the February, 1890, issue under the title "Old and New Metaphysics." In it she notes a number of ancient teachers—Buddha, Jesus, Appolonius, Vyasa—who taught very much as Christian Science does today. Indeed, she says, "The most ancient teachings known to master minds of the wise men are identical with the science of this hour." Many of their teachings were essentially Christian Science teachings but "taught in a little different fashion."

This of course could never be tolerated by Mrs. Eddy or her devoted followers, who seem to have regarded her revelation as the starting point, or at least a restatement of Jesus' teaching.

In 1887 Mrs. Hopkins conducted a large class of some 250 pupils in San Francisco. There was no limitation at that time upon the number who might be taught in a Christian Science class—and be it remembered that she was still calling her teaching Christian Science. Annie Rix Militz was one of her pupils and also Mrs. Cramer, though possibly not in this class. She taught large classes in Kansas City, New York, and Boston. It was in her New York class that Dr. H. Emilie Cady was a member. An Emma C. Hopkins Association was formed and held annual meetings In Boston itself, citadel of Christian Science, she had, it is reported, as many as a thousand students. She put much stress on the Bible, commenting regularly in the Chicago newspapers on the International Sunday School lessons. She developed metaphysical biblical interpretation in much the same manner as did Mrs. Eddy in her *Key to the Scriptures* and as it was expanded later by Charles Fillmore in *The Mysteries of Genesis* and other books, and was probably influential, thinks Dr. Raymond C. Barker, in putting New Thought on a firmer biblical basis than earlier teachers had done.

Eventually she ceased using the name Christian Science and indeed ceased public or class teaching, continuing however to teach individuals. She took up residence in New York, though for a time she was in London, where she worked out part of her *Higher Mysticism*.

Mrs. Hopkins' seminary, called the Christian Science Theological Seminary, was founded by her in Chicago in 1887. A copy of what is titled *Christian Science Theological Review and Christian Science Seminary Catalogue*, for the year ending November 30, 1893, locates it at 72 Auditorium Building, Chicago. Mrs. Hopkins was president. Other faculty members listed were Annie Rix Militz, professor of Scripture Revelation; George Edward Burnell and Mary Lamereaux Burnell, professors of Pure Metaphysics; and Edith Adele Martin, secretary. Included in its statement of purpose was the following:

The Bibles of all times and nations are compared; their miracles are shown to be the result of one order of reasoning, and the absence of miracles shown to be the result of another order of reasoning. . . . the teachings of inspired writers are proved to be identical with the native inspirations of all minds in common. . . . We perceive that inherently there is one judgment in all mankind alike. It is restored by the theology taught here. With its restoration we find health, protection, wisdom, strength, prosperity.

It is stated that the class register numbers 350 names of those who have received the first twelve lessons of Christian Science announced in the seminary classroom, and that there is an ordained ministry of 111 persons who have had in addition the theological course, apparently a prerequisite of ordination.

The plan of education in the seminary, it is declared,

is wholly different from that everywhere else pursued, in that so-called students are addressed from their first moment of entrance into class as already knowing all that is to be known . . . and Truths held in careful seclusion by the religious metaphysicians are not considered too abstruse to meet instant response when spoken to the youngest members.

Three types of classes are offered: regular seminary classes of twelve lessons for which the fee was $50.00; the theological course, open to those who have taken the seminary course, fee $50.00; and what is called "Reviews," open only to theological students, beginning August 20 and January 1 each year, leading to ordination at its close for those deemed prepared. In addition there was a 12 o'clock service daily which ministers, professors, and others were warmly invited to attend "and see for themselves what reviving energy there is in the divine truth fully expressed."

An article concerning the seminary gives something of its educational philosophy. Its purpose is that of "teaching men the spirit that giveth life—awakening in man the realization of the Christian Principle—the God in them and in all things." It does not, therefore, have "chairs of Church History, or Homiletics, or Ethics, or Dogmatic Theology, as is usual in Theological Seminaries. Things taught in such schools are never of first importance, often of no importance, and as a rule distinctly diverting from the main things." Not, the writer hastens to say, "that the main thing is not taught by beautiful spirits often found in these schools," but it is not the nature of such "chairs" to "teach the pure Christian doctrine."

One suspects that here is a fundamental characteristic of the whole teaching philosophy of the metaphysical movement in general, one that probably accounts for the meager formal training required by all the groups of those who minister or who teach in them.

Mrs. Emma Curtis Hopkins lived until 1925. After her death her sister Estelle Carpenter took over, aided by a teacher, Eleanor Mel. A Miss Ethelred Folsom, who had studied with Mrs. Hopkins and apparently had accompanied her on a trip to Europe, either had or came into some money. She married a Mr. Helling who was also interested in Mrs. Hopkins' teachings. She decided to set up an organization to perpetuate Mrs. Hopkins' influence and as a result bought a rather large farm, as farms go in Connecticut. This was called Joy Farm. Here people were invited to come for classes in Mrs. Hopkins' teachings, and her works were published and distributed under the name "The Ministry of the High Watch." The organization was duly incorporated by Mrs. Helling and the sister, Estelle Carpenter. For a time Mr. Helling served as teacher, but he became dissatisfied, sought a divorce from Mrs. Helling, and went out to the West Coast.

For quite a period there was no teaching at the farm, but it was a lovely place and a good many people continued going there for their vacations. Here they had access to the books and were able to meet Mrs. Helling—who now was calling herself Sister Frances—and of course Mrs. Carpenter. This resulted in the continued circulation of some of the Hopkins books.

Then Charles P. Wade came into the picture and resumed classes in the Hopkins teaching. Mrs. Bogart, for some years secretary to Mrs. Myrtle Fillmore of Unity School of Christianity, had while at Unity read some of Mrs. Hopkins' material and was deeply impressed by it. She went to Joy Farm and studied it under the leadership of Charles P. Wade. She conceived an interest in collecting the comments of Mrs. Hopkins on the International Sunday School lessons, which had been published in various periodicals. She went to Chicago, found many of them in the old *Chicago Inter-Ocean,* and had photostats made of them. But how to get them published? Printing was so expensive. Finally she was able to acquire a Multigraph on very favorable terms and began their publication and distribution. Meanwhile, Charles P. Wade left the farm, because of family need, and went to Wisconsin. He later became a Presbyterian minister. This brought to an end the formal teaching program at the farm, though Mrs. Carpenter and Sister Frances continued to fill orders for such books as remained. When Mrs. Carpenter died she willed the books to a real estate man, Leon T. Wilson, who continued for a time to send out the books under the name of the Emma C. Hopkins Publishing Company. Then he lost interest in them and in 1951 wanted to sell them.

Mr. and Mrs. Bogart bought them, and as they were sold money was saved for further publication. *The Higher Mysticism* had been published in a series of twelve small volumes. The Bogarts put it into one good-sized volume. They continued from time to time to bring out additional Bible lessons, now to be found only in old newspapers or magazines or in manuscript.

At one time Dr. H. B. Jeffery taught courses on Mrs. Hopkins' teaching at the Unity School of Christianity. He had been more than a student of hers, really an associate, at one period. Members of classes and particularly other teachers continued to buy and recommend her works. Considerable numbers are sold through the Devorss and Scrivener bookstores in Los Angeles, and the Bogarts have a small but steady sale for them.

High Watch Farm, which replaced Joy Farm as the name of the original property, was eventually sold. The Bogarts carry on at Cornwall Bridge, Connecticut, not far from the farm, under the name "High Watch Fellowship."

H. B. Jeffery, who as we have said taught classes on Mrs. Hopkins, himself wrote books definitely similar to the Hopkins teaching. His *Mysticism* is strikingly like *The Higher Mysticism* of Mrs. Hopkins. At his passing the remnants of his publications were acquired by the leaders of the Christ Truth League of Fort Worth, Texas.

In contrast to Mrs. Eddy's Christian Science, a term which, though used before Quimby and by him, became increasingly associated with her teaching, the name Mental Science, employed by W. F. Evans in describing the psychological aspects of the new healing, began to be widely used. Julius A. Dresser wrote at one time *The True History of Mental Science*. Those who, like the Dressers, practiced this mental science also taught their philosophy and method of healing, and some of those taught in turn healed and taught others. The inevitable result was the formation of little groups of interested persons, each operating independently of the others. There was no general disposition at first to leave the church, though some did so, the New Thought being such as to render them unhappy under the orthodox teachings. If the groups met it was at an hour which left them free to attend also the traditional church services. Some of those who were healed and who undertook to teach and heal were ministers. It was one of these, J. W. Winkley, a former Unitarian minister, who, naturally enough, first organized his group as a church in Boston, calling it the Church of the Divine Unity, incorporating thus, as an integral part of the new emphasis, the element of worship.

Individuals who were in no sense organization-minded also began to lecture, to write, and to publish. Some of them, as for example W. J. Colville, came to their interest through Spiritualism. But Colville became also an able exponent of the general New Thought point of view, and was later a frequent speaker and leader in New Thought congresses. His *The Spiritual Science of Health and Healing* (1889) was widely circulated throughout the English-speaking world and he lectured all over America, Great Britain, and New Zealand. Others came to New Thought via Theosophy and interpreted the new healing on a theosophical basis, a trend which is still found in some parts of the world, notably in Germany.

Groups were springing up in widely separated sections of the United States: that of Mrs. Cramer in San Francisco and on the West Coast, also that of Annie Rix Militz, both described more fully in a later section respectively as Divine Science and Home of Truth; that of the Brooks sisters in Pueblo (and later Denver), Colorado, co-founders of Divine Science; and the Unity School of Christianity founded by the Fillmores in Kansas City, Missouri, besides those of Mrs. Emma Hopkins and Mrs. Ursula Gestefeld. A one-time student of Mrs. Eddy, Mrs. Elizabeth G. Stuart of Hyde Park, New York, began to teach, and Leander Edmund Whipple, another of her students, began to heal and teach in Hartford, Connecticut, in 1885, making Hartford an important center for the development of the new movement. Whipple was later to found and edit the influential *Metaphysical Magazine* in New York; to organize the American School of Metaphysics; and to write several volumes which are among the more important early publications in the field, including *The Philosophy of Mental Healing* and *The Manual of Mental Science*.

It was in Hartford also that another distinguished leader, C. B. Patterson, began his work in 1887. He was later to become the leader in the wider organization of the new movement, as writer and publisher of distinction and editor of perhaps the most important of early New Thought magazines, *Mind*.

Leander Whipple in New York and the groups in Boston began to use the term "metaphysical" to describe the new philosophy of spiritual healing, also called Mental Science. The earliest attempt to bring together the Mental Science leaders of Boston led to the formation in 1895 of the influential Metaphysical Club, which later played a significant role in the formation of an overall organization which finally became the INTA.

At this period there was the greatest divergency of thought among the various leaders. There was no common statement of belief. Healing, achieved chiefly through the mental processes, was a central emphasis. Mental science was an apt description of this, yet both in Quimby and in Evans it had been more than merely mental—it was in the case of both of them, as indeed in Mrs. Eddy, the method of Jesus. Horatio Dresser distinguished quite sharply, indeed rather more so than it seems to this writer is warranted by the facts, between what he calls the Mental Science period and the New Thought period. And he makes the dividing line about 1890, though recognizing that it cannot be fixed at any particular year.

While there is some merit in his distinguishing the earlier and the later periods, it is more accurate to say that from a very early date both interpretations are to be found: what might be called a merely, or predominantly, mental or psychological emphasis, which one might with some justice term a secular interpretation, and a more highly spiritual or religious interpretation. While it is certain that Evans sought, as I have indicated, to show that the logical application of a thoroughly idealistic philosophy leads to "mental healing," his dominant emphasis is a religious one, and so too was that of the Dressers in their teaching.

Handwritten notes taken by a student of the Dressers, Harriet S. Hemenway, Blue Hill Farm, in a class they gave in January, 1887, show that the first lecture deals with "opinion," a characteristic Quimby touch. "Medical opinion is simply an opinion and not the truth but if accepted as truth will influence the patient accordingly." Just "mental" science. But the second lecture begins thus: "The Christ is the God in Man, all attributes of God, love, strength, wisdom—are God in man, so we cannot take any credit to ourselves if we have any of these good attributes, as it is God and not ourselves—so man is nothing apart from God—all that he is in reality is God." Certainly a profoundly religious emphasis. In the third lecture we find, "We are each a separate thought of God. . . . These so-called bodies of ours are God's expression of his thought and idea, real to us, but not real in themselves. The Universe about us is the expression of God's ideas." If this was a true report of the Dressers' position, it is difficult to see how they should be classed, as Horatio Dresser does classify them, as belonging under Mental Science rather than New Thought.

One rather clear distinction there does seem to be between the earlier and later period, namely that health was the principal interest in the earlier day. One looks in vain in Quimby or Evans for any preoccupation with what fills rather a large place in the later years, the emphasis on prosperity, "supply," or abundance. One finds a section on it in Frances Lord's *Christian Science Healing* (1887), in which some five pages (pp. 379-84) are devoted to a treatment for poverty, consisting of numerous denials such as "No belief of my parents in poverty can make me poor," followed by affirmations such as "God is my life and there is no other," "God is not poor," etc.

Even in *Science and Health*, Mrs. Eddy writes, "To all mankind and in every hour divine love supplies all good (494:13-14), and later Christian Science leaders came to emphasize supply and abundance, and to treat for these things as well as for healing. There are two articles attributed to Mrs. Eddy herself in a collection of *Essays on Christian Science* ascribed to Mary Baker Eddy, edited and published by the Carpenters. One is on "Money Thought" (pp. 72-75), the other on "Supply" (pp. 76-82), and they sound very much like what may be found in Unity publications today. Though they are unsigned and undated, and have been officially dubbed spurious by headquarters, Gilbert Carpenter, Jr., a great devotee of Mrs. Eddy, considered them genuine and coming from a relatively early period of her activity. The present writer doubts this. Certainly the evidence is inconclusive. Yet where did Frances Lord get the idea in 1887? A careful check in the writings of Ursula Gestefeld reveals little if any emphasis upon supply or prosperity. And if Emma Curtis Hopkins taught it, it was certainly not attributed to her by any of her pupils.

An important figure in the emergence of New Thought was Mrs. Sarah J. Farmer, who established the Greenacre Conferences in Eliot, Maine, in the summer of 1894. The conferences were an outgrowth of interest in the great religions of the world aroused by the World's Parliament of Religions in 1893. But she was herself a New Thought leader, and Greenacres became rather naturally a center for New Thought summer gatherings, bringing together leaders from various parts of the country, but particularly from Boston and New York. Lectures were given by them, and smaller meetings of more informal character were held in afternoons or evenings.

This was the first of many such centers scattered about the country, some of them still operating, where retreats for special study and development are held during vacation periods. And in more recent years it has sometimes been on an extended cruise that students of New Thought have had the stimulus and guidance of leading teachers, thus combining happily the fun and relaxation of foreign travel with self-improvement under expert guidance. Other early centers were at Oscawana, New York, where C. B. Patterson was an outstanding leader, and at Jackson, New Hampshire, where Henry Wood organized the Jackson Lectures.

In Boston the first organized New Thought group with a regular leader was the Church of the Higher Life, which grew out of Sunday services begun by Mrs. Helen Van Anderson in 1894. It soon outgrew its first meeting place and quickly developed quite an elaborate program of services, including a corps of letter-writers to write letters of cheer to invalids and lonely persons, a Young Peoples Club, an Emerson Study Club, mothers meetings, spiritual training classes, and healing services each Sunday. Not first, but perhaps most important of the Boston organizations was the Metaphysical Club, begun in 1895. It brought together a group of New Thought leaders and followers including Henry Wood; Dr. J. W. Winkley; Warren A. Rodman, afterward one of the important figures in the rise of the overall New Thought organizations; C. M. Barrows, one of the first writers to see the relationship between Emerson and the burgeoning new movement; Horatio W. Dresser; Mrs. Julius A. Dresser; and Miss Lilian Whiting, a widely read New Thought writer. A Unitarian minister, Reverend L. B. McDonald, was its first president.

Julia Ward Howe, though in no way officially connected with the movement, gave the Metaphysical Club's first public lecture on March 28, 1895; for in order to attract public attention the early lectures were of a general nature. But it became increasingly New Thought in its public activities and proved to be the first permanent New Thought club. Fifty years later, in 1945, its first half-century of existence was celebrated and a brief history of its activities printed in the *Bulletin* of INTA. The club, though much reduced in membership, was still in existence in 1961. One person interviewed at a regular meeting in that year had been a member for over fifty years and knew well the outstanding leaders who had brought the club into being, for Henry Wood and Horatio W. Dresser, J. W. Winkley, and others who had been in it from the first were still prominent in its leadership when she joined. No longer possessed of a center of its own—this having been given up about 1958—it meets in one of the Boston hotels. Its present officers are hopeful of bringing it back to a more active and influential place in the life of the community. Although efforts at wider organization were made in various parts of the nation it was at least indirectly from the Boston Metaphysical Club that the National, and eventually the International, New Thought Alliance developed.

Among the more influential figures in the development and spread of New Thought ideas in the nineties were certain men who exercised much of their influence through writing rather than in the personal professional ministry or as leaders in the organizational expansion of the movement. And their writings carried far beyond the limits of those belonging to the organized movement. Three of these and their work should be noted at this point. They are not original in their thinking, but they rephrased and restated ideas that had appeared in both Quimby and Evans, and gave them a literary form that gained for them a wider reading by the general public, or at least that part of it which was attracted to the currents of New Thought which were beginning to run at that time. Henry Wood (1834-1908) was particularly important. Dresser writes of him as the first to seek to spread the new ideas through publicity. He thinks him representative of the "more rational expression of New Thought" (*History of the New Thought Movement*, p. 167), and at the same time the first New Thought philanthropist. Henry Wood had been a successful businessman before his retirement and, while not a man of great wealth, he was well-to-do. He gave generously, particularly to libraries and public institutions, and provided a special room under the auspices of the Metaphysical Club of Boston, known as the "Silence Room, for quiet and meditation." He was the first New Thought writer to undertake to express his ideas through the medium of fiction, writing two novels, *Edward Burton* and *Victor Serenus*. The latter was made into a drama—probably the first New Thought drama—and was performed in a Boston theater. Unfortunately, it was not a dramatic success. Paul Tyner, writing of him in the *Review of Reviews* (XXV [1902], 313), characterized him as the "first of the New Thought writers to become popular with that omnivorous person, the general reader."

In the preface to *The New Old Healing* (Boston: Lothrop, Lee & Shepard Co., 1908), Henry Wood discloses that in the year 1888, at the age of fifty-four, he was in a mental and physical condition "where life seemed a burden and an overwhelming depression prevailed." More specifically, he says he had suffered "a long period of chronic neurasthenia, insomnia and dyspepsia," and that there was "no promise of recovery or even of partial relief." Medicine and the usual methods brought no relief. Then "a plunge was made without reservation, from a supposedly correct moral and ethical life into the practice and philosophy of the higher thought with new ideals. A sharp corner was turned and a new path entered which led to much that was remarkably favorable." Everything accomplished thereafter he gladly attributes to "the strength derived from the new departure" (p. 7), evidently the principles he was about to state in the book, which had been tested under many conditions and their validity confirmed in hundreds of cases.

He stated also that he was not a professional healer and that he took no specific cases. Nor was it possible, he said, to teach in any systematic manner outside of his public writings. (p. 8)

Before his healing Wood had begun to write. His *Natural Law in the Business World* (1887), had brought him into prominence. This book, recast as *The Political Economy of Humanism,* went through a number of editions. But it was for his writing in the field of religion, interpreting the New Thought, that he was best known. *God's Image in Man, Studies in the New Thought World, The New Old Healing, The New Thought Simplified,* and *Ideal Suggestion Through Mental Philosophy* all set forth the general ideas of New Thought. A pamphlet, *Has Mental Healing a Valid Scientific and Religious Basis?* had sold more than thirty thousand copies prior to 1902.

Some idea of the popularity of Henry Wood's New Thought books may be seen in an advertisement of them in the back of the book, *The New Old Healing.* When this was published, one of his books was in the seventh edition, another the twelfth, still others in the fourteenth, eighth, third, and fourth. How large the editions were is not stated, but that the books appeared in a number of editions is evidence that in comparison with other books they enjoyed considerable popularity.

Paul Tyner characterized Wood's style as "clear, simple and direct" as his thought was "logical and comprehensive," asserting that his appeal lay in his common-sense approach to his subject, "utterly ignoring theological tangle and misty mysticism," and the fact that his teaching was so pointed and practical that it was not easy for the average reader to go astray in applying it. (*Review of Reviews,* XXV [1902], 313).

Wood's *The New Thought Simplified* presents an excellent and simple formulation of what New Thought had come to mean at that period. He characterizes it as

not distinctively a new religion, or even a new healing system, but a new all-inclusive way of life. It is not generally organized as a church though it might not be inappropriate to call it "the Church of the Human Soul," its form of service is soulful aspiration, its sanctuary the spiritual consciousness, its temple the unseen, its social companions ideals, and its communion, living contact with the Universal spirit. (p. 135)

It might be, he thought, that not many would avowedly identify themselves with the New Thought Movement, and that might be just as well, but he was sure that this modern spiritual uplift was so subtle and penetrative that it would sweep through dry and formal systems and give them new vitality. (p. 138)

All the fundamental propositions of New Thought he finds were plainly taught in the New Testament. But philosophy, idealism, and psychology have added each its quota in reinforcing the Bible until, together, they "form an impregnable combination." The Bible and New Thought both, he asserts, present the same truth, the one in ancient oriental form, the other in modern phraseology. But "Truth is one and unchangeable." (p. 145)

He reacts vigorously against the prevalent degradation of making the new philosophy a money-making scheme. "No one can sit down and think money into his pocket, and another cannot do it for him. . . . Material advantage must be incidental and subordinate. The law is Seek first the highest and that which is lower in rank will be added." (p. 95)

He does not, as many were doing, deny that there are such things as sin, sickness, death. They are here, in and around us. But, mark it, he writes, we are their creators.

Not wittingly, to be sure, but gradually and unwittingly we have done so and are in subjection to them. We dishonor God by counting them as inherently belonging to his image. . . . The body faithfully articulates and expresses our belief concerning it. We get just what we have accepted and expected. (p. 30)

The New Old Healing (1908) asserts that "the greatest modern discovery is not electricity, etc., but the recognition of mind as the real seat of causation, and the working philosophy of the conscious and subconscious realms." (p. 27) "God made ideal and potential man in his own image and likeness," he declares, but it is for man himself to bring his own birthright into expression and manifestation.

In *The New Thought Simplified*, in writing of self-treatment, which he equates with prayer—a frequent New Thought usage—

Wood comes very close to what was adjudged by a prominent Christian Scientist as the distinctive Christian Science emphasis (pp. 10-11), as over against that of New Thought, when he writes:

Self treatment or prayer is not a begging for special treatment, but rather a recognition that on the divine part everything already is perfect and that we only need conformity. It is simply a conscious taking of what is already provided. . . . Prayer is an effort toward a realization in consciousness of what already *is*.

Henry Wood was active in the important Metaphysical Club of Boston and a frequent speaker and counselor in the formation of larger units of New Thought organization which began to take form in the early decades of the twentieth century, but his great and lasting contribution was made through his books.

No name stands out more prominently in the telling of the story of New Thought than that of the Dressers. Horatio W. Dresser, son of Julius A. and Annetta Seabury Dresser, was perhaps the most prolific writer yet developed within the movement. He was of comparatively slight importance in the organization of the developing movement, though he did play a part in this also, serving as president of the Boston Metaphysical Club and vice-president of the International Metaphysical League and being listed for several years as one of the honorary presidents of the International New Thought Federation and later the INTA.

But his chief role in the movement was as a writer—a writer of magazine articles and of books, editor of magazines, and interpreter of New Thought in general to the public. The Library of Congress lists thirty-two titles under his name, not all specifically expounding New Thought themes, but all in one way or another carrying something of the spirit of New Thought, because that was the point of view of the author. And besides these, there was—in some ways his most important contribution—the editing and publication of *The Quimby Manuscripts*, which as we have seen made public in extenso what was really the fundamental basis of New Thought. In the controversy over the matter of

Mrs. Eddy's dependence upon Quimby, up until that time, reference had been made often enough to the manuscripts, but Christian Scientists had even denied that such documents really existed. Now it was possible for anyone wondering about the relationship between Mrs. Eddy and Dr. Quimby to make his own investigation of the Portland healer's writings and determine for himself what the probable relationship was. Along with the *Manuscripts,* which Dresser edited so as to eliminate much of the repetitiousness of the originals, he included certain letters from Mrs. Eddy as well as quotations from articles she had published in various New England periodicals lauding the man through whom she had been healed.

Heavy pressures upon the publishers led to the exclusion of this material from subsequent editions, but copies of the original first edition are fortunately available in many of the larger libraries.

During 1961 microfilm copies of the entire body of original manuscripts on deposit in the Library of Congress were made for the Bridwell Library of Southern Methodist University at Dallas and the library of the Pacific School of Religion at Berkeley, California. Thus it is now possible to compare the work of H. W. Dresser with these and discover how faithfully he dealt with them. Meanwhile microfilm reproduction had been made of those parts omitted by Dresser. Examination of these revealed no significant omission of material or obvious slanting of what he used. Others who worked through this material were agreed in this judgment.

Horatio W. Dresser was born in 1866, the year P. P. Quimby died. When the Dresser family returned to Massachusetts in 1882, after several years in the West, young Horatio learned bookkeeping and worked for the editor of the *New England Farmer,* writing shorthand and reading proof, later serving as bookkeeper and business manager. Much of his life was thereafter to be linked with editing, writing, and publishing. In 1883, C. B. Patterson writes, he took up the study of Emerson and other great writers and copied for his father the Quimby manuscripts loaned to him

by George Quimby. A biographical note which he himself prepared tells us that in 1884 (at which time he was only eighteen
years old) he began to practice mental healing along with his
parents.

He had European trips in 1888 and 1889 and prepared under a
private tutor for entrance into Harvard, entering as a special
student in 1891. His father died in 1893 and he was out of school
for a time because of his own ill health, but eventually he completed his work for the A.B. degree.

But before this he had begun to publish. A lecture, "The
Immanent God," was his first publication, issued in 1894 while he
was still an undergraduate. The following year saw the publication of his first full-length book, *The Power of Silence*. Paul
Tyner, writing of Dresser in the *Review of Reviews* in 1902,
speaks of him as "one of the New Thought writers whose vogue
rivals that of the popular novelist." (XXV, 314) By that time,
he said, *The Power of Silence* had gone through ten editions.
The Library of Congress entry of this book is dated 1903 and is
the fifteenth edition. Tyner describes it as "the work of a contem-
plative student essaying an interpretation of the German philosophers with amplification of the bearing of their thought on the
problems of the man of the street."

Meanwhile he had undertaken graduate work in the department of philosophy at Harvard, studying with William James,
Josiah Royce, and others. He received the Master's degree in
1904 and the Ph.D., also from Harvard, in 1907. In terms of formal
education, he was one of the most highly trained men in the
leadership of the new movement. He was an assistant in the
philosophy department at Harvard for several years, and enjoyed
the friendship particularly of William James. It was this, in part
at least, that gave Professor James his insight into the New
Thought Movement, which he classed among "the religions of
healthy-mindedness" in his *Varieties of Religious Experience*.
(See pp. 94, ff.)

All during these years he was writing and publishing. In 1896
he began the publication of a monthly magazine, *Journal of*

Practical Metaphysics, with the avowed object of "being helpful in the conduct of life, to prepare the way for a better, more harmonious, rational, and ethical life, and to derive this help from all the resources of human thought." (I, 15) He welcomed the co-operation of all who "believe that the time has come to place the study of mind in its relation to health and happiness upon a firm scientific basis." It was, it announced on the title page, "devoted to the unification of scientific and spiritual thought and the new philosophy of health." Contributors were drawn chiefly but not wholly from among the outstanding New Thought leaders—Warren Rodman, Henry Wood, C. M. Barrows, Dr. J. W. Winkley, Aaron Crane, Annetta Dresser—but there were also others including a Hindu Swami, writing on Hindu literature and thought. The magazine was published only until November, 1898, when it was merged with the *Arena,* and Dresser became associate editor of that influential magazine. Though Dresser was hospitable to ideas from other than Christian sources, he was by no means carried away by Hindu thought. Indeed he expressed, in a lengthy article on the subject, his belief that there had been a too uncritical acceptance of Vedantism, and that the time had come for a more skeptical critical reaction. For that criticism, he asserted, Western thought alone was able to furnish the standard. And he proceeded to a most thorough and discriminating application of such standards to an examination of the main bases of the Vedanta. Dresser's volume entitled *The Power of Silence,* as already indicated, was immensely popular. Soon followed *The Perfect Whole,* and by 1897 a publisher had brought out, under the title of *The Heart of It,* major extracts from these two books, while the same year he added *In Search of a Soul.* In 1898 came *Voices of Hope;* in 1899, *Voices of Freedom* and *Methods and Problems of Spiritual Healing;* in 1900, *Living by the Spirit,* and *Education and the Philosophic Ideal.* At this time he was still only thirty-four years of age. Meanwhile he was turning out magazine articles and doing editorial work as well. And he found some time for active organizational work in the Boston Metaphysical Club and the International Metaphysical League.

He was in considerable demand as a lecturer, chiefly in and around Boston. His volume on *Education and the Philosophic Ideal* indicated an academic interest beyond mere New Thought lines, and this he was to follow out in his later career when he turned to the teaching of philosophy and psychology. But apparently some change had come over him religiously, for Paul Tyner writes that the rather "coldly judicial attitude" displayed in his earlier book *The Power of Silence,* had in *The Christian Ideal,* which appeared in 1901, been "exchanged for the fervor of the early Christian mystic." *(Review of Reviews,* XXV, 314)

By 1902 Dresser had largely withdrawn from all New Thought organizations, "desiring to be identified only with his own interpretation of Christian teaching," wrote Paul Tyner. But that was in no sense the end of his service of the cause of New Thought. Indeed, he continued to be one of its major interpreters. A number of his later books bear titles which are clearly New Thought: *Man and the Divine Order, Health and the Inner Life, A Message to the Well, Human Efficiency.* Then, in 1917, he edited *The Spirit of New Thought,* a collection of addresses and essays by major New Thought leaders, and wrote *Handbook of New Thought,* one of the simplest and most satisfying statements of the central features of the movement. Then he was invited to write *The History of the New Thought Movement,* which he did, publishing it in 1919. This was for many years the standard work in the field, until finally it went out of print. Two years later he laid the whole metaphysical movement deeply in his debt by publishing his very important *The Quimby Manuscripts.*

He wrote one more book on *Spiritual Health and Healing,* and as late as 1933, when he was sixty-seven years of age, he wrote *Knowing and Helping People.*

At one time he taught philosophy at Ursinus College in Pennsylvania for a period of two years. For a time he was lecturer at the Theological Seminary of the New Church (Swedenborgian) in Cambridge, and in 1919 he was ordained to the ministry of that church, of which a brother, Paul Dresser, was also a minister. But in 1928 he withdrew from the ministry at his own request.

For many years he held no academic or church position, but was engaged in writing and personal counseling. An interesting letterhead found in the archives of the New Thought Movement indicates in part what he did in addition to his writing, which resulted in substantial volumes on *Psychology in Theory and Practice* (1924), *Ethics in Theory and Application* (1925), *A History of Ancient and Medieval Philosophy* (1926), *A History of Modern Philosophy* (1928), and *Outlines of a Psychology of Religion* (1929). The letterhead, to be found in the Eugene Del Mar file in the New Thought archives, was employed for a handwritten letter by H. W. Dresser under date of September 2, 1920. Headed "Correspondence Bureau, Horatio W. Dresser," it lists the services he offered as Manuscripts, Vocational Guidance, Instruction in Philosophy, Letters on Personal Problems, Philosophical Criticism, Books on Applied Philosophy, and Religion and Personal Efficiency.

In his later years Dr. Dresser was a member (nonresident, for he lived at Holyoke, Massachusetts) of the Church of Our Savior in Brooklyn Heights, a Unitarian Congregational church. A flyer from the church announced that he would give a series of four evening conferences on Wednesday evenings in the church chapel on the general topic of Health and Inner Control, be available for personal conference at certain morning hours, and on Friday afternoon would lead a quiet hour of meditation—all of these available without any charge. So to the end, though no longer an active member of the New Thought organization, he was still engaged in giving practical effect to its major interests. If he became more psychological in his emphasis, he never lost the central emphasis upon the spiritual. He only chose to make more conscious use of psychological techniques as the instruments of the Spirit in working within mankind. He resigned only in 1953, and died March 30, 1954, at the age of eighty-eight.

Dresser made no significant new contribution to the development of New Thought, but his books have been and will undoubtedly remain among the most valuable to those desiring to follow the development of this important segment of American religious thought. He was for many years a personal link between early New Thought and its later manifestations. With some of these he had little sympathy. He never gave emphasis to the matter of supply or abundance. He tends to play it down. Certainly he shared in the theoretical belief that "these things will be added unto you," if the major premise, "seek ye first," were observed, but he deprecated the uncritical emphasis upon the principle which had the practical effect of making it an end in itself.

In the preface to the little book *The Heart of It*, which brought together selected passages from *The Power of Silence* and *The Perfect Whole* within two years of the publication of the first of the two, the compiler wrote, mentioning the writings of a number of the prominent early New Thought leaders,

Mr. Dresser's books are a step beyond, the thorough philosophical training of the author giving him an authority not to be lightly questioned, while his power of expression illumines the closest argument. The spirit and power of Emerson are both there, but there is something more. It is Emerson, humanized as it were—brought into more vital relation with the needs, small and great, of daily life.

A younger brother of Horatio Dresser called himself David Seabury, choosing to use his mother's name rather than his father's, perhaps with the understandable desire not to be known only as the son of Julius A. or brother of the eminent Horatio W. Dresser. His field was psychology, a subject which he wrote a great deal about, taught to many, and made the basis of his counseling of innumerable persons who came to him for help. His approach to the field, while not technically or nominally New Thought, was nevertheless closely allied to that of the better New Thought leaders, and he was highly honored and respected by them. He died in 1960.

The third, and without doubt the most widely read, of the writers definitely known as being associated with New Thought was Ralph Waldo Trine, though Emmet Fox may in time surpass him in the number of his books circulated. Certainly no single book by a New Thought writer has equaled the sales of Trine's *In Tune with the Infinite,* which, in English alone, has gone well beyond a million and a half copies. And it has been translated into many of the languages of the world, some twenty all told, including Japanese and Esperanto, and sold in huge numbers. It has appeared also in Braille for the blind, boosting the book's total circulation to well over two million copies. Three or four of his other books have sold over half a million each. A highly significant fact is that much of this distribution has reached far beyond New Thought circles out to the general public, which has bought and read Trine's books without ever knowing that they were New Thought.

Yet the book is an almost perfect presentation of New Thought at its best. Publishers of the latest edition, which appears in its entirety in *The Best of Ralph Waldo Trine,* along with selections from his other writings, studiously omit any mention of New Thought, but remark that the author "has succeeded in putting into popular terms much of the New England thought—specifically that of Emerson—which has become the basis of a good deal of modern inspirational literature." (p. 7)

In the preface to the book its basic New Thought orientation is clearly evident.

There is a golden thread that runs through every religion of the world. . . . This same golden thread must enter into the lives of all who today, in this busy, work-a-day world of ours would exchange impotence for power, weakness and suffering for abounding health and strength, pain and unrest for perfect peace, poverty of whatever nature for fullness and plenty.

Where would one go for a better statement of the promise of New Thought? Indeed, the subtitle of Trine's book, *Fullness of Peace, Power and Plenty,* is an almost perfect description of the general characteristics of New Thought. It has often been called "The religion of peace, power, and plenty."

The preface goes on in true New Thought fashion to declare that each builds his own world, building from within and attracting from without; that thought is the force which builds—and, as thought is spiritualized, it becomes more and more powerful and subtle in its working, all in accordance with law and within the power of every man.

Everything is worked out in the unseen, before being manifested visibly, in the ideal before being realized in the real, and in the spiritual before taking material form; for the effective causes are in the realm of the unseen, the effects in the realm of the seen.

It is Trine's declared purpose to point out simply and clearly the facts and laws which underlie the workings of "the interior, spiritual thought forces," so that men can make use of them in everyday life.

For there is "within, above and below the human will," incessantly at work, the divine will. To come into harmony with this will and therefore with all the higher laws and forces available and to work in conjunction with them in order that they can work in conjunction with man is the secret of all success, for it is "to come into the possession of unknown riches, and into the realization of undreamed of powers."

No new principle is introduced into the conception of New Thought by Trine, but no single writer has expressed its essential message more clearly or more engagingly than he. That has been the secret of the continuing publication and sale of his book. The publisher of the latest edition, that of 1957, well says that "Mr. Trine preceded, as he has outdone and may easily outlast, the current school of self-help 'philosophies.'" (p. 7) The book was first published in 1897. On the occasion of the fiftieth anniversary of its publication, Trine wrote, in the anniversary edition, a Foreword in which he stated what he thought accounted for its wide circulation and long life.

Something indeed of a universal nature seemed to get into it which took it all over the world . . . attested by the vast number of appreciative and grateful letters that have come to me from readers in many countries, letters telling in concrete terms what it has done for them and their families.

This he attributes to the fact that there is in it that which he had ardently hoped for, "the element of use, of human help." And it did help. Henry Ford is said to have attributed his success to reading it, and he gave hundreds of copies of it to other industrialists.

Ralph Waldo Trine was born the year P. P. Quimby died, 1866, in Mt. Morris, Illinois; was educated in Carthage College Academy, Knox College, A.B. 1891; and studied at the University of Wisconsin and later at Johns Hopkins University in the field of history and political science. He was much interested in social and economic problems, having won a $100 prize for an essay on "The Effects of Humane Education on the Prevention of Crime" during his student days. C. B. Patterson, writing of him in 1902, says that he had through his studies in these areas come to the conclusion that "so far as ethics and even the actual safety of society, government, and industry is concerned, socialism is the only basis that can be acknowledged, and is certainly the only basis that can be deduced from an actual living belief in the great fact of the Fatherhood of God and the brotherhood of Man." (*Mind*, IX, 327) He was at that time intending to publish a book "from the viewpoint of a socialist who is such because of his New Thought philosophy." If he published such a book, it is not apparent in the titles of those that later came from his pen.

What influences led to his acceptance of the New Thought outlook are not easily discoverable. Indeed, to find out anything about the man personally is difficult. He was never an organization man in New Thought, beyond being listed among the honorary presidents of the early International Movement. He lived not far from Oscawana and was one of the frequent lecturers at the summer schools held there. Whether he made a practice of healing personally and professionally is not certain. One gets the impression that he made his contribution to the movement chiefly through his books and through lecturing. He lived to the ripe old age of ninety-two, spending his last years in Pilgrim Place, Claremont, California, a retirement place for persons who had engaged professionally in religious work.

Perhaps one explanation of the wide circulation is the fact that, while the central point of view of his books is in the best tradition of New Thought, his vocabulary was one which raised little or no question in the minds of the orthodox, or at least in the minds of the more liberally oriented church-Christians. No other New Thought writer gave a more central place to Jesus than he. One finds among New Thought writers little emphasis upon the historic Jesus—rather, they emphasize the Christ. Trine, on the other hand, constantly speaks of Jesus and his teachings. His book *Higher Powers of Mind and Spirit* devotes at least half of its chapters to a study of Jesus and his teachings and a discussion to which at least the liberal Christian of his day would take little exception. Even the orthodox would be moved by his obvious exaltation of the character of the Master and the manner in which he revealed the inner nature of the Divine Mind and its purposes.

And in *In Tune with the Infinite,* though he employs the term "the Christ" more frequently perhaps than the simple "Jesus," he defines being a Christian in terms of Jesus. It is "to be a follower of the *teachings* of Jesus the Christ; to live in harmony with the same laws he lived in harmony with: in brief *to live his life.*" The great central fact of his teaching was "this conscious union of man with the Father. It was the complete realization of this oneness with the Father on his part that made Jesus Christ." (p. 167)

By coming into this complete realization of this oneness with the Father, by mastering . . . every circumstance that crossed his path through life, even to the death of the body, and by pointing out to us the great laws which are the same for us as they were for him, he has given us an ideal of life, an ideal for us to attain to here and now, that we could not have without him. One has conquered first, all may conquer afterward. (pp. 168-69)

But, he admonishes, "don't mistake his mere person for his life and teachings . . . teach as did Jesus, the living Christ . . . the Christ within." This statement would hardly satisfy the fundamentalist or those who have a strongly dogmatic Christology, but it made a profound appeal to a rapidly increasing number of Americans and others in the late nineteenth and early twentieth century who had become impatient of dogma which made Jesus chiefly a forensic figure in what seemed to many an artificial drama of salvation, and were eagerly following a pronounced movement of the day sometimes called the "rediscovery of Jesus," which in one of its directions led to the remarkable development of the "social gospel."

As the New Thought groups began to hold services of worship as well as classes and lectures, there naturally developed a need for hymns they could use. Of course, some of the great hymns of the churches could be used exactly as they were, or could be adapted to New Thought purposes by the change of a word or a phrase, a line or lines, or even a stanza. Then whole new hymns patterned on the old ones were written by New Thought authors and wedded to old familiar tunes such as "Rock of Ages," "Abide with Me," and "How Gentle God's Commands."

Inevitably, however, poems or hymns by New Thought writers such as Ella Wheeler Wilcox, Angela Morgan, Don Blanding, Ernest Holmes, Fenwicke Holmes, and Victor Morgan were set to music not before commonly used by the orthodox churches, or to music composed by New Thought musicians, and a genuinely New Thought hymnology began to emerge. As early as 1896 *Truth in Song*, edited by Clara H. Scott (New York: R. F. Fenno & Co.), appeared and came to be commonly used by New Thought centers. Among others that have appeared subsequently are *The Divine Science Hymnal* (Denver: Colorado College of Divine Science, 1932); *Songs for the New Day*, New Day Hymnal Association (Hollywood: House-Warven Publishers, 1953); *Religious Science Hymnal*, International Association of Religious Science Churches (New York: Dodd, Mead & Co., 1954); and *Unity Song Selections* (Lee's Summit, Mo.: Unity School of Christianity. Revised edition, 1935, 7th printing, 1962).

6

The History of INTA

THE FIRST STEP in the organization of New Thought was of course the formation of local groups, usually around a healer or teacher. Then followed a tendency for like-minded leaders and teachers to get together. Some of these leaders of local groups established other similar groups in nearby or more distant places, and from time to time organized conventions or congresses of their scattered following. Mrs. M. E. Cramer, in San Francisco, was one of the earliest to do this. As early as 1892 she had formed the International Divine Science Association, founded with the purpose of promulgating "Divine Science, the God idea of perfect unity, harmony and wholeness, associated together in unity of spirit for the healing of the nations and the general good of humanity." It held its first congress in San Francisco in 1894, its second in Chicago in 1895, the third in Kansas City in 1896, the fourth in St. Louis in 1897, the fifth in San Francisco in 1899. Mrs. Cramer was president of the association. Although it was under the name Divine Science, leaders in no way connected with Divine Science, organizationally, appeared on its programs, either in person or through papers prepared for them and read by another to the congress. Among papers so read at San Francisco were three by well-known Boston leaders and writers — Helen Van Anderson, Henry Wood, and Horatio W. Dresser. It was hoped that the association would become really international, but the time had not yet come, apparently, for such an overall organization. In general the leaders, then as now, were strongly individualistic and hesitated to limit themselves by becoming a part of an organization, a characteristic that is still evident in the movement and continues to make difficult any effort to build a strong overall organization.

It was in this same year, 1899, that a start toward the wider organization was made in the East, at Hartford, Connecticut. A New Thought Convention was held at Alliance Hall, in Chapel Street, on February 21-22, which was really the beginning of a long line of development that culminated in the International New Thought Alliance.

Speakers at the February 21 session were J. W. Winkley, M.D., Boston, on "Man's Moral Nature"; Miss Harriet Bradbury, Providence, on "The Great Unawakened"; and Warren A. Rodman, Boston, on "The Need of a Key-Note." In the morning of the 22nd Mrs. Jean Porter Rudd, Norwich, spoke on "The Opulence of Power"; and Henry S. Tafft, Providence, and Mrs. Emma Louise Nickerson, Boston, spoke on "The Irrepressible Conflict." Afternoon speakers were Miss Georgina I. S. Andrews, New York, on "Silent Centres"; Bolton Hall, New York, on "The Fundamental Reforms"; and Miss Walton, New York, on "Unity of Purpose." In the evening, Professor E. M. Chesley, Boston, spoke on "The Pearl of Great Price," and Charles Brodie Patterson, New York, on "Metaphysics and Social Reform."

Notice that it is called "New Thought Convention," the first one held under that name—a distinction given erroneously by H. W. Dresser in *History of the New Thought Movement* (p. 195) to the one held in Boston in October, 1899, which is specifically named in its program "Convention of the Metaphysical League." Alliance Hall was the meeting place of the Alliance of Divine Unity, the name which Charles Brodie Patterson had given the organization he had founded in Hartford five years earlier. He had in the meanwhile moved to New York City, where he was owner and publisher of the *Library of Health* and the magazine *Mind*. Who sent out the call for the convention is not indicated, but in the handwritten "Minutes of the International Metaphysical League," in the archives of the International New Thought Alliance, it is stated that early in February, 1899, the following announcement was sent out to many individuals and organizations in pursuance of a plan which had been talked of for some time:

In order to increase the efficiency of the different organizations in the New Thought Movement, it seems desirable to form a central organization by means of which all who are interested in the advancement of this movement may come into closer touch with one another, and, through occasional conferences receive the benefit of one another's continually enlarging experience, thus bringing about a consolidation of forces.

C. B. Patterson was the chairman of the convention, and was chosen president of the general alliance which was formed there. The newspaper account of the meeting calls it simply a "National Alliance," stating that the body would "comprise all the alliances in New England and the Middle States in the end, being the first step towards a general organization." Other officers were Henry S. Tafft, president of the Rhode Island Metaphysical Association, vice-president; Warren A. Rodman of Boston, member of the Boston Metaphysical Club, secretary; Harry Gestefeld of New York, assistant secretary; and William E. Uptegrove of Brooklyn, treasurer. On the executive committee were persons from Hartford, New York, Boston, Providence, Brooklyn, Philadelphia, Springfield, Massachusetts, and Eliot, Maine.

Evidently the name International Metaphysical League had been suggested and perhaps formally adopted, for the call for the convention at Lorimer Hall, Tremont Temple, Boston, in October of the same year, was sent out in the form of a folder under the name International Metaphysical League, and bearing the slate of officers elected at Hartford in February. The call states that "the first concrete step toward forming a world wide organization" had been taken at Hartford in February. One of the prime objects of the league would be to

extend by all available means a wider knowledge of and a deeper interest in, the aims and meaning of the Metaphysical Movement which had been called the greatest movement of the present age. It was hoped that an organization might be formed which would fully represent this optimistic, constructive movement.

It would be "broad, tolerant, non-sectarian and impersonal."

Through the League those interested in such common aims would come into closer touch one with another, "the efficiency of local organizations would be increased and a rich field opened up for altruistic service of the very highest type in the evolution of man's finer forces and his higher powers." Interestingly enough, the call goes on to say that the principles of the new movement "apply to the solution of social, business, educational, political and international problems as well as those of the individual life and health," a note not always present in later phases.

A convention for permanent organization would be held in Boston in October, at which it was expected that there would be present persons not only from all sections of the United States but also from Canada, Europe, and other areas.

The program of the convention dates it as having been held on October 24-26, 1899. On the first evening's program were Charles Brodie Patterson; Mrs. Ursula Gestefeld, then of New York; Mr. Henry Wood of Boston; and Miss Sarah J. Farmer of Green Acres, Eliot, Maine. A newspaper story headlined NEW THOUGHT SECT reported; "The real home of the sect, or belief, or cult is at Green Acres in Eliot, Maine where many present last night were living during the summer." This may be an overstatement of the case but does suggest the importance of Sarah J. Farmer and Green Acres in the early days of the movement. There were, of course, speakers from the eastern cities—Cambridge, Boston, New York, Philadelphia—but there were also others from Lansing, Michigan; Kansas City, Missouri; Santa Barbara, California; and Chicago, and a paper by Mrs. Cramer of San Francisco was read. The range of topics was broad.

Evidently a constitution was adopted, including the statement of purpose, which reads thus:

Its purpose is to establish unity and cooperation of thought and action among all individuals and organizations throughout the world

devoted to the study of the science of mind and being, and to bring
them so far as possible, under one name and organization. To promote
interest in and the practice of a true spiritual philosophy of life: to
develop the highest self-culture through right thinking as a means
of bringing one's loftiest ideals into present realization; to stimulate
faith in and study of the higher nature of man in its relation to health,
happiness and progress; to teach the universal Fatherhood and Motherhood of God and the all inclusive brotherhood of man; that One Life
is dominant in the universe and is both center and circumference of
all things, visible and invisible, and that One Intelligence is in all,
through all, and above all, and that from this Infinite Life and Intelligence proceed all Light, Love, and Truth.

The statement was to be regarded as tentative and "implied
no limitations or boundaries to future progress and growth, as
larger measures of light and truth shall be realized."

Reports of the convention of the International Metaphysical
League stated that nearly a thousand persons attended the first
session—about nine-tenths of them women. The addresses and
proceedings of the convention were later edited and published in
a volume. Officers elected were C. B. Patterson, president; Col.
Henry S. Tafft, vice-president; Warren A. Rodman, secretary.
Members of the executive committee included M. E. Cramer of
San Francisco, and others from Portland, Maine; Brooklyn; Denver; Kansas City (Charles Fillmore); Santa Barbara, California;
and Chicago. A newspaper headline stated that even the "Aus-
tralians wanted to enter the fold."

The Second Annual Convention was held in Madison Square
Garden Concert Hall, New York City, October 23-26, 1900. In
the announcement of the convention vice-presidents were listed
from twenty-four states and from Canada, New Zealand, and Australia. Included were the well-known H. W. Dresser of Massachusetts, Mrs. Helen Wilmans Post, of Florida, Annie Rix Militz,
of California, and Mrs. Fannie B. James of Colorado. Among
southern states represented were Virginia, Maryland, South Caro-
lina, Florida, and Mississippi.

Among the speakers at the New York Convention who were
to become significant figures in the developing movement were

Annie Rix Militz, founder of the Home of Truth; Mary E. Chapin, later to be elected president of INTA; and Ralph Waldo Trine, perhaps the most popularly read New Thought writer in the whole history of the movement, who spoke on "Our Social Problem in the Light of Certain Spiritual Truths." A prominent Indian, Swami Abedhananda, spoke on the "Universality of Vedanta." A physician, J. Arthur Jackson, M.D., discussed "The Physician's Relation to Mental Therapeutics." B. O. Flower, later editor of the *Arena,* spoke of the relation of the New Thought to social and economic progress.

A quote from the Constitution and By-Laws indicates that such had been adopted at the first convention. At the New York Convention Dr. R. Heber Newton was elected president; Annie Rix Militz, vice-president; Warren A. Rodman, secretary; and C. B. Patterson, treasurer.

One newspaper, the *Denver Post,* carried this story of the convention, indicating at least its unusual makeup:

In the audience were the dark faces of the Indian Buddhist, the long pale faces of New England Spiritualists, the high foreheads of occult scientists in Boston, followers of the Persian philosopher, Omar, in fact, representatives of all divisions of modern metaphysical thought. It has members in England, France, Germany, India and many other countries, Any one who is interested in the occult can join.

At this convention a practical problem arose. Christian Science has often enough found itself in trouble with civic authorities concerning its healing method. Now New Thought healers were also experiencing trouble. In their case it was with the Post Office Department, which, it was alleged in a memorial presented to and passed unanimously by the convention, had in several cases confiscated or prevented the delivery of letters addressed to mental healers "acting thus under an arbitrary ruling of the department condemning all healing at a distance, or absent healing, as fraudulent." Since it was reported that the department, "presumably at the instance of prejudiced and interested persons, moved thereto by professional jealousy," intended to continue this course of action, the convention resolved: "That we most respectfully and earnestly protest against said ruling—and all action under it as tending to discredit and degrade not only the individual healers immediately concerned but all mental healing and the entire metaphysical movement." Further it was resolved:

That we denounce the said action of the postal authorities as an indefensible and dangerous violation of the rights of the individual citizen to choose the means and method of therapeutic treatment he requires, as contrary to facts and laws now accepted by a vast and constantly increasing number of people of enlightenment the world over, and which are demonstrated by modern scientific investigation and knowledge, and as opposed to the principles of freedom and progress.

They resolved further that a committee be named to frame a memorial to the department concerning absent healing, and request a "revision of the obnoxious and ill-advised ruling," or the holding of a hearing at which the whole matter might be properly presented for adjudication.

As to whether any such protest was made or a hearing held, I have seen no evidence, but the question came to the courts a few years later when Helen Wilmans Post, an early New Thought healer, was charged with fraudulent use of the mails in advertising her ability to heal by absent treatment. According to an article in the *Federal Reporter* (CXXXV [April-May, 1905], 2 ff.) which summarized the case, she graduated from an Illinois college at about the age of twenty-two and for some twenty years engaged in teaching and literary pursuits. At about thirty she became a student of Christian Science and Mental Science. She rejected Christian Science "so far as it relies upon divine power to heal," but became a believer in Mental Science. About 1885 she moved to Georgia and worked as a mental healer, at first treating her patients at home, and later using the U.S. mails to treat her patients by absent treatment. In 1892 she located in Florida and began the practice of mental healing there, treating patients at a distance by correspondence and advertising her ability to heal by absent treatment. She had between seven thousand and ten thousand patients and employed several clerks and assistants. She received many testimonials of healing from her patients. Her business was conducted quite openly. That her belief in mental healing was sincere was evidenced by her employment of a mental scientist to treat one of her own family. She wrote books and lectured. In the case against her she was charged

with claiming to possess power to cure all or nearly all diseases; to remove the conditions that produce poverty, and to inspire, or cause those conditions that bring success; to restore hair to its natural color, and to grow it on bald heads; ... to remove evidences of old age and to restore youth, if the patient had faith that it could be done; and she further claimed that by "absent treatment," through a second person, she could cure a third person without the latter having knowledge of the treatment. (p. 3)

On the first trial the judge gave instructions to the jury which on appeal resulted (CC.A. 3/28/1905 #1,352) in a declaration that the court was in error in his instructions setting aside as without value testimony favorable to the defendant and putting upon her the burden of proof in establishing her good faith, which was really the only question involved, since mental healing has a recognized legal standing. Her offer to heal by mail could not be construed as criminal if she herself believed sincerely that she had the power alleged. And as to determining whether she did mentally provide treatment there could be no reasonable disproof. Petition of the U.S. government for a rehearing was denied and the case apparently closed.

The next convention was to be held in Chicago in October, 1901, and a committee was set up to plan it, incorporating the program outlined in an Executive Meeting in Hartford February 22, 1901. An interesting note on the final page of the minutes was the suggestion that the name of the organization be changed to "The International New Thought League." The proposal was

fully discussed and, while no formal action was taken, the sentiment of the group was that it would be desirable to present
the matter at the Chicago convention.

But the Chicago Convention was not held in October, 1901,
as planned. The International Metaphysical League had quite
intended to hold it, expecting that the Chicago group would
co-operate. But for some reason that co-operation was withheld
and IML did not participate in the convention, designated in the
published program as an International New Thought Convention,
held under the auspices of the New Thought Federation of Chicago, not in October, 1901, but on November 17-20, 1903. This
convention was designated later by Eugene Del Mar in an article
in *Mind* of March, 1904, as the Third Annual New Thought Convention, the Hartford Convention of 1899 being regarded as a
preliminary conference as a result of which the First Annual New
Thought Convention was held in Boston in October, 1899, and the
second in New York, in October, 1900, both under the auspices of
the International Metaphysical League.

The Chicago Convention, even if labeled "International," was
distinctly local or western in its management, and predominantly
so in its speakers. The only well-known names associated with the
East were Paul Tyner and Ursula Gestefeld, but the latter was
now located in Chicago. Eugene Del Mar, later associated with
the East, had been a New Thought leader in Denver. Of western
leaders later prominent in the INTA, there were Charles and
Myrtle Fillmore of Unity, Nona L. Brooks of Divine Science, and
Harry Gaze.

Eugene Del Mar had lectured widely over the country, both
East and West, and was founder of the Church of the Living
Christ in Denver, working closely in co-operation with James A.
Edgerton, later to serve for many years as president of INTA.
He left Denver in November, 1903, went to Chicago as one of the
speakers at the convention, and was named secretary of a committee of seven set up to consider the organization of an International New Thought Federation and the holding of an International New Thought Convention in St. Louis during the St.

Louis Exposition in 1904. The resolution passed November 18, 1903, "recognized and accepted the Principle of Unity, as made manifest in Brotherhood and cooperation, to be the fundamental basis of the New Thought" and recognized and accepted "Association and Organization as the means whereby Brotherhood and Cooperation are realized, and the Principle of Unity is made manifest." The committee consisted of Eugene Del Mar, New York; Helen Van Anderson, Boston; Nona L. Brooks, Denver; R. W. Miller, Chicago; J. D. Perrin, St. Louis; and Margaret G. Bothwell, New York.

The committee, called the Committee on Organization, presented its report on November 20, recommending the formation of a New Thought Federation which would be international in scope and character; expressed the desirability of a comprehensive and definite formulation of the essential significance and meaning of New Thought; recommended a statement of purpose; and formulated tentatively a statement of the significance and meaning of New Thought. The report was accepted and the Organization Committee as constituted was made the Executive Committee, with power to appoint a Convention Committee to plan for the International New Thought Convention in St. Louis in 1904.

What happened next is told by Eugene Del Mar in a letter to the secretary of INTA, dated April 8, 1939. Pursuant to this delegation, he writes, "I proceeded to New York City and there persuaded Charles Brodie Patterson and the officials of the dormant International Metaphysical League to be absorbed by the New Thought Federation," of which he served as Secretary.

An announcement appeared shortly, headed "The New Thought Federation," with a roster of officers as follows: president, R. Heber Newton; secretary, Eugene Del Mar; assistant secretary, John D. Perrin; treasurer, N. Bradley Jeffery; auditor, Bolton Hall. The Board of Directors consisted of the Executive Committee—Margaret E. Bothwell, New York; Eugene Del Mar; Bolton Hall; H. Bradley Jefferson; and C. B. Patterson—and the Advisory Committee—Nona L. Brooks, Denver; John D. Perrin,

St. Louis; Charles E. Prather, Kansas City; Helen Van Anderson, Boston; with others yet to be selected.

The announcement stated that by directive of the Chicago convention the Executive Committee had formed the New Thought Federation with which the International Metaphysical League had united and would merge its work. A tentative statement of the meaning of New Thought and the purpose of the Federation was made, with the announcement of the forthcoming St. Louis Convention of 1904, which would be the Fourth Annual New Thought Convention. A later advertisement in *Mind* added Ursula N. Gestefeld as vice-president and certain others to the Advisory Committee, all to serve only until the convention in St. Louis, which would, it was expected, effect a permanent organization and elect officers and directors for such terms as it might determine.

Here was a Federation of New Thought on paper at least, with a full staff of officers, and plans were laid for a great convention in St. Louis. One day was designated as New Thought day by the management of the exposition. It was hoped that there would be a large and enthusiastic attendance. Later publicity reported that some five thousand adherents of New Thought would be present during the convention, of whom two thousand would be regular members of the Federation. The letterhead used by the secretary in sending out letters inviting the participation of speakers and others in the convention carried, in addition to the names of the officers and directors, a list of forty-one honorary vice-presidents of the New Thought Federation which reads like a *Who's Who* list of early, important New Thought leaders. Among them were George E. Burnell, associated with Mrs. Emma Curtis Hopkins in her Theological Seminary in Chicago; Alice Callow, leader of the Higher Thought Center of London; W. J. Colville, world traveler, lecturer, and writer, whose approach had been through Spiritualism; Horatio W. Dresser; James A. Edgerton, later to serve longer than any other individual as president of the International New Thought Alliance; Charles Fillmore of Kansas City, founder of Unity; Horace

Fletcher, better known for his dietetic teaching but also a New Thought teacher; Fannie James, sister of Nona Brooks, associated with her in the beginnings of Divine Science in Denver; Anne W. Mills, wife of James Porter Mills, one of the first to introduce New Thought into Australia; the redoubtable editor of *Nautilus*, Elizabeth Towne; Ralph Waldo Trine, most popular of New Thought writers; Ella Wheeler Wilcox, New Thought poetess and writer of a syndicated newspaper column in the Hearst papers; Lilian Whiting, author of numerous New Thought books; J. Stitt Wilson, popular lecturer and leader of liberal reform movements; and the illustrious Henry Wood, whose books were widely read both in New Thought circles and far beyond them. How could a convention so sponsored, and held in connection with a great world's fair, fail to be a success?

An article printed in *Mind* (May, 1904) on the New Thought Federation, written almost certainly by the secretary, Eugene Del Mar, had properly noted that the degree of success to be attained by the Federation rested entirely with the New Thought people. To the extent that unity and co-operation remained unmanifest and therefore unpracticed, to such a degree would the Federation be lacking in vitality and usefulness. It was confidently expected that the Federation would receive such hearty co-operation and support as to make it representative of all that was best in the New Thought Movement and that it would show forth in living form the Principle of Unity which lay at the basis of all New Thought teachings.

But the St. Louis Convention was not a successful one. Although the new Federation was, with the exception of a few leaders who had little use for organization, widely representative of New Thought, it had not been well supported by New Thought publications, which had little or nothing good to say concerning either the Federation or the convention. The result was that though twenty-five officers attended the convention, there were only 210 members present at its opening.

Speakers at the convention included the president, R. Heber Newton, on "The Significance of the New Thought," and Ursula

Gestefeld, on "Curing and Healing." Among others at its opening
and closing sessions were Eugene Del Mar, Miss Harriet Rix,
S. A. Weltmer, Mrs. Fannie B. James, Charles and Myrtle Fillmore, Mrs. Helen Van Anderson, A. P. Barton, Mrs. Malinda E.
Cramer, Paul Tyner, and W. J. Colville.

Because so few voting members were present, the right of
voting was extended to all those in attendance who were sufficiently interested to pay one dollar and thus secure a convention
badge and a printed copy of convention proceedings. Some
seventy persons availed themselves of the opportunity. Because
of the meagerness of this support the Executive Committee did
not project any plans beyond the convention itself. The proposed
constitution was approved, article by article, but, writes Eugene
Del Mar in *Mind* (December, 1904), "not the slightest thought
was expended upon the practicability of the instrument as a
whole." Election of officers was haphazard. There was no nomi-
nating committee. Officers who had volunteered for re-election
withdraw their names and others refused to accept nomination.
Elected president was Henry Harrison Browne; vice-president,
D. L. Sullivan; and on the Board of Directors appeared names
not earlier prominent in the organization. Charles Fillmore, Paul
Tyner, and M. E. Cramer did accept places on it.

Eugene Del Mar, writing in *Mind*, said that clearly both
Chicago and St. Louis had demonstrated that New Thought
people in general were not prepared for co-operative or fed-
erated work. Disillusioned, he withdrew from any official connection with the Federation, and from "further public connection with the New Thought Metaphysical League." Happily,
he did return to serve the movement in conspicuous fashion.
H. W. Dresser erroneously reported (*History of the New Thought
Movement*, p. 199) that R. Heber Newton and others were
elected as officers at the St. Louis New Thought Federation
Convention in 1904. These had been chosen by the committee
appointed at the Chicago convention and served as officers of
the St. Louis convention, but the officers noted above as elected
were for the ensuing year.

The Fifth Convention of the New Thought Federation was held in Nevada, Missouri, under the auspices of the Weltmer School of Healing, on September 26-29, 1905. The constitution adopted in St. Louis was revised. The officers elected for the following year and for the Sixth Convention, planned for Chicago in October, 1906, were T. G. Northrup of Chicago, president; Mrs. Grace M. Brown of Denver and Judge H. H. Benson of Kansas City, Missouri, vice-presidents; Ernest Weltmer of Nevada, Missouri, secretary; A. R. Heath of Chicago, assistant secretary; Mrs. Charles H. Besly of Chicago, treasurer; and Charles Edgar Prather of Kansas City, Missouri, auditor. The name was changed from New Thought Federation to "The World New Thought Federation." But the convention was not held as scheduled.

Eugene Del Mar, commenting on the "Early History of the Alliance" in 1921, remarks that after the St. Louis Convention of October, 1904, the Federation "was given over into new hands, and it soon got lost in the Far West."

H. W. Dresser notes (*History of the New Thought Movement,* p. 199) that the last three conventions had been less successful than earlier ones because "it was not easy to find common ground among representatives of individualism in the West and Middle West."

But in the East there was a persistent desire for a closer union of those interested in New Thought. A circular dated April 26, 1906, was sent out from Boston bearing on its letterhead the words, "Office of the New Thought Metaphysical Alliance." It states that initiatory steps had been taken at the "late New Thought Convention held in Boston" to form a working association of those in the New Thought Metaphysical League. When the convention was held is not stated, nor has any other notice of it been found. It may well have been a group from the older International Metaphysical League which met. It will be recalled that this organization had merged with the New Thought Federation to hold the St. Louis convention of 1904.

H. W. Dresser says that a meeting had been called at the

headquarters of the Boston Metaphysical Club on April 26, 1906, by C. B. Patterson, J. W. Winkley, and others, with the object of organizing a society with the best interest of New Thought in view and to promote the original purposes and plans of the International Metaphysical League. Probably this is the meeting referred to as the "late New Thought convention." A committee appointed for the purpose suggested the new name, the New Thought Metaphysical Alliance, and headquarters were set up in Boston. A constitution was adopted and officers were elected. As president R. Heber Newton was chosen, with J. W. Winkley as vice-president; W. J. Leonard, secretary; C. B. Patterson of New York, treasurer; R. C. Douglass of New York, assistant secretary, and M. Woodbury of Boston, auditor. Directors named were Ralph Waldo Trine, New York; Mrs. Harriet A. Sawyer, Boston; Rev. M. K. Schemmerhorn, Poughkeepsie; Mrs. Josephine Verlage, New York; Mrs. Sarah Meader, Lynn, Massachusetts; Mrs. Louise B. Randall and Miss Anita Trueman, New York; Rev. Helen Van Anderson, New York; Rev. D. T. Van Doren, Norwalk, Connecticut; and Rev. Henry Frank, New York. R. Heber Newton and C. B. Patterson had held the same offices in the International Metaphysical League.

This was a distinctly eastern group, only Massachusetts, New York, and Connecticut being represented in the official lists, though it was stated that an Advisory Committee would be named "to share in the general management, and to consist of a large number of members, representatives of and chosen by various New Thought Societies in different parts of the country." So, though it was made up chiefly of "organizations, clubs, leagues, centers as well as individuals in any way identified with the noteworthy spiritual cause named the New Thought, especially in the Eastern States," the new organization hoped to bring into its fellowship those in the more distant parts of the country as well. One method of achieving its purposes was through the holding of conventions under its auspices in the larger cities and centers of population. The constitution declared, "The Alliance shall in no wise interfere with, infringe upon, or be responsible for the interpretations, methods of work, either of New Thought individuals or organizations."

A convention which H. W. Dresser names as the 7th Annual New Thought Convention was held a year later, in April, 1907. Notable among the speakers were Professor Josiah Royce, famous Harvard professor of philosophy, and Dr. Richard C. Cabot, who was later to play a significant role in the rise of the movement within the churches expressive of a concern for training their ministers for a ministry to the sick, the development of clinical training of theological students, and the serving of internships in hospitals and sanitaria. A seminar with the participation of local Boston ministers considered "The Relation of the Parochial Ministry to Spiritual Healing." A third convention of the Alliance, the 8th New Thought Annual Convention, held also in Boston, presided over by R. Heber Newton, who had been confirmed as president, revised the constitution and changed the name to the National New Thought Alliance, the name by which it continued to be known until 1914, when it became the International New Thought Alliance.

Rev. Henry Frank of New York was elected president for the ensuing year, and Mr. James A. Edgerton was chosen vice-president and R. C. Douglass secretary, with Dr. Julia Seton Sears as associate secretary and Amelia H. Ames as treasurer.

At the fourth New Thought Alliance convention in 1909 (the 9th New Thought Annual Convention) at Chickering Hall in Boston, Mr. Edgerton was elected president, a capacity in which he served longer than any other person in the history of the Alliance. Four vice-presidents were elected—Rev. Stephen H. Robbin, Rev. D. T. Van Doren, J. W. Winkley, and C. B. Patterson.

Eugene Del Mar had written in *Mind*, October, 1904, an article about the Summer School as a phase of New Thought activity. Green Acres had been the earliest of these schools, but others had sprung up and were being held regularly in many parts of the country. The one at Oscawana-on-Hudson, a few miles north of New York City, had been organized first in 1902, largely as the realization of a dream of Charles B. Patterson, who presided at many of the sessions, lectured frequently, and taught classes. It was a New Thought affair, but its interests were broad. It was in fact a kind of Chatauqua with a New Thought emphasis. The general pattern called for classes in the mornings and some evenings, with an afternoon lecture, followed by recreational opportunities, nature walks, etc., and in the evenings entertainment, dancing, or concerts. The School usually lasted about eight weeks. Leading New Thought speakers including Ralph Waldo Trine, R. Heber Newton, Eugene Del Mar, James A. Edgerton, Mrs. Helen Van Anderson, H. B. Jeffrey, and Mrs. Josephine Verlage, spoke or taught classes in New Thought. Edwin Markham read some of his poetry, and there were lectures on philosophy, science, music, art, and literature of interest to others than New Thought visitors. H. W. Dresser says that there was an attempt to make Oscawana replace the older Green Acres summer gatherings, but that it lacked the prestige and atmosphere of Green Acres, and failed to fulfil the expectations of the organizers. (p. 203)

So far the reorganized movement had attracted mainly eastern New Thought followers. The Congress held in New York City on May 13-15, 1910, saw the reappearance of representatives from the Middle West, some of them speaking to the convention. These included A. P. Barton of Kansas City, Missouri, and Ernest Weltmer of Nevada, Missouri. The officers elected were the same as the previous year with the addition of Dr. Ellis B. Guild as associate secretary.

Meanwhile, conventions under the auspices of the National New Thought Alliance were being held in various centers. A program of one held in December, 1910, in Boston included a symposium on "New Thought in Its Concrete Application," various speakers considering it as applied to individual unfoldment, to physics and metaphysics, to constructive living, to hospitality, to healing, and to morality and ethics. Among the speakers was Mary E. Chapin, later president of INTA, and Warren A. Rodman of the Metaphysical Club was the moderator. Other speakers were Dr. Ellis B. Guild of New York; E. H. Pratt, M.D., of

Chicago; Rev. Martin K. Schemmerhorn, of Poughkeepsie, on "The Therapeutics of Socrates and Jesus"; H. W. Dresser on "What is Truth"; and Rev. Kershaw of Pittsburgh on the rather striking theme, "Life in the Infinite Automat." Thus it was by no means merely a local affair, at least in respect to its speakers.

Then once again on June 18-25, 1911, the convention went west, to Omaha. An innovation here was the introduction of classes as well as single addresses, eight being offered on various phases of New Thought. It was at this conference that Mrs. Annie Rix Militz brought her organization, Home of Truth, into the Federation, a notable event from the viewpoint of developing co-operation among the various New Thought groups.

A similar plan was followed at the 1912 convention in Los Angeles, held June 25-30, called "The Convention at School," in which six day courses were conducted by Annie Rix Militz, Harriet Hale Rix, Dr. F. Homer Curtiss, Perry Joseph Green, Harry Gaze, and others. Speakers on the general program included Anna W. and James Porter Mills, Harry Gaze, Harriet Hale Rix, the Bartons of Kansas City, Missouri, and for the first time Victor Morgan, later "poet laureate" of the movement, a former Universalist minister who was to be highly influential in the creation of New Thought hymnology. William Farwell was founder of the considerable group known as the Christian Assembly, which had numerous local centers up and down the California coast. His own headquarters he made in San Jose, California.

Detroit was host to the 1913 convention of the National New Thought Alliance (June 15-22). It must have been at this conference that talk of an International New Thought Conference in London was first seriously engaged in. Certainly there had been a dream of a World Federation of New Thought as early as the convention at Nevada, Missouri, in 1905, which changed the name from National New Thought Federation to World Federation, but that dream quickly disappeared. And there had been repeated visits of American New Thought leaders to Great Britain and a few to distant Australia and New Zealand. A report in the English New Thought magazine, organ of the British Section

of INTA (*INTA Recorder*, Vol. I, No. 1 [1927], p. 6), has it
that Dr. Julia Seton, in conjunction with the Higher Thought
Center of London, organized an International Conference at
Bechstein Hall in London in 1913, and a committee either of
this conference or of the Higher Thought Center—the statement
in the *Recorder* does not make it entirely clear which it was—
invited the National New Thought Alliance to hold its annual
Congress in London in 1914. The invitation was accepted and
the congress was held there, June 21-26. But a preliminary convention which H. W. Dresser lists as the ninth of the reorganized
movement was held in New York on June 7-8 of that year.

President James A. Edgerton accompanied by a number of
prominent New Thought leaders was in attendance at the London
Congress. Among the speakers were Mrs. Annie Rix Militz; her
sister, Harriet Hale Rix; Mrs. Mary E. Chapin, James A. Edger-
ton, Harry Gaze, Miss Villa Faulkner Page, and Miss Leila
Simon. Among the oustanding British New Thought leaders
present were Judge Thomas Troward, Alice Callow, Mrs. Heard,
J. Bruce Wallace, and J. Macbeth Bain. From other parts of the
world came representatives. Those from France were Mr. F. A.
Maren, representating the Ligue Internationale de la Nouvelle
Pensée, and Miss Helen Boulnois, La Societé Unitive of Paris.
And there were others from the Continent and from the British
Colonies, Australia, and South Africa.

At the close of the congress a meeting was held which formally
organized the many representative individuals and groups into
the International New Thought Alliance, which it was intended
should be represented in various parts of the world by regional
sections. At once the British Section was organized, with Judge
Thomas Troward, who had been elected vice-president of the
INTA, as president, and Mrs. Heard as chairman of the London
Committee. At a meeting held in the interests of promoting peace,
plans for a great International New Thought Congress, to be
held in 1915 in connection with the Panama-Pacific Exposition,
were reported.

Following the London Congress a Continuation Conference

was held in Edinburgh, in which a number of the principal speakers at the London meeting also participated. Thus, with a preliminary congress in New York, the International Congress in London, and a Continuation Conference in London, were the beginnings made of the INTA.

Did the London Congress adopt any formal constitution? The writer has not seen such a document. There is a printed copy of the constitution dated October, 1916, indicating that the head-quarters of the movement were at Washington, D.C., but it bears no indication of when it was adopted (it was probably at the San Francisco meeting in 1915). In organizational details it differs but little from the constitution of the New Thought Federation adopted at the 1904 St. Louis Convention. The Board of Directors of the earlier organization consisted of not more than twenty-one members, including *ex officio* the elected officers; the 1916 Constitution limited the Board to a compact working group composed of the president, four vice-presidents chosen by the president, the secretary, the treasurer, and the auditor. Any three members of the Board could form a quorum for the transaction of business. The later constitution had designated also as officers as many honorary vice-presidents as might be selected by the Alliance, and as many field secretaries as might be chosen by the Executive Committee, or elected by the Alliance. Thus formal recognition was given to what had earlier been the actual practice of honor-ing outstanding leaders as honorary vice-presidents. Also there was no mention of any Advisory Committee within the Board of Directors.

Both documents spell out the same broad terms of member-ship, admitting any person in sympathy with the purposes of the organization and paying the annual dues of one dollar. Additional categories of membership are, however, provided in the 1916 Constitution: sustaining membership for an annual payment of $10, and Life Membership on payment of $100.

The earlier constitution could be amended by the Board of Directors at any time by a two-thirds vote, the 1916 Constitution at any annual meeting by a two-thirds vote of members voting.

The 1904 constitution had had a rather elaborate statement of purpose: to aid human development through unfoldment of its consciousness of unity, and in the manifestation of this consciousness by way of co-operation; to stimulate faith in and study of the higher nature of man in its relation to health, happiness and character; to teach the Universal Fatherhood and Motherhood of God, and the all-inclusive Brotherhood of Man; to secure rightful liberty in pursuit of the purposes of the Federation; to foster the New Thought movement in general; to publish such literature as may be found essential, and to take an active part in all matters appertaining to education along the lines proposed. "In accomplishing these purposes, the Federation in no wise shall interfere with, infringe upon, or be responsible for the interpretations, methods or work either of New Thought individuals or organizations."

The statement of purpose of the 1916 constitution was much more concise and direct: "To teach the Infinitude of the Supreme One; the Divinity of Man and his Infinite Possibilities through the creative power of constructive thinking and obedience to the voice of the indwelling Presence which is our source of Inspiration, Power, Health, and Prosperity."

Omitted entirely was the article of the earlier constitution entitled "The Significance of the New Thought" which read as follows:

That One Life is universal in the universe, and is both center and circumference of all things, visible and invisible; that every soul is divine, and that in the realization of this truth each individual may express and manifest his highest ideals through right thinking and right living. These statements are tentative and imply no limitations or boundaries.

But that some statement of principles was desirable soon became evident.

Great preparations were made for what has come to be regarded as the First International New Thought Congress in San Francisco in 1915. It was the year of the Panama-Pacific

International Exposition. Great crowds would, it was hoped, be there from all over the world. As at St. Louis, the management would designate one day as officially New Thought day. Mrs. Annie Rix Militz made a round-the-world trip lecturing and promoting the congress. Local New Thought groups made a special effort, not alone during the congress but all during the exposition, from February to December, to bring aspects of the New Thought before the public. Under the auspices of the California New Thought Exposition Committee, lectures or classes were held at the Hall of the Metaphysical Headquarters and Library, mornings, afternoons, and evenings every day of the week, given by local or visiting leaders, some from abroad. Dr. Frank Riley of London, for example, gave an evening class one week on "The Bibles of the World" and Annie Rix Militz a morning class on "Child Unfoldment in New Thought." How well they were attended, there is no way of knowing now.

Though publicity releases stressed the international character of the gathering, "visitors and speakers from every part of the globe," it was, alas, mostly only American in leadership, whatever its attendance may have been. The elaborate and beautifully printed souvenir program lists only three speakers from abroad, all from England, three from Washington, D.C., three from Boston, and six from New York; but there were thirty-nine from California, two from Oregon, and one each from Connecticut, Kansas, Illinois, Colorado, Missouri, and the state of Washington. Out of a total of fifty-nine who appeared on the program at least once thirty-nine were from California, thirty of them from San Francisco. Dynamic Elizabeth Towne, editor of *Nautilus,* was a speaker, and was henceforth to be one of the Alliance's most vigorous supporters and leaders.

The next congress was held in Chicago, though H. W. Dresser, in his *History of the New Thought Movement,* located it in St. Louis. (p. 212) More speakers from the eastern part of the country participated. James A. Edgerton was continued as president. A considerable number of honorary presidents was named, including such stalwarts as H. W. Dresser, C. B. Patterson, Annie

Rix Militz, W. W. Atkinson, C. D. Larson, and, for the first time, the popular author and editor of the widely read *Success Magazine,* Orison Swett Marden, as well as poets Edwin Markham and Ella Wheeler Wilcox. Vice-presidents were chosen representing various areas in the United States and abroad.

Evidently a need was felt for a Declaration of Principles on which the diverse groups and individuals could agree. Elizabeth Towne, editor of *Nautilus,* was a member of a committee of five to consider the matter and report at the St. Louis Congress in 1917. As a basis for their report, the committee sought statements from leaders of New Thought, both within and without the Alliance, and Mrs. Towne printed and presented to members of the congress complimentary copies of a pamphlet containing them, as well as the constitution adopted at San Francisco in 1915.

The immediate reaction of one respondent was one of shock. He had observed that successive efforts of the human spirit to free itself from bonds that had begun to chafe and gall had ended only in "exchanging one harness for another somewhat looser, one check-rein for another, giving slightly more liberty of movement to the ranging mind." (p. 8) Creeds, she thought, had value as museum pieces giving some measure of the mind's grasp and the soul's aspiration at various periods. There seemed to her to be one basic principle involved: "the conviction that it is the function of mind to control matter—or that it is the high privilege of man's spirit to dominate his physical nature, also his physical environment, and all thereto pertaining." If that foundation principle was assumed as the basic creed, then all who held it ought to be welcomed into New Thought societies. Nevertheless, she went on to add a few extra requirements before she had finished.

Another very great New Thought leader, W. W. Atkinson, declared that New Thought had no fixed principles, settled rules, governing laws, or formal creeds. It took its own wherever it found it, adding to the list every day while at the same time discarding what it had outgrown. New Thought, he said, based itself upon an Infinite Presence-Power, which being infinite eluded definition. All that could be said of it was that it was "One, and One Only, without parts and Indivisible, Immutable and Incapable of Change—though eternally manifesting a world of experience in which there is the appearance of infinite number, infinite variety, and infinite change." New Thought, he held, teaches "the Identity of the Real Self of the individual with this Infinite Presence-Power, and the manifestation of the Divine Individual in effective activity in this World of Experience." (p. 8)

But he went on to say that New Thought, being essentially individualistic, could not be "organized," or formed into an institution and that all attempts to do so would "result merely in dwarfing and stultifying it, and in a denial of its essential substance and thought," an attitude extremely widespread among New Thought leaders both in the earlier period and now, which makes effective organization and co-operation extremely difficult.

Elizabeth Towne could not wait to get the floor at the congress and give her counteropinion. Her printed comment was that, truly, New Thought could not be "formed into" anything, but that New Thought was a soul "which could form as many bodies or organizations as it wills."

Sixteen different statements were printed. While there were considerable differences, particularly in detail, there was a rather high degree of unanimity among the respondents. For example, in reference to God as Universal Life, Good, Love, Wisdom, Infinite Presence, Omnipotent, Omniscient, Immanent, there is complete agreement. There is almost equal unanimity in the estimate of man as at least potentially divine, expressed in a great variety of ways—for example, he is "some part of the Infinite," "a part of the Infinite Perfection," "the expression of the One Life," "a spiritual being," "a reservoir of Divine energy." Stress upon the inner life is a constant running through most of them. Concern for health and healing were emphasized as an integral part of New Thought by most respondents. Life everlasting or heaven as a present experience was frequently stressed. The creative power of thought, divine and human, was held to be

central by most. The oneness of Truth—and man's right and duty
to seek and express it each in his own way—is offered over and
over.

In the end the congress voted to make its own, with a very
few changes, the Declaration offered by its president, James A.
Edgerton.

A notable feature of the varied Declarations of Principles
presented by the committee was the relative lack of emphasis
upon Christ. Eleven out of the sixteen omitted any mention of
Jesus or the Christ, though two of these made a reference to
Christianity. Six, only, mentioned Christ. And the statement as
adopted speaks only of "the teaching of Christ," and says nothing
as to his person or his relation to God. This proved disappointing, particularly to Charles Fillmore of Unity School and his
followers, who had been from the start much closer, at least in
their terminology, to orthodox Christian theological belief.

Therefore at the Cincinnati Congress of 1919 Unity proposed
the addition of a paragraph which had appeared in the *Bulletin
of INTA* No. 17. It read as follows: "We affirm the Christian
standard in all things. The world has never yet had a real Christian movement. This gives us a good opportunity to have one
now. We build our house upon this rock and nothing can prevail
against it. This is the vision and mission of the Alliance." It was
passed unanimously.

After the convention E. V. Ingraham of Unity wrote that,
on the basis of talks with Charles and Lowell Fillmore, he would
suggest a slight revision of this as better expressing the desired
ideal from their point of view. It meant simply including a part
of the paragraph from *Bulletin* No. 17 immediately preceding
the statement already added. The administration was disposed
to accept it, but in order to make it legal, printed a ballot embodying the suggestion and sent it out for a vote of the membership.
A slight change was made in the interest of better grammar and
greater clarity and it was printed as adopted on p. 2 of *Bulletin*
No. 21, December 1, 1919.

The added paragraph now read:

We affirm that the Universe is spiritual and we are spiritual beings. This is the Christ message to the twentieth century, and it is a message not so much of words as of works. To attain this, however, we must be clean, honest, and trustworthy, and uphold the Christ standards in all things. We now have the golden opportunity to form a real Christ movement. Let us build our house upon this rock, and nothing can prevail against it. This is the vision and mission of the Alliance.

Thus revised, the St. Louis Declaration of Principles remained unchanged until 1950. Printed prominently in almost every issue of the *Bulletin,* and in successive congress programs, it read in full as follows:

DECLARATION OF PRINCIPLES
International New Thought Alliance

We affirm the freedom of each soul as to choice and as to belief, and would not, by the adoption of any declaration of principles, limit such freedom. The essence of New Thought is Truth, and each individual must be loyal to the Truth he sees. The windows of his soul must be kept open at each moment for the higher light, and his mind must be always hospitable to each new inspiration.

We affirm the good. This is supreme, universal and everlasting. Man is made in the image of the Good, and evil and pain are but the tests and correctives that appear when his thought does not reflect the full glory of this image.

We affirm health, which is man's divine inheritance. Man's body is his holy temple. Every function of it, every cell of it, is intelligent, and is shaped, ruled, repaired, and controlled by mind. He whose body is full of light is full of health. Spiritual healing has existed among all races in all times. It has now become a part of the higher science and art of living the life more abundant.

We affirm the divine supply. He who serves God and man in the full understanding of the law of compensation shall not lack. Within us are unused resources of energy and power. He who lives with his whole being, and thus expresses fullness, shall reap fullness in return. He who gives himself, he who knows and acts in his highest knowledge, he who trusts in the divine return, has learned the law of success.

We affirm the teaching of Christ that the Kingdom of Heaven is within us, that we are one with the Father, that we should not judge, that we should love one another, that we should heal the sick, that we should return good for evil, that we should minister to others, and that we should be perfect even as our Father in Heaven is perfect. These are not only ideals, but practical, everyday working principles.

We affirm the new thought of God as Universal Love, Life, Truth and Joy, in whom we live, move and have our being, and by whom we are held together; that His mind is our mind now, that realizing our oneness with Him means love, truth, peace, health and plenty, not only in our own lives but in the giving out of these fruits of the Spirit to others.

We affirm these things, not as a profession, but practice, not on one day of the week, but every hour and minute of every day, sleeping and waking, not in the ministry of a few, but in a service that includes the democracy of all, not in words alone, but in the innermost thoughts of the heart expressed in living the life. "By their fruits ye shall know them."

We affirm Heaven here and now, the life everlasting that becomes conscious immortality, the communion of mind with mind throughout the universe of thoughts, the nothingness of all error and negation, including death, the variety in unity that produces the individual expressions of the One-Life and the quickened realization of the indwelling God in each soul that is making a new heaven and a new earth.

We affirm that the Universe is spiritual and we are spiritual beings. This is the Christ message to the twentieth cenutry, and it is a message not so much of words as of works. To attain this, however, we must be clean, honest and trustworthy and uphold the Jesus Christ standards as taught in the Four Gospels. We now have the golden opportunity to form a real Christ movement. Let us build our house upon this rock, and nothing can prevail against it. This is the vision and mission of the ALLIANCE.

The adoption of the amended Declaration removed the objections of both Divine Science of Denver and the Unity School of Christianity, and both became members of the Alliance. Nona Brooks wrote to Mr. Edgerton (November 18, 1919), stating specifically that the action of the Board of Trustees of Divine Science was a direct result of the "definite stand taken by your body at its last convention. You set up the standard of the Christ then, and we believe that with a large body of consecrated workers—consecrated to the realization of the Christ life on earth—there is powerful effectiveness ahead of us."

Dr. A. C. Grier of the Church of the Truth, Spokane, another of the New Thought groups that had developed out of Dr. Grier's ministry, wrote in 1920 (*Bulletin* No. 23, p. 13), saying he had kept his own church out of the New Thought Movement because he felt his own revelation

was so high and of the order of Christ's message that it was a violation of holy sanctities to confuse it with teachings on spiritualism, occultism, palmistry, theosophy, astrology, science of numbers, color, and vibrations, and even of suggestive therapeutics and mental science. And as New Thought had shielded and embraced all of these and many more he had been compelled to stand aloof. . . .

But now that the New Thought Alliance had put itself squarely on the Jesus Christ basis, he was happy to unite forces with it. The resolution adopted at the Cincinnati Congress, he could subscribe to with all his heart.

This, wrote President Edgerton, "completes the union of all important groups in the Truth movement." (p. 2) And there was of course great rejoicing in the Alliance. (*Bulletin* No. 22, January, 1920)

The Declaration of Principles adopted at St. Louis in 1917 was printed as amended unchanged, usually on the back cover of *New Thought (INTA Bulletin)*, until the Spring, 1950, issue. In the Summer, 1950, issue appeared for the first time, in the form of a Responsive Reading, a condensed version of the Declaration of Principles. It read as follows:

We affirm the freedom of each soul as to choice and as to belief, and would not by the adoption of any declaration of principles, limit such freedom. The essence of the New Thought is truth, and each individual must be loyal to the truth he sees.

We affirm the Good. This is supreme, universal and everlasting.

We affirm health, which is man's divine inheritance.

We affirm the divine supply. He who serves God and man in the full understanding of the law of compensation shall not lack.

We affirm the teachings of Christ that the Kingdom of Heaven is within us, that we are one with the Father, that we should not judge, that we should love one another, that we should heal the sick, that we should return good for evil, that we should minister to others, and that we should be perfect even as our Father in Heaven is perfect.

We affirm the new thought of God as Universal Love, Life, Truth and Joy, in whom we live, move and have our being.

We affirm these things, not as a profession, but practice, not on one day of the week, but in every hour and minute of every day, not in the ministry of the few, but in a service that includes the democracy of all.

We affirm Heaven here and now, the life everlasting that becomes conscious immortality, and the quickened realization of the indwelling God in each soul that is making a new heaven and a new earth.

We affirm that the Universe is spiritual and we are spiritual beings.

This is the Christ message to the twentieth century, and it is a message not so much of words as of works.

Comparison of this with the complete Declaration reveals that the omitted material is mainly explanatory or hortatory, with the possible exception of the omission from the eighth paragraph where the clause "the communion of mind with mind throughout the universe of thoughts, the nothingness of all error and negation, including death, the variety in unity that produces the individual expressions of the One Life" is left out. This might have been significant, but no serious protests seem to have appeared.

At the Congress of 1953 the president appointed a committee, with Dr. Ervin Seale as chairman, to bring in a revised Declaration of Principles. This was done and the results were presented to the Congress of 1954 and adopted on July 22, 1954. It reads: (*Bulletin* XXXVII [Autumn, 1954], 18-19)

We affirm the inseparable oneness of God and man, the realization of which comes through spiritual intuition, the implications of which are that man can reproduce the Divine perfection in his body, emotions, and in all his external affairs.

We affirm the freedom of each person in matters of belief.

We affirm the Good to be supreme, universal and eternal.

We affirm that the Kingdom of Heaven is within us, that we are one with the Father, that we should love one another, and return good for evil.

We affirm that we should heal the sick through prayer alone, and that we should endeavor to manifest perfection "even as our Father in Heaven is perfect."

We affirm our belief in God as the Universal Wisdom, Love, Life, Truth, Power, Peace, Plenty, Beauty and Joy, in whom we live and move and have our being.

We affirm that man's mental states are carried forward into manifestation and become his experience through the Creative Law of Cause and Effect.

We affirm that the Divine Nature expressing itself through man, manifests itself as health, supply, wisdom, love, life, truth, power, peace, beauty and joy:

We affirm that man is an invisible spiritual dweller within a human body, continuing and unfolding as a spiritual being beyond the change called physical death.

We affirm that the universe is the body of God, spiritual in essence, governed by God through laws which are spiritual in reality even when material in appearance.

A comparison of this with the revised St. Louis Declaration makes it clear that much of the old is carried forward into the new, but stated in slightly different fashion.

Notable are the omissions of a plank on health as man's divine heritage and the affirmation of supply, though both are perhaps implicit in the sixth and eighth paragraphs. More notable perhaps is the total omission of any reference to Jesus or the Christ, though clear reference is made to Jesus' teaching of the Fatherhood of God, the loving of one another, the returning of good for evil; that the kingdom of heaven is within us; and that we should be perfect as Our Father in heaven is perfect.

The characteristic affirmation of the Oneness of God and Man, made in the first paragraph, is a declaration of at least man's potential divinity which becomes a reality through spiritual intuition, and the declaration that man can reproduce divine perfection in his body, emotions, and in all his external affairs is only another way of stating what seems clearly implied throughout the older Declaration.

What is really new in the revised Declaration is the making more explicit of how the results man desires are to be achieved.

And this seems to the writer to be an essentially Trowardian declaration. It is also certainly found in Ernest Holmes's teaching. But nowhere in the older Declaration had it been made clear. Nowhere in that statement is there any mention of the operation of Law, or that Love, Wisdom, Good, all express themselves not according to Divine arbitrariness, or caprice, but through Law. Here it is clearly asserted that the universe, spiritual in essence, is governed by God through laws, spiritual in reality even when material in appearance. And in the seventh paragraph it is affirmed that it is through the "Creative Law of Cause and Effect" that man's mental states are carried into manifestation and become his experience.

A slight amendment was adopted by the 42nd Congress in 1957. The Declaration as then established is the same as the 1954 statement except that the word "alone" after "heal the sick through prayer alone" is omitted; and thus it stands.

Any organization attempting to bring together individuals and groups must obviously operate under well recognized and accepted rules. This had been evident in the earlier attempts at federation. INTA, at least from the San Francisco Congress in 1915, which seems to have adopted the first formal constitution and by-laws, has worked under a definite set of rules modified from time to time as this has seemed necessary. In the archives of the movement these successive printed editions of the constitution are preserved, and there seems to have been one other about 1926 of which, as it was finally adopted, no separate printed copy is available. It is, however, printed as amended in the *Bulletin* for August, 1926.

Comparison of the first published constitution (1916) with that of the present time (latest printing 1949, with a few subsequent changes) shows that the name has remained constant, although efforts have been made to change it to the InterNational Truth Alliance.

The purposes as stated in 1916 were: "to teach the Infinitude of the Supreme One: the Divinity of Man and his Infinite Possi-

bilities through the creative power of Constructive thinking, and
obedience to the voice of the Indwelling Presence, which is our
source of Inspiration, Power, Health and Prosperity."

In the constitution as amended and adopted at Denver in
1921, the words "as taught and demonstrated by Jesus Christ"
are added to this. How this was brought about is not disclosed,
but it must have come, as did the revision of the Declaration of
Principle, from Unity and perhaps Divine Science, both having
come into the Alliance in late 1919. It is not without significance
that an issue of the *Bulletin* in which a letter announcing the
adherence of Divine Science to the Alliance appears states for
the first time, on the front cover in a conspicuous box, "Stands
for The Full Christ Message—D' 'ine Healing, Divine Supply,
Divine Immanence and Divine Love." With some changes this
continued to appear throughout the whole year.

In addition, there is in the 1921 constitution a section indicating as the Alliance's further purpose "to unite for mutual
benefit the metaphysical student centers and schools of the world,
and to promote cooperation and understanding among its members. To this end it shall maintain a central office."

At the Congress of 1940 there was a substantial revision of the
constitution. Gone was the older statement of purpose as Article
II, and in its place was a preamble which reads thus:

We the members of the International New Thought Alliance in
order to form a more perfect union, to provide a basis for common
effort of the various units of the New Thought world, to promote those
activities which cannot of their very nature be accomplished by each
group working alone, to disseminate and publish the good news of the
New Gospel of Christ, and to build a spiritual fellowship which will
secure the respect of man and the blessing of God, do establish the
Constitution for the International New Thought Alliance.

And so it remains in the current constitution as amended in 1949.

Article I of this constitution states definitely the role of the
annual congress, which from the first had been a chief feature
of the movement, but the powers of which had not been clearly

defined, though its legislative function had been generally recognized and accepted. Now its membership is carefully defined as being made up of leaders and laymen, "all ministers, leaders and teachers of churches, colleges and centers recognized by the Alliance, lay delegates from these schools and colleges and individual members at large." It is given power to determine its membership; to admit or expel; to call an annual meeting of its qualified membership; to hold business meetings each day of the congress if needed; to fix the quorum necessary; to establish general standards of procedures, ethics, methods, and ideals for the movement, requisite for membership in the Alliance; to publish an official organ and other needed literature; to appoint and send out lecturers, to create districts and appoint district presidents and field secretaries, and broadly "to do anything else not specifically reserved to the members herein."

Article II, which appears first in the 1940 constitution, has as its title "The House of Recognized Ministers and Leaders." Its membership is limited to leaders, ministers, ordained or not, "actively engaged in the teaching work with some established headquarters and a local organization." That is, the lay members and delegates to the congress do not participate in its activities. Its purpose is stated as that of concerning itself "with the work of the groups, and adopting plans and resolutions for the furtherance of such groups and their work." Any such resolutions or plans are designed "to have the effect of law" unless overridden by a three-fourths vote of the congress. The vice-president of the Alliance is designated as president ex officio of this group. Actually it has come to be a sort of planned workshop of the professional leadership in attendance at the congress, and has not usually formulated plans for adoption. It is rather a sharing of experience in the conduct of their ministry in which members engage—one of the very profitable features of the congress program.

Gone, however, from the 1940 recension is a provision appearing in the 1925 constitution as Article XII under the title "House of School Leaders," which provided for a group of fifteen persons representing the leaders of Schools of Truth recognized by the Alliance, the number to be increased as new schools appeared and were recognized. Six of these represented the six recognized schools and the others were to be elected by the congress. Its function was defined as that of conducting the Alliance Council on Methods, with full power also to organize itself and conduct other activities for co-operation with the congress and the executive board of the Alliance. It was to meet two days previous to the opening day of the annual congress. Whether it ever functioned effectively is not apparent in the records, but it was dropped somewhere along the way, not appearing in the 1940 constitution.

Conditions of membership have remained constant, though they were made a bit more explicit in later revisions. Any group, society, or association in sympathy with the purpose of the Alliance was the original requirement, defined further as "any church school, center, or other teaching group whose purpose is the promulgation of religious and metaphysical teaching in conformity to the general standards and ideals, to be interpreted by the Executive Board." The 1940 version leaves the membership fee on a "love offering" basis, the 1949 version as well as the 1919-20 specifying a minimum fee of $10.00.

Undoubtedly as a measure of security of freedom of action by the various groups, it is clearly stated that each constituent group member is an "autonomous unit," and "nothing in the constitution shall be construed as limiting the freedom of thought and action of any group so long as it conforms in a general way to the ideals and purposes of the INTA."

Membership may be refused an applicant by a two-thirds vote of the executive board. Different classes of membership—individual, group, sustaining, Century Club, or life—are made available on certain conditions.

Slight differences appear in respect to officers. The number of vice-presidents was raised from two to four. The executive board consists of the elected officers and six others elected for three-year terms. It carries on the business of the Alliance in the

interim between congresses. Formerly the executive secretary
was a member of the board, but he is now an appointee of the
president. A quorum of five members is necessary for the conduct
of business.

Later revisions of the constitution provide for a headquarters,
but without stipulating always where it is to be. Actually it was
in Washington, D.C., for many years, later in New York, and
most recently in Hollywood, at the church where the president
of the movement is pastor. For some reason, probably quite
obvious at the time, a section was entered in Article VIII stating
explicitly that since INTA is one organization with one headquarters, "no local center is entitled to use the term New Thought
Alliance, or Local branch of the INTA." Groups may properly
use after the name of their center "Affiliated with the INTA,"
and individuals after their names, "Member of the INTA."

Amendment of the constitution is relatively a simple matter.
Formerly it was required that five or more persons announce
their intention to propose an amendment in the *Bulletin*, at least
thirty days before the congress meeting, and the proposed amendment must have been read at two business meetings before being
voted on. Then if two-thirds of the members voting agreed it was
adopted. The present requirement is simply that the proposed
amendment be printed in the issue of the *Bulletin* immediately
preceding the congress. Then, after two readings, the two-thirds
vote is all that is required for adoption.

In the thirties there was considerable agitation for changing
the name of the Alliance. The Scottish section, it seems, refused
to come in under the name New Thought. The South African
section was actually using the term Constructive Thought instead
of New Thought. Some of the British leaders indicated a desire
for change and some dissatisfaction had appeared both in Australia and in the United States. Therefore, according to a report by
Mr. Edgerton, the Congress of 1933 voted to change the name
to International Truth Alliance. An advisory vote of the various
sections was sought and the response was adverse. At the Congress of 1936 the change was again voted, but final action was

to await a vote of the next two congresses. The name of the *Bulletin* was actually changed to *International Truth Bulletin*, and published by INTA.

At the Washington Congress in October, 1938, the matter was again brought up in a business meeting. The New York Congress of 1937 had voted in favor of the old name. After discussion pro and con, the Washington Congress voted unanimously to retain the name originally adopted, and so it has remained until now.

Probably the most important feature of the work of the INTA has been the annual congress held regularly every year except two, one during the great depression and one during World War II, when travel restrictions made it advisable to omit the gathering. The congress has been the one place where the members of diverse groups have had opportunity to meet, get to know each other, exchange ideas, pass necessary legislation, receive inspiration and instruction, and not least of all have a thoroughly good time. The pattern of the congresses has differed little across the years. They are held usually in the best hotel, or one of the best ones, in some great American city. An attempt has been made to meet in various sections of the country so that the membership of every area will sooner or later be able to enjoy a congress without too great an outlay of expense. How conscious the planning in this respect has been is not certain, but a fairly equitable distribution is apparent over the years. Of forty-six congresses held, counting that at San Francisco in 1915 as the first, fifteen have been held in the East; fourteen in the Midwest; eleven in the West and Far West; and five in the South. In the East, six different cities have been hosts: Philadelphia and Rochester once each; Boston and Buffalo twice; Washington, which was for many years the headquarters city, four times; and New York five times. If one goes back of the technically INTA period to the congresses of the organization out of which INTA developed, four additional would have to be credited to Boston and two more to New York.

In the Midwest, stretching west from Ohio to the Colorado border, nine cities have been hosts: Detroit, Milwaukee, Minneapolis, Indianapolis, St. Louis and Kansas City, Missouri, each once; Cleveland, twice; Cincinnati and Chicago each three times. In pre-INTA days conventions of New Thought had also been held once each in Chicago, St. Louis, Nevada, Missouri, Omaha, and Detroit.

In the West and Far West, from Colorado to the Coast, congresses have been held once each in Sacramento and San Diego, California; two in Denver; three in San Francisco; and four in Los Angeles, which had also been host to a pre-INTA convention in 1912.

The South, which has never had large numbers of New Thought groups, has had probably a disproportionate number of congresses, Atlanta, Miami, and Nashville having had one each and Louisville two.

Congresses are times for a great deal of speechmaking. The list of speakers across the years is a fairly good index of the more outstanding leaders of the movement, though there have always been some who for one reason or another have refused to participate in the activities of INTA. Popular figures appear year after year among those asked to speak. Most speakers are from among the movement's own number, though an occasional outsider is heard. Sometimes there is an announced theme of the congress and to some extent participating speakers relate their remarks to the theme. One gets the impression, however, on examining a long series of programs, that in general the speaker has chosen his own subject, and it may or may not relate to what others are saying. These larger meetings are open to the public, and often substantial audiences are present. An International Congress is sure to get fairly good coverage by the local press, and not a few persons are first attracted to New Thought in this way. There are, however, sessions which are not open to the public, but only to accredited members of the congress, where subjects of vital interest are discussed. Such a session is the time when the business of the Alliance is transacted, reports of standing committees are given, officers are elected, and the report of the executive committee which effectively manages the affairs of the Alliance in the interim between congresses is received. It offers the occasion for special closed meetings of ministers and full-time workers for the consideration of their particular problems and a healthy exchange of ideas and of techniques that have proved to be successful.

Sometimes a panel is the format of a program or series of programs. In a series at the Sacramento Congress, for example, a group of panelists discussed "Psychiatry and New Thought or Psycho-Analysis and Spiritual Treatment" one day; the next day the discussion by a different panel was of "Goals of the Alliance"; another panel discussed the Declaration of Principles—should they be shortened, restated, and made clearer and more definite; and the following day the discussion was of "New Thought and Christian Science."

In recent years a new feature has been added which has proved popular. It is a seminar, occupying two hours of each morning, at which usually two distinguished leaders provide instruction on announced themes. To insure a serious purpose in attendance, and also to raise funds for the Alliance, a substantial fee is charged those registering for the seminars. For example, the seminar of the 1960 Congress dealt with "The Impact of New Thought on Civilization." Under seven different leaders, the seminar took up successively seven aspects of this subject. Always there is a morning meditation, usually at about 8:15. And always there is a healing meeting, and usually, in recent years, at least, someone made available at an appointed place announced in the official programs, every half-hour of the day during the congress, not for lectures or instruction, but for healing.

An amazing number of persons find some place in the program and/or on committees which seek to make plans for and carry out the work of the congress. In the Prayer Clinic alone, the healing hour, at least fifty different persons were used at the Denver Congress. And besides this Prayer Clinic where healing was central, there were two announced healing meetings in the grand ballroom, the general meeting place of the congress, at

midday and in the early evening. There was a total of nine
scheduled addresses at the major meetings of the congress,
besides the healing meetings, the Church at Work meetings, and
the Youth Congress, which as usual had its own program.

There are many luncheons or dinners at which special groups,
such for example as members of the smaller New Thought groups
like the Church of the Truth or the Church of the Healing Christ,
which have only a very loose organizational structure, get
together, or regional representatives, or persons interested in
special phases of New Thought—possibly its extension by radio
or T.V. or it might be in its Sunday Schools or youth work, or in
drama, or in church architecture; and of course endless committee meetings, for much of the business is first discussed around
the breakfast, lunch, or dinner tables. And climaxing it all the
annual banquet on the closing evening, a truly gala occasion,
often attended by hundreds in the major ballroom of the hotel.

Without the congresses, it is difficult to imagine that the Alliance would continue to function. It is one united effort in which
representatives of the diverse New Thought groups and individual members engage, and in so doing are knit more firmly
together. It is a time for charting the future, year after year,
setting goals, planning programs, and generating the necessary
zeal and enthusiasm for the carrying out of the high purposes
expressed at the meetings. There is a warm fellowship among the
leaders—sometimes there are disagreements, of course, but disagreements among friends who measurably well understand each
other are more easily surmounted than others.

Most of the effective work of New Thought is done, of course,
within and through the various constituent groups. As we have
said, there are no local branches of INTA. A local group functions
either as an individual unit or as a member of some of the larger
groups that are essentially New Thought, such as Divine Science
or Unity or Religious Science, whether they as groups are constituent members of INTA or not. Unity, for example, as a group
does not belong to INTA, but a great many local Unity groups
do belong and participate actively in its programs.

One of the united projects carried out by a committee appointed at one of the congresses that has been extremely useful was the publication of the book *Mind Remakes Your World* (New York: Dodd, Mead, 1941). Edited by Ernest Holmes, founder of Religious Science, it brought together in one volume the best thought of representatives of the widely diversified field of New Thought, as to their understanding of their faith. In no other single source can there be found a more representative sampling of the rich variety of thought and practice of a group which underneath all the differences presents such a solid basis of agreement on certain fundamental issues. Incidentally, in the brief introductory paragraphs concerning the writers, one gets an interesting picture of the organizational framework of the movement as a whole. Of course, in an examination of the back files of the New Thought magazine much the same variety could be found, but here it is brought together in the limits of a single modest volume that furnishes a remarkable cross section of the prevailing ideas and attitudes of acknowledged New Thought leaders at a particular period of their history.

INTA has been fortunate in the leadership it has had from its presidents. Not all have possessed the same qualities of leadership or possessed them in equal measure, or have had to the same degree the executive skills requisite to hold together and advance a cause representing such a wide diversity of interests. Some served too briefly to make a deep and lasting impression on the movement. They are today only names to most of the rank and file membership of it, though they served ably the single year in which it was their responsibility to lead.

First of all the presidents, not of INTA but of the International Metaphysical League, was Charles Brodie Patterson, elected president of the first convention held in Boston in 1899, and chairman of the preliminary New Thought convention out of which the International Metaphysical League grew. His fame has been rather that of editor, publisher, and writer, as well as lecturer, *Mind*, which he published from the first and edited for several years, being perhaps his most important contribution to the developing movement.

As president the New York Convention selected—I suspect at the suggestion of C. B. Patterson—Rev. Heber Newton, who, curiously enough, was not a New Thought leader at all, in the technical sense, but an influential clergyman of the Episcopal church, pastor for many years of All Soul's Episcopal Church of New York City. His acceptance of the post did not represent a sudden unaccountable interest, for he had favored the movement long before it had attained the popularity it had gained by 1900. He had frequently been under attack because of his advanced views on life and religion, but he was a man of rare courage who, regardless of the pressures brought to bear upon him, followed what seemed to him the truth wherever he found it; and he had found a good measure of it, apparently, in the burgeoning new movement. Naturally, his acceptance of leadership in a movement that was looked upon at the time "as the most heterodox in the Christian World" brought upon him immediate disapproval. But he was, writes C. B. Patterson, "beyond doubt the best equipped of any preacher of the present time to hold such an office."

He served as president not only that year but the following also, and when the attempt was made to unite the Western Federation and the International Metaphysical League at the ill-fated St. Louis convention in 1904, he was willing to have his name proposed as president of the new federation. Later, however, along with other officers proposed he withdrew his name, and Henry Harrison Brown was elected. But Newton continued as president of the largely eastern group which met in conventions in Boston in 1906 and 1907, giving it distinguished leadership, and he wrote frequently during these years and subsequently for the magazine *Mind*. Yet he always retained his place as an Episcopal clergyman, apparently in good standing, though he was severely criticized by many of his clerical brethren, both within and without that branch of the Christian church. (Article by C. B. Patterson in *Mind*, IX [October, 1901], 7-8)

James A. Edgerton served the Alliance longer as president than any other person. In the 1890's he was a newspaperman in Denver, writing editorials for the *Denver News and Times*. Friends reading his editorials told him he was writing New Thought. This led him to try to find out what New Thought was, and discovering it, he remained a constant exponent of it until his death. Naturally his search brought him into contact with Nona Brooks and her sisters in Divine Science. He met Charles Fillmore, founder of Unity, and Eugene Del Mar. In co-operation with Del Mar he founded in 1901 the Church of the Living Christ, and thereafter continued its ministry for some years. Mr. Del Mar left Denver in 1903 to attend the Chicago convention of New Thought and, as we have seen, became chairman of a committee to prepare for the Federation Convention at St. Louis in 1904. After being elected secretary, he worked in New York City, where he was later active in founding the League of the Higher Life, to which he gave much of his time and effort. He was invited to be one of the speakers at the International Metaphysical Alliance Convention at Boston in 1906, but, deciding not to attend, designated Mr. Edgerton, who had come to New York in 1905, as his alternate and furnished him with credentials and letters of introduction to leaders in the Metaphysical Alliance. Mr. Edgerton was deeply impressed by his contacts thus formed and very enthusiastic about the Alliance. As a result of his interest and activity he was elected its president in 1908, and became the first president of the National New Thought Alliance when it emerged, and of the International New Thought Alliance when, after the London Conference in 1914, it was organized. In a real sense James A. Edgerton was for many years the INTA, and no other figure in its history did more to determine its course and activities than he.

Mr. Edgerton was a layman, a government employee in the Post Office Department with his office in the national capital. It was natural, therefore, that Washington should become the national headquarters of INTA. Offices were opened there in 1915, and the movement was legally incorporated in the District of Columbia on January 22, 1917, as a non-profit organization in perpetuity, with the expressed object

to federate various groups of people throughout the world who are teaching and practicing spiritual healing and applied Christianity, and to that end send out lecturers and organizers, hold conventions, issue bulletins, collect and distribute funds, conduct circulating libraries; to do all such things in general consistent with the purposes of the institution, that it may secure standing before the business world and command the admiration and respect of all people.

For a number of years Mr. Edgerton gave much of his time outside his business hours to the work of the Alliance. At the Cincinnati Congress in 1919 it was voted to pay him a salary of $5,000 annually if he would give all his time to the work. Mr. Edgerton at once resigned from the Post Office Department, but the resignation was not accepted until March, 1920, and Alliance funds even at that time were not sufficient to put the plan into operation. Mr. Edgerton continued to give large blocks of his time as lecturer, visiting some twenty different states while still employed by the government. Since money was not available, he was drafted as Federal Prohibition Director for New Jersey, but with the understanding that he would resign at once if arrangements for full-time employment with INTA could be arranged. Meanwhile he was offered a part-time salary ($2,000) for the time he was giving it. A letter from headquarters apprised the membership of the situation and sought contributions.

Whether funds were actually raised and Mr. Edgerton was paid a full-time salary, the extant records do not disclose. A report for the year 1923 reveals expenditures of $4,041 for salaries and $2,865 for clerical salaries.

Mr. Edgerton early appointed a committee to gather and publish statements from distinguished New Thought leaders, teachers, and writers, under the title *Truths That Work*, and published them along with a list of the major publications of each contributor. This, printed as a thirty-two-page pamphlet, was circulated widely in the attempt to interest people in New

Thought and to give an idea of what the term meant. Twenty-five "messages" were included. Mr. Edgerton declared in a Foreword that New Thought was not a sect, "but a forum where those who have perceived and developed 'new' thought may find a sympathetic hearing," and that "to preserve and develop the spirit of ceaseless and fearless quest for the absolute" was one of the commonly accepted principles of New Thought. He finds in all the diversity represented in New Thought a concern for "The Constructive Power of Right Thinking and Right Acting—the truth that can be demonstrated because it is based on cosmic law—the attitudes of mind that lead one to inward peace, health, harmonious adjustment to environment and all that goes to make up the more abundant life here and now." (p. 4)

He gathered and published for the first time a list of all teachers and healers who were members of INTA. For a number of years revised editions of these were published, then their publication was made a feature of the *New Thought Bulletin,* so that more frequent revision was possible. In 1915 Mr. Edgerton conceived a plan of operation of the Alliance which has been followed more or less faithfully throughout most of its history, that of dividing the United States and the rest of the world into districts, with officers either elected by the districts or elected or appointed by the Alliance to preside over the sections. Field secretaries were to be appointed whose responsibility it would be to seek to unify the centers and workers more closely, interest them in the Alliance, and extend New Thought teaching into unoccupied areas. Those presiding over the various regions were to be vice-presidents of the Alliance.

There was opposition to the building up of regional groups on the ground that this might tend to detract from interest in and work on behalf of the Alliance, and in some cases the facts have borne out the fears expressed. Nevertheless, it did provide machinery for a more united and effective impact of the existing New Thought groups in the different areas. One finds congresses of considerable size and importance, for example, in New England, in Virginia, on the eastern seaboard, in the Northwest, and in Southern California. And there have continued to be regional rallies, less formal than conventions, briefer and less formally programed, yet serving to bring together in a common fellowship considerable numbers of representatives of the divergent groups.

Mr. Edgerton prepared a mimeographed letter of instructions and regulations for vice-presidents and field secretaries, later to be published in printed form and serve the Alliance as new vice-presidents and field secretaries were elected or appointed. At first, at least, there was a definite form which the individuals signed, affirming that they had read said instructions and accepted the responsibilities and duties that went with the office.

In the edition of the instructions published in 1923 appears an interesting section on "Teachings and Ethics," with two paragraphs which undoubtedly reflect situations which had developed and must therefore be prevented from recurring. New Thought has from the first been plagued, and still is, by what some call "fringe" accompaniments which seem to the leaders to lower the dignity and prestige of the movement, however sincere and convinced their exponents may be. The president is therefore constrained to say that "while the Alliance would not limit the liberty of any one individual or group within its membership," it does nevertheless "require its Field Secretaries, Lecturers, District President and other officials and representatives to refrain from teaching certain things such as names, numbers, colors, sex, psychic phenomena, astrology, black magic and hypnotism." Why? Because, states a minute adopted by the executive board on November 9, 1920, "1st; It is not in essential harmony with our Declaration of Principles, or with the Christian Standards; 2nd, because they tend to create confusion in the public mind; and 3rd because they distract attention from dependence on the God within." (p. 13)

But the problem still persists. One of the most popular and widely known figures in the New Thought field dealt in prophecies based upon a study of the Great Pyramid. Others embrace astrology and numerology also, and some of the early New

Thought greats, such as W. J. Colville, were notable also for their preoccupation with psychic phenomena.

One of the problems faced by the president as editor and publisher of the *New Thought Bulletin,* now the quarterly *New Thought,* has been just what advertisements or advertising claims shall be accepted, for all sorts of "fringe" type ideas seek the use of its pages. The fact that there has been a rather rigid concern at this point has not prevented criticism of the editor and therefore of the INTA as a whole. This is notably true at the hands of groups that have become accepted by the general public to some greater degree than the movement as a whole, and indeed are locally, at least in some places, "prestige" groups. They feel that to be known as associated with a movement which permits these so called "fringe" ideas to appear in its official publication is to run the risk of losing their standing.

In 1958 the *Bulletin* (Vol. XLI, No. 1) carried an article by Dan Custer, "Psychic Science, Good or Evil?" It is stated that he is chairman of the Committee on Psychic Research appointed at the 42nd Congress in Los Angeles. Other members of the committee were Ernest Holmes and Joseph Murphy.

This does not of course indicate a reversal of the general attitude toward Spiritualism in its popular form, but is a declaration of interest in phenomena which have enlisted the scientific concern of universities such as Duke and others that have established departments of parapsychology dedicated to research in the field of supersensory experience. Already there had appeared within the orthodox churches organizations which represented at least an open mind in their willingness to risk serious investigation of the whole realm of psychic experience. In America it was the Spiritual Frontiers Fellowship, founded in 1956, that drew together a substantial number of persons from the various denominations for such an exploration.

As to the other special requirement, less exception could reasonably be taken. It had to do with the promotion and sale of stocks while discharging one's duties as field secretary or regional vice-president. Such persons, traveling about as they did from place to place and often meeting and speaking to quite large audiences, enjoying the prestige of leaders in a substantial movement, were in a position to do just that. By an adroit reference in public address, or in private conference, interest might easily be awakened in a particular mining venture or other business opportunity. It was undoubtedly the occurrence of certain rather well-publicized cases of this sort, in which the leader was almost certainly himself sincerely convinced of the worth of the specific stock he was promoting but which resulted in substantial financial loss both to himself and those to whom he sold or recommended it, that led to this restriction. It should be said that New Thought leaders are not the only religious leaders who have figured in such cases. There is an unfortunate history of some very great leaders within the fold of orthodoxy who have lent themselves to the exploitation of some of their faithful followers.

It was Mr. Edgerton as president who appointed the committee to gather statements of the Principles of New Thought, with Elizabeth Towne as chairman, and it was Mr. Edgerton's statement that was adopted, with only slight changes and additions. So it was he more than anyone else who gave definition to the common beliefs and purposes which formed the basis of the Alliance. Mr. Edgerton also began the publication of the *Bulletin*, which developed from a simple occasional issue to a well-edited, informative, and thoughtful magazine of New Thought.

It was no easy task to weld into a solid organization groups and individuals of such widely divergent views. And the fortunes of the Alliance ebbed and flowed. There was the financial problem, never an easy one. There were the group rivalries, the insistent fear that one group or individual would get more than his proper share in the direction of the movement, or that the Alliance would itself prove a serious rival for the loyalties owed to the constituent groups. One gets hints of this in such letters as remain in the archives. But Mr. Edgerton was remarkably successful under stresses and strains.

He served continuously from his election as first president of

INTA in 1915 at San Francisco (he had been president of the earlier pre-INTA organization since 1908) until 1923, when after being re-elected he resigned and was succeeded by Mrs. Elizabeth Towne, colorful editor of the influential *Nautilus*. Other presidents followed, eight of them during the next ten years, when Mr. Edgerton was again called to lead the Alliance, and remained at its head until 1937. When he finally laid down the office after some twenty years all told (including the pre-INTA period) as its head and moving spirit, the tributes to him were numerous and genuine. He died in 1938.

He was something of a poet and dreamer as well as a man of action. Occasional poems of his appeared in the *Bulletin* and in other periodicals. He traveled widely and lectured innumerable times all over the country, besides publishing several volumes.

When James A. Edgerton finally ended his long career as president of INTA, Mrs. Erma Wells became his successor and for three years headed the movement. She was minister of the Church of the Truth of Spokane, Washington, successor to A. C. Grier, who had founded the group, when he left Spokane to take up work in Pasadena, and later to succeed Dr. W. John Murray as pastor of the Church of the Healing Christ in New York City.

It was under Mrs. Wells's presidency that the depression finances of the Alliance hit the all-time low of $1,080. Then the tide turned. In 1939 income rose almost 50 per cent, and this improved total was more than doubled in the third year of her presidency. With improved income the activities of INTA were substantially increased. Perhaps the most notable contribution made in her period as head of the movement was the setting in motion of the editing of an important book, *Mind Remakes Your World*, though actual publication came after John S. Garns had succeeded her in that office. As editor she could have made no better "choice" than Ernest Holmes, founder of Religious Science, and he and a committee set about getting the contributors to what was perhaps the most representative symposium on New Thought that has yet appeared. It may be confessed that there was nothing strikingly new in it. Almost everything had been well said over and over in the various books and periodicals of New Thought. But it had never before been possible to see quite the total picture of New Thought in all the richness of its varied expressions, as it was here expressed in a single volume.

Thomas Parker Boyd was another Episcopal clergyman—Rector of St. Paul's Episcopal Church in San Francisco—who without, at the beginning at least, relinquishing his pulpit in that church, became quite active in the New Thought Movement. He was one of the speakers on the program at the San Francisco Congress in 1915, speaking on the theme "The New Ministry." He was head of the Emmanuel Movement on the Pacific Coast, had been listed among the honorary presidents of the INTA for several years, and had served during 1919-20 as a field secretary of the Alliance. In 1920 he was announced as one of the national lecturers. He made effective use of Frederick W. Rawson in his church in San Francisco and with him visited other Episcopal churches on the West Coast. In 1930 he became president of the Alliance, in which capacity he served it for two years. In those early years of the great depression he had great financial difficulty in keeping the office open and in publishing the *Bulletin*. His views as to the needs of the Alliance were expressed in the *Bulletin* of May, 1931 (pp. 11-12). He favored (1) either a delegated body for legislative purposes, or an every-member vote in person or by mail on important questions; (2) a departmental organization rather than the looser type the Alliance actually had; (3) a board of publication authorized to publish a real magazine (the *Bulletin,* he felt, had, in the effort to avoid rivalry with publications of the constituent groups, been too long a mediocre periodical); (4) a National School for the preparation of accredited teachers; (5) an active Board of Lectureship; (6) a missionary fund, a necessity if the movement were to extend its ministry. And of course, that meant there was need of money. How it was needed in those days, and how difficult it was to get!

Thomas Parker Boyd organized the Society of the Healing Christ and a number of local groups affiliated with it. Dr. Edna Lister, who served as president of INTA in 1933, was one of his most loyal followers and his successor. She is still active, with headquarters now in Seattle, Washington, from which she continues to circulate the literature of the Society.

Raymond Charles Barker came to the presidency in 1943, probably the youngest person ever to have been chosen for that office. He was trained at Unity Training School and was at the time of his election minister of the Unity Center in Rochester, New York. Dr. Barker had grown up in New Thought. He was enthusiastic about it and entered actively into the affairs of INTA, though Unity had already withdrawn from any official connection with it. He had served on committees, attended congresses, worked in regional groups promoted by INTA, and in general warmly supported INTA in its various activities.

Dr. Barker brought to his new position of responsibility all his optimism, enthusiasm, and energy. It was during the difficult war years that he served. Travel restrictions made holding of a congress impossible in one of the three years of his term, and made it extremely difficult for him to travel through the field. But that, he felt, was what the president must do. He therefore traveled more widely than any previous president had done. He went during his presidency to every major city in the country where he could get local groups to open the doors to him, holding rallies in the name of INTA. He averaged about two months each year on the road, usually working "one-night stands." His being an accredited minister of Unity made it possible for him to get into Unity Centers that are not ordinarily open to INTA officers who are not so related.

Thus he brought the New Thought message and in particular the objectives and services of INTA to centers where they were little known, and along with it he brought something of his own contagious optimism and enthusiasm. While subsequent presidents have traveled more than those who preceded him, none of them has traveled as much as Raymond Charles Barker.

He was later to affiliate with the Church of Religious Science and become the leader of the First Church of Religious Science in New York City and president of the IARSC. But his deep interest in INTA has never flagged. So far as is known, he has never missed an annual congress, and he has always had some place of importance on its program or served on some of its major committees. His skill in money-raising insures him a high place in administrative circles of the Alliance.

Dr. Barker has a keen sense of the value of history. He was, during his years of the presidency and editorship of the *Bulletin*, vitally interested in gathering and making public such knowledge as was available of some of the earlier leaders of the movement. He has supported warmly the decision to make a university library the depository of the older archives and of as full a set as possible of the publications of INTA.

With the election of Dr. Ervin Seale to the presidency in 1946, it was decided to close the Washington office, which had been kept open ever since its establishment, and to move the office to New York. Henceforth it was really to be wherever the president of the period happened to reside. A nominal mailing address was maintained for a time in Washington. Indeed, the *New Thought Bulletin* continued to carry the Washington address until late 1948, when it was shifted to Los Angeles with the election of Dr. Ernest Wilson to the presidency. Here it remained during his two-year regime. Then it was moved to Hollywood when Robert H. Bitzer assumed the presidency. Office space quite apart from that of his own local center is provided in the First Church of Religious Science in Hollywood, and here the executive secretary and assistant secretary, working with Dr. Bitzer, publish the magazine and carry on the administrative activities of the movement.

Both during the years of his presidency and since that time Dr. Seale has consistently sought to raise the prestige of the Alliance, discouraging the fostering of smaller group loyalties. He believes that even though the term New Thought may not be completely satisfactory, it nevertheless represents the most comprehensive description of the whole metaphysical movement. Instead of fleeing from it, he feels, those perhaps imperfectly described by it may in time, through the enthusiastic support of the Alliance, make New Thought a term which will command respect in the world of religious movements. He has consistently held his own great church—nominally related to the Church of the Truth, which is no longer an active organization—as an independent church, with its primary relationships with other metaphysical groups through the International Alliance. He has consistently insisted that no individual group could do the job that all of them working together could do.

In late 1947 a widely circulated Sunday magazine carried an article under the title, "Psychoquacks." It was close enough to some of the things for which New Thought stands so that several sent copies of it to Ervin Seale, then president of INTA. He wrote an editorial in the Winter, 1947-48 issue of the *Bulletin* (Vol. XXX, No. 5), in which he asserted that it was rightfully a concern of the Alliance whom it should recognize as properly trained for the important work of counseling and healing. Indeed this had been the subject of a panel discussion at the Rochester Congress, though unfortunately no concrete suggestions emerged as to how such matters should be dealt with. The Alliance has no schools, but did accredit such, and it was already determined, he stated, that a spring meeting of the executive committee would consider the matter. But then he went on to make certain other observations provoked by the article.

First, he challenged the calm assertion of secular thought that only those with intensive training in medicine and psychiatric work were to be regarded as reputable workers in mental health. After all, psychiatry is a relatively new field with only about a half-century of development. It is, he said, both "unwise and unscientific" to suggest that psychiatry is the only legitimate science in dealing with the human mind. Indeed, the really capable and successful practitioners of psychiatry have already learned by experience that there are limitations in their field and have been led to appreciate the approach of the metaphysician.

Recognizing and making due allowance for the inadequacies, educational and otherwise, in the field of spiritual healing, one must emphasize that the science upon which New Thought healing practice rests "is simply the knowledge of the One Cause and all things, conditions, movements, functions as the effects of this One Cause." And he continued:

We are not in the position of treating effects as causes, nor trying to combat powers which do not exist save in the mind. The student or practitioner who is convincingly aware of One Cause only in himself and his world is afraid of no other. The implementation of this principle in prayer and mental treatment is the road to mental health and a happy estate.

New Thought recognizes, of course, that not everyone can or will work from this high principle and that there will be need therefore for various other types of practice, "all good and proper in their own sphere." New Thought co-operates with all, since "all are needed by some." But that does not mean that "we are compromising with our principle. All is not science which is called science, as all is not gold which glitters. It is still true as Paul declared, 'The wisdom of this world is foolishness with God.'"

The election of Dr. Ernest C. Wilson as president brought to the leadership one of the outstanding leaders of Unity School of Christianity. As we have seen, Unity had officially withdrawn as a constituent member of the INTA. But that did not mean that all Unity Centers or Unity leaders withdrew their memberships. As a matter of fact, many of them have continued not only as members but as active leaders as well. Of course, it is true that Unity headquarters does officially approve or at times disapprove of New Thought leaders as speakers in Unity pulpits.

Ernest Wilson, pastor of Unity's largest church on the West Coast, had been active in Alliance affairs. He was a member of the executive board before his election as president. Perhaps the most notable change effected by his administration was the "new look" given the *Bulletin,* which was spruced up with color and with photographs interspersed throughout the reading section. These changes made of the official *Bulletin* the attractive magazine which it has ever since continued to be.

Robert H. Bitzer was elected to the presidency at the Los

Angeles Congress in 1949, and next to James A. Edgerton has served longer as head of the Alliance than any other person. He had been active in the League for the Larger Life in New York City for some years, then went to Boston where he was minister of the New Thought Church founded by Dr. Julia Seton. While so engaged, he was invited by Ernest Holmes to come to Holly-wood and establish there the first recognized branch of the Institute of Religious Science.

Dr. Bitzer accepted this invitation and began his work, using one of the rooms at the Roosevelt Hotel on Hollywood Boulevard for his lectures and classes. The response to his ministry was enthusiastic, resulting in the forming of what is now called the Hollywood Church of Religious Science on Sunset Boulevard, where an extremely attractive as well as functional center was built and a vigorous program carried on by Dr. Bitzer and his staff. Fortunately there was room to house the secretariat of the Alliance adequately, quite apart from the offices of the local church and center.

For years each retiring president who had answered calls upon his time for wide-ranging travel and speaking, far beyond the call of duty, had recommended that at least a part-time salary be paid the president, so that he could afford to dedicate more time to the affairs of the movement. In the earlier day this had been the plan, but it had never been fully carried out. The depression had reduced to a mere pittance the amount available even for hiring a secretary. But finances had improved. For some time an executive secretary had been paid a reasonably fair salary to look after the details of the office and the publication of the magazine, working always under the president's direction.

The first full year under Dr. Bitzer's presidency the total receipts were nearly $10,000, and they increased notably each year, from $10,000 in 1949 to $23,000 in 1955, and on up to $44,000 in 1958. Even so, no salary item for the president appears until 1953. What was happening? Was there a great influx of new members? No, though there was a substantial increase. But it was in the other categories of membership that the increase was chiefly registered, and probably because the president and his staff worked more intensively in that area. For example, receipts from sustaining membership, which means a five-dollar-a-month payment, had been running from $300 to $700 a year previous to 1949. From that time on this item never dropped below $1,300 and in 1955 it went as high as $4,900, averaging well over $3,000 per year.

Life memberships representing payments of $100, which had only once (1947) brought in as much as $2,000, rose from $750 in 1949 to over $5,000 in 1952, and averaged more than $3,000 annually. Group membership, meaning a minimum of $10.00 per year, had accounted, previous to 1949, for from almost nothing to a little more than $600 annually. Now it increased substantially, falling below $900 only once and reaching as high as $1,640, and averaging well over $1,000 per year.

How account for the increase? Well, for one thing Dr. Bitzer was able to do more traveling, make more public presentations of the claims of the Alliance, meet more frequently the leaders of the movement in various sections of the United States, and so stimulate greater interest, activity, and enthusiasm. This was bound to result in increased contributions. Furthermore, with a more adequate and better-paid staff, he was able to maintain mail contact with all parts of the field, the district presidents, the other officers, and also with individual leaders in local centers. The keeping accurate records, seeing that bills were sent out and collection of moneys due made, and the careful watching of all the business details of the office, in themselves led to economy in expenditures, and in the end to more effective employment of such funds as were forthcoming. Partly, of course, it was due to the fact that these last years, save for two minor recessions, have been years of increased income for almost everyone and of increased giving in all churches. But even so, proper cultivation of the field has likewise played an important role.

Realizing when first elected that the INTA was international only in name, Dr. Bitzer took the stand that it should either drop the name "international" or enlarge its scope of operation. It was

voted by the Congress of 1950 that the Alliance extend its international interests, and to effect this they sent Dr. Bitzer to Europe
in 1951. There was, he reports, only a nominal but quite inactive
local group called INTA in London. He held a series of meetings
in London and Blackpool, and went on to speak to groups in
Paris, in The Hague, and in Germany. Later the same year, at his
urging, Dr. Raymond Charles Barker covered much the same
territory, and as a result of these contacts interest in the worldwide movement was intensified and maintained.

Again in 1953, Dr. Bitzer visited England, speaking in various
centers, and again he spoke in Paris for Unité Universelle, and
visited a number of centers in Switzerland, Germany, and
Holland. All these contacts served to promote a renewed interest
in the Alliance.

Another trip in 1958 took him to Scandinavia. A wealthy
donor who wanted very much that New Thought be brought to
the land of her birth gave a substantial sum which made possible
a visit to Stockholm where Dr. Bitzer gave a series of conferences
which were well attended and awakened a definite interest in
New Thought. But lack of any available person to continue what
he had begun prevented any permanent planting of the movement in Scandinavian lands. This trip also afforded Dr. Bitzer an
opportunity to visit England again and to lecture in several of the
principal centers, besides addressing a special conference of leaders. He went again also to France and had an excellent hearing
through Unité Universelle of Paris, then went on by air to South
Africa, lecturing and meeting the leaders in that part of the world.

As a result of these international efforts, increasing numbers
of representatives from the countries visited have been brought to
the annual congresses as participants, bringing a better understanding of their respective movements to American members and
carrying back something of the spirit and enthusiasm of the
Alliance to their own national groups.

Dr. Bitzer felt early in his presidency that if the Alliance were
to attain growth, there should be a definite change in the format
of its annual congresses. Originally organized principally, he

thought, as a convention organization, with its chief purpose that of affording an opportunity for exchange of ideas among leaders, it should, he felt, be made now to attract laymen in much larger numbers. This would require offering a program of the very best speakers who would provide real stimulus and instruction of a high order.

As a step in this direction, there were held at the Chicago Congress in 1952 a series of afternoon seminars, at which outstanding speakers each had an hour. These proved highly successful. Later, a morning seminar of ten hours, with five major leaders having two hours each, was introduced and was enthusiastically received. The congress now had a definite teaching program. And this has continued every year.

Under Dr. Bitzer's editorship of the *Bulletin,* the high journalistic standards set by Ernest C. Wilson have been maintained and advanced. Now called not the *New Thought Bulletin,* but *New Thought,* it takes its place as a worthy quarterly magazine representative of the broad interests of the entire New Thought Movement.

During his period of service as president, Dr. Bitzer has sought increasingly to make of INTA a year-round working organization. He has stood consistently for raising the educational standards of the ministry in the New Thought field. One of the problems attacked in recent years has been the easy acquisition of degrees through schools which have often enough been labeled "diploma mills," since the requirements were so nominal as to bring the degrees into disrepute. There is no doubt that some valuable instruction has been given, but the granting of a doctor's degree for, at most, only a very few short courses and even these usually given by correspondence and to students who have only the equivalent of a high-school education, has not only brought the schools offering the degree into disrepute, but has the effect also of discrediting to a certain extent the whole New Thought Movement. The two schools principally involved are in the process of increasing their requirements, and there is some indication that they will give up entirely the granting of degrees and award only a diploma or certificate indicating the work the students have completed.

Having carried the load of the presidency for a dozen years, Dr. Bitzer announced at the Miami Congress of 1961 that he would not be a candidate for re-election at the expiration of his term at the 1963 Congress.

The financial support of any overall organization such as INTA always presents formidable difficulties. Most basic of all is that for the great majority of its members it is not their primary loyalty. In the case of INTA, while it is quite possible for an individual to join who belongs to no other New Thought organization, either local or group, the fact is that most individuals who belong to it are first of all members of some New Thought group such as Unity, Divine Science, or some local group which has no affiliation with any organization save INTA. Thus their first responsibility is not to INTA.

Also, since membership is both individual and group, most local groups that hold membership in INTA are also members of one of the several organizations such as Religious Science, Home of Truth, or other. Again the primary loyalty is not to INTA but to one of its constituent groups. When money is scarce and difficult to get, it is easily seen that there might be reluctance to share it with the overall International Alliance. It is a difficulty shared by all city, state, national, and world Councils of Churches.

To maintain itself and carry on its work INTA must seek support from various sources. Dependence has been in part upon individual memberships, but these have been so modest in amount that they have never yielded a very substantial sum. Group memberships, usually $10.00 per year, have sometimes also been on a purely "love offering" basis, and at other times, "love" beginning to operate above a minimum $10.00 fee. These have held up fairly well, but fluctuations invariably occur with changes of administration and the general environmental circumstances. Then sustaining memberships, with publication of the names of donors, have been offered successfully. A considerable number have become members of the Century Club, made up of those who give $5.00 per month to the Alliance either in a lump sum or on the instalment plan. This has proved attractive and brought in quite respectable amounts. More recently individuals and groups have been encouraged to honor past leaders by giving at least $100 and having the leader's name listed in the Memorial Fellowship together with the donor's name in occasional issues of the quarterly *New Thought*. In 1960 more than three hundred Life Members were listed, and in a slightly earlier issue some twenty or more were listed in the Memorial Fellowship, among them Nona Brooks, Dr. Emmet Fox, and former president James A. Edgerton.

But there is seldom enough money to carry out all the plans suggested, and even plans already set in motion have sometimes had to be curtailed for lack of funds. The Alliance has had its share of year-end deficits.

Complete financial records for the years prior to 1927 are not available, but in that year the income of the Alliance stood at the highest figure it was to reach in the next eighteen years: nearly $9,000. After 1927 annual receipts fell in successive years until they reached a low of $1,080 in 1938. But even then retrenchment made possible a surplus of $22.75! The depression had really hit and hit hard. Gone was the dream of a salaried, full-time president, and the poor office secretary was reduced to a pittance. But a headquarters was maintained and a *Bulletin* was published, though not always as frequently as desired and planned for. At least some central INTA affairs were kept going. Somehow the annual congress was held every year, and it was probably this fact that kept the movement alive and provided part of the support, for most congresses, though expensive, are productive of income for the general work of the Alliance. This is the best time to raise funds, it seems.

Beginning with 1939 the financial situation began to improve. In that year over $1,500 was received; 1940 receipts were double that sum. By 1945 income finally surpassed the 1927 level, climbing to more than $10,000. Later years have seen receipts soar to $17,000, to $20,000, to $28,000—and to an all-time high, in 1958, of $44,500. But 1959 saw income reduced to $30,800, and 1960 to $27,700.

How account for the substantially larger income in the years since World War II? Of course, there has been a general upsurge in giving to religious and philanthropic causes. People have had more money and have been more generous in their giving. But that is only part of the answer. Perhaps more than anything else the increase in income is the result of the fact that the movement has undertaken to pay an adequate salary to the president and provide him with sufficient clerical and other help. An organization of the size and complexity of INTA requires more to carry it on effectively than any person or persons can afford to give out of active careers and work obligations to which they owe their first effort.

INTA, like all overall organizations, of course has no independent life of its own. It has no local programs, though it sponsors conventions, retreats, and congresses. It has no radio or TV program going out over the air. This activity, too, is carried out by the constituent bodies, or by individual leaders or local groups. INTA can only be or become what its constituent members want it and will permit it to be. It is first of all a symbol of unity within the general field it represents. If the spirit of the constituent groups is primarily separatist, giving only a meager lip service to the desirability of a unified metaphysical approach, then INTA will not flourish. If they are fearful that a strong INTA might overshadow their own group efforts, it will get but little support from them. INTA has no teaching function in the sense of providing for the training of ministers, teachers, and practitioners. That is done by the constituent groups themselves, though the idea of a united training effort, which would still permit the special emphasis of the different groups, is not outside the realm of possibility—as proven by the experience of certain nondenominational seminaries which train candidates for the ministry of the various larger denominations.

PART II

New Thought Groups in America

PART II

New Thought Groups in America

7

Unity School of Christianity

UNITY SCHOOL OF CHRISTIANITY, now with headquarters at Lee's Summit, Missouri, a suburb of Kansas City, about fifteen miles from the center of that thriving midwestern metropolis, had its beginnings in the late eighties, in Kansas City. It was founded by a real estate operator, Charles Fillmore, and his wife, Myrtle. Thus, it was like so many nineteenth-century American religious movements, a lay movement developed to meet the needs of laymen and laywomen which the churches of the time were evidently not adequately meeting.

Charles Fillmore had had only meager educational opportunities. He never saw the inside of a college or seminary, though his wife, Myrtle, was a graduate of Oberlin College. He had grown up in a relatively poor home—a broken home during a good part of his childhood—and had been forced early to work to support his mother and himself. He worked as a railroad clerk in Texas and as a mule team driver and prospector in Colorado, and finally became a real estate operator, first in Pueblo, Colorado, where he was quite successful while the boom there lasted.

From Pueblo he went to Kansas City, Missouri, which was experiencing a boom at the time. He prospered greatly by laying out and developing certain subdivisions of the rapidly growing city. But the boom there also "busted," and the family fortunes fell on evil days. In addition, Myrtle Fillmore, who had come from a family with a history of tuberculosis, then called consumption, fell a victim of that frequently fatal malady. The future looked dark indeed.

233

Meanwhile Emma Curtis Hopkins, who had been editor of the *Christian Science Journal* but had been removed and had broken with the Eddy school of Christian Science, had founded her Christian Science Theological Seminary in Chicago and taught classes in her conception of metaphysical truth. One of her students, Dr. E. B. Weeks, was sent to Kansas City in 1886 to give some lectures. A friend recommended to Charles and Myrtle Fillmore that they go and hear him. Myrtle's condition by this time was almost hopeless. They had tried everything they knew. Nothing helped. They were willing to try anything. So they went to one of Dr. Weeks's lectures. Charles Fillmore was not impressed, but to Myrtle Fillmore it was the great turning point in her life. As she later told it, one sentence of the lecturer came to her as a true revelation. It was this: "I am a child of God, and therefore I do not inherit sickness." She went home repeating it, and her whole outlook toward herself and toward life underwent a change. It was the beginning of her healing, and really the beginning of Unity, for had she not been healed it is quite unlikely that Unity would ever have appeared.

The healing was not instantaneous. It took time—some two years—for it to become wholly effective, but she knew at once that she would be healed. People seeing the change in her became curious as to how it had come about, and some sought her out for her help. She wanted nothing so much as to share the good that had come to her. Some remarkable healings resulted from her efforts, and her fame spread throughout the neighborhood. Her husband, "a hard headed business man," was at first skeptical. But the patent evidence of his wife's own healing and those of some of his neighbors set him to reading and studying diligently. He and his wife studied with Joseph Adams, who came also from Chicago, and they later went to Chicago and studied with Emma Curtis Hopkins herself. Gradually Charles Fillmore became convinced of the truth that these people were trying to express, and once he was committed to it, it became necessary for him to do something about it.

He was still selling real estate, but more and more he neglected his business in his concern about these new ideas. He himself had been a chronic sufferer from a mishap that had left one of his limbs withered and shorter than the other, so that he had to walk with a crutch or a cane. He began to apply the principles he was learning to his own case and found that his condition definitely improved.

A depression was on in Kansas City at the time, and business was no longer prospering. A third child, Royal, had come to join Lowell, born in 1882, and Rickert, born in 1884. Nevertheless, in that year Charles Fillmore began the publication of a new magazine, *Modern Thought*. Though he continued for a time to carry on his business, he had irrevocably launched himself upon a career which was to demand all his time and attention, as well as that of his entire family, and would eventually become Unity School of Christianity, largest of the movements which are generally thought of as being in the New Thought tradition.

A proper name for the new movement was not at first forthcoming. Christian Science was at the time still a rather loose term used by a good many teachers who were not at all in full agreement with Mrs. Eddy's version. An early reference in one of Mr. Fillmore's magazines was to "Mrs. Eddy's version of Christian Science." Some have supposed that Unity was an offshoot of Christian Science, since for a year the title *Christian Science Thought* was given to the magazine. But Mr. Fillmore and his wife were never students of Mrs. Eddy, and the former was to state explicitly that when he used the term Christian Science, he meant by it "all the metaphysical schools" and he felt it his duty to inform the public that "our views are not those of organized Christian Science." (*Modern Thought*, second issue).

In 1890 Myrtle Fillmore announced the beginning of a new department of the magazine under the name "Society of Silent Help." Believing in the possibility of absent treatment, which meant that "bodily presence is not necessary to those in spiritual harmony," she stated that a little company of people in Kansas City had agreed to meet "in silent soul communion every night at ten o'clock all those who are in trouble, sickness, or poverty, and who sincerely desire the help of the Good Father." She invited all who wished to join this society to "sit in a quiet retired place if possible, at the hour of ten o'clock every evening for not less than fifteen minutes, and hold in silent thought the words that shall be given each month by the editor of this department." (*Household of Faith*, p. 82).

At first the little group that met consisted only of the Fillmores and a few friends and neighbors. It was quite informal. Sometimes they sang a hymn or two, then one of the Fillmores usually led in affirmative prayer, remembering those who were in special need and had asked for help. Mrs. Fillmore supervised the department, but the response was so immediate that soon the two of them were thoroughly caught up in it. Letters streamed in from all quarters from persons seeking help—the sick, the unhappy, the frustrated, and those who wanted a deeper unfolding of their spiritual natures. The hour was changed to nine o'clock to make it easier for farm folk to participate. In addition to the remembering of people's needs in prayer by the group, Myrtle and Charles Fillmore wrote letters of counsel and encouragement. A new prayer or affirmation, later two, were printed each month for the use of members of the society. Later, prayers and affirmations to fit any conceivable need were printed and circulated among those seeking help. The early concern of Silent Unity, as it came to be called in 1891, was largely that of physical healing, and later of financial need and supply; but as time went on, almost every human need was brought at one time or another to the society. Most of the people whom Silent Unity has helped have never even talked personally with any of the Silent Unity workers.

Communication was at first largely through correspondence, later by telegraph and telephone. Eventually Silent Unity was to offer round-the-clock service to persons in need, so that at any hour of the day or night there was always someone awaiting to take a call or receive a telegram.

While the original group was meeting in Kansas City, others were encouraged to meet at the same time anywhere that "two or three might be gathered together." Start with a few, two persons only, if necessary, they were urged. "Two persons in perfect harmony will do more than a hundred in discord," they were told. The growth of the society was rapid. There were ten thousand in 1903, fifteen thousand by 1906. Today Silent Unity receives more than six hundred thousand requests each year for prayer.

It soon outgrew the capacity of the Fillmores to supervise it. Gradually other helpers were added, until at the present time there are about 150 workers engaged in responding to the numerous requests for help that flow in daily to Silent Unity, which now occupies one large wing of the Unity buildings in Lee's Summit. The workers, each occupied with a "case load" of requests, sit at desks in a large open room, over which at one time Charles Fillmore and Myrtle presided, engaging in affirmation and prayer, as well as in the writing of letters of counsel and encouragement to those who have sought Silent Unity's help. Miss May Roland has now for a number of years been at the head of Silent Unity, which is at the very heart of Unity and ministers to multitudes of people who never attend Unity Centers or have any connection with organized Unity. One will find among the letters asking for help the names of many members as well as ministers of the orthodox churches, both Protestant and Catholic, who have not left their churches and probably never will.

Silent Unity has furnished the model for other like services of other groups. Whether the imitation is conscious or not—and in some cases there is no doubt that it is conscious—a number of other religious groups now maintain something quite like Silent Unity. One of those more recently established is that of the Oral Roberts evangelistic group at Tulsa, Oklahoma — organized shortly after a visit by a delegation of workers from that group to Unity at Unity Village.

Charles and Myrtle Fillmore had no notion that they were founding a new movement. This unfolded gradually and took form in unexpected ways. At the heart of it were certain convictions and principles according to which they worked. One was that Truth is one, and that no one organization or school of thought has a monopoly on it. Not even Christianity, though the loyalty of the Fillmores and Unity to Christ, as they understood and interpreted him, is exceeded by no branch of the Christian church. Mr. Fillmore was hospitable, as the contents of early issues of his magazine clearly disclose, to Truth wherever found, whether in the other great ethnic religions or in some of the newer formulations of faith in his own day. The Bible, he believed, formed an adequate basis for a living faith, but his interpretation of the Bible in "metaphysical" fashion drew sometimes from other than distinctly Christian sources.

Religion was not something external to life, but integral, related not alone to "spiritual" values, but concerned as well with every aspect of life, including man's physical health and well-being, his material substance or "supply," and his happiness. Here he was in the truly New Thought tradition, as he was also in his insistence upon the power of thought and in the generally optimistic view of man. Religion was something eminently practical. The organized work which was carried on by the Fillmores locally in Kansas City bore the name of Practical Christianity, as did the work of Unity Centers in some other places.

Healing experienced by the Fillmores was something to be shared with others, so they had to develop some kind of a channel through which the sharing could be effected. First it was the private help in healing by Myrtle, then the publication of the magazine, then the beginning of the Society of Silent Help. At first they operated entirely from their own home, then from the real estate office where Charles Fillmore still continued to make his living selling properties. Later they rented offices in the Deardorf Building, where some other metaphysical groups also had their offices. Here the beginnings of a metaphysical circulating library were made. Still later, there was a move to the Hall Building, where there was more room for meetings and a Knights of Pythias Hall served as a meeting place for the Sunday gatherings which had begun, held not at the usual hour of Sunday morning church services, but in the afternoon and sometimes in the evening. There was no desire to keep persons from attending their own church services. The Fillmores had no desire to function as a church.

Sometimes Mr. Fillmore spoke, sometimes there were lecturers from other metaphysical groups. Several of Emma Curtis Hopkins' students spoke, and she herself came repeatedly to speak and to teach classes—one with a membership of eighty-seven persons, the largest held in Kansas City up to that time. Mr. and Mrs. Fillmore went to Chicago in 1890 and attended one of her classes. They had a wonderful time and came to know many of the leaders in the metaphysical movement. They attended a New Thought Congress in connection with the World's Fair in Chicago in 1893, and an International Divine Science Association held there also in 1895. They invited the congress to meet in Kansas City, and the invitation was accepted. This congress of the movement later to be called the International New Thought Alliance brought together most of the leaders in the metaphysical field. For a number of years the Fillmores took an active and continuing role in the development of the larger movement.

The growth of Unity, as the movement was now called, forced another move in 1898 to a house at 1315 McGee Street, and for two years it sufficed. Then a public hall had to be rented for the accommodation of the larger crowds that the Unity meetings were attracting. By this time the movement was large enough to support its own work, and Mr. Fillmore could give up his real estate business and devote all his time to the work.

The public meetings were not typical church services. There was great informality, and a give and take between leader and people. Charles Fillmore was more a teacher than a preacher, and he welcomed questions and discussion of the subject with which he was dealing. By 1902 he was suggesting the need for a building, and a building committee was hopefully named and a fund started. In 1905 there was but $601 in it. Nevertheless, a property was found at 917 Tracy Avenue, and on it a three-story brick building was erected with space for offices, an auditorium seating two hundred persons, and room for a printshop that would handle the publishing activities. It was dedicated in 1906, a proud day for Unity, which for the first time in its seventeen years of existence now owned a home of its own.

How had the work been financed? Mr. Fillmore had poured into it his own resources, once fairly substantial, but later much reduced because of a depression following the "busting" of the Kansas City real estate boom. He had a growing family. His increasing preoccupation with the work of the magazine, to which all the members of the family contributed their services, led to a still further reduction of income from his business. Yet from the first Charles Fillmore and his wife believed that whatever they did should be done freely and without price, depending on what they called the law, "With what measure ye mete, it shall be measured unto you." In January, 1891, Mr. Fillmore had written concerning the magazine, "This publication is turned over to and is now under the complete control of Principle." While a nominal charge of $1.00 had been made in compliance with a governmental regulation that there must be a subscription price, this was only nominal, "as the value of Truth cannot be measured in dollars and cents, and no specific charge can be made for it." This paper, he wrote, "will trust the law (as above stated) and go far and wide freely and generously to all seeking the Truth."

As the healings occurred no specific charges were made. As the benefits of Silent Unity brought health and abundance to people, no bills were ever sent them. If they felt grateful and sent in a gift it was acknowledged gladly, but no price was ever set upon its services, or indeed on any Unity has performed.

It was not until 1942 that the real secret of the Fillmores' financial policy was revealed, when a document in the handwriting of Charles Fillmore, and bearing the signatures of both husband and wife, was discovered among the papers of Myrtle Fillmore after her passing. It was designated, "Dedication and Covenant." Bearing the date of December 7, 1892, just fifty years earlier, it had never been made public, but had steadily guided

Mr. and Mrs. Fillmore in all the years of their developing movement. This was what they wrote:

We, Charles Fillmore and Myrtle Fillmore, husband and wife, hereby dedicate our selves, our time, our money, all we have and all we expect to have, to the Spirit of Truth, and through it, to the Society of Silent Unity.

It being understood and agreed that the said Spirit of Truth shall render unto us an equivalent for this dedication, in peace of mind, health of body, wisdom, understanding, love, life and an abundant supply of all things necessary to meet every want without our making any of these things the object of our existence.

In the presence of the Conscious Mind of Christ Jesus, this 7th day of December, 1892 A.D.

CHARLES FILLMORE
MYRTLE FILLMORE

This has been the policy in general of the Unity movement ever since. Unity has never put a price upon its services other than a nominal one, because of legal necessity, on its publications. But the fact of an announced price has never kept persons who lacked the necessary funds from getting any literature or other services by Unity. Unity has given freely, and yet there seems always to be money available to meet any obvious need.

The building that had been dedicated in 1906 was soon outgrown, and a much larger one was built on an adjacent lot, at 917 Tracy Avenue. Dedicated in 1914, it was to be enlarged four times to meet the increasing demands for space to house Unity's growing staff and expanding activities. There were now hundreds of employees, many of them Unity followers, many members of other churches. There was always something of a family spirit among them. They were paid as much as or more than persons doing like work in other enterprises. Mr. and Mrs. Fillmore knew most of them personally and were interested in them. Lowell Fillmore, during his many years as president of Unity, has followed the same pattern.

An early provision was a lunchroom — vegetarian, in keeping with Mr. Fillmore's own eating habits. It was clean and well appointed and served wholesome, if meatless, meals. It was primarily for workers, but was open also to the public. In keeping with Unity's general principle of putting no fixed prices on its services, the restaurant functioned for a time on a pay-what-you-wish basis. But eventually it was found that this kept people from coming there to eat, because of the embarrassment of wondering whether their contribution had been sufficient. So modest prices were put upon the meals. But always employees could count on "seconds" and extra coffee or tea without any extra cost.

Unity's labor relations have always been good. People like to work for the organization. Long before most businesses began to add "fringe benefits" to the wages, Unity was providing recreational and other facilities for the use of its workers. It was partly in order to provide such facilities that Unity farm was purchased and developed at Lee's Summit, out about fifteen miles from the heart of Kansas City. Here, the Fillmores began to dream, could be brought together in a wonderful rural setting all the departments of their work, in a group of buildings that would be more adequate and have room for indefinite expansion, and at the same time would provide space for residences for at least a part of the workers and adequate recreational facilities for all the employees.

When Rickert Fillmore returned home from World War I, the dream began to take shape. Together he, Lowell, and Charles Fillmore found and bought a suitable place, a fifty-eight-acre tract of land, partly wooded, partly in cultivation or pasture, near Lee's Summit. Little by little they have added adjacent properties until now Unity owns some 1,300 acres. They had little money to develop it, but through the gifts of loyal Unity followers and of those who have benefited from its ministries the money has come. Unity Village now comprises a marvelous complex of buildings, including its great tower which dominates the countryside and provides seven stories of office space for various phases of Unity's work.

Rickert Fillmore has been the chief developer of Unity Farm. He has drawn the master plans for the whole and has been the architect of most of the buildings, master landscaper and gardener, superintendent of construction, ingenious inventor of improved building methods, and manager in general of the farm and all its numerous departments.

First, residences were built, a swimming pool, golf course, tennis courts, picnic places, a hotel where guests attending the developing training classes could be housed. Then came a building for Silent Unity, occupied first in 1929, but for only a little while, when the great depression made further progress impossible. It returned to 917 Tracy Avenue, where it remained for almost twenty years. Building operations were resumed in 1940. By 1947 the printing department was moved to the new location. In 1949 the entire Unity School left its Tracy Avenue home and was moved bodily to Unity Village.

It would be difficult to find a more beautiful set of buildings than that which Unity now occupies, or one in lovelier surroundings. It has recently been incorporated as Unity Village. Appropriately enough, Rickert Fillmore was elected mayor.

Unity developed along four major lines: (1) the issuing of literature, getting its message out to the world through the printed pages of books, pamphlets, leaflets, and magazines; (2) the work of healing and help in meeting, through Silent Unity, the practical problems of men and women through the ministry of prayer; (3) the work of teaching, as indicated in its name, Unity School of Christianity; and (4) its activity as what it was perhaps never intended to become, but has actually become, a church.

Much of the work of Unity is done through its literature. Besides the active work of ministers and teachers in local Centers who are of course all distributors of Unity publications, the Unity School of Christianity carries on a tremendous mail-order business that reaches literally to the ends of the earth in the sale and free distribution of its periodicals, books, pamphlets, cards, records, and other articles used by the churches, the Sunday Schools, and individuals in the practice of the faith as taught by Unity.

Unity is a publishing house of substantial proportions. It owns its own presses, beautifully housed in one large wing of its buildings. It publishes all of its own books. The current list carries some seventy titles of full-length books in English, selling for two dollars or more, besides twenty or more foreign translations in at least nine different languages, including Greek and Russian. A special list of foreign language publications carries more than 140 titles of magazines, books, pamphlets, cards, etc., available in twelve languages, including French, Finnish, German, Portuguese, and Spanish. *Unita*, a digest of articles from all the Unity magazines, is published in Italian.

The current foreign list carries twenty-one items in French, nine of them books; sixty-five in German, including nine books; four in Greek, comprising four books; ten in Italian, four of them books; three in Japanese, including one book; one book and two pamphlets in Russian; fifty items in Spanish, including seven books; and nine in Swedish, including three books. It is Emilie Cady's *Lessons in Truth* that has been most frequently translated, appearing in nine different languages besides English. It is, of course, the primary textbook used in Unity. No record of its sales from 1894 to 1923 is available, but since that time just under a million copies have been circulated.

How this book came into being makes an interesting story. It might have been supposed that some book by Charles Fillmore, or by his wife, would have been chosen as the textbook for Unity. And of course their books are studied and made the basis of some courses required of those training to become Unity leaders or ministers. But the one book taught everywhere in Unity, and it should be said very widely also among other New Thought groups, was the work of a practicing homeopathic physician, Dr. Emilie H. Cady of New York City, a former schoolteacher who had turned to medicine.

She was a devoutly religious person who, like so many others who have been prominent in the New Thought field, studied with Emma Curtis Hopkins. She wrote and published a little booklet, *Finding the Christ in Ourselves,* which eventually came to the attention of Myrtle Fillmore. She was deeply impressed by it and asked her husband to read it. He did so and wrote the author asking permission to print and distribute it. At the same time he invited Dr. Cady to write for his magazine. Her first article, "Neither Do I Condemn Thee," appeared in *Unity* in the January, 1892, issue, and others appeared frequently thereafter.

One day a letter came to Charles Fillmore suggesting that there was a need for a simple, clear set of lessons setting forth the principles of divine healing, and suggesting Dr. Cady among others as eminently fitted to prepare them. She was reluctant to accept Mr. Fillmore's invitation. She was a busy physician who had little time for writing. But the Fillmores persisted in their request until at last she consented and the first lesson, now the first chapter of *Lessons in Truth*, appeared in the October, 1894, issue of *Unity*. Eleven other chapters followed. There was an immediate and enthusiastic response from readers. The lessons were printed subsequently in three booklets of four lessons each, at 25 cents per booklet, the series for 75 cents. After several years they were put out in one volume, the familiar *Lessons in Truth* as known today, the most popular book ever published by Unity. It is found on the literature tables of local New Thought Centers almost everywhere, whether these are related to the Unity School of Christianity or not.

Unity believes in pamphlets, for it lists over 150 different titles at 5 cents each, $4.00 for 100 of each title, or $3.00 for 100 selected by Unity, with other assortments at special prices. Titles of some of these are revealing as to Unity's interests. For example, concerning health and healing: *Curing Colds, Health Through Right Thinking, How I Found Health*. Concerning prosperity: *How to Handle Substance Spiritually, Prosperity in the Home*. Concerning prayer: *The Atomic Prayer, Unity's Interpretation of the Lord's Prayer*. Typically New Thought emphasis: *Accept Your Good, The Christ Mind, Reform Your God-Thought*. In addition, some twenty or more pamphlets are for free distribution to anyone requesting them. Unity has also made much of simple cards with a prayer, a blessing, an affirmation, or some helpful reminder of proper attitudes or thoughts during the day's work. Typical are these: "An Airplane Blessing," "An Automobile Blessing," "A Salesman's Prayer," "A Student's Prayer," "Beatitudes for a Housewife," "Your Divine Self." How many of these have been put into circulation no one knows, but they continue year after year to be issued and used by large numbers of people.

How, besides through the efforts of ministers and teachers of Unity, are these publications gotten into circulation? Partly of course through advertising in the regular periodicals published by Unity. These alone are read by millions of people. We have already mentioned *Unity* magazine, perhaps the best known of Unity's publications, but it is only one of several, each reaching a substantially different constituency.

There is *Wee Wisdom,* a magazine for children which circulates far beyond the limits of the membership of Unity Centers. It is a first-class children's magazine, ably edited, in no sense a house organ for the advancement of Unity, but edited of course from a general, though never an obtrusive, Unity viewpoint. It is the oldest children's magazine in the country, having begun in August, 1893, as an eight-page paper. For a short time it appeared as a department of *Unity,* but later was again published separately, by Myrtle Fillmore. From the first it was sold at less than the cost of production. This has been true during most of its history, but has not prevented its publication. The circulation in 1960 was nearly a quarter of a million. It is published also in Braille, and is sent to any blind child where there is need, free of charge.

Daily Word, first issued in 1924, is a monthly magazine, pocket sized, containing in addition to an article or two, a poem, and a few short prayers or affirmations, a brief devotional page for each day of the month. It starts with an affirmation, followed by a brief comment or meditation, ending with an appropriate Bible verse. It is edited under the supervision and inspiration of Silent Unity and has a circulation of some 800,000. Every issue carries advertisements of some of Unity's publications. Its outreach has been increased enormously in recent years through its use on radio and television.

Weekly Unity appeared first in 1909 with Lowell Fillmore as editor. Long before this Charles Fillmore had wanted to publish *Unity* on a weekly basis, but circumstances made it unwise to change from a monthly to a weekly schedule of publication. With the expansion of Unity's activity, a weekly bulletin of some kind became a necessity not adequately met by monthly *Unity*, which was not really a news periodical at all. The weekly bulletin, largely local in interest, centering in the activities primarily in Kansas City, proved of interest to other followers of Unity elsewhere in the country, and the result was the decision to issue *Weekly Unity*. It appeared first on May 15, 1909, and has been effectively the news sheet of Unity ever since. Its present circulation is not far from a quarter of a million.

But it is much more than a newssheet. Every issue, usually of eight pages, quarto size, has one or two general articles. A typical issue carries a two-page article on "In My Garden With God," a page-and-a-half article on "Creativity in Modern Art," and departments: "Things to be Remembered," conducted by Lowell Fillmore, "The High Watch," "The Society of Silent Unity," "Because Someone Prayed," "Field Activities," "Notes and News," and a Bible Lesson giving Unity's interpretation of the International Sunday School Lesson. An occasional poem, a meditation, some affirmations, and advertisements of some of Unity's classes and publications, or music, or records usually complete the issue.

Unity's concern for young people is expressed through a monthly magazine published since 1924, called first *Youth*, then *Progress*, then *You*, and finally once again, *Progress*. Currently its format is that of *Reader's Digest*, and it usually runs to sixty-four pages. It is slanted specifically to youth and covers a fairly wide range of subject matter presumed to be of interest to young persons. It has stories, poetry, discussion of youth's problems, articles of scientific or social interest, some specifically religious articles, and some of a generally inspirational nature. Some articles are by young people as well as for them, and in more recent

times a young adults' digest of especially helpful ideas gleaned
from other Unity publications has been featured.

Finally, Unity's concern for the practical application of its
teachings to the world of business is expressed through its magazine *Good Business*, founded in 1922 as *The Christian Business
Man*, later *Christian Business*, and still later, just *Good Business*.
The magazine, now in its seventy-eighth volume (two volumes
per year), is presently a forty-eight page periodical dedicated to
the idea that Christian principles are the best for business. Stories
of business success through the practice of the Golden Rule are
frequent. A typical issue carries a story of a new film version of
Pollyanna, reflecting of course the general optimistic outlook of
Unity; an article on "Prosperity for You," which had continued
through several numbers; "Give Your Best in Your Role"; "Experiment in Selling"; "On these Two," a story of two rival small-
town papers, one of which, the successful one, was being run on
the principles of the Golden Rule; two or three other short
articles; and the regular departments: "Prayers of the Month,"
"Research in Truth," "Shop Talk," "Calendar of Activity," and
"Unity Business Peoples Clubs," which lists a score or more of
such clubs in as many cities in a dozen states. The "Calendar of
Activity" is a two-page spread at the middle of the magazine
containing a calendar for the month and providing in the square
for each day of the month a brief affirmation. "Research in Truth"
is a kind of Bible study, a suitable text for each week, with suggestions as to how to think of it. There are repeated testimonials
as to the help derived from reading the magazine, or from reading some particular article in the area of business. Writers are not
limited exclusively to Unity followers, nor does every article
mention Unity, but the general selection of material and outlook
is directly in line with that of Unity.

Besides advertising its literature constantly through its various
publications, Unity has a special department called the Silent
Seventy, organized in 1910, which has as its major function the
free distribution of Unity literature throughout the whole world.
Maintained by the gifts of friends devoted to its particular mis-

sion, the Silent Seventy gives away freely enormous numbers of pieces of Unity literature. Its purpose is "to spread Truth teachings" and to awaken an interest in individuals who receive it to seek further help.

Silent Seventy offers for free distribution back numbers of the various periodicals, many pamphlets, and prayer cards to those who wish to co-operate. It will furnish literature free of charge in any quantity to chaplains in the armed services, to military hospitals, libraries, reading rooms, recreational centers, and clubs. A Good Neighbor Fund, administered through the Silent Seventy, provides for free literature for persons in foreign countries and for those confined in hospitals and other institutions both at home and abroad; offers the textbook, *Lessons in Truth*, and one or more free subscriptions to Unity periodicals for reading rooms, convalescent homes, orphanages, libraries, hospitals, and other institutions.

Silent Seventy has a special concern for those in prison. On receipt of a prisoner's name and address some literature is sent him. If interested he will be given a copy of *Lessons in Truth* and a free subscription to one of Unity's periodicals. A large number of prisoners take advantage of the offer, with some surprising but logical results.

Unity is also greatly concerned about a ministry to the blind, and Silent Seventy distributes three of Unity's magazines and the textbook in Braille to blind persons whose names are sent them.

All this is entirely free, sustained by gifts of interested persons. When Miss Wright, presently in charge of this service, was asked, "What would you do if some chaplain asked for a thousand copies of a given item?" she replied without hesitation, "We would simply send them." When unusually large requests are received, she consults Lowell Fillmore, president of Unity, and never once, she has said, has he told her that she could not fill a request.

Closely related to the distribution of literature as a means of making Unity's message known is its use of radio and television. Through the medium of the air, Unity reaches far beyond the

limits of its own membership and its organized centers. It goes
into homes of persons of every religious faith and none, and while
it can be switched off or on with the turn of a button, it actually
gets a wide hearing, as evidenced by the requests for literature
or help or further information concerning Unity's teaching. This
is also one of Unity's major means of advertising its literature
and so increasing the number of its readers.

The Fillmores early recognized the possibilities of a ministry
of the air. Unity was one of the first religious organizations to
broadcast its message. As early as 1922, speakers were broadcasting through a local Kansas City station. Frances J. Gable spoke
from the window of a downtown store where people could watch
the novel proceeding. In 1924 Unity purchased station WOJ and
set up a studio and tower. Mr. Fillmore usually gave two or three
talks a week, sometimes for an hour each time. Radio was still
a novelty. Few if any stations operated through the night, so the
air waves were virtually unemployed during the late night hours.
Mr. Fillmore would often advertise in his periodicals very early
morning programs, and listeners all over the United States could
hear him. It was a time when owners of radio sets played around
with them, trying to get distant stations. Not a few had their first
introduction to Unity in this way, picking up one of their programs by chance.

But the maintenance of a radio station was expensive, and in
time it became evident that a wider audience could be reached
over widely scattered commercial stations at no greater cost in
money, and probably less in effort. So in 1934 station WOJ was
discontinued, and the radio department, now an extremely important one, sought to secure outlets for its programs as widely as
possible over the country.

Wherever possible local Unity ministers broadcast over their
home stations, but from Unity headquarters every effort was
made to get commercial coverage, furnishing transcribed, prepared programs freely to stations which would use them as part
of their sustaining programs, and paying for time where this was
possible. Some seventy stations carry a program currently

known as "Unity Viewpoint," mostly at commercial rates. And these rates can vary from $8.00 to $32.00 for five minutes. Since this is a frankly propaganda type program, it has greater difficulty finding an outlet than a television program which Unity has developed recently, recognizing the importance of capturing a viewing as well as a hearing audience.

The "Daily Word Program," a five-minute TV program featuring a brief talk by Rosemary Grace Fillmore, daughter of Rickert Fillmore and granddaughter of the founders of Unity, is produced by a department of Unity and furnished free of charge to stations requesting it. It is filmed for TV and in transcription for radio, a daily dated program for each day, and is shipped on a monthly basis to stations using it.

The program, based on the little *Daily Word* magazine, is advertised as a nondenominational religious program. It includes a passage from the Bible applying to the day's dated message in the *Daily Word*, read by Rosemary Grace, followed by the meditation for that day, and closes with an inspirational "thought for the day." In 1960 it was being shown by sixty stations in thirty-four states, including Alaska and Hawaii. A number of stations use it twice a day at sign-on and sign-off time, with genuine appreciation. It is heard at almost every hour somewhere over some station or other. How many people see or hear it no one knows.

The radio program is heard outside the United States in Australia, Canada, and Panama, and in Spanish on six stations in Puerto Rico. Within the United States it is broadcast in twenty-three states and the District of Columbia, California leading with eighteen outlets, no other state having more than three. The head of the radio department has estimated a listening audience of two and a half million persons. Some seventy thousand letters are received each year from listeners, many of them seeking further information concerning Unity. There is, however, no network that carries the Unity programs.

To the publishing activity the Fillmores soon added the teaching of their ideas of practical Christianity to individuals and classes. There was at first nothing formal about it, no specific enrolment, no fixed body of instruction, just small groups gathered chiefly about Mr. Fillmore, asking questions, entering into discussion. Thus he sought to make clear to himself as well as to others what he really thought.

After a few years he had worked out a set of twelve lessons growing out of his own experience. In 1897 he was giving these lessons to regularly enrolled students in a period of two weeks, in twelve nightly sessions. Anyone who wished might enrol, but no new students would be admitted after the first session. No fee was set for the instruction or the treatments which accompanied the class when needed. Expenses, he announced in *Unity*, would be met by free-will offerings.

Mr. Fillmore was more teacher than preacher, preferring even in the larger public meetings to have free discussion if anyone wished to raise a question. It was the Fillmores' purpose to set up a school rather than establish a church. When Unity Society of Practical Christianity, the name of the local Kansas City group, was incorporated, it was not as a church but as an educational and scientific institution. And the name of the overall organization as it exists today is the Unity School of Christianity.

Repeated classes were taught by Mr. Fillmore in Kansas City. For a time summer classes were taught in Colorado also. But many requests for instruction came from distant points. It was in response to these that a correspondence course was developed, which has been taken by many thousands of persons. It has become a basic requirement of all who seek to become teachers or ministers. It was begun in 1909. The lessons were sent out to those requesting them on a free-will offering basis. Within two years, two thousand had enrolled. They wrote in from Canada, Cuba, Hawaii, England, and eventually from nearly every quarter of the world.

A great deal of the Fillmores' time was taken up in teaching. They taught classes in healing, prosperity, prayer, Truth principles, and many other subjects. Most of their students at first were local, though always there were some from farther away.

In order to make it possible for persons to use their vacations in studying Unity principles, the Fillmores organized summer courses, called Intensive Training School, which lasted two weeks and attracted students from far and wide. It was out of this that Unity Training School eventually grew.

Training for what? It is at this point that the fourth direction of Unity's organization becomes evident, and this is inextricably bound up with the educational department.

At first instruction was primarily for the personal development of the student—what is termed in New Thought generally "one's own spiritual unfoldment." But as in the case of the Fillmores themselves, this personal spiritual unfoldment brought with it a desire, even a compulsion, to share the good that had come to the student, and he in turn wanted to minister to others. This led to the formation of related groups through which Unity principles might be practiced and passed along to others who felt the same needs. Thus there soon began to be other Unity groups, and these required leadership. This meant that some kind of training was a necessity. And as the need arose, provision for meeting it had to be made. It was this that finally brought about the organization of the Training School. The multiplication of Unity Centers and groups led first to an informal meeting together of those charged with group leadership for a discussion of their common problems, and finally to the formal organization of the Unity Ministers Association.

Although this was definitely not their purpose, for as we have said, the Fillmores had no notion of establishing a church, something very much like a church began to emerge.

How should these groups in distant places be related to Unity School of Christianity? In general, the New Thought Movement had stressed individual reliance upon one's own inner experience as a guide. This had led to extreme individualism among New Thought leaders, and to a tendency for each to go his own way organizationally. But here were persons being taught and trained in a definite point of view and going out to start other centers of their own. If they were to bear the name of Unity, should there not be some measure of control from central headquarters? It was the problem which Mrs. Eddy had faced, and she had chosen to insist upon rigid controls for those who wished to call themselves Christian Scientists. Charles Fillmore had resented this attempted control, and refused to accept it. But in doing so he ceased to use the name Christian Science for what he was teaching. Precisely how Unity developed in this respect it is not easy to discover, but eventually a Field Department was set up through which outlying groups were affiliated with the movement. Standards were set for groups which wished to be Unity Centers and the qualifications determined for those who were to minister and teach in these centers. And of course Unity Training School came to furnish the necessary training for ministers and teachers.

Unity ministers naturally organized themselves into a formal Association which through an Annual Conference, in close co-operation with the Field Department of Unity, decides most questions concerning the life of Unity regarded as church. This Association, formed in 1933, operates under a Constitution and By-Laws which gives a clear picture of the relationship between Unity School and the churches and their ministers. On examination, it proves to be probably the most tightly organized and centrally controlled group among the various New Thought or Metaphysical bodies except Christian Science.

This is perhaps most clearly seen in the definition of a Unity Center in Article VI of the By-Laws, where it is stated that a Center must have as its minister a member of the Association who is accredited as licensed minister or a teacher working under the dispensation of the Field Department. According to Article III of the Constitution, membership shall consist of recognized Unity ministers who are working in co-operation with the Field Department. New applicants for membership must have been ordained by the Unity School "after having been approved by the Field Department, The Unity Training School, and the Unity Ministers Association's Executive Board."

It is thus abundantly clear that Unity School has a large

measure of control over the local groups if they wish to be a part of Unity. In the case of New Thought groups in general, it is not infrequent that a local group will call as its minister one from another New Thought group. Would this be possible in Unity? Certainly not on a literal interpretation of the articles cited. Theoretically he would first have to join the Ministers Association. But all new applicants must be ordained by Unity School, and this can only occur after the approval by the Field Department and the Executive Board of the Ministers Association.

Would they approve? A clue as to the answer may be found in an article in the By-Laws which declares that a Center, in order to be recognized as a Unity Center, "shall adhere to the Unity Teachings and text-books; and shall eliminate and avoid presentation of all text-books and teachings that do not conform to the Christ Standard as recognized by Unity School of Christianity." The loophole is in the following sentence, which reads, "This does not exclude any books or lessons that conform to this standard." Presumably, if the ideas and outlook of the candidate conformed to the Christ Standard as recognized by Unity School, he might get approval. The point is that Unity School, not the Center, will finally determine whether or not he does conform. This may be good; it may be bad; but it seems to be a fact.

The Ministers Association stipulates that the candidates for ordination must have completed the Correspondence Course, along with forty-five credits in the Training School, or completion of the Ministerial Training Program at Unity School, which presupposes that a student will have completed the Correspondence Course.

The forty-five credits are earned by taking sixteen courses of four weeks each. One credit is awarded for each class hour taken during a four-week term. Thus for a class meeting four times a week, the student earns four credits during the term. In other words, a single credit means four hours of class attendance, and the fulfilment of whatever class assignments the instructor may require. The full training course is therefore the equivalent of 180 hours of class attendance and required work.

Not more than four courses may be taken during any four-week term, nor more than eight courses in any single year. Working at the maximum rate a student could complete the course in two years of eight weeks' training each year—this of course in addition to the Correspondence Course. The school recommends that something less than maximum work be carried, so that the student may have more time for relaxation and reflection. Perfect class attendance is required for credit.

The curriculum provides certain work in four different fields: (1) Unity Fundamental Principles, which comprise Lessons in Truth, a study of Emilie Cady's *Lessons in Truth*, and Christian Healing, using *Talks on Truth* by Charles Fillmore as text, and healing practice; (2) Bible History and Interpretation, including courses in both the Old and New Testaments; (3) Courses in Center ministry including Public Speaking, Ideals and Ethics, Spiritual Counseling, and Organization and Operation; (4) General and General Required Courses which include Comparative Religion or the History of Christianity, a Seminar on the Sunday School, and Youth Work, altogether eight credits out of the total of forty-five.

There seems to be no specific educational requirement for admittance to the school. The Prospectus simply says:

Any adult 18 years of age, or older, who is interested in the teachings of Unity and who is physically and mentally able to care for himself may apply for enrollment in the Training School. However, the ability to express oneself adequately in both written and spoken English is required of those who take the course for credit.

Presumably one might enter with only a grade school education or less, and receive the certificate provided he could express himself adequately in spoken and written English and meet the demands of the teachers of the courses.

It is carefully stipulated, however, that classwork and credits alone do not insure eligibility for leadership in Unity, where poise, stability of character, and general education are considered as well as spiritual understanding.

That as much is required as appears in the published statements reveals a concern for a trained leadership. And the variety of courses offered indicates an attempt at least at a fairly well-rounded education. It is only when it is considered in comparison with standards in other churches that the meagerness of preparation is seen. Certainly it represents a distinct advance over the requirements of Christian Science, which offers only two courses of not more than twenty-four lessons in the Primary Class Instruction and Normal Class Instruction, of which the great majority take only the first. Also, there is considerable repetition in the second series of material covered in the first series. There are of course lectures by teachers to their Association meetings, and individual study of Mrs. Eddy's writings is required; but there are no formal requirements beyond these classes.

But in contrast with the modern three-year graduate seminary courses offered to, if not always specifically required of, candidates for the ministry of many of the established denominations, the Unity training appears very meager indeed. Take for example the Bible. The total offering in Unity is 64 class sessions, covering the entire Bible. Most seminaries give a general introduction to the Old and New Testaments which runs through three terms of eleven weeks each, or two terms of 16-18 weeks, meeting four times a week. A single term of 11 weeks would call for 44 class hours. The entire year of 33 weeks or more would mean 132 or more class hours, and this only the introductory course. In addition to this there are courses in the Life and Teachings of Jesus, of Paul, the Prophets, etc. Unity has made a good start, and it may be confidently expected that the standards will be raised with the passage of time. Happily, Unity gives a short postgraduate course for Unity ministers and teachers each year, just preceding the Annual Ministers Conference which takes place at Unity Village.

The Training School holds its first two terms in the spring, in April and May, and the third and fourth terms in August and September. Adequate accommodations exist in the Village in the form of cottages and motels, and Unity Inn on the grounds pro-

vides meals. It is still vegetarian, though vegetarianism is not a
necessary belief or practice of Unity. Modest fixed charges are
made for room and meals, but tuition is still on a voluntary or
"love offering" basis.

With its magnificent plant, its lovely country setting, and its
comfortable accommodations, it is little wonder that there is
almost a constant round of activities at Unity Village throughout
the year from March to December. There are retreats of various
sorts, Conferences, Ministers Association meetings, short-term
training courses, and when Unity itself is not conducting some
of its numerous activities, some other church or society is making
use of the facilities; for example, the Camps Farthest Out, the
Glenn Clark organization, has an annual session of one of its
groups at Unity. And always when facilities are available there
are individuals who come for a few days or a week or more of
quiet relaxation, meditation, and soul growth. The fact that
visitors are free to attend certain of the classes during the training
School session makes a stay at Unity an opportunity that many
covet.

Unity is broadly tolerant of others' beliefs and practices, but
in its Training School activities it adheres closely to Unity principles. Students who come to Unity, they say, have a right to
expect that only Unity teachings will be presented. Then follows
in the prospectus this rather unusual statement. "To this end,
the cooperation of every student is requested to avoid the public
discussion of other metaphysical beliefs and doctrines, however
meritorious." Somehow that does not seem to fit well with the
spirit of Charles Fillmore, at any rate in the earlier period of his
teachings, when he seemed to welcome questions of every kind
and a discussion of whatever seemed to be troubling the student.
Is this evidence of a tendency to crystallize at a certain point,
as so many movements in the past have done, notably Christian
Science?

Unity centers are now found in thirty-nine states, Washington,
D.C., and Puerto Rico. In addition there are centers in Africa,
Canada, and England. And in France, Germany, Italy, Finland,

and Brazil, Unity publications are available at certain places. The number of Centers of Unity far outranks any of the other groups which are currently, or have in the past been, related to the International New Thought Alliance.

What has been and what is Unity's relationship to the INTA? For a number of years, Charles Fillmore considered his work as a definite aspect of the New Thought Movement. He attended their congresses, spoke for them, was host to some of the International Congresses, and was a close associate of a number of the outstanding New Thought leaders. But as early as 1905, in an article in *Unity*, Mr. Fillmore wrote that so far as the Unity Society of Practical Christianity was concerned, he felt that its teachings were widely different from those of the majority of New Thought leaders, and that he did not feel at home in the average gathering under that name, though it was always his attempt to harmonize with all "seekers after Truth."

After attending a New Thought Congress in Chicago in 1906, he wrote again his growing dissatisfaction with the movement. He found, he wrote, that it had been appropriated by so many cults that had new theories to promulgate, that it had ceased to express what he thought to be absolute truth. It was attempting to "carry this load of diversity" until it seemed to him that it could not succeed. There were too many divergencies to harmonize successfully. He had come to the place where if this was really New Thought, then he must find a new name for his own philosophy. He had decided, he wrote, that he was no longer a "New Thoughter." He had a standard of faith that was true and logical, he thought, and to this he must conform his teaching. He called it Practical Christianity, and under this name he would henceforth do his work. (Quoted in *Household of Faith*, p. 104.)

This was the beginning of the separation of Unity from the INTA, though leaders of the overall movement were good friends of the Fillmores and were often invited to speak for the Unity Society. Repeated efforts were made to bring Unity back into the movement. In the meantime a formal declaration of principles had been adopted at the St. Louis Congress of INTA. On the basis of this Unity's acceptance was sought, but they felt that there was still something lacking, and proposed an additional paragraph which was adopted by the Cincinnati Congress in 1918. Unity then once more became a member of the Alliance. Royal Fillmore, son of the founder of Unity, and S. V. Ingraham, a member of the Unity staff, were added to the INTA Executive Board. Unity invited the congress to meet at Kansas City in 1920, and it did so, Unity acting as host. The congress was a successful one and the breach between the movement and Unity seemed to have been repaired. But not for long. In 1922 Unity left INTA again, and has never returned, though many local Unity Centers and individual ministers of Unity are members, and some have even served as officials—one, Rev. Ernest C. Wilson, as president. But Dr. Wilson has since withdrawn. His name and that of his church last appeared in the *Bulletin* as members in 1957. There remain, however, a goodly number who identify themselves with the Alliance and give it their warm support.

Unity has no creedal basis. Charles Fillmore once, at the urgent request of some of his followers, wrote out a *Unity Statement of Faith*, which is published by Unity as a pamphlet. But there is nothing ironclad about it. It is not even mentioned in another pamphlet also published by Unity, entitled *What Unity Teaches*. And Charles Fillmore added to this statement of faith this further declaration:

We have considered the restrictions that will follow a formulated platform, and are hereby giving warning that we shall not be bound by this statement of what Unity believes. We may change our mind tomorrow, and if we do we shall feel free to make a new statement of faith in harmony with the new viewpoint.

In his nineties Mr. Fillmore was still saying, "I reserve the right to change my mind." (*Household of Faith,* p. 170)

Charles Fillmore himself believed in and taught the doctrine of reincarnation or rebirth. Indeed, he once told the author that in an earlier incarnation he had been born as St. Paul. He had come to believe also that he had achieved physical immortality, but these beliefs apparently are no official part of Unity's teachings. While the doctrine of reincarnation is taught by some Unity leaders—Dr. Ernest C. Wilson, pastor of the important Unity Temple in Los Angeles, has published a book in support of it—others do not so believe. It is not even mentioned as such in the officially published pamphlet, *What Unity Teaches.*

If Unity differs from New Thought, it is mainly in the degree of emphasis upon what Mr. Fillmore called the Jesus Christ teaching. It is much closer in its use of language to the orthodox Christian faith, yet it clearly distinguishes between the Jesus of history and the Christ, and in its use of such terms as "the Christ in you," "the Christ consciousness," and other like phrases it is distinctly in the New Thought tradition. It speaks also of "the Omnipresence and Allness of God," the "power of creative thought," the divinity of man. "Unity holds that the higher self of man which is the true self is divine, spiritual . . . Divine Mind's perfect idea of man." It practices affirmation and denial as major techniques; its concern about healing by the Christ method is central; it affirms the availability of substance, prosperity, and well-being. All these are earmarks of New Thought, even if clothed in slightly more orthodox terminology than in the more "intellectual formulations of New Thought." But Unity displays a more warmly evangelical emphasis than most other forms of New Thought. Perhaps this is what gives it its appeal to larger numbers of people than are attracted to other New Thought branches.

Unity's growth has been steady and substantial. Its dependence wholly upon voluntary love offerings for its maintenance and extension has been a notable feature. Though it is in a way big business in the number of persons employed, its outreach, and its financial operations, it is singularly unbusinesslike in its procedures.

In an interview with Lowell Fillmore, its president, I asked concerning the financial operation of the movement. "How large is your annual budget?"

"We do not operate on a budget," he replied. "The question

is often asked, but we simply do not do it. We just go ahead and do what seems to be best or needed, and somehow it gets paid for."

"Have you any debt?"

"None," was his reply. "Some of our Centers do, but we have none at present except some current bills that have not yet been paid. Oh, yes," he added, "we did put a mortgage on a $100,000 press we bought recently in England, and we are paying it off month by month. But we have a substantial bank balance which would more than pay any outstanding indebtedness."

"Do you have any endowment?"

"None," he replied, nor did he seem interested in building up one.

"Do you have any large givers who provide large sums—an 'angel,' in common parlance?"

"None," was his answer. "Oh, we have had some fairly large gifts. One man gave us half a million dollars which came in very handy in meeting some obligations, incurred, I believe, in building."

"What would you do if someone gave you, say, a million dollars? Wouldn't you put it away and use only the income?"

"Oh, I suppose so," said he, "but we have never depended on anything like that. Father always said, if you have faith your needs will be met by the Divine Substance, of which there is no limit. We have followed that plan and it has always worked. Sometimes people do give us fairly good-sized sums, $5,000 or $10,000, on which we are to pay them interest during their lifetimes, with the understanding that it goes to Unity at their passing." This is in effect the annuity system, employed by many organizations, though he did not call it that.

"And," said he, "we now and then get a legacy. Indeed, we have a list of persons who, we hope and expect, will leave us money. But usually the legacies come to us from persons we had not thought of as likely to favor us thus."

But as I understood him, unless a gift is designated for a particular purpose, it is simply thrown into the general fund of the movement, the capital as well as income, to be spent if this is believed necessary.

"We have, at times," he remarked, "incurred a debt. Once we sold bonds to the amount of $300,000 and when they came due most people didn't want the money returned to them.

"We went into debt for land at the beginning of the purchase of the farm, and for building at various times, but always it has been paid off in due time. Bankers have come to understand our method of operation, and while at first they raise objections, when we don't know just how much a given building or other enterprise will cost, they have come to trust us."

I sought to get an estimate of the probable value of the present investment in Unity Village. Lowell Fillmore would not even suggest a figure. Rickert Fillmore said, "Somewhere in the neighborhood of $5,000,000. At least the replacement of all the facilities at present prices would reach that sum." My own guess is that it would cost considerably more.

When I asked Lowell Fillmore if he had some rather definite plans for the future, he said, no, they just did what seemed to be needed, the thing to do as things developed. He did say that Rickert Fillmore had plans for future buildings, filling out the general ground plan.

Unity has developed distinguished leadership apart from the Fillmore family, and there are able men and women who are quite capable of carrying on its far-flung ministry if called upon to do so. At the present time, however, it is still a Fillmore inspired and led movement of very considerable proportions. Of the younger generation, Charles Rickert, the son of Rickert Fillmore, is carrying heavy responsibility in the Unity enterprises. And his sister, Rosemary, is the voice of Unity over an increasing number of TV and radio stations.

8

Divine Science

FOR A LONG TIME Divine Science, one of the major constituent members of the INTA, has had its headquarters in Denver, Colorado. Probably in the minds of most people who know of Divine Science at all, it is connected with Denver. But Divine Science did not begin there. Indeed it, had two separate beginnings in the experiences of two women, neither one known to the other, and distantly removed one from the other — both experiences of what they called Divine Healing. Mrs. Cramer was healed in San Francisco, apparently a year or two previous to the healing of Nona L. Brooks in Pueblo, Colorado; but in both cases healing movements developed as a result, along lines so closely similar that when some years later they discovered each other, it was natural that their movements be fused. The name taken for the united movement, Divine Science, was one that Mrs. Cramer had adopted for her teaching.

Nona L. Brooks was born in Louisville, Kentucky, on March 22, 1861, only a few days before the firing on Fort Sumter signalized the beginning of the Civil War. She was one of a large family, one quite prosperous and comfortable, which had come from Virginia to Kentucky. They enjoyed every convenience and luxury of the day and the children were educated in private schools. Nona attended one such school in Louisville, and later graduated from the Charleston Female Academy. A typical daughter of an upper middle class family, she entered fully into the social life of the time and the community. She fell desperately in love with a young student of the University of Virginia, who

264

later went to Union Theological Seminary — and became engaged to another girl. And there were other men. She really wanted to marry and rear a family, but none of those who courted her attracted her sufficiently. Then her mother's health required a change of climate and she went to Colorado. The father's business was suddenly swept away by the discovery of a cheaper way of supplying the product upon which his fortune was based, and too late to begin over again and recover his lost wealth, he entered a new business, mining. Worried and frustrated by the effort required, he suffered a heart attack and died, leaving the family almost penniless.

They were now in Pueblo, Colorado, living on a very much lowered standard. Some of the girls married. Fannie became Mrs. Ben James, and Alethea, Mrs. Charles Small. The latter was a partner in real estate of Charles Fillmore who was later to found Unity in Kansas City, whither he had gone when the Pueblo real estate boom collapsed.

Several of the family were in extremely poor health. Nona Brooks herself developed a serious throat ailment, and finding it difficult to eat solid foods was losing weight steadily. She was under the care of a Pueblo physician, who tried by various remedies to stop the disease; but instead it grew steadily worse.

A friend of Alethea, Nona's older sister, a Mrs. Bingham, fell ill. She sought help from local physicians, but receiving no help, she went to Chicago to consult a specialist. He told her that an operation was required, and that it might take as much as a year of treatment before she could return home. But she had a family to look after. She could not take so much time. Then a friend of hers who had taken classes with Mrs. Emma Curtis Hopkins recommended that she seek her out and see if she might not be healed. She did so and in fact was healed. She returned home, enthusiastic over her healing and ardent in her desire to help other people. She invited the Brooks sisters to attend a class in which she taught what she had learned from Mrs. Hopkins. But the sisters, good Presbyterians, at first declined Mrs. Bingham's invitation.

Finally Mrs. Bingham's importunity won their reluctant consent to attend her class, but only as a mark of their friendship for
her. They were sure nothing would come of it. At the close of the
first lesson, they talked it over on their way home. Why, she said
nothing new, they said, talked mostly of Omnipresence in which
they of course already believed. Maybe the next lesson would be
better. But it was little different. Again she stressed Omnipresence. But she gave them certain things to say, even, she said, if
they did not believe them at the time. They were to repeat,
"God is my health, I cannot be sick." But Miss Brooks's throat
was a constant reminder that she could be sick. "God is everywhere, God is all, God is here," was easier to say, for of course
they had always believed this. If they saw anything less than
perfect they were to repeat again the affirmation of the Omnipresence of God.

On the third day, on the way to the class, they stopped at the
doctor's office. He examined Nona's throat. It was worse. "I have
tried about everything on it," he said, "but there is one thing
more." He gave her a prescription. "If this doesn't take care of
it, then —" he shrugged his shoulders, without finishing his
statement. They went on to Mrs. Bingham's class, and again it
was Omnipresence that she stressed. The sisters sat listening and
repeating whatever she asked them to. Then it happened. Nona
wasn't conscious of just when it occurred. But suddenly, she knew
that she was healed. It was like the light, she said afterward.
The whole room was filled with light. She thought everyone
saw it. She simply knew that she was healed. When she told
others and her sister, "I am healed," they thought she was only
affirming health. But that evening at supper for the first time in
months she ate what the rest of the family ate. She had actually
been healed.

Little is known about Mrs. Bingham, or what she did afterward. But through her, Emma Curtis Hopkins had once more
touched a life and given a start to one who was to make New
Thought history, for Nona Brooks was the cofounder of Divine
Science.

Other healing experiences occurred which deepened her wonder at and faith in the power of the consciously realized Omnipresence of God. Her niece, Alethea's daughter, was ailing. One day, just as they were returning from class, she was reported as bleeding badly. This was dangerous, for she was an easy bleeder. "You, Nona, treat the child," said Alethea, "and I'll treat for you." They had been instructed that two persons should not treat a case at the same time, though one might treat the other, thus intensifying the power of the treatment. Nona demurred. She had never done such a thing, she didn't know how, she said; but following Mrs. Bingham's directions she tried, and, amazingly, the bleeding stopped almost at once — never to recur again, as it afterward proved. A little later she heard the testimony of an old miner to a remarkable partial healing, through the treatment of Mrs. Bingham, and then actually saw the completed healing take place before their eyes, to the utter astonishment of the man who was healed.

Here was incontrovertible proof of the healing power of God. The church ought to hear about it. The sisters called the pastor of their church and told the story. He asked Nona to come to prayer meeting the following Wednesday night and tell just what had happened. She was in an agony of fear at the thought of speaking publicly, but before the appointed hour the pastor called her and withdrew the invitation, at the request of his elders, and in addition both she and her sister were relieved of their posts as teachers in the primary department of the Sunday School. The church rejected them. And so it came about that a great minister, who was to bring healing and blessing to multitudes, was forced to join — or more accurately to help in the creation of — a healing movement outside the church.

But this did not come to pass at once. Other healings occurred in cases Nona Brooks was called upon to treat, though always at first she did so very reluctantly. She attended normal school for preparation for teaching and even had a year at Wellesley College. She became a teacher in the Pueblo public school system, and later moved to Denver to pursue her career as teacher. On one occasion she came very close to marrying, but in the end decided against it.

Meanwhile, her sister, Fannie James, had begun teaching classes, just as Mrs. Bingham had done, in her newfound faith. She held the classes at first in her own home in Denver, though her husband refused to allow her to go out and give treatments. She had corresponded enthusiastically with a woman in San Francisco, Mrs. Malinda E. Cramer, who through a personal healing had come to something like the same ideas regarding healing that the Brooks sisters had, and who used essentially the same methods. She had given the name Divine Science to the system of teaching which she utilized, and had been ordained a minister.

In the year 1885, Mrs. Malinda Cramer was living in San Francisco. For twenty-five years she had been an invalid, and for twenty-three years had been under medical treatment. Living in upstate New York, she had been advised to seek a more salubrious climate and had moved to San Francisco. But the change had had no appreciable effect upon her health. She says that she had been declared incurable by a dozen doctors as well as healers — magnetic, electric, etc. — and by most of her friends. But she kept on going to physician after physician. One day the doctor who was treating her advised her to see a specialist.

Suddenly, and not at the moment understanding why, she said, "I will not see another physician." Asked then what she would do, she replied, "Get well, of course."

When later, in an hour of meditation and prayer, she asked herself why she had made the remark, she was given to know, she says, "that if I ever got well, it would be by the power of the Holy Spirit. . . . There is one way out of these conditions. I must seek that way, the Truth of the presence of Spirit." And this was the beginning not alone of her own personal healing, but of a new grasp of the nature of God,

an all absorbing realization of a presence and a power not before realized. This presence was more than personal, it was Omnipresence . . . it was real, and permanent. It was so vivifying and illumining I knew I was one with it. . . . It was as a "consuming fire" in that all things became It, and were this One Presence manifested.

Before, the presence and omnipresence of God had been a vague belief only. Now it was realization.

She was not instantly healed, but "at once saw the unreality of the condition of dis-ease and was free from the belief that they had any power or could control for either good or evil." Thus, she writes in *Divine Science and Healing* (rev. ed., Denver, 1923), "the ax was laid at the root of the tree and the old conditions passed away as fast as I disowned the old habits of belief." But she did recover completely, and was soon being asked by friends for treatment. To this she consented and with success. Soon she was setting aside one afternoon a week for the free treatment of any who might come — fifteen to twenty persons usually. This led to her teaching also, for those she treated wanted to know how to heal too, and as she sought to formulate her ideas in order to present them intelligibly to others, she was led to further meditation and further spiritual experiences. One day after treating seventeen patients, she writes, she experienced "spiritual wholeness beyond all her former conceptions. I realized," she writes, "the passing from and the blending of the individual into the Universal Spirit of consciousness." (p. 24) She experienced "the true relation existing between Cause and effect. . . . the Unity and at-one-ment existing in the Mind Infinite, its actions and the result of action." (p. 25) Now she knew "that God never thought without producing form; that the universe of form was within Omnipresent Being. This consciousness of Being was the actualization of the Truth of the Allness of God." And she asserts that this Consciousness of Being had been the one and only basis of all her work.

But is this the whole story? Did Malinda Cramer come to these ideas purely as a result of her own experience, and her reflection upon that experience? She definitely declares that the Truth she had taught for seventeen years at the time of the first publication, in 1904, of her *Divine Science and Healing*, had "been derived from no book, but from the Omnipotent Source of all Truth." (pp. 27-28)

Had she read nothing of Christian Science or the earlier New Thought writers? Warren Felt Evans had been writing for nearly twenty years and his books enjoyed a wide circulation. The *Christian Science Journal*, under Mrs. Eddy's editorship and for a time under that of Mrs. Emma Curtis Hopkins, had been appearing since 1883. Was it known in California by 1885, when Mrs. Cramer had her experience in healing? *Science and Health* had been published in 1875 and in ten years had undoubtedly become known on the West Coast. It was in 1886 that the California Metaphysical Institute was established in San Jose. Mrs. Cramer refers twice to *Science and Health* in *Divine Science and Healing*. If indeed it was only to refute one of its statements, her referring to it does indicate some degree of acquaintance with the book. But of course her own book was published years after the experience and might reflect later reading. Mrs. Emma Curtis Hopkins taught a class in San Francisco in 1887 — later, to be sure, than Mrs. Cramer's healing, but long before the publication of her book — and so could have influenced her thinking about the experience she had had and thus might have aided her in the formulation of her system of thinking.

Mrs. Cramer also mentions other books and quotes from the Hindu Bhagavad Gita, mentions the Kabbala and Hermetic philosophy, and quotes from the mystic Jacob Boehme.

If, indeed, her system was an original discovery arrived at on the basis of no previous reading or contact with persons holding "metaphysical" concepts of healing, then Malinda Cramer stands out as an unusual figure in the story of the rise of New Thought.

One day, she says, while seeking ways to express the Truth she felt, she suddenly saw clearly "The Law of Expression" which she characterizes as the distinctive thing in her teaching, to which she gave the name Divine Science. "It is," she writes, "the very bottom of Unity; it proves that we are the All-Good in Being, at one with God; we proceed forth in perfect action at one with Him and in perfect result at one with His result or creation."

She had suddenly seen in this law or trinity—Creator, Creative Action, and Creation — the Unity and fulfilment of all law; a method by which humanity could free itself "from the false race belief of separation from God, and from all errors or beliefs resulting therefrom." (p. 28)

By early 1888 she had become convinced that she must devote her entire time to teaching and healing. In May of that year she chartered the Home College of Divine Science "for educational, ethical and religious purposes; for instruction in Divine Science and its therapeutic application — the Christ method of healing." (p. 29) In August of the same year, though without financial resources to maintain it, she launched on faith, somewhat against her husband's judgment, her magazine *Harmony*. The cover page carried the statement, "A monthly magazine of Philosophy devoted to Truth, Science of Spirit, Theosophy, Metaphysics and the Christ Method of Healing."

The contents of one of the early volumes reveals a considerable acquaintance with the scriptures of other faiths — indeed, each issue carried a section called "The Bible of the Ages," which presented from time to time selections from the Hindu, the Chinese, the Egyptian, and other scriptures along with selections also from mystic writers including John Woolman the Quaker, whose presence is accounted for perhaps by the fact that Mrs. Cramer was of Quaker background. The magazine also carried news of the developing New Thought Movement, including an account of a successful class which Mrs. Cramer herself had held in Denver. For she had begun to travel and lecture and teach her newfound faith. It was this Denver visit which brought her into contact personally with Nona L. Brooks and Fannie James, the cofounders of Divine Science, though she had corresponded with the latter.

Fannie James, influenced by Mrs. Cramer, suggested to her class that they too call their teachings Divine Science. The teachings are scientific, she declared, "because they are proved in our experience," and as to the term Divine, "the entire subject concerns the understanding of God as Omnipotent." Thus Divine Science came to Denver, and has ever since been thought of as associated with that city. It was New Thought, though not so recognized by name. Mrs. Cramer's coming to Denver and holding largely attended classes and lectures gave added strength to the infant movement there. The understanding between Mrs. Cramer and the Brooks sisters was complete, and they willingly co-operated throughout the years.

Though deeply indebted to Mrs. Bingham, the Brooks sisters and emerging Divine Science moved gradually away from some aspects of her teaching on its theoretical side, particularly in respect to its concept of matter and mortal mind, in which Mrs. Bingham followed the view held by Mrs. Eddy. There can be, Nona Brooks came to believe, no Mortal Mind and Immortal Mind, but "one Mind, and that one God, Perfect! Everywhere present! Not two minds, but one." (Hazel Deane, *Powerful Is the Light: The Story of Nona Brooks,* Divine Science College, Denver, 1945, p. 88) It is like light and darkness, she said: "In the light of God's Presence the darkness disappears." Is there then no evil, no matter? These exist in fact, she thought, "but only if we in our thought and feeling misuse the spirit within us which is God, First Cause, and so create evil." (p. 88)

Later, in a formal published statement of *Divine Science: Its Principles and Faith,* evil was to be defined as "a false belief in a presence and a power other than God.... So long as a man believes in a lie, he is subject to it in his experience. As soon as he sees clearly, he sees no evil." (p. 10) And matter was defined as "Pure divine energy manifesting as form. There is no such thing as matter, meaning the opposite of Spirit, for Spirit and matter are two aspects of the same substance," a definition closely akin to that of Warren F. Evans.

Nona Brooks continued teaching. It was her living, for the family fortunes had left her no legacy, even after her mother's passing. She wanted to devote her time to teaching her newfound faith and healing. Fannie's classes had outgrown her home and one of the grateful patients who had been healed under Alethea's treatment offered them rooms, rent free, in a downtown building which provided a classroom which would accommodate a hundred people and smaller rooms for counseling and treatment. Alethea asked her sister to take over the work during the summer vacation which would give her a chance to see if that was what she really wanted to do. Within a month she knew. She sent in her resignation from the school system and though sometimes during the first years she was tempted to return to teaching, she never did so. It was the beginning of a lifelong commitment to the ministry of Christian healing.

At first it was mostly incurables who came, she says. If there was any hope of healing at the hands of materia medica, the people preferred it, for those who made a religion of healing were considered queer. It was a great shock to the more affluent relatives that the sisters had turned to the practice, and they kept it as quiet as possible back in Kentucky.

Soon there arose the question of payment for treatment. Often there was no mention of any payment at all, only a "thank you, Miss Brooks." She was embarrassed, yet she had to have an income. She allowed herself no luxuries, yet she was hardly able to pay for her room rent and board. But she would not turn back to teaching. Even as she worked long hours, far longer than she had worked at schoolteaching, she was learning and growing in her skill and ability to meet the considerable problems that continued to arise.

In 1898, the group that had begun in Fannie James's home and were now in the Moffatt Building downtown incorporated as the Divine Science College. They offered classes in the "Fundamentals of Divine Science," a Bible Course, and a Normal Course for the preparation of teachers of Divine Science. As texts they used Mrs. Malinda Cramer's *Divine Science and Healing* and a new book by Fannie James, *Truth and Health*. The latter is still published by the movement, and continues to be used even today, though supplemented now by a number of booklets by Nona Brooks and other Divine Science writers.

What Nona Brooks and her sisters were reading during those years her biographer does not state. She mentions the writings of Quimby, Evans, Mrs. Eddy, Helena Blavatsky, Emilie Cady,

Ralph Waldo Trine, Henry Wood, and others, but says that the sisters "paid these writers no heed at all, but evolved their own theory, accepting this and discarding that, out of the very business of living." (p. 108) In the natural course of events absent treatments were undertaken, with success. After all, it was logical that if Mind were everywhere, as the idea of Omnipresence would imply, then distance should be no obstacle to treatment. Nona Brooks was inclined to follow Mrs. Bingham in the single treatment instead of repeated treatments and she would sometimes spend long hours in one, remaining with the patient until the healing came. But as multiple demands were made upon her time this was not always possible, and she would begin a treatment at one time and continue it later until she had the assurance of healing.

Her failure to prevent a patient from dying at first deeply troubled her, until she came to realize that she should treat not against death, but for life, and it came to her that life went on, only on another plane. We are immortal now if we are immortal at all, she believed. Death was only a passing incident in a life. Man, as it was later to find expression in *Divine Science: Its Principles and Faith,* "is immortal. God knows each man as an individual expression of Infinite, Eternal, Everlasting Life." (p. 10)

In 1898 Fannie remarked to her that the ladies of their following wanted to have a morning church service, and wanted her to lead it. They had been holding a meditation meeting on weekday mornings and a Sunday five o'clock vesper service. But, a Sunday morning service! That would put them in direct competition with the orthodox churches which held their principal service at that time, and it would, she suddenly thought, make her a minister. There were few women ministers in those days. At first she refused. Anyway, to do this she would have to be ordained and that would mean going to California and having Mrs. Cramer do it, and for that there was of course no money. But the money was forthcoming, and to California she went, was ordained, and returned the Rev. Nona L. Brooks, to hold the first Divine Science Sunday morning church service on January 1, 1899.

As minister of the church and president of the college, she served for a generation. The early meeting place was soon outgrown. In 1902 she began publication of a small inspirational monthly magazine which she edited, called *Fulfillment*. This was published until 1906 when it was superseded by the *Divine Science Quarterly*, which appeared for six years, then gave way to *Power Magazine* and was continued under that name until 1915. In December of that year the publication of *Daily Studies in Divine Science* was begun. The studies of the first issue were prepared by Mrs. Alice R. Ritche, as were those of many issues in the years following.

This, so far as I have been able to discover, was the first of the New Thought publications to publish such daily studies, though it is done regularly now by several of the groups. For example, *Daily Word* of Unity, *Religious Science* of the IARSC, and *Science of Mind* regularly issue such daily studies. Among non-New Thought groups several similar periodicals appear, some of wide circulation. For example, *Upper Room*, published at Nashville, Tennessee, originating in the Methodist church but serving a vast number of other churches as well, is issued in thirty-eight editions, thirty-one of them in languages other than English. Oral Roberts' organization is one of the latest to enter the field, with a publication patterned closely after Unity's *Daily Word*, though of course highly orthodox and conservative in its theological point of view.

In 1930 the *Daily Studies* were incorporated into the *Divine Science Monthly*, and in 1951 this in turn became *Aspire*, which continues the numbering of the volumes begun with the *Daily Studies*.

The official publication of Divine Science has never aspired to be a magazine of general circulation, though it has been widely read beyond the limits of Divine Science itself by followers of other branches of New Thought. Its main function has been and is the inspiration and instruction of those who follow the way of

Divine Science. It is in a real sense a house organ of that segment of the New Thought Movement. It has maintained the same pocket-size format for most of its existence, and the contents have been of about the same nature across the years. Usually there are a few devotional or inspirational articles, sometimes a historical article — as for example that by Nona Brooks in the November, 1938, issue, telling of the early days of the movement — an occasional poem or two, then the daily studies for each day of the month.

This usually consists of a brief passage or two from the Bible, with appropriate comment from some New Thought leader, generally one from within Divine Science. Frequently specific suggestions are made for some practical application of the daily study, and affirmations are supplied in keeping with the thought for the day. It becomes in effect a guide to daily study of the Bible and Truth from the standpoint of Divine Science. Occasional news of what is happening in Divine Science Centers is included, together with the names, addresses, and hours of availability of all Divine Science practitioners; a directory of all Divine Science Centers; and in more recent years a listing of the members of the Federation International of Divine Science Churches and Colleges.

Naturally, the special services of Divine Science are kept before the readers of the magazine. There is the Prayer Ministry, which is somewhat similar to that of Silent Unity. Also announced are the Home Study courses, conducted by correspondence for the benefit of those who may be unable to attend the regular courses offered at the college in Denver. And of course the readers are kept posted on the literature of the movement, as well as other Truth literature. The issues run from forty-eight to sixty-four or occasionally more pages.

Meanwhile, Divine Science was spreading. Mrs. Cramer had held a convention as early as 1894 in San Francisco, and others followed in successive years, held in Chicago, Kansas City, and St. Louis.

In the earlier years of the movement, treatments were given

only for the healing of physical ailments. But it was apparent that some of these arose from financial and other emotional worries, so it seemed logical enough to treat for these also. Miss Brooks came to depend on treatment for supply in connection with the mounting expense of maintaining her work. And it seemed to be effective. Sometimes it was for hymnals that were needed, or sometimes a new rug, or furniture, and eventually a new church building. At first it was her custom to treat for specific things, but then she came to treat more and more for "the spiritual equivalent of things." (*Powerful Is the Light,* p. 145) "Abundant supply is mine for every financial demand made upon me," she would affirm until she established "the certainty of abundant supply." When this certainty came, she wrote, "all burden of action falls away." (p. 145) Never, she learned, should she limit "the direction from which her good was to come." At length she came simply to say, if need arose, "You'll have to take care of this, Father." And, she adds, "invariably the need was met." (p. 147)

Students were being trained in the classes at the college, and were going out to found new centers. They were not always called Divine Science centers. There was as yet no firm overall organization of Divine Science churches.

In the summer of 1917 Dr. W. John Murray asked Miss Brooks to occupy his pulpit in New York while he took a much-needed long vacation. His was the largest New Thought group then in the city. It was called the Church of the Healing Christ. He was speaking to huge crowds at the Waldorf-Astoria Hotel, and his Astor Lectures were widely read and influential. He asked that his church might be called the First Church of Divine Science as well as the Church of the Healing Christ, and this was done. On his return to his pulpit Miss Brooks was asked to remain in New York and start another center there. But she was certain that her work lay in Denver.

It had become the custom to list in the monthly periodical the various centers where Divine Science was established. In 1916 there were but three Divine Science churches with a resident minister listed. They were located in Denver, in Oakland, California, and in Seattle. There was one also listed in Oklahoma with only a practitioner, not a minister, in charge. There were twenty-one workers in the list, but only three of them were ministers. The rest were either teachers, practitioners, or teachers and practitioners, and one was rated as an "individual instructor." Fourteen of these were in Denver. In addition there were "student groups," each under a leader, five in Colorado cities other than Denver and one each in Illinois, Maryland, and California.

By 1918 there were churches also in Boston, Portland, Spokane, St. Louis, New York, and by 1925 churches had been opened in Los Angeles, San Diego, and Sacramento, California; Topeka, Kansas; Washington, D. C.; two in Illinois; one each in Iowa and Cleveland, Ohio; and two additional ones in the state of Washington. The movement was expanding steadily.

Meanwhile the old building in Denver had long been inadequate. Land had been bought in the early years of World War I, but the time was not then propitious for an ambitious building campaign. It was not until after the end of the war that a still more suitable location was found and purchased and plans for actual building were set on foot. Then the money came in with an ease that surprised the Board, which was made up predominantly of businessmen. In 1922 the church, a $90,000 structure, was dedicated, and in 1925 the final indebtedness was paid off. The church and college were now housed in a dignified, architecturally handsome edifice with a large sanctuary and numerous rooms for the educational and social ministry which they were carrying on.

Meanwhile James A. Edgerton, former Denver newspaperman, had become prominent in the growing New Thought Movement, was president of the International New Thought Alliance, and had interested Miss Brooks in the work of the Alliance. She took her movement into the INTA in 1922. She attended their annual congresses and spoke often on the platform there and at regional conventions. She served on important committees, and became one of the most trusted and influential of the leaders in that organization.

As early as 1918 she had attended a congress on the West Coast, where she had met for the first time a young man, Ernest Holmes, who was just getting started in the work which was eventually to become the Church of Religious Science. He had recognized in her a speaker of power and watched her carefully. "Why," she asked him, "do you watch me so closely?"

"Because I want to find out why you are a leader. I want to discover where you get your power."

Here was a young man who would be a distinguished leader himself, trying to discover the secret of the success of a leader he admired. He found, he said, that she got it from "Omnipresence." "You continually hark back to Omnipresence," he declared. He was right.

Now Nona Brooks was often asked to speak at important gatherings. In 1927 she was given a trip abroad by her friends, and spoke in various foreign centers. And she was receiving coveted recognition at home as well. She was asked to serve on Boards for various civic and philanthropic purposes. For years she was a member of the State Prison Board. She had never joined the Ministerial Association, but nearly thirty years after the beginning of her ministry she was welcomed to membership in it.

At the height of her popularity, she decided to resign as minister of her church. Against great opposition, and only after a man had been found who might replace her temporarily, she was permitted a leave of absence from the church, though continuing for a time as president of the college.

For a time she was undecided as to what to do. Then came an opportunity to go to Australia, and she spent a year there, working in Melbourne, Sidney, and Adelaide. This was a memorable visit to the Australian New Thought Movement. A Divine Science Church is still listed at Adelaide, South Australia. After that Miss Brooks spent some time in Chicago, serving there in one of the centers; spoke often in summer conferences of New Thought; and spent her winters in San Antonio, Texas.

In 1938 she was invited back to be president of the college,

and served it until 1943, when Dr. Irwin Gregg, former popular
Unity minister in Detroit, came to take over the pastorate of
the church and the presidency of the college. It was that year that
Dr. Raymond Charles Barker, then president of INTA, introduced
her to a great congress meeting as "Our best loved leader," to the
enthusiastic applause of the entire gathering.

Two years later, on March 14, 1945, only eight days before
her eighty-fourth birthday, Nona Brooks passed away, one of the
really "greats" of the entire New Thought Movement.

She wrote very little, only a few small booklets, most of them
still circulated by the Divine Science Church and College:
*Mysteries, Short Lessons in Divine Science, Studies in Health,
The Prayer That Never Fails,* and *Truth Prayers for Little Folks.*

While most of the leaders of Divine Science have received
their training at the Divine Science College of Denver and have
gone out to start Divine Science groups in other cities, by no
means all of them did so, and some of those taught at Denver
did not call their organization Divine Science. Also some who
did take the name Divine Science founded and maintained Colleges of Divine Science which likewise trained leaders, who in
turn established centers, or served as registered workers, the
name usually given to practitioners.

But the relationship between Divine Science groups had not
been cemented by any firm sort of organization until the Divine
Science Federation International was organized. It was the feeling of need for some more definite sort of organization that led
to the formation on January 15, 1957, of the Divine Science
Federation International, a union of co-operative Divine Science
organizations, standing firmly on the Omnipresence of God. While
each member is almost entirely autonomous, the Federation brings
them together into a more closely knit overall body, and local
churches find mutual help and reinforcement because of their
membership in it.

Membership in the Federation is open to Divine Science
churches and to individuals who are properly sponsored by one
of the member organizations. There are three classes of member-

ship, patron, regular, and associate, the difference being in the respective membership fees, presently $18.00, $12.00, and $6.00 per year.

The controlling body of the Federation is the House of Delegates, composed of the individual members of the Federation who attend the session and as many official delegates as each member organization chooses to appoint. However, they do not vote individually, but by organizations, and non-officially appointed members who may attend have no vote at all. Presumably the organization vote is determined by a majority vote of its officially appointed delegates. The freedom of the floor is allowed to all who attend the Federation's annual meeting.

The House of Delegates elects a General Council of five members with staggered terms, which carries on the affairs of the Federation in the interim between annual meetings.

"Unification without regimentation" is one of the aims of the Federation, in the belief that Divine Science can be advanced and its purposes achieved better through united effort than by the various organizations' operating separately. Practical ends better served thus are the republication of older books now out of print and the publication of new literature; the improvement of the general plan of religious training for children and youth, through the issuing of more suitable lesson materials and helps; the publication of a new hymnal, etc. And it was hoped that through their combined efforts the standards of the training of ministers, teachers, and practitioners, as well as individual members, might be continuously raised.

At first member organizations were listed on a page of *Aspire*, the monthly magazine published by the First Divine Science Church in Denver, which had been considered generally as the headquarters of Divine Science. In another section were listed other Divine Science churches and approved regular "workers." Now only member churches and colleges are listed in *Aspire*, which, though still published by the First Church in Denver, is declared to be the official organ of the Federation. The Federation does publish a *News Letter*. Headquarters of the Federation is in the First Church in Denver, which is now considered simply as one of the constituent churches.

Membership in the Federation has grown steadily. A recent *News Letter* lists four new organization members added during the past year. Gradually the other Divine Science institutions are taking membership in the Federation, and new ones are being formed or added from other sources. A list published in a 1959 issue of *Aspire* showed thirteen member organizations; the 1962 listing in the November *News Letter* of that year included twenty-six. There is no published report of the number of individual members.

The Federation has published a pamphlet, *Divine Science: Its Principles and Faith,* which sets forth, as I have nowhere else found it, a concise statement of the beliefs commonly held by Divine Science. It is not presented as a formal creed to which all members are required to subscribe, but it does offer a good idea as to what is generally held by followers of Divine Science.

Like Unity, Divine Science tends to use terms familiar to members of the orthodox churches, but a meaning is given to them that is less orthodox. If there is any one point on which Divine Science insists with reference to its belief in God, it is that God is Omnipresence. A statement of what the term "Divine" stands for is this: "The Fatherhood of God as Omnipotent Life, Substance, Intelligence, Power." (p. 6) But the pamphlet goes on to say that Divine Science does not conceive of God as a person, but as a "Universal Mind Presence." The Trinity, of which it freely speaks, is "Mind, Idea, Consciousness" or in other terms "Spirit, Soul, and Body." The nature of God is "wisdom, love, knowledge, understanding, power, life, joy." (p. 8) The stress upon the idea of God as Mind clearly reveals the close kinship of Divine Science with New Thought generally.

All bodies and natural objects are seen as "Ideas in the mind of God, taking form according to the original divine pattern." (p. 8) Man is defined as "the individualized expression of God . . . the Christ Idea in Divine Mind." He makes his own world "to the extent that he measures his good to himself in terms of thinking." He does not create the good that he experiences in his own life, for God, Mind, is the only Creator, but "through his right thinking he becomes aware of the good that is always at hand." (p. 9)

Evil is thought of as a "false belief in a presence and power other than God. . . . As soon as he sees clearly, he sees no evil." Man is immortal as "an individual expression of Infinite, Eternal, Everlasting Life." Death is not what our senses report it to be, but "an incident in an unbroken and endless life." The individual goes on existing, learning, and unfolding in the same Divine Presence, guided by the One and only Presence and Power. (p. 11)

Divine Science affirms that it no longer separates the Christ and Jesus, as do most metaphysical groups, for it declares: "He who was the historical Jesus of Nazareth became the full embodiment of Christ Consciousness, which earned for him the title Christ Jesus." It is difficult, however, to see how this differs greatly from the usual New Thought pattern.

Divine Science teaches the principle of healing, as it believes this was taught and practiced by Jesus Christ. It does not deny the fact or reality of disease, but declares that "The Power of Love that freely forgives all our iniquities, just as willingly heals our diseases. We know the same Source for health as for forgiveness, and one is as surely granted as the other." (p. 11)

And the characteristic New Thought attitude toward Abundance or Supply is expressed in the statement that "All the richness of God is ours. His good awaits our acceptance in every area of our lives. We bring it forth through the law of realization which comes from affirmation and action." (p. 12)

Perhaps Divine Science stresses prayer more than do some of the New Thought groups, but prayer is defined as simply

acknowledging, affirming, and acting according to the true nature of being. Prayer is a state of receptivity in which Truth is accepted. It is communion with God and realization of the Divine Presence. Affirmative prayer opens man's mentality to the flow of the great Universal Mind, and he receives what has been there all the time for him. (p. 9)

The dual origin of Divine Science in the experience and work of the Brooks sisters in Colorado and of Mrs. Cramer on the West Coast is recognized in the official textbook, *Divine Science: Its Principle and Practice,* which is a compilation from *Divine Science and Healing,* by Mrs. Cramer, and *Truth and Health,* by Mrs. Fannie James.

9

Religious Science

LATEST TO EMERGE of the larger groups usually considered to be a part of the New Thought Movement was the Church of Religious Science. Not that they called themselves New Thought, or even considered themselves a part of the movement known as New Thought, in the earlier days. Indeed, some who shared in the earlier phases of what is now called Religious Science have rather indignantly insisted that they were never "New Thought-ers." But if they differed in some important respects from other recognizable New Thought bodies, their emphasis upon the aims common to New Thought groups—the centrality of Mind, their concept of man as divine, their insistence upon the immanence of God to a point scarcely to be distinguished from pantheism, their clear distinction between the Jesus of history and the Christ, and their practice of metaphysical healing—these and other characteristics unmistakably indicate that they are one part of a general movement which rightly or wrongly has come to bear the name New Thought.

Furthermore, for years they have actively participated as a constituent movement in the International New Thought Alliance. The founder, Ernest Holmes, was himself an active member, speaking frequently at INTA congresses and serving as officer or chairman of important committees and as editor of one of the few publications put out by the Alliance, *Mind Remakes Your World*. One of his books bears the title *Dictionary of New Thought Terms*, and a substantial percentage of the local churches of Religious Science and/or the ministers of these churches are listed as active—many as Life—members of the Alliance.

The Church of Religious Science was founded by Ernest Shurtleff Holmes, though it was only in more recent years that the present name came to be employed. It was his mind that conceived the particular formulation of ideas that is basic to the movement. It was his pen that wrote the textbook, *Science of Mind,* which is the basis of its present teaching; it was he who launched the magazine, *Science of Mind,* which has been its main literary expression. He also is author of numerous books and articles supplementing his text. All these writings not only furnished stimulus, inspiration, and positive instruction in the realm of thought, but also spelled out the methods by which the ideas they discuss might be practically implemented and made to function in the lives of individuals and society. On the organizational side he has been less of a creative force, and has sometimes had to be pressured into taking the necessary organizational steps to insure the permanent effectiveness of his message.

Ernest Holmes came from away down East. Born January 21, 1887, in a rural section of the State of Maine, the youngest of the nine children of William N. and Anna C. Holmes, he spent his boyhood in a home of relative poverty, which knew nothing of the comforts and conveniences, to say nothing of the luxury, in which his more mature later years were to abound. But though they were poor in this world's goods and forced by financial reverses to move about from place to place, thus making it hard for Ernest to get even the meager schooling provided in the district and small town schools where the family lived, it was, on the whole, a happy wholesome family life they lived. An older brother, Fenwicke, has written a biography of Ernest Holmes in which he brings alive in graphic fashion the family life of the Holmeses as the children were growing up. It is a fascinating story of a typical family of the period.

There were three books, as Fenwicke tells it, that were in constant use by the Holmes family. The first was the Bible, the second *The Story of the Bible,* a larger book containing many pictures of biblical scenes, some in color, which from his description seems to have been the one the writer remembers poring over endlessly as a boy, sometimes lying stretched out flat on the living room floor, the book lying open in front. The third, strangely enough, was the famous *Natural Law in the Spiritual World,* by Henry Drummond, which, says Fenwicke, his parents somewhat secretly read. It could be that Ernest's later emphasis on science, as indicated by the name of his book and of his magazine, *Science of Mind,* and the Institute of Religious Science which he later founded, stems ultimately from Drummond's relatively scientific approach to religion.

Ernest did not get to college. His only degrees were honorary ones which came to him much later in recognition of the remarkable extent to which he succeeded in educating himself through his wide reading and his contacts with minds which had enjoyed the advantages of formal schooling.

Fenwicke, four years Ernest's senior, was more fortunate. He entered and completed the course at Colby College, then went on to study at Hartford Theological Seminary and enter the Congregational ministry. In 1912 he went to Venice, California, a suburb of Los Angeles, and started the Congregational church in that city. During his six-year pastorate he won a numerous following and built a substantial new church.

Though he had little formal schooling, Ernest was a great reader. From boyhood he was always seeking answers as to why things were as they were. He early got hold of Emerson's essay, "Self Reliance," which made a deep impression on him and became one of the great formative influences in his life. This was the period of Chatauqua lectures, and Ernest must frequently have heard them. It was perhaps this that inspired him to want to become a platform speaker. He entered the Powers School to prepare for such a career.

He made a trip West to visit Fenwicke in California, liked it, and spent the rest of his life there. Once he entered Pomona College, but he didn't like that and quit. He began to help Fenwicke in his church in Venice, often giving dramatic recitals there. He found employment as a playground director for the city, and this he liked very much. Fenwicke became involved in a political affair. Ernest helped him, and they won the campaign.

He continued reading widely. Meanwhile, Fenwicke had become interested in and had read some of the books of W. W. Atkinson, who wrote under the pen name of Swami Ramakaracha. He is considered one of the early and great exponents of what is now called New Thought. Together the brothers took a correspondence course with Christian D. Larson, another of the influential New Thought leaders. This was with no idea of ever becoming themselves followers of the new faith. A great many ministers have privately read and studied the works of writers in this field without ever becoming "New Thoughters," and have greatly enriched their ministry by so doing. Others, as for example William H. D. Hornaday, now pastor of the great Founder's Church of Religious Science in Los Angeles, who was a Methodist minister in California when he began to listen to the broadcasts and read the writings of Ernest Holmes, have found in his teachings a deeper satisfaction than in their own faiths and have eventually become members of the Religious Science clergy.

Ernest had read *Science and Health*, the Christian Science textbook, while a student in Boston, at the age of eighteen. He became interested in the similarities between Christian Science and New Thought. In later years after he was firmly established it was told of him that his mother was a Christian Science practitioner. But this was not a fact. She did, years later, become an effective and much loved Religious Science practitioner, but at no time was she ever a Christian Scientist, much less a practitioner.

Throughout his long life Ernest never lost interest in the techniques of mental science healing. Whenever he met a practitioner of any school he would immediately ask him to explain his system in detail. This was true in regard to Christian Science. While he never himself became an adherent, he held great respect for it, and when he became acquainted with a practitioner in Los Angeles, he asked her to give him a full course of lessons in practice, which she did. After some months she told him he knew all she could teach him.

It was at this time that he became acquainted with the writings of Thomas Troward, onetime English judge in the Punjab, India. He was elated to find there an elaboration and confirmation of conclusions he had reached from his own wide reading and study. "This is as near to my own thoughts as I shall ever come," he said. The first lecture he ever gave was to a group of people in a private home in Venice, California, in which he explained passages in *The Edinburgh Lectures* by Troward.

Meanwhile he was reading and memorizing poems by Walt Whitman and Robert Browning, as well as prose and poetry by Ralph Waldo Emerson, both because of their metaphysical content and his love of verse. Suddenly aroused by the common denominator in all he was reading, which included the Bible, he became enthusiastic about the idea of devoting his life to the formation of a synthesis of all of them. This he began to do— a task which occupied his entire life, coming to climax in 1960, when *The Voice Celestial* was published. On the jacket of the book the two brothers, Ernest and Fenwicke, indicate its content in these words, "Questions all thoughtful men have asked, answered by the wisdom of the ages."

In his later life Ernest gave generous tribute to his sources, emphasizing particularly Troward and Emerson. But, as a matter of fact, asserts Fenwicke, "they were but percussion caps, exploding his own mental energies," thus helping him along the road toward the synthesis he ultimately achieved in his fully developed Religious Science, his major contribution to his world. Whatever the degree of his indebtedness to Troward—and it is probable he generously overstated it—there can be no doubt that Ernest Holmes was one of the main channels through which Troward's influence has been felt in American circles. Nor is there any doubt that the combined influence of Troward and the Holmes brothers has made the term "Mental Science" or "the Science of Mind" known to millions of readers in this country and abroad.

In 1917 Ernest and Fenwicke Holmes joined forces to found

the Metaphysical Institute and to launch themselves as full-time teachers of their individual interpretation of Mental Science. They founded a magazine called *Uplift* and published it under Ernest's name. In 1919 they merged this with *Truth Magazine,* published by A. C. Grier of the Church of Truth. During the years 1917-19 the brothers lectured in the Grand Theater, Los Angeles, as well as in Long Beach. About the same time they established also the Metaphysical Sanitarium in Long Beach. In 1918 they moved out of Long Beach into Los Angeles. Meanwhile both men were also engaged in writing, and both published their first books in 1919. Ernest's title was *Creative Mind* and Fenwicke's was *The Law of Mind in Action.* Both went into more than twenty printings during the next forty years.

About this time the interest in a metaphysical approach was great in the eastern cities, particularly New York and Boston. Dr. W. John Murray was attracting large crowds to his Sunday lectures and classes. Both Ernest and Fenwicke made trips East in 1920 and gave a series of public lectures and classes in the Colonial Room of Hotel McAlpin. They were billed as the Holmes Brothers, Founders of the Southern California Metaphysical Institute, Los Angeles, California. The lectures were free, the classes at a price. Their announced topics included "The Meaning of the New Movement," Fenwicke; "The One Law of Mind and Matter," Ernest; "The Law of Wholeness," Ernest; "Beating the Law of Karma," Fenwicke; "The Thought and the Thing," Ernest; and "Our View of God," Fenwicke.

The series was successful—and profitable. It was repeated again and again in the next few years, in New York, Philadelphia, Boston, and other cities. Free lectures drew full theater audiences, and in the classes there were sometimes as many as a thousand, at a fee of as much as twenty-five dollars for a course of lessons.

But Ernest Holmes liked Los Angeles and wanted to settle down there. About 1923 he began lecturing in the Philharmonic Theater. His following grew steadily. He was an excellent platform man, a speaker of genuine power, but he also liked to teach. Fenwicke preferred the lecture platform. There was no disagreement between them but in 1925 the brothers dissolved their partnership and each took up his preferred work. Fenwicke went East and had phenomenal success as lecturer and writer. Ernest put his roots deep down in the rapidly growing city of Los Angeles and grew with it.

Through these years Ernest broadened the scope of his reading. He was attracted by Eckhart and the other great mystics. Some of the writings of Emma Curtis Hopkins came to his attention. Though well along in years, she was still teaching, at least individuals. He sought her out and was ushered into her presence. She was always the grand lady, formally dressed and wearing a hat as though about to go out. She greeted him coolly and began to talk. She talked steadily for an hour, and then he knew he had had his first lesson. He returned again and again. She eventually unbent and they became fast friends. His association with her added a new dimension to his thinking. He was to rate her along with Eckhart as the greatest of the mystics. It was not, says Fenwicke, through this experience that he had his first intimation of "cosmic consciousness," but here it became a basic element of religion to him. What it was and meant the brothers much later attempted to say in their epic poem *The Voice Celestial* (New York: Dodd, Mead, 1960) which was finished only a little while before Ernest Holmes's passing in 1960. An experience essentially ineffable and indescribable, something of its nature is nevertheless set forth in the section of the poem called "Illumination and Intuition."

> I stood upon the shore of
> The Larger Life, I heard its swelling tide,
> I felt its lapping waves upon my feet.
> Uninvited, the unknown became the known,
> The invisible was seen. A voice spoke
> And I heard it. Beyond all reasoned thought,
> It spoke a language that feeling and only feeling
> Can interpret . . . but *real*, oh, so real!
> Illusive, fluidic, but substance of
> All substance, Illumination came! (p. 157)

In his later years, says Fenwicke, Ernest had frequent experiences of world or cosmic consciousness. It came to him almost at will, and at times he remained for considerable periods immersed in it. It had the effect of lifting his personal treatments to higher levels.

In 1926 Ernest Holmes published his *Science of Mind*, the textbook designed for study by all those who sought seriously to follow his teachings. Fenwicke had written a book under the same title two years earlier, but did not object to Ernest's using it also. His book has been repeatedly revised, of course, across the years, but it still stands as the basic formulation of the Ernest Holmes philosophy and teaching, which is followed in all of Religious Science.

If, as has been alleged, the heart of Ernest Holmes's teaching is to be found in the first four introductory chapters of *Science of Mind*, then in very brief summary this is what he finally evolved as his synthesis of the great ideas of the founders of the world religions and the philosophers of the past, including the philosophers of New Thought, for which he declared in another connection that he was a natural candidate.

There is first of all the Thing Itself. The very study of Science of Mind is a study of First Cause, Spirit, Mind, or that invisible Essence, that ultimate Stuff and Intelligence from which everything comes, the Power back of creation, the Thing Itself. It is apparently that which elsewhere, he says, he finds at the heart of every religion, One Reality, an Unseen upon which men of all faiths have an instinctive reliance. This Mind, Spirit, Causation, is beyond the complete grasp of an individual mind. "We are It to the extent that we grasp It," he says; but being finite, we can never encompass it entirely because it is infinite. Mind is subjective and objective. There are not two minds, but one; the objective is the conscious, the subjective the subconscious, the latter being that part of the mind which can be set in motion as a creative force by the conscious state. Man has thus at his command limitless power because he is one with the whole on the subjective side, "for there is but one subjective Mind."

What we call our subjective mind, he says, is "really the use we are making of the One Law. Each individual maintains his identity in Law through his personal use of it. And each is drawing from Life what he thinks into it." (p. 29) Everyone on the subjective side of Life, he explains, is universal and only individual "at the point of conscious perception." Every time we make use of our own minds we make use of the creative power of the Universal Mind. And all thought is creative. "There is that in each one of us which partakes of the nature of the Divine Being," and we are therefore divine.

Now, how does it work? The essence of the whole teaching is, he suggests, that the Thing Itself, Mind, Intelligence, Spirit, finds "conscious individual centers of expression through us." Man's intelligence is indeed, he asserts, this Universal Mind "functioning at the level of man's concept of It. It works for us by working through us. It can work in no other way." But it can become power to us "only when we recognize it as Power." Hence our belief in it sets limits to the demonstration of a power which is itself limitless Power. "Only as much as we can believe, therefore, can be done to or for us."

What does it do? Well, it works through us, and according to Law. Once understood, any law operates quite impersonally. Love is the essence of the Thing, yet even "Love rules through Law." (p. 43) "Love points the way and Law makes the way possible." It is necessary that the mind conceive before the creative Energy can produce a desired result, and we humans have to be the channels through which it works. We are forever surrounded by Infinite Good. But only so much of it is ours to use as we can embody. Treatment is a conscious direction of the creative energy in a particular way, which if done in faith is effective. The greater one's faith that his thought has power, the more power the treatment will have in effecting a desired end.

How then may we use it? By conscious thinking we make use of the Universal Law of Mind, and cause It to do things for us through us. It responds quite without respect to persons. It is ever ready and willing to operate in obedience to our creative belief. This law we did not create, nor can we change it. As we understand it and use it according to its true nature, "it works for us by flowing through us." As a result of right treatment, Holmes says, "the mold formed in the subjective mind makes possible a concrete manifestation." Treatment is an intelligent Energy in the invisible world, he asserts. "It is a spiritual entity working through the Law of Mind, and is an actual force now consciously directed. Therefore it must produce specific results." (p. 57)

The implications of these fundamental ideas for practical living are drawn out in greatest detail in his further teaching and writing. While there is stress upon meditation and the inner life, the outcomes of this have rich meaning in health, happiness, and the enjoyment of the good life. Nor are these values delayed until a future life, though the teaching with regard to the continuing life of the spirit is clear and constant. Along with the stress on the inner life goes a vigorous gospel, ethically based and deeply Christian in spirit, for both the individual and social life of man.

This is of course only a brief glimpse of the thought of Ernest Holmes. Each of these great ideas he argues and embroiders in a thousand ways, seeking to make them intelligible and relevant to every man, through his textbook, his lectures, and his many other writings. He had a rare way of making old theological concepts meaningful in a new way to a changing age—for example, his resolution of the difficult Christological problem of the two natures, human and divine, in Christ. And his use of the Bible is constant, though he quotes freely also from scriptures of other faiths as well.

Wealthy and influential friends again wanted Ernest to organize. They insisted that a group, organized around an idea or a point of view, would be much more enduring than an unrelated number of individuals who might come under his influence. Holmes demurred. He felt that organization might rob him of time and of independence. As he was operating, he was quite his own master, and while his independence entailed some financial risks, still his profits were his own to use as he thought best. If he became involved in organization, he felt he would lose much of his freedom. He would have to accept a fixed salary. On the other hand, he felt he might be freed from many onerous details which he disliked and of the necessity of personally supporting his work. Substantial sums were available, if he would consent to organize.

In the end he yielded, and in 1927 the Institute of Religious Science and Philosophy was founded and a charter was obtained from the state of California. A building on Wilshire Boulevard was selected and rented, and a headquarters was set up. Public meetings were first held in the Ambassador Hotel, and when that was outgrown, the Ebell Theater was taken.

Under the charter a Board of Trustees was created and made responsible for the conduct of the Institute and its various activities. Ernest Holmes was naturally made a permanent trustee, as were others once elected, and any vacancies in the membership of the Board were to be filled by the Board itself. It was thus a self-perpetuating body completely free from outside dictation or control. Later the term of membership on the Board was fixed at four years, but re-election was always possible by vote of the members of the Board.

The same year Holmes started the monthly *Science of Mind*, to be published by the Institute, the purpose of which was, he wrote, "to instruct ethically, morally and religiously from a scientific point of view of life and its meaning." He characterized the magazine as a semireligious periodical, ethical in tendency, moral in tone, philosophical in its viewpoint, seeking

to promote that universal consciousness of life which binds together all in one great whole . . . to show that there is such a thing as Truth, and that it may be known in a degree sufficient to enable the one knowing to live a happy useful life, wholesome, healthful and constructive; . . . to feel certain that his future is in the hands of an eternal Power and Goodness, and that nothing real can ever cease to be. (Vol. I, No. 1, p. 21)

Under able editors to whom Holmes's counsel and guidance

as well as his facile pen were always available, the magazine grew steadily in circulation. It got on the public newsstands— one of the comparatively few essentially religious magazines that have done so—and after more than a third of a century it enjoys a circulation quite out of proportion to the number of followers of Religious Science, and surpassed by comparatively few religious periodicals save those of mass character.

In 1937 a beautiful building, formerly headquarters for a noted architectural organization, was acquired at Sixth and New Hampshire streets. It still continues as headquarters of the movement. Here in the midst of beautiful furnishings and works of art were conducted classes in a wide range of subjects— psychology, philosophy, history of religions, and others—often taught by teachers brought in from the faculties of the several colleges and universities in the region. Here were offices of the director, Ernest Holmes, and an increasing number of staff members, secretaries, and practitioners. And from here as a dis- tributing center went out a steadily broadening stream of litera- ture promulgating and interpreting the central ideas of Religious Science.

Meanwhile, in 1927 Ernest Holmes had married Hazel Gillen, a wealthy widow, and lived at the Palms, the spacious comfort- able home he had built. Mrs. Holmes was an ardent believer in Religious Science and became a very successful practitioner. She was said to have something of P. P. Quimby's clairvoyant ability to know, without being told, the ills from which patients suffered. Ernest Holmes was sometimes able to do this, but not regularly, according to his brother. Later, Holmes's father and mother came to live in the home. His mother was finally con- verted to Religious Science and also became a successful prac- titioner. She lived to a ripe old age, loved and revered by all who knew her. Every one of the sons was present for the celebra- tion of the older Holmeses' fifty-fifth wedding anniversary.

At first Holmes was apparently not interested in extending his organization. But as he continued year after year to train people in his mode of thinking and practice, it was inevitable that some of them should start centers of their own. And some of them, like Holmes, became popular figures, drawing large crowds to their theater meetings and classes. They taught largely as Holmes thought, used his textbook, *Science of Mind,* circulated his magazine and other writings. They thought of themselves as in some sense extensions of the Institute of Religious Science and Philosophy. Robert H. Bitzer, who had studied under Dr. Julia Seton and was a New Thought minister in a church she had founded in Boston, was invited by Holmes to come West and to form the first branch of the Institute, in Hollywood. Although he did not encourage others to think of their organizations as branches of the Los Angeles Institute, Ernest did not forbid it and so a number of them came to be known as Institutes and to function in the same way as the original Holmes Institute.

This may seem rather strange. Why should he be so loath to organize? He was certainly not unaware of the value of what he was doing, at one point saying: "I am not going to be modest. We are doing here the most significant piece of work that is being done in the country." Was it because of that inherent distrust of organization felt by so many in the metaphysical field? Arthur Corey reported a conversation he had had with Holmes in which he said he had always distrusted organization, and resisted it, but that a few years previously he had surrendered to pressures and launched an organization to expand and perpetuate his work.

Each of the local Institutes seems to have been quite independent of the control of the original Institute, though the Holmes textbook as well as other literature was used. Only the personal loyalty of various former students of Holmes held them together. But it became evident that Ernest Holmes was not always happy with some of the things they did. If they were to bear the same name as his own organization, should there not be some means of exercising control over them, at least of preventing them from doing things of which he obviously disapproved?

Students of Christian Science will recall an almost identical situation in the early days of that movement. Mrs. Eddy made every effort, though not always successfully, to exert control over those using the name Christian Science.

When one of the groups under the leadership of Dr. Carmelita Trowbridge purchased property in a Los Angeles suburb, Alhambra, and put up a sign indicating that it was the site for a new building for the Church of Religious Science—the first public use apparently of the word "church" as descriptive of the teaching—the news got quickly to the Institute, and she was told she could not do that, that Ernest Holmes didn't want a church. But Dr. Trowbridge had long since come to the conclusion, she has said, that her group could not continue to function permanently as only a teaching institution, that it should really be called a church; and that that was the only way in which she could continue the work.

Other groups followed the same pattern, and in a short time there were several churches which called themselves Religious Science churches, functioning both in Southern California and beyond. Common problems led the ministers of these churches to set up an informal association of Religious Science ministers in Southern California. This met from time to time to discuss their common problems. It had no legal standing, no legislative powers, was related in no way officially or organically to the Institute in Los Angeles, of which Ernest Holmes was the beloved head. Holmes himself was a member of the group.

He seems to have seen in this loose organization the possibility of achieving what he found it difficult to achieve through the Institute itself. At his request, Robert H. Bitzer, who was president of the ministers' association, named a committee to study the whole organizational setup. Dr. Carmelita Trowbridge, Dan Custer, and Wayne Kintner were named to the committee. They made the suggestion that an International Association of Religious Science Churches be formed. This was done and the organization was incorporated under the laws of the state of California under that name. Ernest Holmes became a charter member and honorary president.

The Association was authorized to grant charters to local

groups which might be formed under conditions determined by the Association, but a minister in order to be able to teach must go to the Institute for his training, and over the educational policy of the Institute the church had no control. The Institute had its own Board of Trustees, as stated above, which was self-perpetuating and therefore not subject to democratic controls of any kind. On this board the churches had no representation. Thus the ministers felt themselves to be a part of a two-headed affair, and in time this became a source of dissatisfaction to some of the leaders.

A first step toward a solution to the difficulty was to seek representation of the churches on the Board of Trustees, and this was granted. The churches were permitted to name two representatives to the Board of the Institute, and two members of the Board of Trustees became members of the Council of the International Association of Religious Science Churches. This of course left control precisely where it had been before, for the majority of the board was still self-perpetuating. The churches, or at least a significant number of them, were not long satisfied with the arrangement. They felt, whether rightly or wrongly, that the board's interest as a whole was centered in Dr. Holmes and the Institute, and not in the churches. Indeed, some believed that they did not even want expansion through the churches.

Meanwhile, within the Institute, which was, perhaps naturally enough, the main interest of the board, a field department was set up through which the relationship between the churches and the Institute was maintained, somewhat after the fashion of the Unity centers or churches and the Unity School of Christianity at Kansas City. This proved not to be a highly satisfactory arrangement, for the International Association of Religious Science Churches was not always willing to accept field direction. Something had to be done, it seemed. A number of factors entered in to bring about change. Ernest Holmes himself seems never to have wanted his movement to become a church, and only in the last few years of his life did he become interested in a church building, with its accompaniment of religious symbols, its dim light, and its unique atmosphere of meditation. And when, only shortly before his death, he spoke at the dedication of the magnificent new Founder's Church in Los Angeles, he said: "This church was not my idea. It was Bill Hornaday's." William H. D. Hornaday, Ph.D., was the man he had chosen to be the minister of the group as he grew older and wished to relieve himself of one and another of the responsibilities he carried.

However, not only Hornaday but others as well were thinking more and more in terms of church. Another factor which may have had its influence upon the board was the fact that there were certain tax advantages in having the corporation listed under the title of "Church" rather than under that of "Institute." Mounting financial and property assets and the desire and need for increasing income may have influenced the board in its decision.

At all events, whatever the underlying causes, a new form of organization was resolved upon which it was hoped would take care of the relation of the Institute or the central organization and the Religious Science churches which looked to it in some sense as the head of the growing movement.

A new church would be formed, the Church of Religious Science, which would, under a Board of Trustees, make place for and carry on the church which had come to be called the Founder's Church, the educational work of the Institute in the conduct of classes for the training of ministers and practitioners, as well as general classes for the lay public and instruction through correspondence of those not able to attend classes, and the churches in the field which desired to be affiliated with the central organization. This latter would consist obviously of the churches which had formerly been grouped under the name International Association of Religious Science Churches. But this was a more or less well-organized group with its own elected officers and functioning under a constitution and by-laws.

Whether this group as a whole would have accepted the relationship had the opportunity been allowed for careful democratic discussion of the whole matter will never be known. It could conceivably have meant the dissolution of the IARSC as an organization, or it could have meant the continuation of IARSC, recognized as in affiliate relationship to the central body.

Stories as to just how the matter was handled differ at some points. One side says simply that leaders of the IARSC were not asked if they would accept the arrangement. They say they were simply told that this would be done; that a lengthy statement, drawn up without any consultation with them, was suddenly presented to them without their even being furnished a copy which they might study and discuss.

This was too much for a highly individualistic group of influential leaders to take. Some of them have even remarked that it looked too much like a repetition of the formation of the Mother Church of Christian Science in Boston. Indeed, they said that the Founder's Church was sometimes spoken of informally as the Mother Church by leaders who advocated the proposed organization. Although the central controlling authority was by no means as rigid as that of Boston, it nevertheless lacked the democratic controls which some of the IARSC leaders felt were essential. Therefore, they, and the churches they represented, refused to accept the proposed arrangement. The result was that the IARSC remained intact under its state charter and the Institute and as many of the local churches as were willing to do so resigned from it and accepted the relationship of Affiliated Churches of the Church of Religious Science. It is somewhat a point of honor to the members of IARSC that they do not constitute a group which broke away from the Church of Religious Science. They are, rather, they affirm, the original IARSC from which the others withdrew.

Actually, according to the published lists of churches at the time of separation, forty-six churches or fellowships accepted the new setup. Nineteen churches remained within the IARSC. There were a few which have preferred to remain independent of either group, although they are clearly Religious Science churches in belief and general practice, using as little or as much Religious Science literature as they desire and having what contacts they may wish with both the bodies, but retaining complete freedom from the control of either.

There is an occasional shift of a church from one group to the other. Both have continued establishing new churches in new territories, and the relationship between the groups is cordial and co-operative. There is occasional exchange of pulpits among ministers of the two groups. They continue to study and teach Ernest Holmes's *Science of Mind,* and apparently are not different ideologically in any sense. It seems to be a purely organizational matter and the primary difference is in the degree of central or authoritarian control each is willing to take.

The leaders of the IARSC appear to be rather more adamant than the others in respect to the reuniting of the groups. The IARSC, they say, will never accept what they regard as a tendency toward the "Mother Church" control which they think they see in the Affiliated relationship.

Did Ernest Holmes believe that his teaching was the final revelation, which at all costs must be maintained in its purity as the authoritative basis of Religious Science, as in the case of Mrs. Eddy, necessitating tight measures of control designed to preserve it? If his brother Fenwicke is right, he evidently did not, for Fenwicke told me in personal conversation over and over again that Ernest had no notion that he had evolved the final answers to all the great questions. He would say, "This is my revelation—not yours. It must always be open at the top for new understandings and insights." He evidently did not expect that his writings would crystallize into hard and fast doctrines which, as in the case of Mrs. Eddy's, must be considered the final word.

It might be well at this point to indicate precisely what is the organizational setup of the rival organizations as these exist today. First, the Church of Religious Science, successor to the Institute of Religious Science and Philosophy:

The Church of Religious Science is organized under the laws of California as a nonprofit corporation, governed by a Board of Trustees, of which Ernest Holmes, Founder, was, while living, a permanent member. The others are now elected, each for a term of three years; but they may be elected again and again by their colleagues if they so desire. Twelve of the trustees—eleven now, since the number one place vacated by the death of Ernest Holmes will never be filled—are elected by the board, making it to that extent a self-perpetuating body, subject to no recall by any democratically constituted body. Seven other trustees are elected by the Convention of the Affiliated Churches, each for a three-year term, and therefore hold their posts as trustees subject to election by democratic processes.

Under the Board of Trustees are various departments. There is a Department of Education which has its own Board of Regents of eleven members, seven elected each for a term of five years by the Board of Trustees, and four chosen by the board from a panel submitted by the Church Council. This is the department which oversees the total educational effort of the church and the training of its teachers, practitioners, and ministers, and determines the curriculum of instruction in each case and the conditions under which instruction may be given, as well as the qualifications of authorized teachers, a provision against which the IARSC had raised powerful objections.

The Department of Church, of the Church of Religious Science, has to do with the Founder's Church which, unlike the Affiliated Churches, is under the direct supervision of the Board of Trustees. There is a Congregational Council, but its function is that of service, not direction or control, for it is the Board of Trustees which chooses the ministers, sets salaries, says for what the church building may be used, determines who may speak from the pulpit, and makes major decisions concerning the conduct of the affairs of the church. Founder's Church does send elected delegates, to the maximum number of ten, to the Convention of the Affiliated Churches which does elect a part of the Board of Trustees. Besides Trustee members and Congregational members, there is a provision whereby members of Affiliated Churches may also, if they desire, hold Associate membership in the Founder's Church, an arrangement not

wholly unlike that in Christian Science which makes it possible
for members of local churches to be also members of the Mother
Church in Boston. But these members have full voting privileges,
which Associate members of Founder's Church do not enjoy.
Comparatively few, I was told, avail themselves of the Associate membership privilege.

It is in the Department of Affiliated Churches where the
democratic participation in the management of the affairs of the
churches is most in evidence. Affiliated churches which have
been duly chartered by the Church Council are entitled to send
at least three delegates, one of whom must be the minister, and
one additional delegate for each fifty members beyond the first
one hundred members, to the Annual Convention of the Church
of Religious Science. And as indicated above, Founder's Church
may send as many as ten delegates. The convention meets each
year in January at the headquarters in Los Angeles, or in such
other places as may be designated by the Board of Trustees. The
chief functions of the convention are to elect the seven members
of the Board of Trustees; to elect the Church Council; to determine the quota or apportioned contribution of each church; to
make recommendations for action by the Board of Trustees; and
to determine ecclesiastical policy relating to the denominational
activities of the Department of Affiliated Churches.

The election of seven members of the Board of Trustees is
democratically a clear advance over the earlier complete lack
of any representation, and then of representation by two members; but it is pointed out by the IARSC leaders that this still
leaves control where it was before, since a majority vote in the
Board of Trustees is all that is required for most matters that
come before it. It is true that the convention representatives
participate also in the election of the eleven non-convention representatives, and that in some cases trustees, originally elected by
the convention as their representatives, are chosen as among the
eleven non-convention members, thus possibly introducing gradually more of the convention point of view into the board as a
whole.

The Church Council is composed of thirteen members, twelve of whom are elected each for a three-year term, and not more than six of whom may be active ministers. Office number one of the Council is held ex officio by the Dean of the Institute, or one named by the Board of Trustees. It is the Council which determines the conditions under which churches may be chartered, ministers licensed or ordained, and practitioners certified. It names the administrator of the Department of Affiliated Churches and his deputies for the oversight of the churches, and determines their salaries and terms of employment, subject to formal approval by the Board of Trustees. The Council may and does suggest to the convention matters that should be determined by it. It also names a panel from which the Board of Trustees may elect trial boards for hearing cases calling for disciplinary action.

This department issues a monthly *News Letter* for ministers and board members, and there is presently under consideration the publication of a periodical for the general membership of the churches which will provide them with church news in a way the *Science of Mind,* which is in no sense a house organ or news reporting periodical, cannot do.

The *News Letter* for March, 1961, reported a total of 59 fully chartered churches and 8 Religious Science Fellowships, a total of 67, with a membership of 12,683, a gain of 8½ per cent during the year, in comparison with a gain of less than 3 per cent among a number of the major denominations.

Religious Science, like most movements, has had the problem of recruiting and training leadership. A few men trained for the ministry in other churches have been converted to Religious Science and brought to their ministry the advantage of a college and even seminary training. In most instances this has not been the case. Laymen and laywomen, failing to find their needs met in the churches, have been attracted to the lectures or classes of Ernest Holmes or others of the men who have won substantial followings through their theater or other public meetings, or it may be through their radio ministry. Finding a gospel that

seemed to them adequate they have, with the zeal of new converts, wanted to share what they have found. In order to do this
they have attended a series of classes and then undertaken to
build groups of their own. Perhaps it has been the influence of
Christian Science which has never required more formal training
than its Primary and Normal Class Instruction, in addition to
private study of the Textbook and Mrs. Eddy's other writings,
that was responsible for the rather uncritical acceptance of a
meagerly trained leadership. Or was it the practical necessity
of using what was immediately available at the time? Undoubtedly some of these untrained leaders have achieved marvels
through their ministry, but by no means all, and it was early
recognized that more was required than zeal. Ernest Holmes
himself believed in teaching. His own lack of formal training
may have caused him to see the need of more formal instruction.

At present there is a real concern for the proper training
of ministers. As we have seen, a special education department
has been set up to make sure that the standards are continually
raised and that properly qualified persons are given the necessary training. The Board of Regents which is responsible for
the educational program concerns itself with all the leadership
and educational activities, determining what shall be studied
and for what periods by those desiring to become ministers or
practitioners. It grants no degrees such as are granted by accredited academic institutions authorized by the state, but does grant
what it terms "recognitions" for the completion of certain
required courses of study, using—unfortunately, as it seems to
an outsider—the clearly academic designations for degrees. Thus
BRSc, i.e., Bachelor of Religious Science, and the MRSc, or
Master of Religious Science, are given. Also, it is authorized to
confer the Doctorate of Religious Science, DRSc, on an honorary
basis.

There has been a steadily stiffening program of study, carefully detailed in the catalogue issued by the department, and
plans are under way for a still further tightening of requirements.
Judged on an absolute basis the present requirements seem to an

outsider low. But said one of the leaders, "You ought to see from where we have come!" And perhaps that is a fairer way to judge the situation. The day is envisaged when at least college graduation will be required of candidates who wish to be ministers, and they will then be required to take the special courses relating to Religious Science. And there is a dream of a day when a candidate for ordination will have had full seminary training in addition to the specialized Religious Science instruction.

Certain of the courses required for ministers and practitioners may be taken under properly accredited instructors in some local churches, and of course general instruction may be and is given by local ministers, but certification comes from the department at headquarters. In addition, correspondence courses are given by a special bureau at headquarters in Los Angeles, and hundreds of persons take these each year. But when all the required work has been taken and properly certified by the department of education, ordination does not automatically follow. Candidates for ordination must be passed upon by the Church Council before they are ordained. Thus the Council, the representative of the Affiliated group as a whole, does have the final word as to who shall minister in the name of the Affiliated Churches.

According to a folder published by the International Association of Religious Science Churches, its purpose was that of unifying spiritually, strengthening, and assisting in the work of all the member churches and the expansion of Religious Science into an effective spiritual movement encircling the globe. Its declared beliefs do not materially differ from those of Affiliated Churches. A later mimeographed copy of the by-laws of IARSC adopted on January 6, 1960, and incorporating such changes as had been made prior to May, 1959, states specifically that "true spiritual unity among men can be most effectively manifested under a democracy wherein the inherent freedom and divine individuality of all members may express for the good of all in understanding, brotherly love, justice and equality." Further on it adds this: "We believe that the future good of Religious Science can best be manifested in the consecrated hands of the many under a spiritual democracy than in the hands of even the most capable few."

Authority for the conduct of the affairs of IARSC is vested in a democratically representative Congress meeting annually, composed of the minister of each of the component churches and one delegate for each fifty members of each local church. The Congress elects a Board of Directors which serves as the executive and judicial body of the association. It is composed of eight ordained members and six lay members, each elected for a three-year term. The officers elected by the board from its own membership serve as officers of the Congress. The board meets at least quarterly for the conduct of necessary business. It has such broad powers as those of rescinding charters of local churches, setting "standards of procedure, ethics, methods and ideals" for the Association and its churches and ministers, determining the qualifications for ministers, teachers, and practitioners, and maintaining the integrity and standards of the teachings of Religious Science and Science of Mind; employing or dismissing personnel, and suspending or expelling for just cause any church leader, pastor, or minister member of the Association. However, all such decisions may be appealed to the Congress and may presumably be confirmed or rescinded. Definite procedures are provided for such appeals. Thus in all important matters the democratically elected representative congress stands as the final authority.

The organization is thoroughly congregational at the local level. Each church is autonomous in respect to ownership of property and administrative rights. But to be a chartered member of IARSC, it must act in conformity with the Articles and By-laws of the IARSC. Local churches are required to pay the treasurer a determined quota which apparently is variable, in order to maintain their voting rights in the Congress.

Formerly the IARSC depended chiefly on the Institute in Los Angeles for the training of its ministry, though the Council reserved the right of admission to ordination. Each of the larger Religious Science churches belonging to the IARSC offers class instruction which is basic to the training of all ministers. But the specifically ministerial training course is given only in Hollywood and in New York.

The IARSC honors the credits for courses taken in the Institute in Los Angeles, but the acceptance of credits is not reciprocal. IARSC grants no "recognitions" such as those granted by the educational department of the Church of Religious Science in Los Angeles, but does confer the honorary degree DRSc.

A comparison, then, of the Affiliated Churches and the IARSC reveals no great differences save at one point. Final control in the case of the Affiliated Churches rests with the Board of Trustees of the Church of Religious Science. Conceivably the board might consent to every democratically taken decision made by the Convention of Delegates in their annual meetings, and might approve of every action or recommendation of the Church Council, but on the other hand they might approve of none. Actually the report is that they have quite frequently approved, and sometimes have recommended reconsideration or modification before giving their approval. In the case of the IARSC, the Congress has the final decision, and the decision is democratically taken. One is theoretically—however it may operate practically— authoritarian, the other democratic or libertarian. Each local group must choose which it wishes to follow. In this respect Religious Science churches are as all the rest of the churches. Some like it one way, some another.

What was the effect of the break upon IARSC in terms of member churches which were lost? In *Science of Mind* for December, 1953, there were listed sixty-nine churches and prechurch groups chartered by the Institute of Religious Science. Whether all belonged to IARSC is not disclosed. But the December, 1954, issue reports only forty-six, a loss of twenty-two member groups. In the December issue of *Religious Science,* the magazine published by IARSC, nineteen groups were reported, a combined total of three less than the ones listed the preceding year. This may not mean an actual loss to Religious Science as a movement, but only that some churches had not yet made up their minds which group to follow, or had chosen to remain independent of any overall relationship. The growth of the IARSC by years from December, 1954, to March, 1961, was as follows: 19, 26, 33, 36, 34, 29, 30, 31; that is, there was a rapid rise from 1954 to 1957, then a drop through 1959 and a slight gain through 1960 and 1961.

The pattern of growth of the Affiliated Churches for the same period was: 46, 54, 57, 59, 61, 64, 69, 71, a steady growth though not large in any one year save 1955, when eight churches were added. IARSC had gained 63.1 per cent up to March, 1961, while the Affiliated Churches had gained 54.3 per cent. The combined Churches of Religious Science had made a healthy gain of 56.9 per cent. This says nothing about the number of members, since this is not reported for both groups; but in the number of churches the gain is substantially above that registered in the case of the major denominations, where the number of churches in some had fallen off, owing to the consolidation of local groups and the elimination of many formerly rural congregations. Of the larger denominations, the Southern Baptists, the fastest growing of all, showed a gain in the number of churches of only a little over 8 per cent; the Church of the Nazarene increased 19 per cent, the Mormons 40 per cent. This, it should be recalled, is only with respect to the number of churches, not members.

Since Religious Science got its start in California, it is natural that California should have the largest number of churches. Before the division 51 of the 68 chartered churches listed in *Science of Mind* were in California. Only New York had as many as three; Colorado and Washington two each; and Hawaii, Idaho, Florida, Minnesota, Missouri, Oklahoma, Pennsylvania, Texas, Canada, and South Africa each figured with one church.

After the division, IARSC reported 13 in California, two in New York, and one each in Arizona, Colorado, S. Africa, and Washington, a total of 19. The Affiliated Churches reported 36 in California, two in Oklahoma, and one each in Colorado, Florida, Idaho, Pennsylvania, Washington, and Hawaii, a total of 46. In March, 1961, IARSC reported 14 in California, or a gain of but one church. The Affiliated Churches reported 59 in the home state, a gain of 23. The gains of IARSC have been mainly east of the Mississippi, being found in the District of Columbia, Illinois, Maryland, Ohio, New Jersey, New York, and Canada, with foreign groups in South Africa and the West Indies. The Affiliated Churches have no member churches east of the Mississippi except in Florida, where there are five, nor have they increased their number of churches in any western state except California. They reported two churches each in England and South Africa and one in France.

The growth of Religious Science churches registered in the combined churches was, by years, from 1954 through March, 1961, as follows: 65, 80, 90, 95, 95, 93, 99, 102; and this does not take into account a number of churches which are definitely in the Ernest Holmes tradition, using the textbook and loyal to the general Religious Science point of view. In combination Religious Science has churches or active groups in Arizona, California, Colorado, District of Columbia, Florida, Idaho, Illinois, Maryland, Minnesota, Missouri, Nevada, New Jersey, New York, Ohio, Oklahoma, Oregon, Texas, and Washington, in continental United States; in Hawaii, Canada, the West Indies, England, France, and South Africa. That is to say, they are found in about one-third of the states of the United States, and in several overseas areas.

10

Other New Thought Groups

MANY LOCAL New Thought groups have not affiliated with any other, save perhaps the INTA. Others arising from the work of a particular New Thought leader have formed a limited, usually regional, group under his personal leadership. For example, the Society of the Healing Christ was organized by Dr. Thomas Parker Boyd, a former president of INTA, and spread chiefly along the Pacific coast. A few churches still use the name, and their leaders hold an informal meeting at the annual congress of the INTA. Miss Edna Lister, successor to Dr. Boyd, also a former president of INTA, heads the group.

Another group, the Christian Assembly, grew out of the work of William Farwell at San Jose, and spread regionally through the nearby area of California. Three churches under that name appear in the current list of affiliates of INTA. The Christ Truth League, under the leadership of Alden and Neil Truesdell of Fort Worth, Texas, carry on a more than local ministry through the publication and distribution of books by Dr. H. B. Jeffery.

Space forbids even the attempt to list all such groups that have arisen, some later to disappear completely and others to carry on in limited fashion. But some have played so important a role in the extension of New Thought ideas that they must be given at least brief mention.

One of the early New Thought groups which, beginning as a local institution, came to have centers in a number of places, chiefly on the West Coast, but also elsewhere in the United States, was called Home of Truth. Like a number of other groups it was

312

the result of influences set at work by that remarkable New Thought teacher of teachers, Mrs. Emma Curtis Hopkins.

It was in one of her classes in San Francisco in 1887 that Mrs. Annie Rix Militz became one of her students and found her life-work, as she told her sister, Harriet Rix, after the third lesson. A fellow-member of the class, a Mrs. Gorey, had a small metaphysical bookshop, and when this woman asked her to give up her teaching — she was a public school teacher — and join her in the bookstore, Annie Rix did so, and began soon to conduct classes there in what were essentially the teachings of Mrs. Hopkins.

Her work in the bookstore gave her the opportunity to read widely in the metaphysical field, and she absorbed a great deal from her reading. It was perhaps this experience which accounted, in part at least, for her broad tolerance and sympathy for the thought of others who differed from her. She was never creedally bound by any one teaching, though she herself held profound views as to the nature of the universe, of God, and of man. Her one basic belief she said, was in "The Allness of God," no matter where or how she found it. "Those who take the stand that the Real Self is God," she said, "give the most perfect liberty to each individual to carry out his idea of God, and do not dictate his method." (*Bulletin*, XXVIII [Summer, 1945], 6)

Mrs. Militz and Mrs. Gorey quickly outgrew the bookshop and secured a new place of several rooms over a store. Growth of their work soon led them to take over the store also and convert it into a hall where they could hold their meetings. They called their Center "Christian Science Home." It is known that at this time Mrs. Eddy was making every effort to control the use of the name Christian Science. Whether any pressures were brought to bear upon the leader to abandon the use of the name is not known. A Home of Truth writer later explained the change of name as due to the fact that Christian Science had "come to be associated with a sect or denomination of people." In any event, the name Home of Truth was substituted for that of Christian Science Home.

Why this name? What was probably a later rationalization was given in a paper found in the archives of the INTA, evidently one read at some meeting but apparently never published. It says:

A Home of Truth is a composite, as it expresses both the individual and universal ideas of what a Home should be; and the mothering spirit there goes out not just to one household, one family, or one set of so-called religious people, but to all people, all nations, all families, all religions; in fact to every creature who lives on this earth-plane of consciousness or some other. As the individual mother [in the home] directs and guides those of her fold in the way of Truth, so have these universal mothers taught thousands this universal principle of the brotherhood of man, or better still, the divinity or the Godhood of man. In fact we are taught that the one and only mission of every creature is to express his divinity and to see that same divinity in our brothers and sisters; that we are all of one happy family, and that loving service is the only thing worth while.

For three years Mrs. Militz worked in the Home; then she was called to teach as a member of the faculty of the Christian Science Theological Seminary, in Chicago, of which Mrs. Hopkins was president. She left the San Francisco Home in charge of her sister, Harriet Rix, and Miss Eva Fulton.

When, in 1896, Mrs. Militz returned to the West Coast, she found the San Francisco Home in such flourishing condition that she went to Los Angeles and started another there. Beginning in a modest way it quickly outgrew successive locations on Flower, Figueroa, and Georgia Streets, and was in more adequate quarters on Union Avenue, where it was functioning at the time the paper we have mentioned was written.

The movement spread to other cities. Soon there were Homes of Truth all up and down the coast from San Diego, California, to Victoria, British Columbia.

It was in Los Angeles that Mrs. Militz began the publication of one of the earlier and more outstanding New Thought magazines, the *Master Mind*, which attained a wide circulation and an influence far beyond the limits of her own movement. She herself was much in demand as a lecturer and teacher. She traveled widely both at home and abroad. She became very active in the INTA. She was one of those present in London in 1914 when the first International Congress was held and the INTA came into existence. She made a trip around the world in 1914 lecturing and promoting the San Francisco Congress, held in connection with the Panama-Pacific Exposition in 1915.

The content of the Home of Truth teaching is set forth in the *Bulletin* in 1931. (February issue, p. 17) As stated by Harriet Rix, the Home of Truth teaches "that God the Good is All in All, the only power and intelligence, including life, love, truth, mind, substance or spirit, prosperity, health and strength. There can therefore be no reality, no truth, power or intelligence in materiality, sin, evil, sickness, poverty, sorrow or death." That man, as the idea of God, is absolutely what God is, all good, not a sinner, perfect, as God is perfect, immortal in the same way that truth is; that God is his health, power, strength, and wealth; that he is spiritual, not material. Man's purpose is to manifest God in the fullness of joy, beauty, peace, power, and immortality, to describe in mind, body, and affairs that perfect state known as the Kingdom of Heaven. The soul of man is birthless and deathless. The healing methods of the Home of Truth are spiritual, through silence and prayer. The word of God is spoken both in denial and affirmation, and no material means ever resorted to, and no suggestion or autosuggestion is recommended. "The chief teacher and founder is Jesus Christ, the great authority for our faith is the Holy Spirit within each one, and the church is the whole body of divine humanity everywhere, visible and invisible, and we are all one in the Father-Mother God."

The organization was never a tight one. Though the working basis of the various Homes of Truth was essentially the same, each was completely autonomous and distinct from all the others. There was no formal membership — there was really no way of joining the organization. People affiliated themselves with it simply because they liked the practical Christianity they found expressed in the writings of Mrs. Militz and her co-workers, and the kind of activities they were carrying on in the Homes. There were no dues or quotas to meet. Everything was on a voluntary basis. No fixed charge was made for any of their services, yet there was no lack of material support.

Homes of Truth were listed or mentioned from time to time in the magazine *Master Mind*, which, incidentally, had a news section of what was happening not only in Homes of Truth, but in the general New Thought field. Aside from those in California and on the West Coast, others appear in New Orleans, Miami, Manchester, New Hampshire, Colorado Springs, Chicago, and Boston. And one was reported in Rome in 1925.

How many still are in existence today it is difficult to say. There is no longer any publication, nor is there any overall organization binding together the Homes that may continue to function. Miss Eleanor Mel, leader of the Home of Truth in Boston, may be considered the present head, if there is any. Hers is the only Home listed as a member of INTA at present.

But Annie Rix Militz will always be regarded as one of the "greats" of New Thought. Her editing and publication of *Master Mind*, one of the most distinguished New Thought periodicals, from its beginning in 1911 until her death in 1924, would insure that. She was a magnetic speaker, a leader of far vision, a valued counselor in organizational matters in INTA, and an inspiring teacher. Her sister, Harriet Rix, carried on *Master Mind* under the name *The Christ Mind* until it ceased publication.

One of the smaller New Thought groups included within the INTA is the Church of the Truth. At one time a fairly extensive group, with its own periodical, the *Fountain*, it no longer functions as a separate organization, except in a very loose fashion. Its ministers meet, if at all, in a very loosely knit Ministerial Association, in connection with the Annual Congress of INTA, and it does continue to decide upon who shall be ordained as its ministers. At present there are some ten churches actively carrying on their ministry.

The most widely known one is that which met in Carnegie Hall in New York City until October, 1962, when it moved to Philharmonic Hall in Lincoln Center. It is under the ministry of

Dr. Ervin Seale, one time president of INTA. Though representing a different branch of New Thought than did Emmet Fox, who in his day spoke to probably the largest congregation meeting in New York City, he carries on in Philharmonic Hall a remarkably effective ministry.

The Church of the Truth had its beginnings in the healing of a Universalist minister into whose hands fell a New Thought book on prayer and healing, at a time when he was suffering grievously from stomach ulcers. As a result of this, he began actively to preach spiritual healing. His church was liberal, at least theologically, but it was not liberal enough to accept such teaching. So Albert C. Grier left the Universalist church and founded what he called the Church of the Truth in Spokane, Washington.

Various persons who were attracted by Albert C. Grier's ministry and teaching extended the Church of the Truth to other cities. Edward Mills carried it to Portland, Oregon, though he later returned to Spokane. Erma Wells, who was later to become president of INTA and an important figure in its development, came under his influence, became his associate, and was later, for a long time, the president of the University of Metaphysics which was developed in Spokane, as well as pastor of the Church of the Truth.

Albert C. Grier himself eventually left Spokane and took over a small Unity group in Pasadena, California, forming it into a Church of the Truth. When he was later called to New York to succeed Dr. W. John Murray of the Church of the Healing Christ, one of a succession of New Thought leaders to have captured the popular interest in New York City, he was succeeded by Edward Mills, who bought property, built a substantial church, and served as its leader until his death, being succeeded by his much beloved wife, affectionately known as Mother Mary. Dr. Grier eventually left the Church of the Healing Christ, to be followed by Emmet Fox, and started *de novo* a Church of the Truth, which he led until his retirement.

His daughter, Gladys Grier, who had come as his assistant, carried on the work until 1940, when Erwin Seale, who had had his apprenticeship under Dr. Erma Wells in Spokane, became minister and began to build up his extensive following. It was after the untimely death of Emmet Fox that Dr. Seale moved his congregation into famous Carnegie Hall.

Erma Wells had done her work well, both as teacher and minister, and had sent out not a few to found and minister to other Churches of the Truth in other cities, among them Tom Williams, one-time student of John Garns of Minneapolis, newspaper editor and politician, now minister of the Church of the Truth in Pasadena. A University of Metaphysics is currently maintained in Portland, Oregon, with Mary Prendergast as its president.

Erma Wells had the misfortune to suffer an automobile accident which ended her active career and made a further speaking ministry difficult. Her church brought in a new minister, and it has since affiliated with the Unity School of Christianity and is no longer counted among the Churches of the Truth. When the writer asked various members of the Church of the Truth in attendance at the INTA Congress at Denver in 1960, "What is it that causes your little group to go on maintaining its separate identity?" the chief reason alleged was personal loyalty to Erma Wells. All were co-operating actively in INTA and were content to do so. Most of them, except for sentimental reasons, would probably be willing to lose their separate identity in the larger ongoing New Thought Movement.

Another who brought the gospel of New Thought to millions, most of whom were reached through advertising, either direct mail or through newspapers and magazines, was Frank B. Robinson, of Moscow, Idaho, founder and director, in the thirties and forties of this century, of the movement known as Psychiana.

A pharmacist, son of a Baptist minister in England, trained in a Canadian theological school, for a time a member of the Salvation Army, but finally disillusioned with organized religion, he became an atheist and almost violently antichurch in his attitudes. Then he was converted. It was not the old type evangelical conversion, at least in respect to the content of his new faith, but a New Thought conversion to which he brought something of the old evangelical zeal that frequently characterizes the orthodox convert. Once convinced of the Truth, he simply had to do something about it.

On a rented typewriter he pounded out a series of lessons, trying to bring to others what had come to him in his conversion experience. But how to get people to read it? He would advertise it. So with borrowed capital he inserted in *Psychology Magazine* an ad which an advertising agency in Spokane, Washington, had refused to try to place, because they said it was so badly written that no one would read it.

But they did read it. "I talked with God," it boldly proclaimed, insisting that others might have the same experience, and telling what the results had been in his own case. It became probably the most widely read advertisement of any period, eventually appearing in almost every magazine or newspaper that would print it. And the replies came in by the thousands.

The story of this man has been told often enough. (See the writer's *These Also Believe* [New York: Macmillan, 1949] or Marcus Bach's *They Found a Faith* [Indianapolis: Bobbs-Merrill, 1946].) Sometimes called "The Mail-Order Prophet," Dr. Frank B. Robinson, during the years of depression and the war years, sold more than a million copies of his lessons and his books. There was no organization. He even refused at one time to give to persons in a given area the names of others taking his lessons in the same community, so deep was his distrust of organization. As a result, when he died in 1949 there was no organization to carry on the work. His son continued for a time to circulate his lessons and books, but without "Doc" Robinson there just wasn't really any Psychiana movement, and so it was liquidated.

But enormous numbers of people from every walk in life had gotten his message. He used to advertise in the most unlikely places—on match covers, for example, which might be found in a saloon, or a brothel even. And many a man and woman found some new hope when they answered the ad of the man who had "talked with God." He more nearly followed the injunction of Jesus to "go out into the highways and hedges and bring them in" than probably any other man on the contemporary scene.

His teachings were New Thought all the way through—New Thought ideas proclaimed in highly dramatic fashion, designed to catch and hold the attention, and New Thought techniques through the employment of which health, well-being, prosperity, peace, happiness—all the proper heritage of man—might be achieved. It may well be that more were attracted to Psychiana because of the promise that those who "talk with God" may be expected to prosper, or to gain health, than for any spiritual benefits they might hope to derive from it; but that multitudes, as attested by letters which came to him by the thousands, received spiritual benefits there can be no doubt.

PART III

New Thought Outreach in America

11

New Thought Periodicals

EVERY MOVEMENT of any significance in a literate culture eventually produces a literature of its own. This is certainly true of the New Thought Movement. Its literature consists of books, pamphlets, articles in the public press, and weekly, biweekly, monthly, bimonthly, or quarterly periodicals published by some individual or group within the movement. In an article on "The Metaphysical Movement," published in the *Review of Reviews* (XXV [1902], 312-20), Paul Tyner says that the periodical literature of New Thought "has grown steadily until now it numbers more than one hundred monthly and weekly publications in this country alone." (p. 313)

Many of these periodicals quickly disappeared, but numerous others took their places, flourished for a time, and then vanished in their turn. What the total number of such publications is, it is impossible to guess. Some did continue over a considerable period of time and were influential in the spread of the movement.

One of the very earliest of the magazines that were of importance in the formative years of the movement was *Harmony,* which was edited by Mrs. Malinda E. Cramer, cofounder of Divine Science. According to the cover page, this was "a monthly magazine of philosophy, devoted to TRUTH, Science of Spirit, Theosophy, Metaphysics, and to the Christ method of healing." It was published in San Francisco from October, 1888, to 1906. The intention of the editor was stated in part as:

To teach that God is infinite and ever present, and that there is no other power; that there is but one Mind and one Life. To teach that

Faith is Wholeness, Health and Happiness; that Truth is religion and that religion or truth frees us from all error and sorrow; that Matter has no power over Spirit or Divine Mind; to supply a simple method by which to come into full realization of Truth and the Christ method of healing. To supply to students and practitioners of Spiritual Science information and practical lessons on Treating and Healing; to expand individual thought universally; to bring about Unity of Thought and effort . . . and to apply to all problems of life a simple method of interpretation . . .

The issues of *Harmony* contained, typically, weekly meditations, selections from the scriptures of various religions, stories and articles, a Bible lesson, questions and answers, correspondence, and notes, including testimonials of healing and some news of the general movement. Little is to be learned concerning Mrs. Cramer herself, except what is revealed in her many contributions to the magazine, in which she made frequent reference to her college and to her fellow-workers. Although much was said in the magazine of Mrs. Eddy's Christian Science, her name was not usually mentioned.

Some of the New Thought magazines have been definitely house organs, designed to present a specific point of view of a given branch of the movement and to serve the interests of that particular group. Others have been of a more general nature, concerned mainly with ideas rather than organizations. Among the latter, one of the most widely read and ideologically important was *Mind*.

Mind appeared first in October, 1897, and was published monthly by the Alliance Publishing Company of New York City. On the inside of its cover the purpose of the magazine was set forth at length. It was pointed out that a need had been felt for a strictly high-class periodical representing all phases of New Thought. The fundamental principles of the different phases were regarded as identical, and it was felt that "the establishment of this unitary basis would greatly facilitate the work in the field of action." The editors therefore announced the publication of *Mind*, "owing no allegiance to any school, sect, system, cult or person." Its sole aim would be, they promised, "to aid in the progress of mankind through a cultivation of the knowledge of Truth wherever found regardless of individual prejudice and preconceptions." The prevention and cure of disease "through the understanding and application of Law, which regulates life in its varying phases of spiritual, mental and physical development" would be treated both theoretically and practically. Among occult and psychic questions to be discussed were reincarnation, adeptship, psychometry and psychography or automatic writing, clairvoyance, astrology, mediumship, hypnotism, etc. A competent study would be made of comparative religions. While granting due credit to Hindu metaphysics and oriental mysticism, the editors would look more to the development of a Western psychology "that will harmonize with the conditions of life in the Occident, at the same time tending to promote the spiritual welfare of the race as a whole." Clearly this covers more ground than a great many of the New Thought leaders of today would wish to include within their interests.

The closing paragraph of an editorial, "Our Name and Mission," in the first number of *Mind* declares:

Divinity is pure Mind; hence mind in man is an extension or projection of the divine into the human personality. Being the higher element of the soul, its immortal principle, it inspires the understanding to develop impressions into distinct thought and purpose. The province of this periodical, therefore, will be to encourage the higher thinking, the evolving of profounder motives of action and the bringing up through the lower and external nature of better concepts of life and truth, duty and real knowledge. (p. 54)

At one time or another, most of the widely varied subjects envisioned by the editors were actually treated. Several articles on Vedanta gave evidence of the interest in this subject among followers of New Thought at that period. Other articles discussed problems of philosophy and psychology. Here and there were notes concerning the organizational structure of New Thought, which was developing rapidly. In Volume VI it was noted that every month showed a decided increase in the magazine's circulation, and that it went to nearly every part of the civilized world and had found a place on the public newsstands.

In the November, 1901, issue, announcement was made of the absorption of the *Arena* by the Alliance Publishing Company. B. O. Flower, editor of the *Coming Age,* which had been acquired by *Arena,* assumed responsibility for certain features of the magazine. J. H. McLean had been restored to the editorship along with C. B. Patterson, who had been editing *Mind* during the previous year and was now to be editor-in-chief of the *Arena* as well. Of *Mind,* the announcement said:

Its leadership in the literary world of the great metaphysical movement which means so much to future generations, is acknowledged everywhere. Its supremacy among New Thought periodicals is conceded. . . . Its special province is progress and research in the Science of the New Metaphysics. It is not engaged in propaganda for any school, and its mission is not to proselyte.

While the *Arena* and *Mind* were now to be issued under the same auspices, the former occupying itself with "reform along economic, political and ethical lines," the two had a common inspiration, "the conviction that only through the upbuilding of the individual can be brought about the upliftment of the race."

An article on "Growth by Absorption," in the issue of March, 1901, stated that there had been an unprecedented rate of increase in the circulation of *Mind* during the previous half-year. Leaders of the movement had felt for some years that New Thought periodicals were too numerous and too scattered for productive and effective work. By concentrating on single features, some of them had contributed to the formation of sectarian groups and a weakening of the energies of the movement as a whole. *Mind* had constantly sought to serve the whole movement; now it was prepared to consolidate, the first step being the merging with *Mind* of *Universal Truth,* the leading metaphysical journal of the West, which had been published in Chicago for over twelve years. The editors of *Universal Truth* were to continue as contributors to *Mind.* Negotiations for similar mergers were under way with other New Thought journals.

In Volume IX appears an article by Elizabeth Cady Stanton on "Women's Right," and another writer re-echoes an earlier plea for the abolition of capital punishment. Here was an appeal to social action, showing that *Mind* was by no means wholly dedicated to individual action only, in social matters. There is also an article on the relation of fear to success — but not success as it is so frequently interpreted, meaning the gaining of wealth and power. Little attention was given in this magazine to the matter of getting ahead or acquiring possessions.

An editorial in the January, 1902, issue of *Mind,* written by C. B. Patterson, inquired, "Has the Metaphysical Movement Found Its Soul?" Many letters had been received complaining of "lack of harmonious action and unity of thought and purpose" among the New Thought leaders. Among other things, there seems to have been almost no public-spirited effort to form clubs, libraries, or reading rooms, or to encourage the giving of free lectures. Where any such efforts were made, they were mainly supported by the newly interested rather than by those long identified with the movement.

Because of this lack, some New Thought followers were known to have joined Christian Science groups. New Thought leaders, said the editorial writer, may not want to found a church, but they ought carefully to consider these corporate aids in establishing the cause of Truth. The difficulty seems to be that the leaders are more concerned with philosophy, psychology, and anatomy, advocating the study of Spinoza, Leibnitz, Heine, and other philosophers to equip themselves for New Thought leadership. But there is a heart as well as a mind to be cultivated. Love is the greatest force in the life of man. What one loves to do, he does.

There is a religious element in human life which cannot and will not be ignored. All the science and philosophy of the world will not satisfy the deeper craving that wells up in the life of man—the desire to know

God, to become conscious of Him as a living Presence.... If the religious element is left out of New Thought and it is simply to be an intellectual renaissance, then it may be of temporary use as a stepping stone to a higher order of development, but it will find no lasting abiding place in the hearts and minds of people. If the New Thought expects to reach the masses with their teaching they must appeal to the heart as well as the head; they must work as well as think; they must be willing to forego petty jealousies and the desire for personal leadership, and setting aside selfish ends, work unitedly for the good of the cause. (p. 296)

A significant article on "The Antiquity and Universality of New Thought," by Henry Frank, appears in Volume XIV (July, 1904). "That which is proclaimed as the New Thought," the author says in his opening sentence, "is essentially as old as the civilized centuries." This does not detract from it, but on the contrary, if through so many years it has reappeared persistently in new forms that were always adapted to the particular age in which it appeared, "it the better demonstrated its essential value to the race, and its unequalled adaptability to the spiritual requirements of mankind." (p. 12)

Mind continued publication until 1906. Judged by the wide range and the nature of its content and the eminence of its contributors—not only New Thought leaders, but others in the field of philosophy and religion, Eastern as well as Western—it stands out as probably the most notable of all the magazines of the New Thought Movement.

Another magazine of slightly different character, but still definitely New Thought in its main outlook, was the *Metaphysical Magazine*, "Devoted to Occult, Philosophic and Scientific Research." Edited by Leander Edmund Whipple and J. Emery McLean, who was at one time editor of *Mind*, it was published in New York City by the Metaphysical Publishing Company. The prospectus announcing its appearance described it as "devoted to scientific examination of the laws of being; to a study of the operation and phenomena of the human mind; and to a systematic inquiry into the faculties and functions, the nature and attributes of the soul—the ego of mankind." The editors and publishers are convinced

> that in the psychic realm there is a sphere of knowledge almost entirely unexplored; that man's highest and best powers are yet to be demonstrated; and that a correct understanding of his own inner nature and endowments will result in a more perfect expression of the idea in creative mind which he is intended to manifest.

In early issues such subjects were discussed as levitation, preexistence, the abolition of capital punishment, the religious training of children, comparative religions, metaphysics in India (discussed by Swami Vivekananda, who introduced Vedanta to America), the Kabbalah, Sufism, Taoism, concentration, and occult philosophy. The freedom of thought which the magazine allowed evidently led many to seek it as an avenue of expression for strange, sometimes highly sectarian, even fantastic views which the editors felt it beyond their province to publish. The magazine showed no evidence of serious bias, unless it be considered that belief in the occult or psychic is in itself an evidence of bias. Nor did there appear any propaganda on behalf of any particular form of New Thought. Yet its publication was in the stream of New Thought, rather broadly conceived; certainly all that New Thought at its highest levels stands for was treated quite freely in its pages. Though it gave considerably more space to the occult and the psychic than does modern New Thought in general, it seemed in no sense a house organ for any group.

Another periodical which is usually considered as a literary magazine rather than a New Thought publication, but which had, at least during a part of its existence, a very definite New Thought character, was the *Arena*, of Boston. There can be little doubt that the *Arena* was widely influential in bringing New Thought to the favorable attention of a wide public that probably would not have read a periodical definitely regarded as a New Thought publication.

During the years 1889-99, the *Arena* had been edited by B. O. Flower as a magazine comparable with the *Forum* and the *North*

American Review. It had espoused the cause of the common man
and had fought the tendency to concentration of economic power
in the hands of the few. In the mid-nineties it was a strong sup-
porter of Populism, and it sided with William Jennings Bryan
and his Free Silver campaign in his first try for the Presidency.
The *Arena* did not, however, limit its interest to these subjects;
it advocated women's rights, birth control, and abolition of capital punishment, and was generally on the side of liberalism and
reform in the field of religion, on which articles frequently
appeared. At the same time it was a magazine of literary pre-
tensions as well and carried articles by many of the better-known
American writers.

It never attained a wide circulation, and earned a profit in
only a few years. It was in serious financial difficulties when in
1897 it was sold to John D. McIntyre, a New York manufacturer
who made John Clark Ridpath, the historian, his editor. He
continued it as a magazine of reform, but within a year it was
announced that it would suspend publication with the September
number of 1898. At this juncture Paul Tyner of Denver, who in
1897-98 had been editor of the *Temple,* a monthly magazine
"devoted to the fuller unfoldment of the divinity of humanity,"
merged his publication with it along with another, the *Journal
of Practical Metaphysics* of Boston, edited by Horatio W. Dresser,
and later also the *Coming Light* (1896-99) of San Francisco.
Dresser became associate editor and B. O. Flower continued as
a contributor. The new management declared the policy of the
magazine to be one of independence from all parties and fac-
tions, dedicating itself to seeking out the truth regarding questions dealt with. During the year only two articles on mental
healing appeared, and none on New Thought as such. Tyner's
ownership of the magazine lasted only a year; then it was purchased and published until 1904 by John Emory McLean and
his Alliance Publishing Company of New York, the concern
which published *Mind.* McLean, assisted by Neuville O. Fan-
ning, edited the magazine for a year; but by 1900 Charles Brodie
Patterson, New Thought lecturer, became supervising editor of

both *Mind* and the *Arena,* but with former editor Flower as managing editor and H. W. Dresser as his assistant editor. During the year 1899 Dresser is credited by *Readers' Guide* with at least four articles in the *Arena* on some phases of New Thought and its relationships. One dealt specifically with "What is New Thought?" one with "The Inner Life," and one with "Christian Science and its Prophetess," which considered to some extent the relationship between Christian Science and New Thought. In the fourth article Dresser gave an interpretation of the Vedanta which had definite relevance for New Thought. The *Arena* was, therefore, in some sense a vehicle for the spread of New Thought ideas, though the agreement in publishing the two magazines was generally to keep it in the field it had first occupied and let *Mind* serve the rising metaphysical movements in a nonsectarian manner. It was during this period of Patterson's supervising editorship that the *Arena* reached its maximum circulation, a little less than thirty thousand. In its first two years it had reached twenty-five thousand, which at that time was greater than the circulation of either the *Forum* or the *Atlantic,* though it never equaled that of *Harper's* or *Century.* The fact that at the time of its peak circulation it was under essentially New Thought editorship is not without significance to the development of the movement.

In April, 1889, a small periodical, *Modern Thought,* began publication in Kansas City, Missouri, under the editorship of a former real estate man, Charles Fillmore. Merged as it was later with *Unity,* this was to be the longest lived of all the New Thought periodicals until now. Beneath the title of the first issue are the words, "Devoted to the Spiritualization of Humanity from an Independent Standpoint." The date of the first issue was April, 1889.

The writer of an article with the title "Our Mission," in the first issue, states his belief that three-fourths of the adherents of the churches have outgrown their creeds, and "long for a religion in harmony with the progress of the age." Many, he asserts, are adrift in an unknown sea of speculation, their intellectual growth having forced them away from the older expressions of faith, and the multiplicity of sects and differences in spiritual interpretation leave them confused. It is for the independent Christian or thinker particularly that *Modern Thought* will have meaning. There is, he declares, "not a periodical in the land devoted to this class." *Modern Thought* hopes to serve by pointing out the good in all religions and philosophies, and by demonstrating to men and women "that they can acceptably serve God without being bound hand and foot by creeds of church or belief of isms." These all have good in them, but none has a copyright on God's truth, "perfection being the prerogative of divinity alone." There is just one standard by which to estimate the truth or error in the beliefs and creeds of men: "By their fruits shall ye know them."

The first issue's lead editorial, on "Modern Thought," stated that it was to the wave of spiritual thought sweeping the land and calling for a publication dedicated to its discussion and dissemination that the new periodical owed its founding, not as an organ of any school of thought, but as "the mouthpiece of all honest souls earnestly seeking for spiritual light." It was hoped that "all who feel the bubbling up within them of the spirit of Universal Love will use its columns to express their views . . . never to tear down, but always to build up." It was to be a journal of progress. The desire was to grow. Man has, of course, here and there touched the truth, but a universe of Truth lies beyond to be compassed step by step. Men were still discovering truth and "inspirations of today are worthy the same reverence as those of former ages." "The influx of new thought [not capitalized] is always necessary to life, and he who writes a creed or puts a limit to revelation is an enemy of humanity." In this Charles Fillmore was quite in line with developing New Thought (capitalized), whose leaders almost all found the limitations of creeds and organizations galling.

From the wide range of interest indicated in the articles included in the first issue of *Modern Thought*, and even more in the advertisements of books and periodicals, it is apparent that the Fillmores were quite interested in the occult, Spiritualism, theosophy, Rosicrucianism, Hermeticism, and other subjects as well as in Christian Science. Incidentally, the term "Christian Science" was being used in a much looser fashion than was pleasing to the founder of that movement. When later for a time the magazine changed its name to *Christian Science Thought*, this brought a sharp rebuke from Mrs. Eddy and the name was shortly abandoned.

The back pages of the magazine list scores of books and pamphlets on sale by the Modern Thought Publishing Company and more than a score of periodicals dedicated to healing, Christian Science, Spiritualism, Rosicrucianism, and the occult in general for which *Modern Thought* would accept subscriptions.

In the second issue a "Christian Science" department is introduced. And in an article, "Is This Christian Science?" the editor states that he feels in duty bound to declare, "our views are not those of orthodox Christian Science." Although instructed by some of its best teachers, the editors "have not been able to accept as truth all that it teaches." Many schools of thought sail under the general name of Christian Science, he continues. Mrs. Eddy of Boston gave the initial impulse to it, and her ardent followers claim the exclusiveness of her inspiration; but this is doubted by others. Orthodox Christian Science, he thinks, has its vagaries as do all movements, and has also some of the fanaticism which seems necessary in the beginnings of a movement. But investigation has led to the conclusion that equally successful healing has been practiced by other metaphysical and faith cure schools quite at variance with Christian Science. Thus "a more rational philosophy is being evolved from the jumble of science and theory with which Christian Science startled a world." Organized Christian Science has outstripped its rivals. Better organized, it reaches more people. The editor admits that he is "partial to Christian Science," but by the term Christian Science he says he means "all metaphysical schools."

In the sixth issue is included a "Mental Science Catechism" written for *Modern Thought* by W. W. Atkinson, which indicates more or less what was currently believed. The fact that it was written for *Modern Thought* is evidence that the ideas expressed differed little, if at all, from those held by Mr. Fillmore at the time. In defining God the writer asserts that "There is but one God and we are but different manifestations of it, and that it is omnipotent, omnipresent and omniscient, filling all space and is Good." A logical deducation from this is that "God or Good and man are one, as Christ and the Father are one." There is but one substance, God substance. Matter is a negative stratum of this God substance, Mind is a positive stratum of the same God substance; that is, they are "different degrees of the same substance, or the same substance in different degrees of development."

Successive issues of *Modern Thought* indicate a growing sense of independence from the orthodox Christian Science movement. Charles Fillmore finds many things emphasized by them to be of little importance, while holding the central principle valid. That it works practically he has often seen demonstrated.

In an article in the ninth issue, that of January, 1890, he writes an editorial under the title "Where We Now Stand." He has espoused definitely the system of scientific religion known as Christian Science, but "because of the narrow sectarian spirit with which Christian Science has been interpreted by many of its advocates, we are loath to come under what we conceive to be a galling yoke." But since listening to Mrs. Hopkins' interpretation a broader conception had come to him and he could now see that Christian Science in its basic statements is an "epitome of the best features of the ethical and religious teachings of the past." He reserves the right, in teaching Christian Science, to "interpret the All Good from our standpoint regardless of the details taught by any school of Christian Science." (p. 8) That is, he would be a Christian Scientist, but free to interpret it as he saw it—a thoroughly Protestant attitude toward what Mrs. Eddy had set forth as Christian Science.

In the notes and comments column it is announced that "the Eddy school of Christian Scientists" have a reading room and free dispensary. In the final issue of Volume I, Mr. Fillmore returns once more to the discussion of Christian Science. He had espoused it because he thought Christian Science had a higher grasp on truth than any extant system, but because Mrs. Eddy claimed it as her exclusive property, he rebelled, yet at the same time "advocated like principles." It is the property neither of Mrs. Eddy nor Mrs. Hopkins, nor of any other person, but as a "manifestation of the Divine Mind for any soul in the universe" Christian Science as he holds it does not claim anything absolutely new in the domain of truth, but does claim to be "a better formulation and practical application of the truth than has heretofore been taught." (p. 8)

Volume II of Mr. Fillmore's periodical makes its bow with a new name, just *Thought*. The "Modern" had been dropped out, and across the term "Thought," on a kind of banner, is written "Christian Science." Thus it is really *Christian Science Thought*. Beneath the title appear the words, "There is no religion Higher than Truth." Now Myrtle Fillmore, Charles Fillmore's wife, is listed with him as editor. A special department which she edits is called "Society of Help."

In the second issue of the new volume, there is an article by Mrs. Eddy, taken from the *Christian Science Journal*, on "Love Your Enemies." This is the only time that anything directly from her has appeared, and she has been mentioned only a very few times.

In the September issue Charles Fillmore discusses the problem of evil under the title, "Good Is All." There is, he writes, no reality in evil. The only true answer to the question of evil is "that evil does not exist at all—it is an illusion of the intellect. The intellect being of the illusory world itself that which it seems to conjure up must of necessity be like it." (p. 1) This is in the best Christian Science tradition.

Volume III appeared in a smaller format. It continued the Christian Science feature of the title. Meanwhile a new periodical, *Unity*, had been begun by the Fillmores and was cutting into the circulation of *Thought*. It cost but half the price of *Thought* and many felt that it was a better paper to put into the hands of inquirers. This had led the Fillmores to consider discontinuing

Thought altogether, but before doing so they wanted the opinion of their readers. Actually *Thought* was continued through Volume VII, Number 6—that is, through September, 1895, when it was announced that the Fillmores would consolidate their publications into one, which would be called *Unity*, thereafter to be published twice a month instead of once. *Wee Wisdom*, said to be the oldest children's magazine in the United States, which had been established in 1893, now became a department of *Unity* and so continued until July, 1898, when it was published as a supplement to Volume XI of *Unity*. *Unity* had been published since January, 1891, as a monthly, and was in its sixth volume when the consolidation occurred. It has appeared continuously from that date until now, though from the time of the consolidation until August, 1898, it appeared twice monthly.

Thought dropped the Christian Science subtitle beginning with Volume IV. Mrs. Eddy had strongly objected to Charles Fillmore's reprinting of her article. She informed him that her articles were not to be used by other publications. This seems to have been but one of several attempts she made to control the name "Christian Science." At about the same time the magazine *Christian Science*, published by Joseph Adams in Chicago, changed its name to *Chicago Truth Gleaner*. In an editorial Adams asserted that the name "Christian Science" had given rise to a new sect which for "jealousy, bigotry, selfishness, unrelenting persecution and deification of personality exceeds any sect of Christendom" with which he was acquainted. (Quoted in *Thought*, III [September, 1891], 252-53) He felt that the name "Christian Science" was misleading and provocative of prejudice and antagonism, and further that Christian Science was being substituted for the gospel itself.

When *Thought* was merged with *Unity*, publication was still in the larger format, usually as a sixteen-page paper. With Volume VII, 1896, it took the smaller size which it has since employed, running annually to some six hundred pages.

From an early day both *Thought* and *Unity* published without charge the names of teachers and healers, metaphysical publishing houses, and metaphysical publications. There was at that time no overall Unity organization, and anyone who worked in the general New Thought field could list himself in the journals. Later there were listed places where the Unity publications were distributed. About 1912 the list was called simply, "Directory." In it a few recognizably non-Unity branches were listed. Then the practice began of registering all accredited Unity Centers and ministers, with an additional list of places where the literature could be found. Finally it became the custom to list simply Unity Annual Conference members and licensed teachers. At present the listing is of Unity Centers and classes and ministers who are conducting a ministry "in keeping with Christ's teaching as interpreted by Unity School of Christianity." Later Unity was to publish the other magazines we have discussed earlier.

Though never an official publication of the New Thought Movement, *Nautilus* was probably the most widely read of the many that have appeared, and was very influential. It was a private enterprise of its editor, Elizabeth Towne, who, originally a Methodist, had taken up New Thought and become a teacher. She was married at quite an early age, but the marriage proved to be an unhappy one which ended in a divorce. She had to support herself and her children. At one period, while still living in Portland, Oregon, she felt the need for added income. Her schooling had been interrupted by her early marriage and she had no background of business experience; but one day, as she tells it herself, it suddenly came to her that she should undertake to publish a small periodical.

She had no capital with which to begin it, but secured some help from her father, $30.00 per month for a six-month period, and so launched the magazine which by a kind of inspiration she chose to call *Nautilus*. Begun in 1898, it continued for more than fifty years until in August, 1953, Mrs. Towne announced that the advancing years of the editor and the increasing costs of production made it seem wise to discontinue publication with that issue.

Mrs. Towne wrote constantly for the magazine and published

numerous books and pamphlets of her own and others' on New Thought lines. It was reported that at one time the magazine subscription list ran to more than forty-five thousand, and that some of her books had sold to the number of a hundred thousand or more. Possibly those were right who said that she had been read by more than a million persons and had influenced them in the direction of New Thought.

From its place of origin in Portland, *Nautilus* moved to Holyoke, Massachusetts. There its publisher married William E. Towne, and together they eventually built up a substantial and even profitable business in the publishing and distribution of the magazine and of New Thought books. Mr. Towne was himself also editor of a magazine and distributor of books. Many famous writers contributed to *Nautilus* at one time or another—some regularly, as for example the well-known New Thought poetess Ella Wheeler Wilcox. Titles of Elizabeth Towne's works reveal her interests. Among them were *Joy Philosophy*, 1903; *Meals without Meat*, 1903; *Practical Methods of Self-development*, 1904; *How to Concentrate*, 1904; *Happiness in Marriage*, 1904; *How to Wake the Solar Plexus*, 1904; *How to Train Children and Parents*, 1904; *Experiences in Self-Healing*, 1905; *You and Your Forces*, 1906. Most of these were pamphlets or booklets of small size.

It is quite evident that Elizabeth Towne was very much the editor of *Nautilus*. The magazine, of course, belonged to her and her husband and not to any organization, though it served the entire New Thought Movement. The issues of the magazine were usually from sixy-four to eighty pages or more in length. Often there were as many as twenty-four or more pages of advertising.

Many of the advertisements were naturally concerned with healing in some form. Most of these were from the general New Thought point of view, but this was by no means true of all. A surprising number involved physical, rather than mental or spiritual, means of healing. In advertisements other than those for health products and systems of healing, complete hospitality would seem to have been extended to all of what are usually called occult systems of thought and practice.

Many of the various New Thought publishing companies advertised in the pages of *Nautilus,* which was an excellent medium for reaching a widely scattered host of readers. Every issue carried a list of distributing centers where New Thought books, magazines, pictures, etc. might be purchased or read.

The articles published in the magazine manifested the same breadth of interest as did the advertisements. There were, of course, those treating of generally accepted New Thought ideas, in their application to all aspects of life. There were articles on science, psychology, research, travel, astronomy, scientific discovery, oriental religions, and similar topics. And there were also discussions of such matters as telepathy, psychometry, hypnotism, rhythmic breathing, clairvoyance, and auras. Altogether, there was material to interest almost everyone.

The best writers of the New Thought Movement appeared in *Nautilus,* as the authors either of articles in the magazine itself or of books reviewed. Probably no book of significance in the field failed to receive mention, either appreciative or critical.

Elizabeth Towne, as editor, wrote on a wide range of subjects. And her writings, especially her editorials, were far from stuffy. Discussing the remark of a reader, "Our dear old grandmothers used to go into the silence when they knelt by the big open fireplace and earnestly prayed for the good of all," Mrs. Towne wrote:

I am not so sure of that. . . . The sort of prayer I've heard of our good old grandmothers praying would have shivered to quivers the deepest silence in space. They hollered as if God were a slightly deaf Old Gentleman on a far distant Great White Throne. And they proceeded to tell God about everybody's sins and perversities and to beseech him to shake them over the pit of hell till their teeth chattered and they begged for mercy.

A correspondent once wrote Mrs. Towne saying that as he understood it all New Thought people were once Christian

Scientists, but because they couldn't keep silence had been ejected from the Christian Science church and had become members of New Thought groups. Said Elizabeth Towne in reply, "Many, yes, but all, hardly." It was true that a good many New Thought people, once Christian Scientists, had become aware that "simply thinking Mary Baker Eddy's thoughts after her was not enough to satisfy themselves or God" and therefore had seceded. Colonel Sabin, she declared, "could not stand the hierarchical nature of Mrs. Eddy's church and therefore proposed to withdraw and start a Protestant Christian Church of his own." Whereupon, numerous Christian Scientists "moved heaven and earth and furiously emitted M.A.M. [Malicious Animal Magnetism] to prevent Colonel Sabin from leaving," keeping it up until he got his church organized.

As for herself, she "never attended a Christian Science meeting or listened to a Christian Science teacher." One of her best friends had turned Christian Scientist after being "a New Thought girl" for several years. She sought to convict Mrs. Towne of ingratitude to Mrs. Eddy for the ideas she had been teaching for a dozen years. "Bless her good little heart," wrote Mrs. Towne. "And I never read over twenty pages in *Science and Health* either, and not those until after I had for several years been teaching classes myself." And she continued, "No, I acknowledge no debt to Mrs. Eddy. I owe most to the Bible and to the theological libraries to which I had access for three years. I owe much to Warren F. Evans who taught New Thought before Mrs. Eddy taught Christian Science, and who learned many things from Quimby." She went on to acknowledge her indebtedness to a man named Childs, whose book she had read forty or fifty years before. And she owed a debt no man can pay, she said, to "the many philosophers of all ages."

As she understood it, she continued, Mrs. Eddy repudiated her debt to these philosophers. But she herself thought that the world owed Mrs. Eddy a debt,

not for *discovering* or inventing Christian Science, but *for organizing a society that systematizes and advertises to all the world the truth that was taught by Jesus and his disciples and by the philosophers of all time including Quimby, Evans and others.* For this I give due credit to Mrs. Eddy.

If, she counsels, you feel the Christian Science spell coming over you, read first the history of W. F. Evans in recent numbers of *Practical Ideals,* and also *The Philosophy of P. P. Quimby,* by Julius A. Dresser.

If then you want to join Christian Science, do so, not because you are hypnotized into imagining that Mrs. Eddy is the only or original discoverer of *anything* or that she is or was ever any more inspired than Quimby or Evans or any other philosopher of any age. They are all inspired in the same way, and by the same old truth. And don't forget it. (*Nautilus,* May, 1908, pp. 10-12)

Nautilus was one of the comparatively few religious journals that were distributed through secular channels, and presumably it was on public newsstands. It is stated in various issues that the American News Company supplies it to newsdealers "on a returnable basis."

Concerning the circulation of the magazine, a statement appeared in the November, 1907, issue that 2,800 copies of the first issue were printed; in the tenth year there were 28,000. By that time some 2,500,000 copies had been sent out. Assuming an average of five readers to each issue, the magazine was reaching some 150,000 persons each month. At the peak of its popularity, some 45,000 copies were distributed monthly.

The magazine among the so-called New Thought periodicals most likely to be available to the general public, and therefore best known to it, is probably *Science of Mind,* for it is the one such publication widely sold currently on the public newsstands. There was a time when *Unity* was also sold on the newsstands, but it is no longer to be found there. *Science of Mind* may not even be thought of as a religious magazine by those who buy it casually. It could be just another of the several psychological periodicals which are currently popular. But once it is examined, its religious character is immediately evident. It is the major publication of the Church of Religious Science, at Los Angeles, and began its life under the title *Religious Science* when first launched, in October, 1927, by Ernest Holmes, founder of the Institute of Religious Science. In December it was called the *Religious Science Monthly,* a name which it bore till November, 1928, when it became the *Religious Science Magazine.* In October, 1929, it took the name *Science of Mind,* the title under which it has appeared now for more than thirty years.

In the first issue (p. 21) Ernest Holmes had this to say about his reasons for founding the magazine:

The purpose of this magazine will be to instruct ethically, morally and religiously from a scientific viewpoint of life and its meaning. A semi-religious periodical, ethical in tendency, moral in tone, philosophical in its viewpoint, it will seek to promote that universal consciousness of life which binds all together in one great Whole. It is to be tolerant, charitable and kindly in its aspect. . . . It will seek to present readers a systematic and comprehensive study of the subtle powers of mind and spirit in so far as they are now known. . . . All truths lead back to one central theme, namely, man and his relationship to the universe in which he lives. It is to be the purpose of the periodical to show that this relationship is real, direct and dynamic; that there is such a thing as Truth and that it may be known in a degree sufficient to enable the one knowing to live a happy and useful life, wholesome, healthful and constructive; to engage in all the activities of life without being depressed by them, and to feel certain that his future is in the hands of an eternal Power and Goodness and that nothing real can ever cease to be.

William H. Brooks was listed as editor at the start. When the titled changed to *Science of Mind,* Ned L. Chapin became editor, and the distinguished New Thought leader, Christian D. Larson, himself former editor and publisher of a widely circu-lated magazine of New Thought, and one who exercised con-siderable influence over Ernest Holmes in his early career, was associate editor and a frequent contributor. Ernest Holmes him-self also contributed frequently and conducted a special Question and Answer department, in which, month after month, he sought to answer questions both theoretical and practical concerning the clear understanding and application of the Science of Mind to the individual and society. Five thousand copies of the first issue of the magazine were published.

Across the years circulation has climbed until at present some ninety thousand copies are issued monthly, of which some thirty thousand represent individual subscriptions, some ten thousand go in bundles for circulation through the churches of Religious Science and other New Thought Centers, and around fifty thousand are sold on newsstands all over the English-speaking world. A large number go to newsdealers in such faraway places as Singapore, Hong Kong, and the cities of Australia and New Zealand and South Africa. This is a record equaled by few religious magazines, not many of which are available on public newsstands even within the United States. The format of the magazine has remained substantially constant during its entire existence. It has varied somewhat in the number of its pages, running from sixty-four to a hundred or more, but even here the difference has not been great. It carries no advertising except for the publications of the Institute and Church of Religious Science. It runs each month, gratis, the list of local churches of Religious Science with their hours of meetings. And it also, for a modest fee, carries the names, addresses, and hours of availability of practitioners of Religious Science.

The magazine is in no sense a "house organ." It carries no promotional features beyond the advertising above mentioned. It carries no news of local churches or of the New Thought Movement in general. It does include, as it has always done, a meditation for each day of the week and month. And it consistently sets forth the Religious Science point of view in every issue. But it does not limit itself wholly to religious matters. It regularly publishes articles of a scientific nature, often written by distinguished scientists who are not themselves in any way to be considered members of the Religious Science church or any New Thought group. Articles by ministers of the orthodox churches, Presbyterian, Methodist, Episcopal, and others, appear from time to time, with an occasional article from a distinguished Jewish writer such as Abraham Herschel or Ernest Trattner. True, the distinctively Religious Science articles and meditations are written by Religious Science writers, but articles are accepted and even solicited from writers who have no connection with Religious Science. The magazine pays modestly for its articles and at times quite substantially for those specially solicited.

Science of Mind is read far beyond the limits of the particular group which publishes it. For example, a Methodist Sunday school teacher in one of the orthodox churches finds it invaluable in her teaching of a class of seventy persons. A Methodist minister wrote Willis Kinnear, the present editor, that he had been a minister for twenty years, but never knew what God was until he began to read the magazine. A man in New Jersey sent a gift subscription for a year at Christmas time to each of sixty-seven of his friends, most of whom probably knew nothing of Religious Science.

The magazine has had a number of editors. Maud Lathem for years carried this responsibility. Willis H. Kinnear has been editor since 1953. There is an editorial board appointed by the Board of Trustees who have general oversight of all departments of Religious Science, but the function of the editorial Board is largely consultative. The editor in general plans the successive issues, outlines the content, solicits special articles, and passes on unsolicited materials. He is aided by a capable staff in both the editorial and circulation departments, in the latter especially by the longtime secretary of Ernest Holmes, Mrs. Carmack.

When asked in a personal interview what he conceived of as the purpose of the magazine as currently issued, Mr. Kinnear replied at once: "To make clear the meaning and function of prayer, and of course in relation to every aspect of life." But the magazine covers a wide range of interests, psychological, scientific, social, theological, philosophical, devotional, etc. And an examination of the file of the periodical bears out his statement. It is broadly and deeply religious, but at the same time avoids narrow dogmatism and is wisely tolerant of differences of opinion among those who hold divergent views as to the nature and function of religious faith.

Religious Science, published by the International Association of Religious Science Churches (IARSC), began publication in December, 1954. In the initial statement it is designated "Your Daily Pocket Guide," for it is published in pocket size. The statement declares further,

This new magazine is a channel for Truth. It replaces none and enhances all. It is streamlined, compact and direct. It will fill the need of many busy people who desire a pocketful of Spiritual Ideas to make easy their day. The action of God takes place through these pages and all who read them will be permanently improved. Truth reveals itself to the ready mind and open heart. God, the One Mind, is both the Writer and the reader. Divine Ideas are its only activity.

Briefly stated, its purpose is "To spread the Principles of Science of Mind as taught in Religious Science." It is under the direction of an editorial board, and Edward Ramsey has been the managing editor during most of its existence. It is published monthly in Los Angeles. Most issues contain one to three short articles; then follows a daily page of meditation, with an appropriate scripture verse, and often a suitable affirmation is suggested for the reader's use. Each issue contains a directory of all the IARSC churches and centers and lists the practitioners, giving their addresses and hours of availability.

In 1957 a new feature was added which has been continued ever since. A series of "Twelve Basic Lessons in Religious Science" was introduced, offering a "brief but comprehensive study of the principles upon which our faith is founded." Subsequent series have covered a wide range of subjects.

The International New Thought Alliance had at first no official publication. But the need for one arose very soon. At first it took the form of the printed programs for the successive congresses which the Alliance organized.

In the one complete file of what most of the time has been

termed the *New Thought Bulletin,* now just *New Thought,* to be found in the Alliance headquarters, the first issue was the program of the San Francisco Congress, held during the Panama-Pacific Exposition in 1915. Number 2 was the program of the Chicago Congress of 1916, and Number 3 was the published report of that congress. Numbers 4, 5, and 6 were published in Washington, D.C., in February, 1916, and February and August, 1917, while Number 7 was again a congress program—that of the St. Louis Congress of 1917. Four-page *Bulletins* were published from Washington on a bimonthly basis during 1918. The program of the Boston Congress of that year, though published, was not counted as a *Bulletin* issue. Still in four-page format through the first two numbers of 1919, the *Bulletin* was enlarged to eight pages during the remainder of that year, except in December, when it appeared in sixteen pages. Again the Cincinnati Congress program was not counted as an issue.

At this congress it was voted to enlarge the *Bulletin* into a regular magazine. But there was some opposition. Up until the end of 1919, twenty-one issues of the *Bulletin* had appeared. In 1920 it became a monthly magazine with from twelve to twenty pages, plus a colored cover.

During the years 1921-24 most issues were of sixteen pages. But with the assumption of the editorship by Elizabeth Towne, who had been elected president of INTA that year, the size of the *Bulletin* jumped to as many as thirty-two, and once even fifty-six, pages. Nor was this the only change effected by Mrs. Towne. The *Bulletin* assumed a sprightliness of manner reminiscent of the *Nautilus.* Nothing Mrs. Towne had anything to do with could fail to register something of the enthusiasm and energy which was her natural character.

Under succeeding editors in 1926-30, the *Bulletin* returned to its earlier and more modest dimensions. Then in 1931, when Dr. Thomas Parker Boyd was editor, the Great Depression made itself felt. Only seven issues appeared that year; and for the next decade the magazine was issued irregularly. At the end of 1941, under the editorship of John N. Garns, the *Bulletin* appeared

in a new format resembling that of the *Reader's Digest*. At this
time it was published in Minneapolis. With Volume XXVII it
returned to its original format and became a quarterly, which
it has remained until the present.

During the nearly half a century of its publication, the *Bulletin*
has been chiefly a "house organ." While of course it has been
edited and published as an exponent of the general New Thought
point of view, its particular purpose has been to advance the
INTA as the overall unifying force in a highly divergent and
extremely individualistic field. It has done this in several ways.
It has been the chief medium for the promotion of the annual
congresses, which have probably been the principal means of
holding the somewhat amorphous New Thought Movement
together, and the regional rallies that have brought together
the leaders and considerable numbers of the followers of New
Thought for discussion of their common purposes and problems,
as well as for personal acquaintance and good fellowship. And
it has not only reported faithfully the decisions reached by the
congresses, but also brought to the movement as a whole something of their inspiration, by printing in whole or in part some
of the more outstanding addresses given by the principal speakers.

It has been the chief means of communication between the
responsible leadership of the Alliance and the field. It has given
the INTA president, who has always been the editor, a means
of contact with the whole membership, a medium through which
to present his ideas and plans for the development of the movement. In a real sense, the periodical has served as a faithful
reflection of the outlook and general point of view of the presi-
dent-editor. Those who served but a single year or even two
years had little opportunity to make an effective impact upon
the magazine. Some have had little drive, some, comparatively
little journalistic ability or interest. But each has left some mark
of his particular personality and point of view upon it.

Most colorful of all was Elizabeth Towne, in many ways a
great editor, as proved by her success in editing *Nautilus;* but
John N. Garns, Ervin Seale, and particularly Raymond Charles

Barker, each brought a special quality to the editorship. James A. Edgerton and Robert H. Bitzer have served as editors longer than any others. It was under Edgerton that the *Bulletin* had its start and developed from a purely promotional periodical to one in which the serious issues of New Thought began to be presented. It was undoubtedly highly influential in keeping the young organization going against a considerable apathy, if not open hostility, on the part of some important leaders. Under Robert H. Bitzer, it has become somewhat less a "house organ," though still definitely that, and more a general magazine, discussing not only organizational aims and problems, but also the general principles embodied in the whole New Thought area.

Editor Barker had a definite interest in the history of the movement. From time to time he published articles on the major personalities in the development of New Thought, together with an occasional article revealing specific historic steps in its unfoldment. These included admirable studies of some of the earlier aspects of the movement, as well as articles on Quimby, Evans, Emerson, and other creative figures.

The *Bulletin* has always carried news, not alone of the Alliance itself, but of the constituent bodies also. It has kept close account of changes in the constitution and by-laws, and has presented in almost every issue the latest formulation of the Declaration of Principles. From very early in its history it has carried a list of its group members with addresses of their centers. It has faithfully reviewed books—not alone those of distinctive New Thought character, but also general books that might be of interest to New Thought readers. It has provided a forum for discussion, through letters to the editor as well as through contributed articles, of any question of major interest to its readers. And finally, through its advertising section it has kept before the public the books, pamphlets, records, radio and TV programs, classes, seminars, and other services available to readers. It mirrors, in short, the whole New Thought Movement in all its diversity, more faithfully than does any other single periodical.

It has never enjoyed a mass circulation. It has probably never printed more than ten thousand copies of any single issue. It is distributed through individual and group subscriptions, besides packages going to constituent groups for sale to their non-subscribing members and the public through the regular book table maintained by practically every New Thought center, and through the efforts of the local literature committees. Considerable numbers of each issue are distributed free in the effort to interest additional persons in New Thought and in subscribing to the magazine itself.

Some of the New Thought magazines published abroad will be discussed later in chapters on New Thought in the various countries—England, France, Germany, South Africa, and Australia. At one time there was also a Spanish periodical, *Mente* (*Mind*), published in Santiago, Chile, described in 1921 in the INTA *Bulletin* as "an attractive magazine of 30-40 pages." At present there is no information concerning any New Thought activity in Chile, or indeed anywhere in Spanish-speaking South America, though there was a Santiago Center listed as late as 1947.

There was reported in 1921 a Brazilian New Thought magazine, *O Pensamento,* in São Paulo, Brazil, issued by the "Esoteric Circle," composed of several thousand members, and this society was said to publish also a weekly paper, but again, investigation reveals no present-day New Thought publishing activity in that country.

12

New Thought Leaders

FROM THE BEGINNING of the organized New Thought Movement there have been outstanding leaders in every period who have been highly influential through their personal lecturing, teaching, and writing for the recognized New Thought groups. But New Thought has of course always been a minority movement. No one knows how many real adherents it has even in its organized form, for most branches of the movement do not make public any figures as to their membership. None of the groups is even listed in the *Yearbook of the Churches* which annually publishes church membership statistics for the United States. In part this is due to the fact that exclusive membership in them is not a requirement on those who join. And not a few continue still as members in the larger denominations while they participate also in the life of the New Thought groups.

But like minorities in almost any area of interest, New Thought groups are influential far beyond the number of their own loyal members. This comes about in a variety of ways. Sometimes it is through powerful individual leaders who by their effectiveness as lecturers, preachers, or teachers attract huge audiences and a personal following that goes far beyond the limits of organized New Thought. Or it may be through their writings that are read by the general public as well as by specifically New Thought followers, so that their ideas are accepted without any recognition that they are New Thought at all, by persons never related in any way to the New Thought organizations.

Or the outreach may be through individual leaders within the organized orthodox churches who in the reading of New Thought literature or contact with New Thought leaders find something which they regard as a valid part of the gospel they are supposed to preach, but which has fallen into relative disuse, or some new method or technique of making effective ideas which they hold to be a part of the gospel, but which they had not before known how to employ.

It would seem to be logical to group together first those who were acknowledged followers of New Thought, in many cases indeed distinguished leaders of it, who have managed in one way or another to get the attention of the world beyond the New Thought organization and to pour out into the general cultural stream fundamentally New Thought ideas and suggested methods of attaining the ends sought for not only by New Thought people, but by all the people. Then, second, to single out at least a few leaders within the orthodox churches who are employing essentially New Thought concepts and certain techniques popularized by New Thought, in their ministry within these churches.

Few if any of these men have been original in their thinking. The main lines of New Thought were laid down substantially before most of them came along. They added little or nothing to what had already been taught by the pioneer leaders of the movement. But they did interpret and express it in new ways, each according to his own genius, attempting to make it more effective and relevant to their own contemporaries. Some were organization men, others were aloof from organization, operating chiefly as teachers or lecturers, while others had little contact personally with the people, save through their writings. Yet all, in one way or another, were able to attract a substantial following of readers or listeners, or both, from among the larger public who never became in any formal sense New Thought adherents.

Three of the earlier writers have already been discussed—Henry B. Wood, Horatio W. Dresser, and Ralph Waldo Trine.

Thus far no single subsequent writer has been so widely read as Ralph Waldo Trine. But in a later day there arose one who, as a preacher, attracted greater audiences than any before him, and the circulation of whose writings bid fair eventually to equal or surpass those of Trine, at least in English. This was the late Dr. Emmet Fox, pastor of the Church of the Healing Christ, founded by Dr. W. John Murray in 1906 and called also the First Church of Divine Science, in New York City.

Dr. Murray had a numerous personal following. He had spoken for years to one of the large congregations in New York, meeting in the great ballroom of the Hotel Waldorf-Astoria. At his passing he was succeeded for a time by Dr. A. C. Grier. Meanwhile, Emmet Fox, who had been a very successful English electrical engineer, had become interested in New Thought, or Higher Thought as it was called in England. He lectured frequently in the various London Higher Thought centers. Then in 1930 he came to America. He spoke at the Church of the Truth in New York and drew large crowds. For a time he lectured and taught independently in a New York hotel, attracting a generous following. But he was only a layman and felt that if he were to minister thus he should be ordained. Unity, when approached, according to Lowell Fillmore, stated that it would ordain only those who had taken the training regarded as a prerequisite. Emmet Fox was already a highly successful preacher and teacher, as proved by the throngs who attended on his ministry in New York. Nona Brooks of Divine Science was quite willing to waive the formal requirements, and so he was ordained as a minister of Divine Science by the College of Divine Science at Denver. Shortly after this Dr. Grier resigned as pastor of the Church of the Healing Christ, and Emmet Fox was called to succeed him.

Thus began one of the most remarkable ministries of any church in America in that or any other period. Dr. Fox's crowds grew larger and larger, necessitating a move each time to more ample quarters, until in the end the great Hippodrome was rented, and for several years he had the distinction of preaching to the largest congregation in New York City, and probably the greatest in all America.

When the Hippodrome was finally torn down to make way for newer and more needed buildings, Dr. Fox and his congregation had to move to the Manhattan Opera House, which was remodeled for the purpose. Eventually another move was made to Carnegie Hall, where he ministered to crowds often overflowing the auditorium and requiring the use of auxiliary rooms to which his voice could be carried by the public address system.

On a cold rainy Sunday morning in May, 1947, the writer attended one of Dr. Fox's services. It was a disagreeable day to be out, yet the main floor of Carnegie Hall was filled, as well as the first two tiers of boxes, and at least part of the first gallery. The crowd seemed to be middle to upper middle class, well dressed, though not flashily so. More were around middle age than under, though not a few were young people. On the great stage were a bank of flowers, a pulpit, and a single chair which Dr. Fox occupied.

The service differed in no particular from an ordinary church service save for a silent healing meditation period. The whole service lasted less than an hour and a half. The silent healing meditation, conducted by Dr. Fox, who spoke with great assurance, seemed to be the most effective part of the service. His affirmations were all positive. They all involved God, his love, his power, his healing, his desire for men's good, not in some distant future, but now. "God is here," he said. "God is Love. God is love now, and you know it. God desires only your good. He never sends ill. He wants you to be well. He is healing you now and you know it." The positiveness, the quiet assurance, and the immediateness of all that went on in the service, recognized by each individual person, made it exceedingly impressive.

The sermon, entitled "Ha, Ha, Among the Trumpets, Says the Bible," had nothing in it which was remotely suggested by the title. It was short, not more than twenty minutes. Dr. Fox spoke much of God, who, he said, "has every personal quality except limitation." He spoke to and of God in the most personal and intimate terms, though occasionally referring to him impersonally. The general tenor of the sermon was, "Don't be too hard on yourself." Apply the Golden Rule to yourself as well as to other people. If you have sinned, repentance is proper and necessary, but just don't sin any more. Don't bear your sin about as a burden. You aren't perfect and don't expect to be. He spoke of his church as an undenominational church of Christ. He said that the love of God and prayer are at the very heart of Jesus' teachings.

In his announcements he reminded the people of the book department in a side room of the building. After watching the great hall empty itself, I stepped into the book room, only to find such a crowd about the tables that I could hardly see what was on them. Most of the books and pamphlets were by Dr. Fox himself, with some others of kindred nature. Three or four women were selling books, and they were all kept busy.

Dr. Fox died in 1951, a comparatively young man, but his influence lives on in his writings which have had a phenomenal circulation, and not simply among New Thought people. His publishers, Harpers, have distributed over six hundred thousand copies of his *The Sermon on the Mount,* which has become something of a Christian classic, found in almost any bookstore in America which stocks religious books at all. Ministers of every denomination read it. The writer has seen it on the bookshelves of many ministers. They do not, of course, read it as New Thought, but they buy it and read it. And over a quarter of a million copies of his *Power through Constructive Thinking,* a sheer New Thought title, are in circulation. Altogether a total of a million and a quarter of his publications have been distributed, excluding the pamphlets which circulate in fabulous numbers.

How can we account for the popularity of Dr. Fox's ministry as preacher and writer? Who can say? He was in no way sensational either in his language, in his ideas, or in his illustrations. Compared to such performances as those of Aimee Semple McPherson, Billy Sunday, or even Billy Graham, his services were models of quiet, thoughtful, prayerful worship. He was very down-to-earth. He made things as simple as profound truth can be made. He was direct. He was forthright. He had a warmth about him that drew people to him personally, though he was not gregarious and had few close friends or associates. But he was deeply sincere. He was hopeful. He was optimistic in the best sense, and so utterly sure of the gospel and its workability that his quiet confidence led men to want to hear him. His message was for "right now." He had a faith in the future—of that no one can doubt who reads him—but his religion was for here and now—and people needed just that. So they listened to him, and they still read him, many not knowing that his was the gospel of New Thought.

The influence of Emmet Fox in the spread of New Thought ideas and emphases lies not simply in the large number of his readers, but in the fact that he is so widely read by ministers of all denominations, who in turn are heard and read by the general public. A check in large denominational bookstores in various cities from time to time has revealed that Emmet Fox's books are in constant demand; and these are the stores in which ministers chiefly buy their books. There is nothing sectarian, certainly, in the titles *The Sermon on the Mount* and *The Lord's Prayer*, nor is there anything about them outwardly to indicate that they are New Thought.

In a number of American cities New Thought leaders, speaking usually in theaters in lieu of buildings of their own, have attracted large audiences; and often in more recent times, through the use of radio, or in some cases of TV, they have spoken to very large numbers of people, many of them quite unrelated to New Thought. This has been particularly true of West Coast cities.

Ernest Holmes, founder of Religious Science, had a very large hearing, both in his home city and when in the earlier day he teamed with his brother Fenwicke Holmes to put on special lectures and classes in other cities, chiefly in the East. Fenwicke, after they went their separate ways, also continued to draw large audiences. And other contemporary leaders have spoken to great numbers of people, many of whom are transients or radio listeners in no way related to organized New Thought.

And now and then some lay figure, a poet, journalist, philosopher, or even a businessman who is in no sense a professional leader, gets a wide hearing or reading for New Thought ideas by the general public. Not known primarily as representative of a minority religious group, they are heard or read without prejudice, and often enough their ideas, when not specifically designated as an expression of a minority point of view, are accepted readily—indeed, often as corroborating what the reader or hearer had himself thought sometimes, though he had perhaps never said so, even to himself. Such a one was poetess Ella Wheeler Wilcox (1855-1919).

She may not have been one of America's greatest poets, but in her time she was one of the most popular, her verse appearing in innumerable magazines and periodicals as well as a number of books. She has probably been read by many more people than poets who have been considered her superiors. While she is no longer read by many, and is largely forgotten, she is still comparatively well represented in the poetic anthologies. In the Granger *Index to Poetry* (4th edition), covering poems published through 1950, she has eighty-eight titles. While this is less than the number from most of the well-known poets of first rank, it is more than the number from Amy Lowell, Eugene Field, or Harriet Monroe, and almost as many as James Whitcomb Riley and Edwin Arlington Robinson have.

A number of her poems are found in as many as five, six, or seven different popular anthologies, mostly of the inspirational type. One very widely used anthology, *Quotable Poems*, edited by Thomas Curtis Clark, contains thirteen of her poems. Another, *Poems That Touch the Heart*, which has gone through more than twenty-five printings, has seventeen, a number exceeded by only one other poet, while *The World's Best Loved Poems*, edited by James C. Johnson (Harpers, 1927), includes seven of her poems. Only Henry Wadsworth Longfellow has a larger representation.

Not all these poems are, of course, New Thought in outlook, for she wrote all sorts of verse. One of her volumes bore the title *Poems of Passion*. Read in the light of today's preoccupation with torrid passion, it seems rather passionless. But of the eighty-eight in the Granger *Index*, eighteen were definitely in the spirit of New Thought, and several others could be considered as emphasizing some New Thought values—as, for example, the unimportance of creeds.

In a dozen or more different poems in one of her books, *Poems of Power*, may be discerned typical New Thought ideas and emphases. Indeed, in the preface she says specifically that the word "power" in the title "refers to the Divine Power in every human being, the recognition of which is the secret to all success and happiness."

In the poem "Assertion" (p. 18) she is really talking about affirmation, which is the heart of New Thought technique. "I am serenity"..."I am good health"..."I am success." The last stanza, ending,

> God is my Father, He has wealth untold,
> His wealth is mine, health, happiness, gold,

can be found, in other words of course, in almost any New Thought writer. Or again, in "Success"—a subject that is a preoccupation especially of the more secular wing of New Thought, the idea is based on the concept of man's divinity:

> ... Man may be
> And do the thing he wishes, if he keeps
> That one dominant thought through night and day,
> And knows his strength is limitless because
> Its foundation is in God.

The power of thought is emphasized, and more, the thought of man as divine, supreme, which is the real answer to man's problems. In the poem "Words" is stressed the necessity of "positive thinking," and the power of affirmation.

> Words are great forces in the realm of life.
> Be careful of their use. Who talks of hate,
> Poverty, of sickness, but sets rife
> These very elements to mar his fate.

Rather let men talk of "love, health, happiness"; "Their names repeated over day by day" become realities.

In "Attainment" (p. 85), she says:

> Use all your hidden forces. Do not miss
> The purpose of this life, and do not wait
> For circumstance to mould or change your fate.

> In your own self is destiny. Let this
> Vast truth cast out all fear, all prejudice,
> All hesitation. Know that you are great,
> Great with divinity. So dominate
> Environment. . . .
> Once let the spiritual laws be understood,
> Material things must answer and obey.

Finally, in her poem "You Never Can Tell," she emphasizes once again the power of thought, a typical New Thought emphasis, in a stanza that was familiar to thousands who had never heard of New Thought.

> You never can tell what your thoughts will do
> In bringing you hate or love,
> For thoughts are things, and their airy wings
> Are swifter than carrier doves.
> They follow the law of the Universe,
> Each thing must create its kind,
> And they speed o'er the track to bring you back
> *Whatever went out from your mind.*

But Ella Wheeler Wilcox wrote not only poetry. She did a great deal of prose writing as well. A number of her essays specifically on New Thought themes appeared in a volume entitled *The Heart of New Thought,* which the publisher's preface described as a "Noteworthy interpretation of New Thought, the backbone of which philosophy is the Power of Right Thought. ... Mrs. Wilcox is ever the voice of the People: what she says is practical, what she thinks is clear, what she feels is plain." The particular edition used here was the tenth thousand. A later edition, published in England, proclaimed itself as the twentieth thousand. In an advertisement at the end of the book it was stated that Mrs. Wilcox would become associate editor of *New Thought Magazine,* published by the publisher of the book, and would contribute to it regularly.

There was nothing distinctive or new in her treatment of New Thought. She called it a science, the Science of Right Thinking. "Do not tell me that you are sick and broken in spirit. The Spirit cannot be sick or broken, because it is of God. It is your mind that makes your body sick." Assert daily, once, twice, or better twenty times a day, "I am love, health, wisdom, cheerfulness, power for good, prosperity, success, usefulness, opulence." But, she warned, growth is slow and patience and persistence are necessary. (pp. 8-10) "Believe in your own God-given power to overcome anything and everything," she wrote. (p. 19).

Her attitude toward the contemporary forms of orthodox religion was typical, and she thanks God that a wholesome religion has taken its place, one which says, "I am all goodness, love, truth, mercy, health ... that I am a necessary part of God's universe ... a living soul, and that only good can come through me or to me. God made me, and he could make nothing but goodness, purity and worth." (p. 35)

She is true to New Thought in her declaration, "Right Thinking Pays Large Dividends." *Think* success, prosperity, usefulness, she writes. "Every time we entertain thoughts of love, sympathy, forgiveness and faith, we add to the well-being of the world and create fortunate and successful conditions for ourselves. Those

may be late in coming to us, But They Will Come." (pp.
50-51, *passim*)

She realizes that men may be attracted to New Thought by
its declaration of men's right to material wealth and his power
through mind to create conditions that produce it, but though
she is sure it is true, woe to those who cultivate mental and
spiritual power for this reason alone, for they make themselves
spiritual outcasts and their wealth will bring them no happiness.
Rather, she cries, "Make your assertion of opulence the last in
your list, as you make love first." (p. 66) The first step to take
in New Thought is self-conquest. The man who wishes to control
circumstances "must love better things than money before he
can succeed. He must love and respect and believe in his creator
and trust the Divine Man within himself, and he must illustrate
this love and trust by his daily conduct in his home circle and
in his business station." (p. 70)

But it was probably as regular contributor to newspapers that
Ella Wheeler Wilcox reached her widest public, for she wrote
syndicated articles for the Hearst papers. Many of these were
simply expositions of the central teachings of New Thought,
though not definitely linked with that minority point of view.
Thus New Thought ideas found an outlet to the public they could
never have gotten through specifically New Thought channels.
Many of these ideas commended themselves to the minds of
readers which might well have been closed by denominational
prejudices, had they come labeled as New Thought.

Mrs. Wilcox was certainly New Thought in her general outlook, but she went much farther than many of the leaders of the
movement in her espousal also of ideas which are regarded as
occult. And some of the leaders were not always happy with what
she wrote. She was strongly drawn to Spiritualism and gave much
credit to oriental—especially Indian—thought, as the source of
many of her ideas.

There have been other New Thought poets. Victor Morgan,
who came to be known as the poet laureate of the movement,

wrote a great many poems which were widely read among New Thought followers. He is really the chief figure in the creation of a New Thought hymnology. Fenwicke and Ernest Holmes also wrote verse, and collaborated on an unusual epic poem, *The Voice Celestial* (Dodd, Mead, 1960), which is a remarkable presentation of the heart of New Thought in poetic form.

Angela Morgan was a devout believer in New Thought and many of her poems express the ideas central in the movement. She did not attain the popularity of Ella Wheeler Wilcox, nor has she fared as well in the anthologies, though some of her poems are still to be found in the better anthologies of religious verse. She published a number of volumes, some of which went through various editions and were read beyond the limits of New Thought. A part of one of her poems was read at the dedication of the tomb of the unknown soldier in Arlington, and another was used in a broadcast on the occasion of a memorial to the late Will Rogers. She was a frequent speaker at New Thought conferences and spoke or read her poetry to many local New Thought groups. Undoubtedly she was a channel for the flow of New Thought ideas into the thought of the general public.

Don Blanding was not always a follower of New Thought. In the biographical accounts of him which appeared after his death no reference is made to any religious element in his career, except one which listed him as a member of the Episcopal church. But in his later years he was quite active in New Thought circles, and at his passing the president of INTA characterized him as "one of the most prominent teachers in the Metaphysical Movement." (*New Thought,* Vol. XL, No. 2, p. 33) He told a *Current Biography* reviewer once that during a period of despondency in 1942 he had found that the study of metaphysics (New Thought) met his need and he became quite active in the Churches of Religious Science. He lectured often in the Los Angeles Religious Science Churches and over the air, and later in New York lectured repeatedly at Town Hall, at the Church of Religious Science, on New Thought subjects. He became a frequent contributor to *Science of Mind* magazine, and conducted "Don Blanding's Page" in *Let's Live*, a monthly health magazine.

Born in Oklahoma in 1894, he had been attracted to Hawaii by seeing a play, *Bird of Paradise*, and spent a number of years in the Islands, where he eventually came to be considered the Hawaiian poet laureate. He contributed a column and verse to the *Star Bulletin* of Honolulu. He became a commercial artist and subsequently illustrated most of his own books. *Vagabond's House*, his most popular book, was first published in 1928 and went through forty-five editions. Other volumes followed, and a number were printed over and over again. It was in his later period that New Thought ideas appeared in his poems.

Typical is his *Today Is Here* (Dodd, Mead, 1946). There is little in the book that indicates any specific New Thought interest, though one or two poems do express the spirit of the movement at one level. The item most definitely New Thought is not a poem but a story, "A Talisman for You," at the end of the book. In a time of deep depression, a Hawaiian friend gave him a cryptic formula, L-I-D-G-T-T-F-T-A-T-I-M, which he had carved on the fireplace mantel in his Vagabond's House.

His friend asked him to repeat the words for which the letters stood, when he had gone to bed and relaxed. He did so. The words were "Lord, I do give thee thanks for that abundance that is mine." At first, he writes, he laughed hollowly, thinking that it was a poor time to be thankful for nothing. What abundance was his? Then he got to thinking and began to list his assets—six feet, one inch of healthy body. He recalled a legless pencil seller, a blind friend, etc. His list of abundance grew. "It is not enough just to say the words, you must say them with conviction," he wrote. "Carve them in your heart even if you don't put them over your mantel." That is excellent New Thought technique.

Don Blanding did not appear in the anthologies of religious verse as often as Angela Morgan or Ella Wheeler Wilcox. In James Morrison's *Masterpieces of Religious Verse*, where Angela Morgan has four poems and Mrs. Wilcox seven, he has only two. One is on war, the other on "The Journey Ends." While not specifically New Thought, for almost any Christian poet might have written much the same thing, his delineation of "death" as "withdrawal" rather than ending certainly fits the New Thought pattern. This is from *The Pilot Bails Out* (Dodd, Mead, 1943):

> I have seen death too often to believe in death.
> It is not an ending . . . but a withdrawal,
> As one who finishes a long journey,
> Stills the motor,
> Turns off the lights,
> Steps from his car
> And walks up the path
> To the home that awaits him.

New Thought finds expression at various levels. Sometimes it is highly philosophical, really an expression of pure philosophical idealism. Again it is profoundly religious, a noble mystical approach to reality. At times it is warmly devotional. But there is another side to it, a practical application of New Thought to matters of supply, and it seems at times very secular in its interest, stressing the power of positive thinking in relation to success measured often in terms of money. At this level it is little different from the secular approach to success, and uses essentially the same methods. It is difficult to distinguish New Thought at this level from the application of merely psychological techniques to the attainment of desired ends. Sometimes those who make this approach have actually come to it through New Thought consciously, but sometimes they have been quite unconscious of any indebtedness to the movement.

One of the most widely read of all those who have stressed especially the ability to accomplish great things through the proper use of the mind was Orison Swett Marden. He was actually an exponent of New Thought, though seldom if ever identifying it as such, and active in some of its organizational forms. Now pretty well forgotten, he was at one time perhaps as widely read, not only in America, but throughout the world, as any American writer of his time, unless it were the popular novelists of the day whose reading public was restricted almost entirely to America, or at most to the English-speaking world. But this man was read literally all over the world.

Thirty of his books—he was a prolific writer—were translated into Spanish. Once a special edition of nine thousand copies of one of his books was printed in Spanish and copies were used as prizes in the Central American republic of Guatemala.

Thirty of his books were also translated into German, and over half a million copies of them sold. All told, it was reported in 1925, three million copies of Marden's books had been translated and sold in twenty-five different languages. One of his books, *Pushing to the Front,* required twelve printings the first year, and a total of 250 editions appeared in America alone. It was translated into some twenty-five tongues, and in Japan alone nearly a million copies were distributed. One Japanese woman was reported to have said, "We call it the Japanese Bible."

Who was Orison Swett Marden? He was the son of poor parents, born on a New England farm in 1850. He attended Boston University, and also Andover Theological Seminary. Graduating from Boston University in 1871, he took an M.D. at Harvard in 1881, an LL.B. degree, also at Harvard, in 1882, and studied at the Boston School of Oratory. During his college days he worked at catering and hotel management and was so successful that he had some $20,000 in capital when he finished his formal training.

Then he went to Block Island, near Newport, Rhode Island, and bought a property which he developed into a thriving resort area. Hardly a background, one would think, for a later literary career. He went on to buy a chain of hotels in Nebraska, but in 1892 met financial reverses and had to take employment once more as a hotel manager in Chicago during the World's Fair of 1893. Then he went back to Boston and started over again.

When he first read Samuel Smiles is not disclosed, but the English writer became his first literary hero and inspired much that Marden wrote and accomplished. Smiles's *Self-Help,* which he had found in an attic and read, did much in the shaping of his career. He once wrote, "The little book was the friction which wakened the spark sleeping in the flint." Later of course he also read Emerson, Oliver Wendell Holmes, Longfellow, Phillips Brooks, and others, but Smiles was the "awakener." It became his ambition, he says, to become the Samuel Smiles of America, and there is little doubt that he achieved his ambition.

On his return to Boston, he began to try to put together his ideas, particularly concerning optimism, which was to be a central theme in his writing—incidentally also a central theme in New Thought. His first book, *Pushing to the Front*, published in 1894, had, as we have said, a phenomenal circulation. In 1897 he founded *Success Magazine,* which reached the enormous circulation, for that time, of nearly a half-million, meaning of course that it was read by from two to three million readers. This periodical ran into financial difficulties and suspended publication in 1912. But once again, in 1918, he founded a new *Success* which was rapidly climbing in circulation when death ended his career, in 1924. This was a magazine of optimism, of confidence in man and his ability to do what he willed to do, a central theme of New Thought.

Marden's book titles express eloquently the outlook of cheerful optimism and confidence. At his death it was said of him that he averaged two books a year, from his first in 1894 to his last just before his passing in 1924, and had some two million words in as yet unpublished manuscripts when he died. There was much repetition, of course, in his successive books, but as they came in a steady stream from his pen they were eagerly bought. T. Y. Crowell alone published thirty full-length books by him, besides numerous smaller books and pamphlets. In the *U.S. Catalogue of Books in Print* for 1912, thirty-one titles were listed under his name, and in 1928, four years after his death, there were fifty-one. Alas, it must be confessed that in the current edition of *Books in Print* only one title remains. Here are a few of his titles: *Rising in the World, or Architects of Fate,* 1897; *The Secret of Achievement,* 1898; *Cheerfulness as a Life Power,* 1899; *Every Man a King,* 1906; *The Optimistic Life,* 1907; *He Can*

Who Thinks He Can, 1908; *Peace Power and Plenty,* 1909; *The Miracle of Right Thought,* 1910; *The Joys of Living,* 1913; *How to Get What You Want,* 1917; *Prosperity and How to Attract It,* 1922.

While most of these books make little or no mention of religion, some do. Marden was rather a writer of essentially New Thought faith than a writer technically on New Thought as such. Actually he was for several years president of the League for a Higher Life, a New Thought organization in New York City of which Eugene del Mar was for many years the effective leader, and of which Robert H. Bitzer, long president of the INTA, was onetime secretary. It is not certain that Marden ever used the term New Thought to describe his faith, but an article which he wrote on the "Rediscovery of God" clearly represents the typical New Thought outlook.

In contrast to the severe theological emphasis on sin and eternal punishment so current in his boyhood is this passage:

The supreme thought of Jesus, Son of Man and Son of God was to impress upon man his divinity, his oneness with his maker, his greatness and vast possibilities as a son of God. . . . He tried to show his disciples that his Kingdom of Heaven was not some far distant place, but that it was within men. He told them that if they would only have faith in the God-Power within them, they would do even greater things than he, Jesus himself, had done.

Note the use of the term "God Power within them," a typical New Thought phrase. (Connally, *Life of O. S. Marden,* p. 301)

He goes on to equate "God" and "Good," to remark that it was unfortunate that the "o" had dropped out of Good and that God had been misinterpreted, he thought, to suggest form instead of Spirit; and to assert that it was a mistake to teach people to think of God "as a person instead of Spirit or Principle—the eternal Principle of Good." (p. 302) God means the everlasting, changeless Principle of Good, he writes, capitalizing both Principle and Good. "God is the heart of all reality," he declares. "He permeates all life, He is life." (p. 303) "The church of the new age will be creedless," is a typical New Thought observation. (p. 307) "The Christ is the kernel of Christianity." He quotes Ella Wheeler Wilcox approvingly:

> A thousand creeds have come and gone
> But what is that to you or me?
> Creeds are but branches of a tree —
> The root of Love lives on and on.

"And what is love but God?" he asks. (p. 308) We do not care so much today, he observes, "about what kind of a lamp our brother uses so long as it lights his fellow-man's path and gives him light— the light of truth, the light of helpfulness, of service, of love, the light that radiates from the All-Good.... The light, not the lamp, the Christ not the creed, is what the hungering world wants." (pp. 309-10)

In an article on "The Great Adventure," the change called death, he writes:

But why should we fear? We have had to trust a higher power than our own every moment of our lives. Not for one instant have we been able to take care of ourselves without this Infinite Power, this Inscrutable Wisdom.... Why in the face of the change called death, why should we then distrust It? Why should we shrink from taking the leap in the dark when Father-Mother God calls us to leap into his Everlasting Arms?

All this is definitely in the New Thought tradition, though it wears the cloak of orthodoxy, and it proclaims Marden as a definite and highly influential figure, whether consciously so or not, in the outreach of New Thought ideas into the general culture of his time.

Typical of the more or less secular expression of New Thought in popular form in the mid-twentieth century is *The Magic of Believing* by Claude M. Bristol (Prentice-Hall). It is little more than another Marden book, dealing with essentially the same forces, looking toward essentially the same end—that is, the achievement of success—but expressed in the language of mid-twentieth century America. Writing when he did, Bristol had a great wealth of psychological experimentation back of him: the whole remarkable work of Freud, Jung, and others who have plumbed the depth of the subconscious, the disclosures of the parapsychologists who have attempted to discover the laws of operation of extra-sensory perception (ESP), as well as the work of writers like Dale Carnegie, who taught his generation *How to Win Friends and Influence People*. And it should be said that he draws upon all these sources rather than upon those of the more properly religious exponents of New Thought.

In his first chapter he tells something about how he came to tap the power of belief. Past fifty when he wrote, he claimed that he had had many years of "hard practical business experience," as well as a goodly number of years as a newspaperman, police reporter and editor of the church section of a large city daily. Here he met all sort of religious leaders, among them "mind healers, divine healers, Spiritualists, Christian Scientists, New Thoughters, Unity leaders, sun-worshippers, and yes, even a few infidels and pagans." He witnessed all kinds of evangelistic efforts, from those of Gypsy Smith to those of Aimee Semple McPherson. He visited Lourdes in France, Salt Lake City and the Mormons, the Dukhobors of Canada, and the learned *kahunas* of Hawaii, by whose powers he was profoundly impressed.

Again, he asserted that he had read literally thousands of books dealing with

religions, cults, and both physical and mental science ... modern psychology, metaphysics, ancient magic, Voodooism, Yogism, Theosophy, New Thought, Couéism and many others dealing with what I call "mind stuff" as well as philosophies and teachings of the great masters of the past. (p.6)

Gradually it came to him that there was a common element running through all of them, *belief*, which made these systems work for those who sincerely applied them. It is therefore of *the magic of believing* that he writes. One night while in the army, on a crowded troop train in France, he made up his mind that when he returned to civilian life he "would have a lot of money." At that moment, he says, the whole pattern of his life was altered. The idea of becoming rich was steadily held in mind. His doodling took the form of dollar signs. Within ten years he had a fortune. Then with a desire to share his good fortune with others he began lecturing on the subject, and finally he put his ideas into a book which he called *T.N.T. It Rocks the Earth*, of which *The Magic of Believing* seems to be an enlargement. He appears to have had an experience too of what he calls "illumination." It seems that something which is called "Cosmic Consciousness" had induced it. He described the experience of a "brilliant white light" to which he had alluded in the first draft of *T.N.T.*, but toned down merely to "light" in the published form. But, says he, "In those few seconds, I received more knowledge and understanding than I had ever received in my years of reading and study." This bears a striking resemblance to the experience of Dr. Frank B. Robinson, founder of Psychiana. And it was a part of Robinson's technique to try to induce the experience of the "white light." The remarkable results Bristol relates sound also strikingly like some of those of Dr. Robinson.

Robinson falls clearly within the New Thought pattern, both in theory and in practice. So does Bristol. It is not insisted that Bristol was at all consciously related to New Thought, but only that in general outlook and technique he falls within the limits of the rather formless area of New Thought in America. Certainly the practical outreach of New Thought is greatly extended through such books, which because of the large numbers in which they are circulated evidently make a considerable impact upon the American mind.

Note the central emphasis of Bristol, the power of mind or thought. Incidentally, he quotes Emerson (p. 28) "that the ancestor of every action is thought," and Emerson is in a sense the high priest of New Thought. While not solely the product of New Thought, many of the sentences in Bristol's books might have come directly from the pages of some of the best New Thought writers. "What you exhibit outwardly, you are inwardly.

You are the product of your own thought. What you believe yourself to be, you are." (p. 29) Of course this parallels a saying of the Buddha out of the sixth century B.C., "All that we are is the result of what we have thought." But it is much more likely to have come to Bristol via Emerson rather than Buddha. He goes on to quote the Irish poet George Russell (Æ), and others who have spoken in like vein, but these seem more likely to be something he found after his great discovery and is using to buttress his position, than to indicate its source. Certainly it is a distinctive New Thought conviction he expresses in saying, "It is the power of believing that alone sets in motion those inner forces by which you add what I call plus values to your life." (p. 36) And he speaks specifically of being convinced by his study "of the so-called mystic teachings, the various sciences and the regular orthodox teachings" that they all work in varying degrees, "but only to the extent that their followers believe." He is certainly part product at least of New Thought teachings.

A second emphasis is upon prosperity, a cardinal emphasis in New Thought. Many of Bristol's illustrations of the power of thought are intended to show how men have achieved financial success and influence through the magic of believing. He reports Dr. Bach, who writes of having asked one of the sons of Charles Fillmore if the Unity teachings could be applied to a real estate venture. The reply was, "If it works at all, it works everywhere." While healing is not stressed as much as success in business, Bristol also champions mental healing. He is inclined to explain it on the basis of suggestion, but whatever the explanation, he believes that many ailments can be cured through the use of the mind and suggestion.

He believes also in the possibility of projecting thought through nonphysical means and so affecting others. He sees in this power, logically, the possibility that if good thoughts can be projected, so also can evil thoughts designed to effect evil results. That is what Christian Scientists call Malicious Animal Magnetism, a thing of which many of them, including Mrs. Eddy, stood in fear, and against which they defended themselves by affirmations and denials carefully designed to offset the evil intended. Bristol solemnly warns, "Never use it for harmful or evil purposes." (p. 25)

Bristol also recommends the time-honored method of affirmation of that which one desires to achieve. For example:

> If you are unhappy, use the words, I am happy.... repeat it to yourself twenty or thirty times.... I am strong.... I am happy.... I am convincing, I am friendly.... Everything is fine ... are a few simple affirmations you can use to change your mental point of view for the better. (p. 122)

Also one must get a clear picture of what he desires to accomplish and hold it before his mind. Suppose, he says, it is a promotion one wants. "Keep telling yourself constantly that you are going to get it . . . the repetition will be the means of driving the suggestion deeply and firmly into the subconscious mind." (p. 122)

He insists that negative thoughts must be avoided.

> When you permit thoughts of doubt or fear to enter your consciousness, it is obvious that the forceful, positive, creative thought will have to give way and consequently you lose your positive state.... One must rather keep his mind filled continuously with positive thoughts in order that their strong vibration may ward off thoughts that are negative or destructive coming from without. (p. 123)

With Bristol, the subconscious is all-important. "Once the subconscious has received your message and understands your desires and ambitions, it will only be a short time when your desires will be fulfilled and your ambition achieved." And it is through the magic of believing sincerely and completely that the subconscious receives the message and understands the desire. (p. 226) Nothing is said here about the worthiness of the desire or the ambition; no moral monitor of the subconscious is suggested. In this Bristol is not quite true to the New Thought which emphasizes always the Good.

Bristol's *The Magic of Believing*, first published in 1948 by

Prentice-Hall, had already gone through seventeen printings by 1951.

One of the most persistent and effective propagators of essentially New Thought ideas beyond the limits of New Thought organizations and institutions was Robert J. Collier, who created no church or local center or society to which one could belong, but who reached enormous numbers of people of all classes through his books, which were sold chiefly by advertising and through the mails. Robert Collier was not an organization man. He had little or no personal contact with organized New Thought or its leaders. So far as I have been able to discover, he never spoke at their conventions, though he may well have been invited to do so. Yet through his books, pamphlets, and correspondence, the basic ideas, attitudes, and techniques of New Thought were communicated to countless persons throughout all America, and to some extent the wider English-speaking world.

A nephew of the founder and publisher of *Collier's* magazine, P. F. Collier, Robert Collier from earliest childhood had been destined for the ministry. This had once been his famous uncle's ambition, but one that was never carried out, and he eagerly encouraged young Robert's entrance upon that career. But the young man disappointed him. Instead he turned to mining engineering and for ten years either worked in the mines, prospected, or studied mining. Then he returned to New York, working in his uncle's publishing house, and for a time was on the staff of the *Review of Reviews*, a widely read magazine of that period.

Then one day he suffered a serious attack of ptomaine poisoning. The aftermath was a long painful period of treatments, chiefly by dieting, which brought no significant improvement. Some of his friends suggested that he try psychology or metaphysics. He had no faith that it would do any good, but was willing to "give it a try." For he desperately wanted to get well. And wonderful to relate, he recovered completely.

This led him to join no cult, but it did set him to thinking deeply of the power of the mind in effecting results. If it worked in the area of health, why not in other areas as well? Why could it not overcome financial lack? Or, for that matter, why might it not be the means of attaining any good for which one might devoutly wish?

What Robert Collier read is nowhere stated, though his son says that "for long months it was just books, books, books, hundreds of books and courses of lectures on everything related to the subject." (*Make Your Own World,* p. 3) In *The Secret of the Ages* he quotes from many sources. A considerable number were psychologists and physical scientists, and a great many physicians, since he concerns himself much with health. Mention of Christian Science is made in such a way as to suggest some familiarity with its claims and methods, an indication that he had done some reading in it.

Among philosophers few were mentioned, William James and Emerson being quoted, and there is reference to the Hindu Upanishads. He mentions, as though he knew something of their teachings, Unity and Mental Science. He never mentions New Thought by name, but he makes reference more than once to Judge Thomas Troward's *Edinburgh Lectures,* and quotes other New Thought writers such as James Allen and Charles M. Barrows. Several times he quotes from O. S. Marden and Glenn Clark who, we have seen, were definitely influenced by New Thought, while Ella Wheeler Wilcox is quoted over and over again.

What he worked out in *The Secret of the Ages,* his most widely circulated book, can safely be characterized as more nearly approximating New Thought than any other recognized system, though in some respects it is closer to Christian Science than to the main line of New Thought. (As we have seen, the line of demarcation between the two is by no means clear and sharp.) It is certainly in the broad metaphysical field, with perhaps a greater emphasis on the secular aims and objectives than on the religious or spiritual. But the terminology all the way through is just what one finds in New Thought. There is great stress on Universal Mind; Mind is All; Mind's creativity; no intelligence in matter; man as entitled to every good thing; the Law of Infinite Supply; the importance of the unconscious or subconscious, (concerning this he uses almost the exact language of Judge Troward); techniques of relaxation; the use of affirmations and denials; the illusory character of illness and lack; man as the perfect thought of God—all familiar to the students of New Thought.

If he took no part in the organized movement and did nothing to promote it by name, he did a great deal to make these characteristic ideas and attitudes known, and he did it largely through the printed page. He first put to the practical test of experience the ideas he had gleaned from his reading and reflection, then, after a few years, issued seven little pocket-sized volumes which he published himself and advertised through the mails and in the public press. The results were amazing. Within the first six months he had orders to the value of more than a million dollars. A company was formed with enough capital to operate at that level and, the partner assuming the task of management, Robert Collier was left free to write and to counsel through correspondence with the large numbers of people who wrote to him telling him their troubles and seeking help. He also published other books. *The Law of the Higher Potential* was widely sold, and he established and published a magazine, *Mind,* through which he was able to offer advice and guidance to those with whom he had no direct contact.

How many persons were influenced by him in the direction of New Thought can only be guessed at, but Gordon Collier, his son, reports that 300,000 sets of seven volumes of *The Secret of the Ages,* first published under the title *The Book of Life,* were sold. Then in 1948 it was revised and printed in a single volume of which by 1961 they had sold 250,000 copies, thus reaching the total of 550,000. All his books and pamphlets are still being published and circulated, though Robert Collier died in 1950. His wife and son Gordon have carried on the business of the Robert Collier Publications, Inc. Gordon Collier has himself written and published several books which have also publicized New Thought ideas. The publishing company operates in Tarrytown, New York.

Not all the persons who were the channels through which at least some of the essential New Thought ideas and techniques have flowed out into the life of America were consciously aware that they were serving as such channels. Many of them had no definite connection with organized New Thought, nor had they known that some of the books which had stimulated their interest in this direction were New Thought books, or out of a New Thought background. In the end it matters little whence the ideas came. The important thing is that the ideas were being popularized and accepted by the public in general. It is not always easy to distinguish between the results of New Thought and those of what has been called the new psychology, by which is here meant not so much the newer schools of psychological theory, but the practical application of known psychological principles to practical ends, such as business, advertising, selling, making friends, influencing people, and of course, health. Books of this character, which reflect the secular level of New Thought, sell by the hundreds of thousands, not to say, in the aggregate, millions. Books such as those of Dale Carnegie, which have had an enormous circulation, undoubtedly owe little directly to New Thought as such, yet the author emphasized as does New Thought the central importance of *thought*.

He finds a very ancient basis for this in the writings of Marcus Aurelius, who said, "Our life is what our thoughts make it"; but he quotes also from Norman Vincent Peale. He also goes on to quote from Mrs. Eddy, who said that she had gained the certainty "that all causation was mind and every effect a mental phenomenon." He disclaims ever being a Christian Scientist, but declares that the longer he lives the more convinced he becomes of the tremendous power of thought. He recommends (*How to Stop Worrying and Start Living*, p. 99) the reading of James Allen's *As a Man Thinketh*, which he says had a profound effect upon his life. This little book, already in its fourth edition and one hundredth thousand by 1908, was still in circulation in 1960 in no less than eight editions, published by as many publishers, varying in format from a paperback edition at thirty-five cents to a de luxe edition at $4.50. The author died in 1912.

Running through Carnegie's books is not alone the theme of the power of thought, but the optimistic view of man which is characteristic of New Thought, and the implied New Thought idea that man has an inherent right to health, success, and happiness.

And this has been true of many books of this kind. At the turn of the century, Frank Haddock sold his books in tremendous numbers, teaching New Thought not so much in its religious form, but rather at the secular level. His *Power of Will* and other similar titles reached a total circulation which for that time was quite the equivalent of the "best sellers" of our own period. Of the book, one reviewer wrote, "If not officially belonging to New Thought, it is hard to separate his work from that cult."

A number of mail-order teaching organizations which have few or no organized activities, but teach by correspondence persons reached largely through advertising, are in some respects close to New Thought, though not identified with it. Mental Physics is more oriented toward Hindu thought, but its teachings at many points differ little from those of New Thought. So also the Ontology Foundation of Chicago. Prosperity Now, operating out of San Antonio, while wholly secular in its emphasis, uses definitely New Thought ideas and techniques.

The Walter Russell Foundation was popularized to some extent by Glenn Clark, who wrote in a pamphlet of Walter Russell as *The Man Who Tapped the Secrets of the Universe*. The language he uses in describing the career of Russell sounds exactly like that of New Thought. And Russell was frequently a speaker for New Thought gatherings. And there are others.

Among contemporary writers who write for the general public, in essentially New Thought terms, should be listed Margery Wilson of Hollywood, whose books have been and are extremely popular. She was a student of Fenwicke Holmes, and according to him is an ardent believer in New Thought. Some of her titles are on the order of some of those of Marden: *Believe in Yourself; You Are as Young As You Act.* She writes much for women, e.g., *The Woman You Want to Be; Charm; The New Etiquette;* but she has at least one book on religion, *Your Personality and God.* Rather than writing about New Thought as such, she is a New Thought follower writing on popular themes and bringing to them the outlook which rules her life.

This often enough happens. A New Thought minister on the West Coast has a son who has become a novelist. He said to his father, "Why, Dad, I am teaching in my novels just what you are from your pulpit." The father, having read his son's books, wasn't quite sure that this was true, but that is one of the ways such ideas make their way into our general culture.

No one who knew Lloyd C. Douglas, a minister of the gospel in one of the established churches, who long before writing his popular novels had been writing serious studies in the field of religion, would consider him as a New Thought follower. But New Thought people regard *Magnificent Obsession* as a New Thought novel. And it has sold in enormous numbers. Wherever it came from, and however it may be thought of by others, New Thought folk think of it as New Thought in literary form.

Thus far no distinctively New Thought novels or plays have won general acclaim. As we have already noted, Henry Wood's play, *Victor Serenus,* reached the stage in Boston, but it was not highly successful, and his novel, *Edward Burton,* enjoyed only a modest success. Probably the movie version of *Magnificent Obsession* brought the essentially New Thought point of view, though it was never so named, to a greater number of people than any other book or drama.

Best known of all the literary figures identified in any way with the New Thought movement was Edwin Markham, whose poem, "The Man with the Hoe," was and is regarded as one of the finest produced by any American poet. Just how much he was really a New Thought figure it is difficult to say. There is little in his poems that can be discovered that marks him as a "New Thoughter." Of course there was his poem, perhaps best expressive of the broad tolerance which is a part of the New Thought movement,

> He drew a circle that shut me out,
> Heretic, rebel, a thing to flout.
> But love and I had the wit to win,
> We drew a circle that took him in.

While it summed up the attitude of the best representatives of New Thought, this poem was equally cherished by other broad-minded minority persons and groups. It is still one of the most widely quoted quatrains in the whole range of American poetry.

Actually, Edwin Markham was listed for some time as an honorary president of the pre-INTA overall New Thought organizations which from time to time bore different names. It is true too that he was a regular contributor to *Nautilus*, Elizabeth Towne's well-known magazine. A letter from a former president of INTA recalls his seeing Ella Wheeler Wilcox, Edwin Markham, and Elizabeth Towne walking arm in arm down the street one day, an impressive sight as he recalled it. At least the New Thought people regarded Markham as one of their own. And his influence was indeed wide.

13

Leaders Outside the Movement

BECAUSE OF the unusual breadth and tolerance of the New Thought Movement—one of its major attractions to many in an age in which sensitive souls find themselves cramped within the narrow creedal lines of orthodoxy—it is not easily defined. To say therefore exactly what is and what is not New Thought is difficult, and the attempt to trace it in its more tenuous forms out into the general culture of America and the world is no easy task. It is the author's purpose not alone to chronicle the more obvious facts of its rise and development, to follow the growth of what can readily enough be recognized because of its organizational form, but in so far as possible to see what leavening effect it has had upon our total culture.

To what degree has New Thought made its way out beyond the well-defined limits of the organized movement into the larger life of the greater community? Has it influenced, directly or indirectly, other churches in their general outlook and practices? Has it had anything to do with the rising emphasis on healing in the churches or on their ways of going about their healing task? Has it had any appreciable influence, say, in the direction of a more marked emphasis on the immanence of God; on the way in which Christ is thought of; on the extent to which man is regarded as essentially divine? Has it made any change in the thought concerning death and the life hereafter; any modification in traditional ways of regarding evil?

What would be the specific things one should look for in determining whether New Thought was exercising an influence?

Though these ideas and emphases are not exclusively the property of New Thought—Christian Science shares most of them—it is nevertheless true that New Thought, more than any other group unless it were Christian Science, tends to define God in terms that are supra-personal, if not impersonal. Though they also use the language of personal relationships in their talk about God, they are likely to stress the Allness of God, and always think of God in terms of Mind. The world of phenomena is the creative thought of God in manifestation. God is good. Evil, whether real or not, is negative rather than positive, and is always impotent in the presence and activity of Divine Mind. God is abundance. In him there is no lack. God is wholeness; in him there is no place for imperfection, weakness, or sickness. Man is God's idea. He shares the divine nature; he is indeed divine, though endowed with free will and therefore capable of error, and consequently subject to sickness and poverty. He need only claim his birthright of health and plenty.

Three or four words pretty well identify the New Thought and those kindred movements that derive from it: health or healing, abundance or prosperity—sometimes even wealth—and happiness. And since the dominant characteristic of God is Mind, thinking or thought is the key to the power necessary to achieve the good ends sought after. Since the achievement of abundance has so often been the measure of success, the terms success and successful living are frequently used in New Thought. To be sure, in New Thought at its best success is to be measured in other than financial terms, but there has arisen a rather superficial cult of success which marks what may be called the secular wing of New Thought. To New Thought in its higher forms such things as health, prosperity, success, or even happiness are only by-products of a higher aim which is the recognition or realization of one's at-one-ment with Divine Mind. They are the natural and logical results of the attainment or near attainment of the primary end for which man should seek.

Thus, though they may have come from some other source, when one finds in common use the familiar terms "power of thought," "power of constructive thinking," "the primacy of mind," "mind control," "think positively," "affirmation," "denial," and others long current in New Thought circles such as "the Christ in you," "the Christ Consciousness," "the divinity of man," he is justified in at least wondering if some New Thought influence has not been at work. Likewise, when one finds a person recommending the use of positive affirmations or of denials, he is likely to think of New Thought or at least of some "metaphysical" influence.

One of the avenues through which New Thought is reaching out into the larger world beyond the membership of New Thought groups is a group of ministers of the major denominations who are directly or indirectly, and it might also be said consciously or unconsciously, making use either of New Thought ideas or techniques in their ministry within their own churches, and through their books, articles, and personal appearances as lecturers beyond their own local churches. Some of them are, I am confident, quite unaware that they are doing so. Some are aware of what they are doing, but never openly acknowledge the source of their teachings or practices. But others unhesitatingly and gratefully acknowledge the effect which some phase of the New Thought Movement has had upon them. An example of the latter is Dr. Lewis L. Dunnington, a prominent Methodist minister, for many years pastor of the University Methodist Church at Iowa City, Iowa, seat of the University of Iowa. Besides his preaching, he has published a number of books which have had a wide circulation, being particularly read by other ministers. His better-known books are *Handles of Power* (Abingdon Press); *More Handles of Power* (Abingdon Press); and *The Imprisoned Splendor* (Macmillan). How many ministers have read them and been helped to accept as their own many of the ideas Dr. Dunnington has written about, can never be known; but the number is undoubtedly large; and how many have been influenced by these "handers on" of essential New Thought ideas and techniques none can ever determine.

Dr. Dunnington himself tells, in a foreword to *The Imprisoned*

Splendor, how he was led to the investigation of one of the New Thought groups, what he found, and how it affected his whole ministry.

He was pastor of a Methodist church in Duluth, Minnesota, when in the course of his pastoral calling he found that a good many of his members were readers of one or more of the publications of the Unity School of Christianity. What pastor anywhere in America has not had a similar experience? Of this fact many ministers from many denominations, including Roman Catholicism, have borne witness. Some of them have been worried by it.

Dr. Dunnington may have worried a bit—he doesn't say so—but he did begin to observe these families. What he discovered was, he wrote, that they were convinced that they had received greater help from the Unity publications than from any other source. Furthermore, he found that they were among the best balanced, most poised, best integrated persons in his parish. He began to investigate the publications. He went farther. He went all the way to Kansas City, Missouri, to meet and talk with Charles Fillmore, the founder of Unity, and his son Lowell, now head of the organization. He was enormously impressed by Charles Fillmore, then ninety years of age, but full of energy and forever dreaming of greater things which his movement might accomplish. He was younger in appearance by twenty-five years than his actual age. Dunnington was amazed to discover that both he and his wife had been near death's door fifty years earlier, but had been healed and had both had a half-century of successful healing. He knew that here was one with the secret of healing power that few know anything about.

He was taken through the immense institution. He was struck by the peace and harmony he found among the more than five hundred employees, the like of which he had seen nowhere else. And basic in it all, as he saw and heard the stories of people who had been brought to new health, happiness, and spiritual attainment through its ministry, he observed, was their living positively, by affirmation.

These people, he wrote, had the "how" of applied Christianity that he had been seeking. "They had something that worked. It solved problems." (p. ix) He returned home and worked out a series of sermons which were ultimately published in *Handles of Power* (1942), and his people were encouraged to test practically the method of affirmation in appropriating the riches of the Kingdom of Heaven that is within us. And, he relates, "wonderful things began to happen to all of us."

Across the years he has been faithful to the method of affirmation, not simply telling people to affirm, but suggesting, in his books and on cards available after sermons, specific affirmations to be used for particular occasions. His whole ministry, he says, was lifted. In his great congregation in Iowa City he had practiced his technique of affirmation consistently, and had seen his attendance grow from an average of some four hundred to over two thousand each Sunday morning. The people, he writes, are spiritually hungry. "They want to be told specifically *how* to appropriate spiritual power, *How* to lay hold of the inexhaustible riches of Christ. This technique is *how*." (p. xi)

In his books Dr. Dunnington makes frequent reference to writers or ministers who are clearly New Thought followers, or who like himself employ many of the same terms and methods. There is, for example, reference to Thomas Hamblin, a famous English New Thought writer and editor. Material is used from the *Aquarian Age,* definitely a New Thought magazine. Unity and Unity publications are referred to repeatedly. He frequently quotes from Glenn Clark, who like himself makes much use of familiar New Thought techniques. Whether he got it from Frank Robinson of Psychiana is not clear, but he suggests an affirmation that Robinson recommended to his students as one to be repeated over and over again, especially just before going to sleep at night: "I believe in the power of the Living God."

Phrases and sentences that are frequently used by New Thought writers spring out at one from the pages of Dr. Dunnington's books. Some of them are: "We are individuated centers of the One Creative Life and Being." "As individuated centers of

the One Creative Life and Love, we all have limitless potential."
"Mind is creative. Every thought creates for good or ill, depending
on whether it is positive or negative." "The great well of the
unconscious mind is the creative repository of the conscious
mind. . . . God works through that repository to answer our
prayers and to bring wholeness of body, mind and spirit through
the constant repetition of great affirmations of faith."

How far is a ministry of this sort reaching in the spread of
New Thought ideas and techniques? Dr. Dunnington had a
regular radio program for years and reached a large public in
this way. He speaks of literally thousands of letters which he
has received from listeners and readers all over the country.
An article on his method in the influential *Christian Advocate* of
the Methodist church and samples of his affirmation and prayer
cards in *Church Management,* he says, brought "a perfect torrent
of letters of inquiry, hundreds of them from every corner of the
country. . . . All sought more information and samples of sermons
and cards." (*Handles of Power,* p. 12)

A number of Episcopal clergymen have, across the years,
quite openly, while retaining their status in their own church,
joined forces with New Thought. We have already written of Dr.
R. Heber Newton and Dr. Thomas Parker Boyd, who served as
presidents of the developing movement. The Rev. L. Douglas
Gottschall of Oakland is president of the College of Divine
Science as well as rector of an Episcopal church. Dr. C. Stanley
Long was actually a member of INTA. His book *You,* already in
a second edition in 1944, was characterized in an advertisement
in the *New Thought Bulletin,* in a statement by a former president
of INTA, as "definitely a *fresh interpretation* of the Principles of
New Thought." That was why it was being read by so many
leaders of the movement and recommended to students. It was
said to be in use as a textbook for class instruction in several
Centers. That it was not alone in use among New Thought
groups, but was warmly recommended to the orthodox churches,
is evidenced by statements quoted from the *Christian Century*
and the *Christian Herald,* bearing out the claim that the book was

influencing the thought of leaders in the churches toward New Thought.

The Rev. Robert A. Russell of the Church of the Epiphany in Denver is another Episcopal minister who is said to teach what New Thought leaders recognize as New Thought, and in his books he has definitely recognized his indebtedness to New Thought. For example, in a book, *Vital Points in Demonstration*, with the subtitle, *You Can Get What You Want if You Return Home*, he announces that it is one of a series of three consecutive "metaphysical" studies of the Parable of the Prodigal Son and the Elder Brother, and at the end of the book he acknowledges material quoted from Unity publications and from Christian D. Larson, Ernest Holmes, O. S. Marden, V. P. Randall, and Emilie H. Cady, all New Thought leaders. A chart in the early pages of the book might well have come from a New Thought teacher's writings. At the center of two concentric circles, there is the word THOUGHT with "positive" above and "negative" below. Toward the top of the figure, from "The Source of Infinite Life— The Father's House," the Divine Energy and Creative Power flow through the positive, upward and outward to "Life As It Is, and Planned by God, manifesting itself in Health, Success, Joy, Happiness, Strength, Divine Wealth . . . Faith . . . Certainty . . . Peace . . . Love . . . Freedom"; and downward through the negative, which is described as "thinking down toward the self," the lines radiate out to "disease, failure . . . sorrow . . . misery . . . weakness . . . discord . . . bondage, or Life as we make it through our Negative Thinking."

"The thing you are seeking," writes Dr. Russell,

is seeking you. It is within you awaiting your release. Deep in the submerged depths of your being is the Power that will, when rightly directed, not only build into your life anything you want, but remove whatever you do not want. It is the Power of God. It is God Himself. It is the greatest thing in you. It is your highest Self. It is the sum total of all your possibilities, physical, mental and spiritual.

Dr. Robinson of Psychiana could not have said it more directly or clearly. "You can get what you want if you realize that man's Power plus God's Power is greater than any obstacle that can oppose itself to your will." (pp. 14-15)

You can have these things, *if;* and then follow some twenty or more statements, most of which are sheer New Thought:

If you know that the world you live in is mental and not physical. . . . If you know always that God is Good and that nothing ever opposes that Good. . . . If you will cultivate a consciousness that entertains only constructive and positive thoughts, and refuse to give attention or power to destructive and negative thoughts. . . .

But interlarded through all runs an orthodox strain as well:

If you will let this mind be in you that was in Christ Jesus. . . . If you seek the Divine Will instead of your own will. . . . If you take time every day to commune with God. . . . If you cast all your burdens on the Lord without dictating and outlining the manner in which His blessings are to come to you. (pp. 16-17, *passim*)

The man through whose ministry essentially New Thought ideas and techniques have been made known most widely in America is Dr. Norman Vincent Peale, pastor of the Marble Collegiate Church on Fifth Avenue, New York. Dr. Peale is a minister of the Reformed Church in America, and asserts his complete adherence to the doctrinal standards of this historic church. Yet, through his preaching in his own pulpit and over the air, through his books, his frequent lectures to national and international conventions of various sorts, many of them of business and professional men, through a syndicated newspaper column, and through the little magazine *Guideposts,* which now has around a million subscribers, he is reaching more people, probably, than any other single minister in America and perhaps the world, and is using consistently ideas and methods which are and have been the peculiar earmarks of New Thought since at least the turn of the century.

This is not to say that Dr. Peale is not, as he claims, orthodox in his doctrinal ideas. His language is certainly orthodox, perhaps inclined toward the liberal, and he has not by any means adopted all the ideas or practices of New Thought. But he has succeeded in weaving into an otherwise unobjectionably Christian orthodox framework some of the basic New Thought ideas and has whole-heartedly adopted some New Thought aims and especially techniques. One finds in his writings numerous words that are very familiar indeed to those who know the literature of New Thought.

Look, for example, at the title of one of his most popular books, *The Power of Positive Thinking*. This is a distinctly New Thought title. To be sure, New Thought has no monopoly on the idea; it might as well have come out of the new psychology, but long before there was a new psychology to popularize the idea, New Thought had been emphasizing the creative power of thought. Indeed, it was insisting that thought was the ultimate creative power in the universe, and it had defined the whole creation in terms of mind. And it had never ceased to make thought—positive thought—central, whether in its deeper religious expression or at its most practical secular level. It was negative thought that produced disease, poverty, and evil, and positive thought that brought health, abundance, and happiness.

In an earlier and widely popular book, *Guide to Confident Living*, Dr. Peale had entitled his last chapter, a kind of a summary of the whole art of confident living, "Change Your Thoughts and You Change Everything." An earlier chapter was on "How to Think Your Way to Success." The announced purpose of the book was, "to lead people to personal happiness and success," goals much more frequently insisted upon among New Thought teachers and writers than among the orthodox. I do not recall any direct statement to the effect that happiness, health, and adequate supply of this world's goods are the inherent right of man as a child of God, as New Thought frankly proclaims, but Dr. Peale's books seem to proceed at least practically on that assumption.

On the whole his optimistic view of man is rather in contrast to the generally low estimate of man entertained in orthodox theology, particularly that of the Calvinistic variety which is the basis of the Reformed Church.

When he declares, as he does in his recent book, *The Tough-Minded Optimist,* that "you have within you all the strength you will ever need to handle anything you will ever have to face" (p. 4), he certainly attributes to man a capacity denied him in orthodox theology, which makes much of the scripture passage, "without me ye can do nothing." Of course, Dr. Peale throughout the numerous books and articles he has written frequently emphasizes, in good orthodox fashion, reliance upon God's help in times of stress and strain.

I once wrote him saying that I had read his books and articles and in doing so had had the feeling that I was reading New Thought. Had he indeed heard their leaders, read their books, and consciously or unconsciously been influenced by them? I had heard among New Thought friends reference to a visit of Ernest Holmes of Religious Science to his church and of the pleasure Dr. Peale had expressed at meeting Dr. Holmes after the service, greeting him as one he knew and deeply respected from the reading of his writings. I had heard and read of at least indirect contacts which Dr. Peale had had with Unity.

His answer, which came not by mail but in a personal conversation by telephone with him, was, yes, that he had read them all and found valuable elements in them. He had read widely in a variety of religious points of view, but he thought that out of it all he had worked out a system of thinking and a method that was truly his own, and had proved it in his own personal experience and in his ministry to others. He had, he told me, written of his background in *The Tough-Minded Optimist* (Prentice-Hall, 1961), and the reading of that book would answer my questions. In Chapter II, under the title "Never Be Afraid of Anybody or Anything," he tells the story of his early years and the background of his ministry.

Son of a Methodist preacher, he attended college and went to Boston University School of Theology to prepare himself for the ministry. The strongly liberal, social gospel emphasis of the school at the time was not to his satisfaction, nor was Fundamentalism, so he chose for himself "the middle road with average sensible people who didn't have all the answers, and who realized that fact but were humbly seeking God." (p. 45)

He went out of the seminary to a run-down Methodist church in Brooklyn with only a handful of members, but in three years had built a new church and had nearly a thousand members. Called to a large church in Syracuse, a university pulpit, he preached to a dominantly intellectual community, and found an increasing dissatisfaction with his ministry. He was, he says, on the way to losing what spiritual vitality he had. Then he began to read certain "spiritual literature" which he found was increasingly getting into the homes of his people. This literature was coming from Unity, Religious Science, Science of Mind, Christian Science, from various "metaphysical teachers," the Oxford Group, from persons like Glenn Clark, who had drunk deeply at the fountains of New Thought, Starr Dailey, Sam Shoemaker, and others. He seemed to find in these something reminiscent of the outlook of his preacher father who had been a physician before entering the Methodist ministry and who had "always wrapped medicine and religion together in a kind of body, mind, soul package." (p. 24) From his father he had seen that "as the mind is healed, so also are body and soul affected," and that "many of the ills of human beings, both of mind and body originate in soul sickness."

But with all this reading he believes he is still orthodox, affirms belief in the cardinal doctrines of his church, but believes also that the ancient faith "can be taught in new and fresh thought and language and applied scientifically and with creative power in human lives; that it can solve the toughest problems of human nature and society too." (p. 30)

It is undoubtedly true that Dr. Peale's borrowing from New Thought has been chiefly method rather than content of thought. In the introduction to his *Guide to Confident Living*, he states specifically that its primary purpose is "to state and demonstrate a simple workable technique of thinking and acting . . . it tells HOW you can achieve your most cherished desires." And the technique most recognizable as New Thought is that of affirmation and denial. Over and over again in his books recurs the admonition, "affirm . . . deny." Another New Thought technique is that of visualization—that is, for example, seeing yourself as that which you wish to be. A formula given Dr. Peale by a businessman who had made a notable success was "prayerize, picturize, actualize," and Dr. Peale's explanation of its operation is definitely in the New Thought pattern, though neither he nor the businessman may have known it. Henry Wood, one of the early greats of New Thought, has a book specifically on this method.

An interesting case in illustration of the principle is told by Dr. Peale in Chapter V. Back in 1941 *Guideposts* had reached a plateau and was failing financially. To put more money into it looked like a waste. A wealthy woman to whom he had looked for rescue declined categorically to put any more money into it so long as he was willing to go along and just maintain it at the approximately 40,000 circulation it had reached.

How many subscribers ought the magazine to have to support it? she suddenly asked Dr. Peale. Hesitantly he replied, "One hundred thousand." Then said she, "Let us see it as having 100,000 and thank God that it is so."

Dr. Peale says that he thought this was pushing the Lord pretty far, but he went along with her. And that was the turning point. Today around a million subscribers receive *Guideposts* regularly. Nearly twelve hundred firms take it for all their employees.

Incidentally, this story is narrated in a chapter headed "Have Prosperity and Enjoy Life," which is hardly an orthodox emphasis, but is a constant in New Thought. In the course of this chapter, Dr. Peale quotes passages on prosperity from New Thought leaders, notably from Charles Fillmore's book, *Prosperity*. "Do not say that money is scarce," he wrote, "the very statement will scare money away from you. . . . Do not allow one empty thought to exist in your mind, but fill every nook and corner of it with the word plenty, plenty, plenty."

Of course Dr. Peale is interested in health and believes in spiritual healing, as New Thought does also. He has linked religion and health definitely by providing a staff of psychiatrists and clinical psychologists in connection with his great church, and he is president of the American Foundation for Psychiatry and Religion. His healing work is thus more closely linked with scientific medical skill, both psychiatric and through materia medica, but religion is an essential element in it. And his books narrate repeated healings of the same sort one finds in the literature of New Thought.

Finally, one finds in his frequent reference to the importance of the subconscious something quite reminiscent of Judge Troward and Ernest Holmes. To cite but one instance among many that occur: he writes of the value of memorizing New Testament passages concerning faith. Let them sink into your mind, he says in effect, saying them over especially as you go to sleep, for they will sink into your subconscious mind "by a process of spiritual osmosis" and in time will "modify and re-slant your basic thought patterns . . . you will have new power to get what God and you decide you really want from life." (*Power of Positive Thinking*, p. 109)

At one time, under heavy criticism from fellow-clergymen, he was tempted to resign from his pastorate and carry on his ministry outside the church. It was his father who kept him from this step by assuring him that what he was preaching and doing was all right. "You have," he told him, "evolved a new Christian emphasis out of a composite of Science of Mind [New Thought], metaphysics, Christian Science, medical and psychological practice, Baptist Evangelism, Methodist witnessing, and solid Dutch Reformed Calvinism." This, it seems to the writer, is a valid judgment, the greatest difficulty being that of justifying the reference to Dutch Reformed Calvinism. Certainly, New Thought is finding an outlet for some of its major insights and techniques through the vigorous ministry of Dr. Norman Vincent Peale.

Another who, without being himself a recognized New Thought leader, has been highly influential in introducing New Thought ideas and techniques into the churches, was Glenn

Clark, for many years a member of the faculty of Macalester College, a Presbyterian liberal arts college in St. Paul, Minnesota. Glenn Clark was a teacher of English and an athletic coach. But he was deeply religious and something of a mystic, a great believer in prayer. He first came into prominence through an article in the *Atlantic Monthly*, "The Soul's Sincere Desire." He then began to be much in demand as a speaker in the churches and in summer camps. Eventually he organized a summer camp of his own to which he gave the name "Camp Farthest Out." Here for a period, amid pleasant surroundings, a group of congenial and serious-minded persons met for a season of fellowship, relaxation, and spiritual renewal, under the direction of Dr. Clark and others of somewhat similar views. In it all prayer and the disciplines of silence and meditation have played a major role. He sometimes called the camps "laboratories for experimentation in the art of praying."

All this was strictly a "within the church" effort. It would have been easy for him to have organized another religious sect; but, a good churchman, he chose to work within the framework of the church seeking to deepen its spiritual life through the new emphasis he gave and the techniques he employed. The Camps Farthest Out multiplied from the original one until in 1961 there were forty-one of them, meeting in almost every section of the country. There is a warm sense of fellowship among those who have had the experience of attending one or more of the camps.

The importance of these camps for our present purpose is the fact that in and through them has been introduced into the life of the churches much that is central in New Thought teaching and practice. The notable thing is that it has been accommodated to the vocabulary of the orthodox Christian faith, and so made an effective part in the ongoing life of the church without most persons' ever being aware that it is so.

Glenn Clark was a Presbyterian, reared in the church, teaching in a Presbyterian college, and teaching also a Sunday School class in his home church in St. Paul. Through a series of experiences told in his autobiography, *A Man's Reach*, he had been brought to an unusual interest in prayer, and it became his major concern and emphasis. It set him to reading especially the works of the mystics and about them and their approach to God. He read Rufus Jones's *Studies in Mystical Religion,* Evelyn Underhill's *Mysticism*—he especially liked her definition of mysticism, "Union with Reality"—and Brother Lawrence's *Practice of the Presence of God.* But he went beyond these. He read Ouspensky's *Tertium Organum,* Bragdon's *Fourth Dimensional Vistas,* and Frank Rawson's *Life Understood.* Rawson, a onetime Christian Scientist who had been expelled from the church, figures among the influential leaders of New Thought in England. The thing that attracted Clark to Rawson, he says, was that "he believed one's prayers could be just as scientifically infallible as the laws of physics and chemistry. He believed that merely to deny the existence of evil would make it vanish away, and to affirm the opposite reality would make it appear." (*A Man's Reach,* p. 159) Rawson came to Minneapolis and Clark heard him, later talked with him personally. To his surprise he learned that Rawson had read almost nothing but science and that he lacked imagination, a fundamental necessity for "converting his science of prayer into an art." "I determined then and there," writes Clark, "to be not a mere follower of his, but to begin where he left off."

A group in the Twin Cities met weekly to study Rawson's book. It included chiefly members of the orthodox churches, but also an active New Thought follower and a teacher of Christian Science. On meeting, the group would go into a Quaker silence, trying to feel the presence of God. Then the leader would read a list of names of people to be prayed for, and the members of the group would try to "deny away" some of their troubles. They discovered, he writes, "that all Mankind was One, and if we cleared *our own mind,* the trouble *of the one we prayed for* would disappear. One strong denial and a number of positive affirmations seemed to be the most effective way to clear our minds," though they also found that "dwelling too long on negatives did more harm than good." (p. 160)

This was, of course, good metaphysical practice, employed by

both Christian Science and New Thought. And Glenn Clark
unhesitatingly adopted it and carried it into his own ministry and
teaching. One finds again and again in his writings whole paragraphs that might have been found in any of the better New
Thought writers. Take for example his book, the title of which
is itself a good New Thought expression, *How to Find Health
through Prayer*.

In this book he says that the process of removing illness consists of releasing first love, then faith, then peace upon the thing
to be removed. One may then deny it away, laugh it away, relin-
quish it away, or know it away. The denial method, he explains,
is first to deny sharply. He suggests such denials as this: "There
is no sickness in heaven." This is to be followed by a strong
affirmation, e.g., "All is harmony, wholeness and health." He
gives an example of how to deal with the specific illness, anemia.
First the denial: "There is no unhappiness nor weariness in
Heaven." Affirmation: "All life in heaven is buoyant, fresh, happy,
joyful." Denial: "There is no retarding of the joy that flows
through the channels of consciousness." Affirmation: "All is joyous,
free and overflowing with gladness, bringing perfect health, perfect harmony, perfect wholeness." (p. 87)

The way of knowing he holds to be the most powerful of all
methods, the method indeed which Jesus used. He comes very
close to New Thought when he says, "It requires making the conscious and sub-conscious minds cooperate as a unit in perfect
understanding and positive acceptance of the great basic principles of life." (p. 93)

His idea concerning man is strikingly similar to that of New
Thought. In *How to Find Health through Prayer,* discussing the
nature of man, Clark says:

The way I overcame anger and its offspring of jealousies, grudges,
bitternesses and unforgivingness was to make a practice of seeing
every human being in a perfect world governed by a perfect God. . . .
Because I always held this view of man as a perfect image of God,
naturally innocent, sweet and pure, I never suffered the pangs of hate.
(p. 25)

The following could have come directly from any one of a hundred books by New Thought writers:

Marvelous results will come if one will turn in thought to God and Heaven, deny the existence in Heaven of the wrong thing felt or thought, and then realize that in God and Heaven the opposite condition prevails. One must dismiss from his mind completely the thought that the wrong thing felt or seen is permanent, and then follow instantly with the realization that the opposite condition exists here and now. (*The Soul's Sincere Desire*, p. 13)

He goes on to make practical suggestions that could be right out of some Unity or other New Thought publication. For money troubles one should realize, "There is no want in Heaven," and turn in thought to certain suggested affirmations. For poor health, realize, "There is no sickness in Heaven," and affirm . . .

For happiness: "There is no unhappiness in Heaven," and affirm . . .

For aid in thinking and writing, for criticism and misunderstanding, for worry, etc., appropriate denials and affirmations are suggested.

I have found nowhere any mention of Glenn Clark's having read *Science and Health*, but his former secretary told me that he did so. She is also authority for the statement that his favorite of all the New Thought writers was Walter Lanyon, the implication in her statement clearly being that he read from others too.

Would it have bothered him to have suggested that he had been influenced by such reading? Not in the least. After the publication of the article that won him fame, and the subsequent publication of his book, *The Soul's Sincere Desire*, by the Atlantic Monthly Press, he relates that the Quakers claimed him; the Catholics thought the book breathed the spirit of Brother Lawrence and St. Francis; and New Thought joined the chorus. The Swedenborgians said that "he may never have read Swedenborg," but that he "states the law of correspondences better than any of our writers have done"; while a New England Bahai was certain that he was a Bahai.

Actually the New Thought people regarded him as one who spoke their language. He was a welcome visitor at the headquarters of New Thought in Washington. The *Bulletin* reported that he met with a dozen teachers and workers and that all were uplifted by this time together and sustained "in our realization of the active power of concerted constructive thought and prayer." He spoke to the INTA Congress held in Minneapolis in 1939, on "The Secret of Jesus," dealing with the healing of the demoniac boy in Mark 9:24 ff. Nearly a page of terse statements are included in the issue of the *Bulletin* reporting the Congress. (Dec. 1939) One of them certainly indicates a fairly intimate acquaintance with some of the leaders. Said he: "If I were to pick a football team, I'd pick John Garns for faith, Nona Brooks for love, Elizabeth Towne for joy, Emmet Fox for power, Erma Wells for selflessness, Victor Morgan for gratitude." He appeared again at the San Francisco Congress where he spoke on "Our Responsibility toward World Peace."

Clark's books and pamphlets are frequently sold on New Thought book tables. The Prayer Tower, which is a continuing part of his ministry, though he died in 1956, is in many respects similar to Silent Unity at Lee's Summit, whether consciously inspired by it or not. Hundreds of prayer groups all over America, largely the result of attendance at Clark's Camps Farthest Out, employ many of the techniques which New Thought employs, and the interest in healing which they carry into the churches, healing not only of souls but also of bodies of men, is quite in the pattern of New Thought, though the vocabulary may be the more familiar one of orthodoxy.

There are several persons carrying on spiritual healing largely within the churches, who are, whether consciously or not, using much the same methods as New Thought. They are found in no single denomination. Rebecca Beard is a member of the Society of Friends, Agnes Sanford is the wife of an Episcopal rector. Both work closely, but by no means exclusively, with the Camps Farthest Out, the organization which carries on the work begun by Glenn Clark. Whether the two women have been under New

Thought influence is not certain, though Rebecca Beard tells of having attended, in 1945, a conference held in Minneapolis for a group of persons practicing spiritual healing, with the hope that they "might be able to pool their findings and share their experiences in healing through prayer." (*Every Man's Search,* p. 5) This group included several New Thought leaders, representing Religious Science, Divine Science, Unity, Science of Mind, and others. But at that time Rebecca Beard had already committed herself to the belief in and the practice of spiritual healing.

Long before, she had largely abandoned the use of drugs. She recognized that they had their place, but when, she says, we learn that there is only one power behind all the agencies of healing and choose to go directly to that power, we lose our sense of dependence upon them and the need of them. This, though New Thought has no monopoly on it, is thoroughly good New Thought doctrine, and wherever it is taught something of New Thought has entered in, whether consciously recognized or not. Her recommended use of the prayer of affirmation, for example, (p. 98) is in good New Thought tradition. It sounds like something out of Unity.

"To pray the prayer of healing," she writes, "we must visualize a change for which we can give thanks." Or, "Dwelling upon the negative will never change it to the positive. We must reconstruct the situation and see all the factors in harmonious order the way we would like to see them. In that way we reverse the power and it will flow in the opposite direction." Either of these statements might well have come out of any one of a score of New Thought books. (p. 96)

Agnes Sanford, born the daughter of a Presbyterian missionary in China, is now the wife of an Episcopal rector. She is one of the best known and widely read of the contemporary "spiritual healers." Her book, *The Healing Light,* written in 1947, had gone through nineteen editions by 1955. She, like Mrs. Beard, is active in the Camps Farthest Out during the summer seasons, but is in great demand in the churches as a speaker on spiritual themes, especially spiritual healing, and is constantly practicing healing, either privately or in conjunction with prayer groups.

The content of *The Healing Light* differs little from what one finds in many New Thought books—especially those of Unity—except for the fact that Mrs. Sanford's language is that of traditional Christianity. She makes four practical suggestions as to methods of prayer, especially that for health. The first is to choose a regular time and place, get comfortable, and *relax*. This matter of relaxation is the new element, in contrast to most Christian practice, in which prayer is anything but relaxation. It is very much so in New Thought. Second, one should remind himself that there is a life outside oneself. To one who is agnostic as to God, she still says that he knows that there is something outside the self. So third, he should ask that Something to enter into him. To a young man who had suffered an injury, but had no particular belief about God, she recommended that his prayer be something like this: "Whoever you are or whatever you are, come into me now and help nature in my body to mend this bone, and do it quick. Thanks." And fourth, she says that he should form a picture of his body as well and perfect, then give thanks that it is so. This is almost perfect New Thought technique.

She recounts an instance in her own experience when, after slamming a heavy door on a finger, she proceeded in the best New Thought fashion. She remarks that if she had said "damn" and fought the pain, her finger would have continued to hurt. Instead, she relates, she simply held her finger up and blessed the pain, considering it really as one of God's healing agencies, then thought, "I am a spiritual being, a Child of God. My spiritual body has a finger, and that finger doesn't hurt." A Christian Scientist might well have differed with the idea that she had a spiritual finger, but would otherwise have proceeded in much the same way. The pain ceased at once, she asserts, and quickly the nail resumed its natural color and the incident was forgotten. (p. 72)

Her assumption throughout, though she does not say it in so many words, seems to be that God never wills ill health, or suffering, or pain. Specifically, in the case of a leaky heart, she declared of a person, "The will of God for him was not a leaky heart but health." (p. 29) In the case of a Mr. Williams, suffering a heart attack and unconsciousness at the moment, she says she talked informally to his heart, assuring it that at the moment the power of God was re-creating it, and that it need no longer labor. Then, she says, she pictured the heart as perfect and blessed it, giving thanks to God that it was being "re-created in perfection." Again, perfect New Thought technique.

Like the New Thought writers, she emphasizes the role of the subconscious, one chapter of the book bearing the subtitle "Re-educating the Sub-conscious." In her chapter on Intercession, which was her method of effecting what New Thought folk call absent treatment, she says that she was experiencing great difficulty in helping or healing people from a distance. Then a lady minister of another church—a New Thought church, one suspects —helped her. The trouble is, said her friend in effect, that you are seeing them sick. If you are to heal them you must see them well. If you continue to see them ill, you only fasten their illness the more firmly upon them. And she was right, asserts Mrs. Sanford, for we pray not alone with our conscious minds. Much of our thinking—nine-tenths, we are told—is done with our subconscious minds, and "the spirit uses the path of the sub-conscious in sending forth the power of prayer." If therefore the subconscious retains the image of the person as ill, there is transmitted at best a mixed picture of illness and health. So she learned that here also, as in present treatment, she must see the patient as being well. When she could do this, she could then say, Amen, so let it be—incidentally a definitely New Thought custom—and the healing would take place.

In her description of how this takes place, she uses definitely orthodox terms, the final stage being "the re-creating of man in the image of Christ through seeing Christ in man," which is little other than the New Thought idea, or Christian Science for that matter. Mrs. Eddy, writing of one of Jesus' own healings, describes the process thus: "In this perfect man [who "appeared to him where sinning mortal man appears to mortals"] the Saviour saw God's own likeness, and this correct view of man healed the sick." (*Science and Health*, 447:2-4). Which is, it would seem, at least the recognition of man's potential, if not his real, divinity. And the divinity of man is a sure earmark of New Thought.

And while God is of course intensely personal in Mrs. Sanford's thinking, and loving in unlimited measure, he always operates through law, just as does Principle, or the more or less impersonal Being of New Thought and Christian Science. Here there is nothing arbitrary or capricious. Love works through law, sometimes through a higher law than man has yet discovered, but always through law.

It would be clearly unwarranted to claim that the undoubted current upsurge of interest in spiritual healing in the churches is wholly the result of the influence of New Thought, or of Christian Science. Christian healing is as old as Christianity itself and in some form has been practiced in greater or lesser degree throughout its entire history. One reads of healings in the period of the Reformation, of John Wesley, George Fox, and other Protestant leaders. And at Catholic shrines particularly, healings have taken place in every century. But never in the history of the church, since the early Christian centuries of its existence, has there been such a widespread belief in or practice of healing. P. P. Quimby, the first of the "mental healers" in America, insisted that he had only rediscovered and was practicing the method of Jesus. And it has been the claim of Mrs. Eddy and her followers that it was she who made this rediscovery and gave it to the world through the revelation to her of the contents of *Science and Health*.

Preceding Quimby and leading to his discovery of the power of mind to heal, to which he gave a religious interpretation, later further developed in Evans, Dresser, and Mary Baker Eddy, in slightly differing fashion, there had arisen a new psychology which had led, quite apart from religion, to healing by psychotherapeutic methods which, like New Thought and Christian

Science, put little or no faith in materia medica as a healing method.

The claims of Christian Science particularly, but New Thought also—though being organizationally less effective and therefore less aggressive it drew less attention to itself—were bitterly opposed by both the churches and the doctors. Both had, aside from any theoretical philosophical objection that might be raised to the new teachings, a very practical interest. The churches were losing members and the doctors patients to these new movements. What to do about it?

To the assertion of these enthusiastic teachers and practitioners of health through religion that they were only recovering a lost emphasis of the church, there could be no reasonable objection. A frank, unbiased study of the gospels was all that was necessary to reveal how great a part of Jesus' own ministry was concerned with the healing of men's physical as well as spiritual ailments. Was the church failing in an essential element of its true mission? One might be quite convinced that the philosophies and methods of healing were all wrong; but that these new groups were operating in an area of concern to Jesus, the head of the church, could hardly be doubted. There was little in the practice of the Roman Catholic church or in the healing extremes of traveling evangelists that seemed to meet the situation.

It was therefore no accident that in Boston, right at the center of activity of both New Thought and Christian Science, an answer should have been found and incorporated into the life of the Episcopal church under the name "The Emmanuel Movement." It was led by two ministers, Elwood Worcester and Samuel McComb, but with the advice and co-operation of a board of distinguished physicians. Its essential features have been described in their book *Religion and Medicine*. In very brief summary, their idea was this: Yes, healing is an essential part of the work of the church. There were, they declared, many maladies, apparently physical, which had no organic basis, but were functional results of mental and spiritual causes. They were anticipating in this the now general recognition of the psycho-somatic nature of illness. In the case of sickness, therefore, a first step should be to diagnose the nature of the ailment and its underlying cause. In this they differed categorically from Christian Science, which places no importance on diagnosis. Since disease is not real, it makes no difference what name may be given to the apparent illness. New Thought has generally been less emphatic in this regard, but many New Thought practitioners have also been indifferent to diagnosis.

If the illness were one which might properly be dealt with by psychotherapeutic methods, including prayer and religious ministrations, then these should be provided by one skilled in either psychotherapeutic techniques or so-called spiritual methods—anointing, laying on of hands, prayer, etc. This might be carried out in private or in the church, before the altar, as seemed best. Included here would be most of the so-called nervous disorders.

If, in the opinion of the diagnostician, the ailments were such as to require medication or surgery, properly qualified doctors would be entrusted with the task of providing the necessary treatment. Of course, the ministrations of religion might be helpfully added to this. Thus the church would have its part in the healing in any case, and so fulfil that part of its mission. Indeed, the first actual effort of the Emmanuel Movement to bring relief to the sick had been an attempt to answer the question whether the poorest consumptives could be cured in the city slums without removing them from their homes, by adding to the then recognized methods of treating tuberculosis, "discipline, friendship, encouragement and hope." And the records carefully kept established, write the authors, that the results of their effort, while carried on under the most unfavorable circumstances, would bear comparison with those of the best sanatoria. (p. 1) It confirmed them in the belief that the church had an important mission in this regard and that the physician and the clergyman could "work together to benefit the community."

The new movement was thus to be a co-operative venture between scientific medical practice and the psychotherapist and the minister. All healing is of God, seemed to be their position.

He uses many means to cure illness. It was absurd to suppose that the use of physical means meant a lack of faith, they declared. They did not believe that the use of one method rather than another "was necessarily more an act of God than the other." (p. 3)

So a very successful movement was begun and spread, especially through the Episcopal church. Ever since the establishment of the Emmanuel Movement, the element of healing has been a constant feature in some segments of the Episcopal church, under such names, for example, as the Guild of Health, as indeed it has also been in the Anglican church in England. The magazine *Sharing*, published in San Diego, carries in its healing directory the names of churches which ask to be included and which provide regularly some form of healing service. The list in a recent issue was over two pages long. And in each case the method employed, whether of anointing or laying on of hands or through prayer groups or some other means, was indicated. In many churches, both Episcopalian and others, a regular staff of physicians, psychiatrists, and/or clinical psychologists, as well as clergymen especially trained for such a ministry, is maintained. Marble Collegiate Church in New York City, the church of Norman Vincent Peale, is a notable example.

Partly as a result of this increase of interest in healing, there has arisen a new type of training for ministers as counselors, often with a required period of internship in some hospital where the student learns to work along with the physician or psychiatrist in a special co-operative ministry to the sick. Almost all theological schools now have specialists in the area to train their students. The National Council of Churches has an active Department of Religion and Health which works constantly to extend the application of the gospel of healing. A study was made in the early fifties by the writer on behalf of the National Council concerning the practice of spiritual healing in the major denominations. This study revealed that healing was practiced to a remarkable degree in these denominations. (See "Spiritual Healing in the Churches," *Pastoral Psychology*, May, 1954). There is every reason to believe that the practice has grown rather than diminished in the years since the study. Certainly the number of books and articles dealing with the subject has not decreased.

It is possible, of course, that the authors of *Religion and Medicine* were right when they wrote, "Our movement bears no relation to Christian Science [or, he might as well have added, New Thought] either by way of protest or limitation, but it would be what it is had the latter never existed," but the writer simply doesn't believe that this is true. The Emmanuel Movement may have taken its stand "fairly and squarely on the religion of Christ, as that religion is revealed in the New Testament," as its leaders declare. But why, at that particular time and place, discover in the gospel that particular emphasis? In the opinion of the writer the impulse arose, consciously or unconsciously, in Boston, the center of both early Christian Science and New Thought, as in some measure a result of insistence upon "the recovery of the gospel of healing" that had been an integral part of the teachings of Jesus and the early church, but that had fallen largely into disuse.

Indeed, in a later book, Dr. Worcester reveals that he was influenced—at least negatively—by Christian Science. New Thought represented much the same point of view in the eyes of the clergy of the major churches, who made little attempt to distinguish between the two movements. Dr. Worcester had, as he remarks, seen "the rise of the great and for the most part irrational healing cults of America." The majority of those who associated themselves with these movements had

done so, not because they are insane, as their opponents so naively imagine, or because they are in love with crude and obscure metaphysical systems which few of them seek to comprehend, but because they desired the kind of help they were not receiving from their physicians, nor yet from the churches.

In view of this, he says, he asked himself,

Is this necessary? Is there any reason why this infection should spread?

If there is help in religion and in ethical ideals, why should such sufferers quench their thirst in shallow and stagnant pools, and not rather drink of the living water from the hand of Christ and the prophets and the other teachers of mankind? (*The Christian Religion as a Healing Power* [Moffatt, Yard & Co., 1909], p. 27)

It was borne in upon him then by this fact that he and his church should try to do something about it. The Emmanuel Movement was the result.

But though he had himself but lately made the discovery of the necessity of co-operation between doctors and clergymen, he says, John Wesley had seen it clearly a hundred and fifty years before, when he wrote in his *Journal*, May 12, 1759:

Why then do not all physicians consider how far bodily disorders are caused or influenced by the mind; and in those cases which are utterly out of their sphere, call in the assistance of a minister; as ministers when they find the mind disordered by the body, call in the assistance of a physician? But why are these cases out of their sphere? Because they know not God. It follows, no man can be a thorough physician without being an experienced Christian. (Quoted in *The Christian Religion as a Healing Power*, p. 39)

Also in a later chapter in *Religion and Medicine* in which his disclaimer of any influence of Christian Science or New Thought appears, in discussing the importance of the subconscious, Dr. Worcester writes, "Concerning the value of the discovery and use of those inexhaustibly subconscious powers which have their roots in the Infinite.... Much has been written of the highest value by the so-called metaphysical school to which I am glad at least to pay my respects." In a footnote he says, "I allude to such writers as Henry Wood, Charles B. Patterson, Horatio W. Dresser, Ralph Waldo Trine, Aaron Crane, also to Horace Fletcher ... and many others, all or most of them well-known New Thought leaders." (*Religion and Medicine*, p. 134)

PART IV

New Thought Abroad

14

New Thought in Great Britain

THUS FAR the outreach of New Thought has been discussed in terms of the persons and means through which its ideas and practices were spread and the organizational forms through which it worked in America. By America was meant, of course, both the United States and Canada. New Thought gradually made itself at home on both sides of the border, developing in Canada no distinctive features and no permanent separate organization. New Thought in Canada, just as in the United States, was often enough accepted by individuals who never left their churches. It was sometimes organized into quite independent local groups. Often these became members of one or another of the movements such as Divine Science or Unity, and many individuals or groups, thus affiliated or not, also became and are active members of INTA. Current issues of *New Thought* list three district presidents in Canada — Eastern, Central, and Western.

But New Thought, while distinctively a product of America, has long since gone abroad. Persons holding essentially New Thought ideas are to be found all over the world, and in some countries substantial movements have developed, each taking its own particular form of organization.

The beginnings of New Thought in Great Britain are not altogether clear. There is, however, an anonymous pamphlet bearing the title *Early History of the Higher Thought Movement in England,* which apparently was written not later than 1915, and possibly as early as 1911, though it bears no date of publication.

Horatio Dresser, in his *History of the New Thought Move-ment,* published in 1919, either did not know of this pamphlet or made no use of it, for he contents himself with remarking simply that in England, as in America, "interest was aroused by Christian Science, then came a gradual reaction and the estab-lishment of independent branches of the movement." (p. 262) But the pamphlet tells a different story. It says that the Higher Thought movement traces back directly to the appearance in London of a married couple, Charles and Susan Bowles, with an extraordinary message addressed to "The Wounded and Sick in the Battle of Life."

Whence the Bowleses came is not disclosed, nor what connec-tions they may have had with any other movements before com-ing. Had they come from some other part of England to London, or had they come perhaps from America? Thus far nothing has been discovered as to their background. They began to hold meetings, first in Westminster, later at Queen's Hall, Kensington, where classes were held three times a week.

Were they Christian Scientists, or were they New Thought people? The class taught was called a "Class for Mental Har-mony," which sounds more like New Thought than Christian Science. Both Mr. and Mrs. Bowles usually spoke. Following the talks by the Bowleses, personal interviews and healing treat-ments were given.

Hugh Studdert-Kennedy, himself an Englishman, in his book, *Mrs. Eddy* (Farallon Press, 1947), writes that the first effective introduction of Christian Science to the British public was an article in the *London Times* of May 26, 1885, written by a cor-respondent in Boston who had attended a meeting at Hawthorn Hall, where Mrs. Eddy was then speaking regularly. There was also in the same issue an editorial on the subject of Christian Science. Studdert-Kennedy goes on to say, however, that the first real introduction to the British Isles through a teacher did not occur until 1888, when a Mr. and Mrs. Coles, who as a result of reading a letter from an American friend purchased *Science and Health,* were thrilled by it and went to America to study with Mrs. Eddy. They formed part of the famous class of March, 1888, of which Edward A. Kimball and others later to become prominent in the movement were members. Then they returned with a Mrs. Laramine, at Mrs. Eddy's request, to open work in Dublin in November, 1888. Mrs. Eddy asked Mrs. Laramine to go on to London, and this she did, opening approved Christian Science work there in December, 1888.

Frances Lord, one of the earliest writers on Christian Science, discovered it while on a trip to America in 1886 and in 1888 published her book, *Christian Science Healing* (Chicago, 1888). In the preface she mentions having taught classes in London between October, 1887, and July, 1888. But since she had been a student of Emma Curtis Hopkins, who had by this time been repudiated by Mrs. Eddy, what she taught would not have been considered true Christian Science by Mrs. Eddy and her "loyal" followers. Thus Charles and Susan Bowles came to London after the *Times* article, but two years before any definite officially approved Christian Science work was begun in Britain, and at least a year before Frances Lord taught her class.

The outline of the teaching of the Bowleses, given by them in a printed syllabus, is quoted at length in the pamphlet. (pp. 3-4) There is not the slightest indication that their teaching was Christian Science. The outline contains nothing about the unreality of matter, or about mortal error, and none of the synonyms for God that play so important a role in Christian Science appear in it. There is healing, yes, but not after the Christian Science pattern.

On the other hand, the presentation is typically New Thought. According to the syllabus, the principles of mental harmony are both positive and negative—the positive, that of holding in the mind the image of the good; the negative, that of casting out of the mind "all images of evil." Thoughts, the Bowleses affirmed, are *things;* they form habits, shape character, and rule destiny. Training of the mind in higher, purer thought makes therefore for a higher and purer destiny.

Health is defined as positive, disease as something negative.

Disease is absence of Truth. Health is more contagious than sickness. "The constant effort of Natural Law is toward the Type and its recovery." Harmony is the basis of health. "Chronic nervous tension is often relaxed by loving and harmonious thought contacts. Even the most materialistic minds can be reached and harmonized by loving thoughts and acts where intellectual efforts fail to reach them."

Let it be granted that the whole rich development of later New Thought is not to be found here; nevertheless the kinship of this teaching with New Thought rather than with Christian Science is abundantly clear.

Who were the Bowleses? The little brochure never connects them definitely with America, except to quote from letters from them written at a later time from Rockford, Illinois, and Oakland, California. It seems that it was their custom to spend a few months each year in London, then go elsewhere for the remainder of the year and do the same kind of work. Among other places they are mentioned as having visited are Cairo, Geneva, and distant Japan. Were they sent by some organization, or were they on their own? How were the expenses of such wide travels paid? The fact that they did later work in America may give some basis for the belief that they originally came from there. But it is only conjecture.

The writer of the pamphlet, who had attended earlier meetings, apparently had left London, then in 1890 returned with the intention of taking up work of somewhat similar character. She was prevailed upon to take over the class during an absence of the Bowleses, and a small permanent group was formed which continued to meet weekly throughout the year, paying expenses by personal contributions. They eventually established themselves in an upper room near Earl's Court, in what was known to them as the Wharfdale Studio. Meetings were held on Fridays and a program that had been suggested by the Bowleses was followed. Furthermore, the Bowleses wrote them frequently, giving advice and encouragement. In these programs and communications appears a religious element not apparent in the syllabus, which made no mention of the Divine or God and only once spoke of the Law of Nature.

One letter reflects at least the desire on the part of some members of the group to make it into a sect or a church. This idea was firmly opposed by the Bowleses; but other teachers were appearing and some of the group members left to follow them. The author of the pamphlet says that they never learned of the controversies in the general field from the Bowleses. They happily read from many sources and felt "very much like the early Christians of the first and second centuries, ready to lend our ears to any voicing the precious passwords, 'All is good.'" This, naturally enough, led to complications.

Teachers noted at the time as influential were Mrs. Emma Curtis Hopkins, Ursula Gestefeld, Frances Lord, and Annie Rix (later Militz). Members of the group were reading Dr. Warren Felt Evans' books. Mentioned especially was his *Divine Law of Cure*. Magazines included the *Blue Bird,* as they called it, or *Christian Science,* or still later *Universal Truth*.

The group continually urged the Bowleses to return and they finally did so, but it did not work out happily. Some break occurred, though the narrative contains no details concerning it. The Bowleses accepted the situation and refused to enter into any controversy, but held meetings in their own quarters, while two or three other leaders had a following also. Ultimately the Wharfdale group found its ongoing life chiefly in the Moral and Spiritual Development of the Women's Educational and Industrial Union in London, led by a Dr. Harriet Clisby, who had attended a Federation of Women's Work in Boston. It lost its own life, says the author, but "permeated with its life-giving waters the whole body of work of which it had become an integral part." (p. 20)

Those who did not work with the Women's Union drifted into other groups and activities to which they brought the metaphysical outlook. Among these was a Pioneer Club, to which Charles Brodie Patterson lectured and gave classes during several seasons. Also, the well-known "Sesame Club," the author points out, contained certain elements of the Mental Harmony teaching.

Swami Vivekananda, coming direct from the World's Parliament of Religions held in Chicago in 1893, was welcomed as a lecturer to several of these groups and undoubtedly contributed much from Oriental thought to the developing movement. There was also frequent interchange of lecturers with the Theosophical Societies. Among Theosophist lecturers was the rising leader Annie Besant, later to become World President of the Theosophical Society. An increasing number of American lecturers appeared before the Women's Union and other New Thought groups.

In 1897 Mrs. Alma Gillen, an independent worker, edited and published the first English magazine, *Expression: A Journal of Mind and Thought,* which was distinctively along the lines of the New Thought, or Higher Thought, as it had come to be called.

The Women's Union was dissolved in 1900, but a group of those interested in the Higher Thought, consisting of Miss Beth-Jones, Miss Callow, Miss Agnes Harvey, Mrs. Oliver, and Miss Grace Western, called a general meeting to see if adequate support could be found for the maintenance of a Higher Thought Center. The meeting agreed that it was possible and passed resolutions setting up such a center for the purpose of serving as headquarters for what was recognized as Higher Thought in all its branches, both in England and wherever found, and providing that it maintain a depository for the sale of books and a lending library. The name Higher Thought Center was at first adopted only temporarily, but it came generally to be the recognized name in England for what in America was called New Thought.

The Center soon found suitable rooms and set up a library. Regular meetings, lectures, classes, and silent meetings were held. Miss Grace Western was chairman of the Committee of Management, as well as teacher of various classes. Named among the lecturers of the earlier days of the Center's existence were Bruce Wallace, Edward Carpenter, Macbeth Bain, Mrs. Kohaus, W. J. Colville, Mrs. Hooper, and others. In 1901 Judge Thomas

H. Troward gave his first lecture at the Center. Harry Gaze, Dr. James Porter Mills, Annie Rix Militz, Charles Brodie Patterson, and J. Stitt Wilson, all from America, appeared under the auspices of the Center. Some who first lectured at the Center later opened other centers in London and elsewhere, and so the movement grew and spread in many directions.

Quite the most outstanding figure in the development of New Thought in England, on the side of the formulation of ideas, was Judge Thomas Troward. He had spent all of his active career in India, during the latter part of it as a judge in what is now Pakistan. After retirement he returned to England and gave himself up to his hobby, painting, and to writing. Up until that time he had apparently had no connection with any New Thought exponents. It is true that according to his daughter he "valued Emerson very highly," but Emerson can hardly be thought of as a New Thought writer, but rather as one of the sources from which New Thought drew a great deal. The daughter is also on record as saying that he "delved deeply into various Indian and other Eastern religions" during his stay in India.

Miss Callow, one of the early New Thought leaders in England, says that during his Indian period he devoted all his spare time either to painting or to the "study of the tomes of sacred Indian lore and the scriptures of the Hebrews and other ancient peoples." From this, she says,

there was unfolded to him as if in a vision, a system of philosophy which absorbed in an undercurrent of thought all the working hours of the day and the quiet hours of the night. Released from his onerous duties at last, he settled in England and a manuscript of some nine hundred folios came slowly into existence.

Most of this, at least, took place before he made any connection at all with the Higher Thought Center in London.

In *My Personal Recollections of Thomas Troward*, Harry Gaze tells the story, related originally by Miss Callow, sometimes called the Mother of the Metaphysical Movement in England, of Troward's first introduction to Higher Thought in England. He was sitting one day in a tearoom in London, working on a manuscript, when Miss Callow entered, and finding no other table vacant, asked if she might be seated at his table. Noting that he was writing in a very large hand which she could not help seeing, she remarked that he was writing what seemed to her either Higher Thought or Divine Science. This remark led to further conversation and his eventual introduction to the Higher Thought Center. Here he found congenial friends, listened to lectures and discussions, and was himself invited to address the group. This he did, not once but many times; and finally he became the most noted of British New Thought leaders, one who influenced not alone British New Thought but, through the publication of his lectures, the thought of the whole "metaphysical" world.

Troward was thus introduced to New Thought as it had developed up to that point. He saw its literature, books, pamphlets, and periodicals, as they were found at the Center, and was to some extent no doubt influenced in his own thought by them; but it seems clear that he arrived at most of his philosophy independently. Perhaps he was influenced by Emerson, as were all the others, and surely he was to some extent influenced by oriental thought. His firm belief in reincarnation seems to have been one of the results of Indian influence. But so were other early leaders influenced by Emerson and by oriental thought. His was an able and original mind.

He was a very diffident individual and shrank from appearing in public. Eventually, however, he consented to give a series of lectures, and in 1904 he delivered the famous Edinburgh Lectures in Queen's Gate Hall in Edinburgh. *The Edinburgh Lectures on Mental Science* has since gone through numerous editions both in England and America. The lectures were given to a small but appreciative group of persons, some of whom hardly understood what he was saying. He was urged to publish them and finally consented. Though he published a number of other volumes before his death in 1916, including the *Doré Lectures on Mental*

Science, The Creative Process in the Individual, Bible Mystery and Bible Meaning, The Law and the Word, The Hidden Power, and his comments on the Psalms, it was *The Edinburgh Lectures* that set the basic pattern of his thought. It represents his thought before he had come under any appreciable influence of the writings of others in the field.

One who felt that he had exerted such influence was Harry Gaze, who pointed out in his *Personal Recollections of Thomas Troward* one or two respects in which Troward followed ideas which he himself had long taught and which Troward had apparently not at first glimpsed. Gaze writes that he had known the Judge personally and had had him in some of his classes as early as 1903, and in what he calls personal interview lessons. He finds in *The Edinburgh Lectures* (p. 11) a restatement of what he himself had published first in his book *Science of Physical Immortality* in 1899, concerning the key to the control of "life, permanent health, and immortality," as lying in the "conscious cooperation with the LAW in individual evolution." But whether this was borrowed from Gaze or was merely the logical conclusion from Troward's own premise that "the supreme principle of life must also be the ultimate principle of intelligence," is not clear.

Gaze seems to have taken it as logical that even death was under voluntary control and could be avoided, so that man could achieve physical immortality. Indeed he claimed, as did Charles Fillmore of Unity, that he had himself reached that stage. He sought to impress this on Troward, who seems to have recognized the possibility on theoretical grounds; but Troward never came to believe that he himself would not die. Perhaps his doctrine of reincarnation kept him from that, and on one occasion he predicted his own physical death. This, says Gaze, is precisely what led to his final physical dissolution, for what man projects into the Universal Unconscious Mind becomes a fact. One cannot help wondering what it was that brought about Gaze's own demise, for he seems continually to have affirmed that he would not see death. His book and lectures on *How To Live Forever*

are well known in the New Thought field. My own conviction
is that if he had any influence on Troward it was but slight, and
was almost wholly in the direction of the practical application of
theory to life. In this Troward was little interested, especially in
the earlier years of his connection with the Higher Thought
group. There is some record of his having been instrumental in
healing individuals, but he was never in any real sense a "practitioner," though remarkable healings have been reported as the
result of the reading and study of his books.

Troward has been read with great respect by eminent leaders
in the field of philosophy. William James characterized his writings as "far and away the ablest statement of the philosophy I
have met, beautiful in its sustained clearness of thought and
style; a really classic statement." (Quoted in Gaze, *Personal
Recollections of Thomas Troward*, No. 2, p. 4)

How much Troward was read by the British clergy it is
impossible to say, but he was a close friend of one of the most
prominent clergymen of the Established Church. A warm personal friendship existed between Troward and Archdeacon Basil
Wilberforce of Westminster Abbey, and Gaze has pointed out
instances in which the thought of Wilberforce seems to have
been influenced by Troward. In his *Spiritual Consciousness*,
Wilberforce writes:

Love being the only quality which cannot be mechanical, automatic,
as is the cosmic consciousness, the life centers who are to manifest
Love must have a measure of volition conferring upon them the
freedom to refuse. All this is luminously expressed in Troward's
Doré Lectures. This refusal of men to be a vehicle, a manifestor, of
God's highest quality means the concentration of his desires upon
self instead of God. . . . The fall of man is his fall from the consciousness of his divinity, his oneness with the Infinite Mind. . . . The
conscious mind held in concentration upon the fact of oneness with
the Infinite Immanent Mind will transform the whole life. The function of the will is to be the centralizing principle of the conscious
oneness with that interior principle as the truest fact of our being.
Affirm "In me is the divine Immanence, that is my real self, the Infinite
Indweller seeks to realize himself in me, He desires to think his
thoughts in me, and his thoughts are thoughts of gentleness, moral

purpose, purity, courage, patience." Then use the will in holding that thought, keep the conscious mind from wandering away from it. (Quoted in Gaze, *Personal Recollections*)

Whether Wilberforce got it from Troward or not, he is clearly echoing him when he writes:

The Cosmic Mind which is intensely intelligent, is subconscious mind; that is, it has no initiative, but is keenly sensitive to suggestion. . . . Now Jesus was the specialization of the Infinite Superconscious Mind which is God. Therefore when he suggested anything to the cosmic subconscious mind, his suggestion was instantly adopted. (Quoted in Gaze, p. 12)

Well might Gaze declare that, in a sense, Troward was vicariously voicing ideas in historic Westminster Abbey of the Church of England through the famous preacher, for he says, "His sermons were permeated with the metaphysical teachings as given in the Troward literature, and in their devoted personal companionship and study." (Quoted in Gaze, p. 6)

Frederick L. Rawson, writing in *Active Service* (I, 650) confirms the close friendship between Troward and Wilberforce. He says that Wilberforce was a great admirer of Troward's works and in his sermons was constantly quoting from them. He quotes from an article in the *Christian Commonwealth* saying of Troward's books, "Their lucidity, insight and logic brought conviction to many. Churchmen especially were attracted by *Bible Mystery and Meaning.*"

It would be a mistake, of course, to suppose that Wilberforce followed Troward in every respect. Indeed, they differed sharply at points, but there is no mistaking the fact that the Anglican divine accepted the basic presuppositions of Troward, however much he may have differed in lesser matters. Wilberforce was one who could gather ideas from many sources. Indeed, in a specific passage in *Spiritual Consciousness* he advises that others assimilate gratefully what groups of different viewpoints have to offer. He says that he has done just that, but that, having gathered honey from many flowers, he "comes back to the hive

of the Catholic Church with a sense of rest, and a renewed satisfaction and appreciation, bringing with me some spiritual honey
from every flower I have mentally explored." But, says Gaze, he
wanted "the form of metaphysical thinking as the keynote of the
Church itself, and not as a separate movement or cult." (p. 8)

While Troward was influential principally in shaping the
thinking of the Higher Thought Movement in England, he has
also been quite influential in the thinking of some leaders of
American New Thought, perhaps most notably that of Ernest
Holmes, founder of Religious Science. Holmes tells how he was
finally successful in the beginnings of his own work only after
some months of complete failure to attract people to his ministry.
One day he loaned a copy of one of Troward's books to an
engineer with whom he was talking. A little later, the engineer,
having read it with interest, asked Holmes if he might not invite
some friends into his home and have Holmes talk to them about
it. This was done, and Holmes was so successful that he was
soon launched into a public ministry through which he was
reaching thousands.

Just how much of what Holmes teaches is from Troward it
is difficult to say. It is significant that in his textbook, where he
is setting forth his basic thought, there is no mention of Troward.
Gaze makes the easy explanation that Holmes has combined
with his own forceful thinking the teachings of Thomas Troward
"in a simplified, breezy, American way." But it is not as simple
as that. It is extremely difficult to sit down with Holmes's books
and discover at just what points he is clearly following Troward.
He has digested Troward's thought so completely and made it
so much his own that it is doubtful if he himself could have
told precisely when or where in his own teaching he was setting
forth Troward's thought. He did teach Troward's thought as
such, as have other teachers of New Thought. Gaze lists a dozen
or more men and women in America who periodically offer
courses in Troward's teachings.

The thing that perhaps distinguishes Troward from other
New Thought writers is the unique fashion in which he arrives

at the theoretical basis for the practical outworking of New Thought in its healing, prosperity, and other aspects. He starts with no revelation of a religious nature. He simply looks at the universe. As he does so he sees that which seems to have about it a quality of livingness and that which does not. The difference is not always sharp. There are, he thinks, degrees of livingness, and when he tries to discover what it is that makes the difference at the various levels, he finds that it is intelligence. Always the degree of livingness is seen to be related directly to the degree of intelligence. That is, livingness is ultimately to be measured by its intelligence.

Motion, which seems also to be associated with livingness, appears, the lower one goes in the scale of livingness, to be more and more beyond the control of the thing in motion, while the higher the level of intelligence, the more control is exercised over motion. From this Troward deduced that the very livingness of life itself consists in intelligence, or in other words in the power of thought. *Thought* then, he concludes, is the distinctive quality of spirit, and *form* that of matter. Matter without form cannot be conceived of; it must occupy space. On the other hand, spirit or thought knows no limit of space and from this he argues that it is also independent of time. It must always, therefore, be something not in the past, or in the future, but always in the eternal now.

If, as he has affirmed, the higher the grade of life, the higher the intelligence, then it seems to follow logically that "the supreme principle of Life must also be the ultimate principle of intelligence." This concept he finds to be supported by a consideration of the evolutionary view of the universe. It must be, he asserts, that there is a great cosmic intelligence which underlies the totality of things. (*The Edinburgh Lectures,* p. 9) In the earlier stages of evolution the cosmic intelligence seems to work by a law of averages which permits a wide margin of loss and failure to the individual. But advance toward higher intelligence is always accompanied by a narrowing of the margin and the removing of the individual more and more from the law of averages, and the individual has a continually increasing ability to control whatever conditions his own survival. That which chiefly distinguishes the cosmic and the individual intelligence is the fact of individual volition. This very power of volition is an outcome of the cosmic evolutionary principle at the point where the highest level is reached. If man is to evolve further, it must be by his own co-operation with the law that has brought him to the stage where he can realize the existence of such a law. (p. 12)

Now he must consciously participate in the creative activity of cosmic intelligence through the use of his own individual intelligence and volition. He must work co-operatively with that intelligence expressed in law. It is a fact that "Nature obeys us precisely in proportion as we first obey Nature." For example, an electrician must work with the law that electricity must always pass from a higher to a lower potential, and as he recognizes this he can make electricity serve him in a thousand ways.

That which seems to differentiate the higher and lower degrees of intelligence is self-recognition, and the more intelligent the recognition, the greater the power will be. The lower level, he thinks, involves only the recognition of the ego and the non-ego, while the higher degree, realizing its own spiritual nature, sees not merely the non-ego in all other forms which are not the self, but in that which is not itself it sees the alter-ego, or that which is itself in a different mode of expression. (pp. 12-13) Here it is that Mental Science operates and produces its results. For when one recognizes self as an "individualization of pure spirit," he finds himself in a position to control lower forms of spirit which do not know the law.

Underlying all substance, says Troward, is what may be called Atomic Intelligence (p. 15), which is distinguishable from individual Intelligence, and it is by the response of the former to the latter that thought is able to produce at the level of matter results such as the cure of disease.

All this helps to understand what is meant by "Unity of the Spirit." Underneath the specific forms there lies an essential undifferentiated unity which supports the forms of individuality which arise out of it. It is quite unlimited by space, nor is there any space where it is not. It is therefore infinite, and infinity mathematically must be a unity. There cannot be two infinities; each would limit the other. Therefore because the originating Life Principle is infinite, the whole must be present at every point at the same moment. Spirit, he therefore deduces, is omnipresent in its entirety, and all Spirit may be thought to be concentrated at a point at any moment when we fix thought upon it. Pure Spirit, as devoid of relation to space or time, is devoid of individual personality, but it is infinite in its responsiveness and susceptibility. It is upon this that as individualized Spirit we "can impress any recognition of personality that we will." It is with these great facts that the mental scientist operates.

Thus far Troward has dealt with metaphysical abstractions. He now turns to the discussion of what he calls subjective and objective mind, as he seeks to lay a solid basis for making practical use of the abstract principles so far deduced. It is in the experiments with hypnosis that he discovers the fact of the dual nature of mind—what he calls the objective and subjective mind, or what would now be called the conscious and subconscious mind. The objective or conscious mind is able to reason inductively, that is, draw conclusions on the basis of a massing of evidence which may then be put to the test of experimental proof, if they are in the area of the physical sciences. The subjective or subconscious, on the other hand, can only reason deductively, as is shown by the fact that it accepts uncritically whatever suggestion may be impressed upon it, and works out in great fidelity whatever may logically follow from the suggestion. For example, if a hypnotized person is told that he is a dog, he acts like a dog.

But it is the subjective or subconscious mind that builds the body, and the subjective mind is under the control of the objective mind, which may suggest what it will to the subconscious. The subjective then proceeds to carry out logically the suggestion offered. This has its great importance in the area of health and well-being. A belief that medicine will heal has its effect. There is nothing wrong in such a suggestion, says Troward. The error lies in the belief that there is no higher, better way. It is, he thinks, just as easy to externalize healthy conditions of the body as the contrary.

Further consideration of the nature of subjective and objective mind leads to the identification of the subjective mind with the all-pervading spirit. It cannot, as *universal mind,* have the attributes of objective mind. It is the creative power throughout nature. It gives rise to forms in which objective mind recognizes its own individuality. (p. 30) As subjective mind the all-permeating intelligence follows the law of subjective mind and will carry "any suggestion that is impressed upon it to its most rigorously logical consequences." (pp. 30-31)

Troward is, of course, at pains in his further discussion to distinguish between the individual personality and that of the universal Life principle which he insists cannot possess the element of self-recognition as individual personality on any scale whatsoever. For it to recognize a selfhood that differentiates one individual from another would be to impose upon itself a limitation which is at once a denial of universality. For it to recognize a point where it ceased and another, or something else, began would be to recognize itself as not universal. (p. 46) Thus the originating Spirit is "the grand impersonal principle of Life which gives rise to all the particular manifestations of Nature." (p. 46)

This principle must possess all the qualities of personality, since out of it come personalities, but "without that conscious recognition of self which constitutes separate individuality." This he chooses to describe by the term *personalness* instead of *personality.* So he speaks of the "personalness of the Universal Mind" as indicating its personal quality, apart from individuality. (p. 47) This runs very close to what a distinguished theologian of the orthodox, though liberal, church used to assert concerning God as person. The term he used was "the personality producing factor" in deity.

All nature is permeated by this "interior personalness, infinite in its potentialities of intelligence, reponsiveness, and power of expression, and only waiting to be called into activity by our recognition of it." (p. 48) As Troward sees it, this operates either wholly by chance or by universal law. Chance, he thinks, would produce chaos. The intelligent order of the universe seems to establish the basis of operation as not chance but Law— but man knows only a few of the laws, nor can he know them all, since he is finite and the universal Mind is infinite. (p. 49) Nature inevitably punishes the infraction of her law. The only way is to co-operate with nature, knowing the Law and working with it. And this Mind, all-producing, infinite, and underlying, must be ready to respond immediately to all those who realize their true relation to it as well as being infinitely susceptible to feeling, and it therefore must produce accurately whatever conception of itself man impresses upon it. (p. 53)

In his chapter "Causes and Conditions," he states that a *primary* cause can never be negative, since "negation is the condition which arises from the absence of active causation." This is the philosophic basis of *denials,* which play so important a part in Mental Science. (p. 64) The region of primary causes is within ourselves, for it is the region of pure ideas. The thought-image or ideal pattern of a thing is, he thinks, the *first cause* relatively to that thing.

We are always, whether consciously or not, impressing some sort of image upon the Universal Mind, but many of these images are the ideas of limitation which we have received from our social milieu. We need consciously to make use of *first causes,* realize that our purpose is not contingent on any conditions whatever; then we can await the result with cheerful expectancy. And the Spirit is independent of time and space. An ideal must be formed now or not at all; so it is necessary that one picture to himself the fulfilment of his desires as already accomplished on the spiritual plane. If the end is secured, then the proper means or steps to the end are secured also, and one need not worry as to the outcome. But since the Law cannot be expected to do *for* us what can only be done *through* us, we must use our intelligence, convinced that that intelligence is but the instrument of a greater intelligence. (p. 69)

In discussing actual healing, Troward holds that "a change of belief" is the universal basis, regardless of sectarian differences in other respects. Often the illness is but an externalization of the wrong belief that some secondary cause, which is really only a condition, is the primary cause. But there is only *one* primary cause, the factor which we call the subjective or subconscious mind. Troward apparently thinks, like Quimby and Evans, that a wrong impression has been made upon our subconscious by factors in our social environment—doctors, folk beliefs, or what not—which externalize themselves as sickness. Now if the individual can but conceive himself in the absolute rather than in the relative, he will know that as "purely living spirit" he is not hampered by conditions of any sort, and therefore not subject to sickness. This, impressing itself on the subconscious mind, will externalize itself as health and well-being. This will not usually happen instantaneously, but continued treatment administered either by oneself or by a practitioner will eventually result in a cure.

When the aid of a healer or practitioner is sought, the function of the healer is to find entrance to the subconscious mind of the patient and to impress upon it the suggestion of pure health. This he is able to do by substituting his own objective or conscious mentality, which he describes as will joined to intellect, for that of the patient. As soon as the healer realizes that the barriers of personality between himself and his patient have been removed, it is possible for him to speak to the subconscious mind of the patient as though it were his own, for, Troward says, both being pure spirit, the thought of their identity makes them identical.

Hence absent treatment can be quite as effective as personal treatment, and perhaps even more so, for in mental treatment neither time nor space mean anything, since it takes place on a plane where time and space do not count. Treatment may,

Troward asserts, be made in sleep—even in the practitioner's sleep, if, before going to sleep, he deliberately impresses upon his own subconscious mind that it is to convey to the subjective mind of a patient a curative suggestion. Troward regards this method as especially adaptable to young children, who would not of course understand the principles of science even if they were told to them. (p. 81)

In what was originally the last chapter of *The Edinburgh Lectures*—three brief chapters on Body, Soul, and Spirit were subsequently added—the author gives an excellent summary of his major theses. He has tried in the lectures to make the student aware of the tremendous importance of our dealings with what he calls subconscious mind. On the scale either of the individual or the universal, he insists, the key to all we are or ever can be lies in our own relation to it. (p. 94) On the universal scale it is "the silent power of evolution"; on the individual, it is "the spring of all that we can call the automatic action of mind and body," and "by our conscious recognition of it we make it, relatively to ourselves, all that we believe it to be." What is needful is to discover how best to put ourselves *en rapport* with it so that what we have been accustomed to think of as automatic action, whether in our bodies or our circumstances, will pass under our control, and we shall be able to control our entire individual world. But how? We come into touch with it by rising to its own level "on the plane of the interior and essential." We come into touch with the absolute "exactly in proportion as we withdraw ourselves from the relative." It is by first formulating clearly in our objective mind a conception of what it is we wish to impress upon the subjective mind. A very down-to-earth method suggested, which has proven to be quite successful, is to say to subjective mind, "This is what I want you to do; you will now step into my place and do it, bringing all your powers and intelligence to bear, and considering yourself to be none other than myself." Having done this, let the subjective mind develop its own ways of working consonant with the laws of its own nature. And if this succeeds in the case of the individual subjective mind, why not also in that of the Universal Subjective Mind?

Troward has, he says, set out three laws of the subjective mind: (1) its creative power, (2) its amenability to suggestion, and (3) its inability to work by any other method than the deductive, whether individual or Universal. It becomes of great significance how we think of the Universal Mind, for "it will infallibly bear *to us* exactly that character which we impress upon it." (p. 99) Jesus, the greatest teacher of Mental Science, he asserts, bade men to picture it as benign Father, loving, compassionate, one to whom prayer should be made with absolute assurance of an answer, and to whom no limits of power or willingness were to be set. And this is, he says, no mere anthropomorphism, but the deepest truth of Mental Science. "As unalloyed Life and Intelligence it *can* be no other than good," can entertain no intention of evil. (p. 101) The deepest problems of philosophy lead back ultimately to the old statement of the Law, "'Ask and ye shall receive, seek and ye shall find, knock and it shall be opened unto you.' This is the summing-up of the natural law of the relation between us and the Divine Mind." (p. 104)

But this does not relieve us of responsibilities. The deeper one penetrates into Mental Science, the more carefully must he be on his guard against all thoughts and words expressive of even the most modified form of ill will. . . . "We must cultivate that tone which we wish to see reproduced in our conditions whether of body, mind, or circumstance." (p. 105)

Only scattered notes, mostly in American New Thought publications, have been available concerning the Higher Thought Movement in England during the period 1900-1914, the time of Judge Troward's activity. Julia Seton's *The Column* says that in February, 1912, the Higher Thought Center, then at 10 Chemiston Gardens, London, had a complete program including lectures by C. B. Patterson and other teachers from America. Patterson was leading the Sunday services at the Doré Galleries, where Judge Troward had given his famous Doré Lectures years before. In July of that year Dr. Julia Seton lectured five times in London to crowded halls, and was considering outdoor meetings in Hyde Park. The March, 1914, issue of *The Column* speaks of a plan for holding an International New Thought Congress in London in June of that year, apparently at the suggestion of American leaders. The Congress was duly held in Knightbridge Hall and the International New Thought Alliance was formed.

Active Service for August 8, 1917, reports that three years later the International Alliance was seeking to bring together the various centers of healing throughout the British Isles. The work was being done from the Higher Thought Center in London. Individuals concerned with calling the conference included Miss H. Bridgman, editor of the *Rally*, a monthly seeking to spread the Truth among the working classes; Mrs. Heard, president of the Higher Thought Center; Mrs. Claus, leader of the Manchester New Thought School; Miss Owen, head of the New Thought Center in London; Miss Alice Callow, secretary of the Higher Thought Center; and Miss Beatrice Hope, assistant secretary of the International New Thought Alliance, a sister of Miss Effie Hogg of *Active Service*. The meeting to be held in the Graften Galleries on September 2-9 would be devoted to reports of work, Spiritual philosophy, True Revolution in education, social and political, divine healing, and Science, Art, and Music from a spiritual standpoint.

It was hoped that the conference would bring the different schools of thought into closer touch with each other so that they might work unitedly, place before the general public in a definite way the divine healing being carried on, and let that public understand better the Science of Right Thinking which results in right speech and right action.

Later issues (September 15 and 22) reported that the British section of the INTA had convened at the Old Bond Street Galleries, London, gave a summary of many of the addresses, and noted certain actions taken by the Congress. Fraternal greetings were sent to the INTA Congress meeting in St. Louis, and an invitation was extended them to hold the next Congress in London. So successful were the sessions that some outdoor meetings were held in Hyde Park. In a closing service it was proposed that a fund of a thousand pounds be raised to give permanence to the British Congress. There is no indication as to whether anything was done toward raising the fund.

Among the persons mentioned as present and participating in the Congress were J. Macbeth Bain, author of *Brotherhood of Healing* and *Christ of the Healing Hand;* Mrs. Heard, president of the Higher Thought Center, and Miss Alice Callow, secretary; Mrs. Mary Gordon and Mrs. Hall Simpson of the London New Thought Center; F. L. Rawson and Mr. Hendry of the Healing Center; Mr. Aldridge of the Wolverton Higher Thought Center; Paul Tyner of the Edinburgh New Thought Center; Captain A. St. John, secretary of the Penal Reform League; Rev. Charles Gardner, chaplain of the Guild of Health; Inayat Kahn, a Sufi; and Harendranath Maitra, a Hindu.

In a letter to James Edgerton, President of INTA, written in 1928, Miss Alice Callow states that during the twelve years when the Higher Thought center was at Chemiston Gardens, a number of lecturers came from the United States to speak to the Higher Thought Center and later established centers of their own. Dr. and Mrs. James Porter Mills established the Higher Health Center and later the New Order of Meditation, carried on later by Miss Antonia Collette and Mrs. Lena Ashewelt; Mrs. Hannah More Kohaus of the Gestefeld School led the Science of Being Center; Mrs. Ursula Gestefeld started a center (not named in the letter) which continued for some years; Mrs. Emma Curtis Hopkins visited London, but did no public work. She did, however, give private lessons to many distinguished persons, and wrote part of her *Higher Mysticism* while in London. Dr. Julia Seton founded a center called the Church of the New Civilization, carried on later by Miss Muriel Brown; Dr. Orlando G. Miller conducted a center in the Old Bond Street Galleries; and there were others.

The most distinguished English teacher of the period, wrote Miss Callow, was Miss Adela Curtis, founder of the Guild of Science, which had a large following. She also founded a Community Home in the country which lasted several years. But during the years following 1917 F. L. Rawson's Society for Spreading the Knowledge of True Prayer was the most active of the English New Thought groups.

F. L. Rawson, like many other leaders in the field of New Thought, was not a clergyman. He was an engineer and business-man. Born in 1859, he had become a distinguished practicing engineer, had achieved a marked success in his profession as consultant and as businessman, and had retired before he founded the Society for Spreading the Knowledge of True Prayer. In *Who's Who in Business* he was called "the principal authority in the city of London on new inventions and discoveries."

Among other things, he was a pioneer in the field of the prac-tical use of electricity and engineer of the first company in the field of electric lighting. He laid the first electric railway in England. But he was also interested in other things. It is said of him that he drew the plans for the first gas-driven automobile and was consulting engineer for the first airship built in Britain. He had the respect of the serious-minded scientists of his day.

He was an active participant in the world of sports, excelling in cricket, tennis, golf, and rifle shooting. He was first violinist in an orchestra for more than a dozen years. He was widely read in the fields of science, and also read philosophy. But it was his scientific interest in some of the remarkable claims that were being made in the areas of religion and the occult which led to his studying them to discover whether or not the claims were true, and if they were, what explanation could be given for the unusual things that were being done.

Christian Science had come to England in the late eighties and had had considerable success. Its claims of ability to heal the most stubborn diseases could not but attract the interest of thoughtful people. The *London Daily Mail* resolved to find out the facts concerning these claims and publish them. The paper commissioned Rawson to make a study of the new cult and write a series of articles on it. Rawson accepted the assignment and began the study of Christian Science, with the result that so far from exposing its errors, he was convinced of its truth and became an ardent Christian Scientist. He became a warm admirer of Mrs. Eddy, believed that she had discovered a long neglected phase of the gospel, and to the day of his death, many years later, was a firm exponent of her teachings. Had the organized church been more pliable, there is little doubt that he would have ended his days as a loyal member of the Church of Christ, Scientist, perhaps the ablest man to have been attracted to it in all its history.

But his was too brilliant and creative a mind to yield itself to a control so absolute as that imposed by the rigid authoritarian organization that Christian Science had become. He was first asked by his local church not to give his testimonies in the Wednesday evening meetings, then was asked not even to attend, and was finally excommunicated from the church by the action of the all-powerful Board of Directors of the Mother Church in Boston. Forced out of the existing institution, he began his own work, which ultimately grew into one of the most active and influential metaphysical healing groups in England, and affiliated itself with the growing New Thought or Higher Thought Movement in that country.

Briefly, the story of the origin and development of his work is this: World War I was on. English soldiers were dying by the thousands in the trenches on the Continent. Unnumbered young men were in active service at the battlefronts across the channel, constantly faced by imminent death. What could people at home do? Of course they could pay the taxes and furnish the arms and ammunition, and feed and clothe the men who were dying in battle. But was that all? Rawson thought not. He had taken Mrs. Eddy seriously. Evil was not real. All this mutual slaughter that was taking place only a few miles away was not real. It was all a ghastly mistake. Only God was real. God was mind, the only mind there was. If this could only be realized fully would it not do away with the seeming evil?

Rawson had gotten hold of an aspect of Christian Science

which many Christian Scientists of his day and our own only dimly understand. Probably most of the healing in Science was and still is done on a purely mental healing basis, and for this there is a sure foundation in *Science and Health.* The healer argues silently and audibly until the mistaken concept in the mind of the patient is erased and the truth is established, and this is the healing.

But others healed on a purely impersonal basis. Indeed, the healing really took place in the mind of the healer, not in that of the patient at all. This was recognized in the Kimball school especially, in which the insistence was that the practitioner must heal himself, clear his own mind of the error, and the result would be the healing of the patient. In 1912 Rawson had set forth this viewpoint in his book *Life Understood,* which was to be revised and re-edited again and again, used as the textbook of the movement he founded, and studied far beyond the limits of his own groups by metaphysical healers the world over.

If the error is in the mind of the healer and healing results from the realization of the truth of the Allness of God, would not this same principle apply in the protection of soldiers? Rawson thought it would, and it occurred to him that there might be an active service on the part of those at home who would undertake to treat for the protection of soldiers. A group might be formed of those who would regularly and systematically dedicate themselves to trying to protect the soldiers at the front through the power of right thinking and right prayer.

To this cause Rawson gave himself. Now retired from business, he began to speak to groups and to write numerous letters. Some marvelous results began to appear. Testimonies came to him from persons benefited by the treatments, and these he passed on through public address and through correspondence. Finally, when the correspondence became so burdensome that it seemed better to resort to printing rather than mere letter writing, *Active Service,* a weekly periodical, was born. It has continued publication from its foundation in 1916 to the present, though recently it has been published monthly rather than weekly.

At first the magazine seems to have been a purely personal venture. There was no organization behind it. For the purposes of publication and teaching, for he was now doing a good deal of lecturing and teaching as well as healing, Rawson set up a headquarters at 90 Regent Street, London, and on August 12, 1916, the first issue of *Active Service* appeared. At the masthead of the first number were the words: "A weekly paper devoted to the spreading of the knowledge of the truth. YE SHALL KNOW THE TRUTH AND THE TRUTH SHALL MAKE YOU FREE." On the cover was the statement of purpose:

To help its readers realize their at-one-ment with God, and to teach them how by their prayers—scientific thinking—they can gain health and happiness, and be able to free others from sin, disease and suffering. It will show how to eliminate fear, and how to hasten the time when all men are found to live in perfect harmony with their fellowmen and joy and happiness reign supreme upon the earth.

The first article in the second issue was "How to Protect Our Soldiers," by F. L. Rawson, with the subtitle: "Or the Practical Utilization of the Power of God by Right Thinking," the title of a pamphlet which he had already issued and circulated. The advertising for the pamphlet states that

it gives the scientific reason for the miracles of Jesus, and shows how those at the front can not only protect themselves, but obtain so-called miraculous results of many kinds. It also shows how those at home can protect their loved ones at the war by true prayer, i.e., by right thinking, in the way taught and demonstrated by Jesus the Christ.

At the Regent Street headquarters, just off Picadilly Circus, Rawson edited his magazine, carried on a large correspondence requiring a dozen or more secretaries, lectured, taught, and gave treatments. Evidently he had become quite noted, for patients came to him in such numbers that to protect himself and to allow time for his other multiple activities it had become necessary for him to make a charge for his treatments. This brought him not a little criticism. On more than one occasion it was explained in the magazine that far from profiting personally, Rawson poured every penny of his earnings from this source into the support of the work of *Active Service*, and that he contributed beyond that from his own private funds. He never made any charge for teaching those who assisted him in his work of healing, and he gave many treatments to persons who were unable to pay. His lectures were so largely attended that it became necessary to charge an admission fee, which was also contributed to the support of *Active Service*. From the first the magazine contained at least a page of testimonials to the healings and other blessings that had come either through Rawson or through members of his staff, or had been accomplished by persons on their own initiative according to the teachings given by Rawson, which he insisted were simply the teachings of *true* Christian Science.

That Rawson instructed a number of persons in his method of treatment is clear from a report which he made in an address before the National Congress of New Thought in September, 1917, only a little over a year after the first issue of *Active Service*. There he said that a number of practitioners and assistants were working from 90 Regent Street, taking patients, and that there were 200-250 patients per week of all kinds. An average of 112 free patients per week were treated during the summer months of 1917.

Reporting on the circulation of *Active Service* in the issue of November 25, 1916 (p. 316), Rawson said that there had been an average of 3,500 printed each week, which he thought meant that some ten thousand persons were reading the magazine. The subscription list was not large, only 588, but it was growing, and an increasing number were being sold on the public newsstands. Additional office space had to be taken to accommodate the added staff which had become necessary.

But as yet there appears to have been no organization. The first step in that direction seems to have been the decision to set up study circles. Apparently no one in particular was responsible for them. It was announced that Rawson's book, *Life Understood*, would be divided into eight sections, each of which might well form the basis of a week's study, making an eight weeks' course in the essentials of his teachings. This plan was set forth in *Active Service,* which also offered to inform persons interested in this study of others who might wish to enter such a class. Those completing a class might then become leaders of other classes which might be formed. Questions were published on each section of the studies as a help to students. And for some time thereafter a note would appear occasionally saying that persons in such and such a place would like to be put in touch with others in the area interested in forming a class.

A second step was the establishment of a Sunday School. Mention of it was almost casual, and it was clearly experimental, for the one who reported on the matter did it in quite tentative fashion. Gradually it became a fixed part of the program, and a weekly page in *Active Service* was given to it.

Before the formation of the study circles occasional lectures were given by Rawson, usually on invitation before some already existing society. Rawson was accustomed to lecture at headquarters each first Tuesday of the month. For these lectures an admission fee of two shillings sixpence was charged. Other lectures were also given by helpers, the one most frequently mentioned in the earlier period being Miss Ethne Tatham.

But in the issue of July 28, 1917, that is, just a little over a year after the appearance of *Active Service,* a still further organizational step is suggested. Someone had proposed that *Active Service* facilitate the holding of weekly meetings. Such meetings, the editorial said, had already been held successfully. But it continued, "We think it is a mistake that such meetings should be connected with us or with any one person." They should be entirely democratic, organized by those in the town, and should not be tied to any particular form of doctrine or belief, other than that of the endeavor "to obtain a better knowledge of God and the right thinking that leads to better knowledge." The editor offered to act as a clearinghouse for an interchange of views or the gathering together of those who wished to meet, and would gladly put those who wrote to him in touch with others desiring such a meeting. He would also be glad to know who might have rooms available for such gatherings. Here appears the distrust of centralized organization which Rawson probably felt as a result of his unhappy experience with the Mother Church of Christian Science.

The atmosphere of the meetings, he went on to say, should always be purified by treatment before gatherings occur, and development should be left to Principle acting on the minds of those connected with the movement. At a Truth Center in America, he wrote, they have weekly meetings for the study of the literature, calling it a Peace Meeting.

In *Active Service* for October 6, 1917, appears the first notice of the organization, under the title, "Notes of a National Campaign." The organization was to be called the Society for Spreading the Knowledge of True Prayer, SSKTP; the method of prayer was to be that of the realization of God, conscious communion with God. A national campaign was proposed to show all spiritually minded and unselfish persons how (1) to bring about speedily a thoroughly satisfactory permanent peace; (2) to demonstrate the results of right thinking in daily life, obtaining relief and ultimate immunity from evil, disease, and trouble of every description.

The Society would not only conduct a campaign but would leave a permanent center in whatever district they might be led to visit. These centers would follow for the most part the policy of *Active Service* and be centers of enlightenment, healing, and emancipation, "tending to bring peace to our land, and to all nations." The campaign would embrace Leeds, Darlington, New Castle-on-Tyne, Edinburgh or Glasgow, and other cities. A national campaign leaflet would be prepared and circulated embodying the principles of the societies. It would not be a creed. The work was to bring together in a body those who, by realizing God, would bring the power of God into operation.

In most of the succeeding issues of *Active Service* there are notes concerning the progress of the national campaign. Miss Ethne Tatham lectured in Letchworth; Rawson and Miss Tatham in Birmingham, where the first center was established with E. C. Kendrick as leader. A little later the campaign had reached Glasgow and Edinburgh. Readers in Southport, Bradford, Canterbury, South Leicester, Wolverhampton, and other cities were visited or had requested visits by the field secretary. One article stated, "We look to the churches to join us in this campaign." Evidently it was expected that with the emphasis on true prayer, the churches would be interested. And actually, some of the lectures were delivered in the churches. In London the message was carried to the public through open-air meetings in famous Hyde Park, near the Marble Arch, where according to the *Active Service* issue of November 24, 1917, as many as five hundred persons heard Rawson at that popular outdoor open forum center, and in proper Hyde Park fashion they asked him all sorts of searching questions.

Meanwhile it had been announced that Rawson had consented to act as chairman of the Working Committee of the newly formed society, and Admiral Grafton would take charge of the organization of the society in London. Temporary offices were acquired in the same building in which the magazine and the Crystal Press, which published and distributed Rawson's books, were located. And *Active Service* was named as the official organ of the society. It still holds that relationship today.

On June 1, 1918, *Active Service* noted that monthly conferences of the London centers were being held, which drew the societies together. A note in July lists four London centers, ten in the provinces, two in Scotland, one in Canada, and one in France. On the cover of that issue it was stated that in addition to being the official organ of SSKTP, *Active Service* was also the official organ of the International Union of Teachers and Healers. In the October issues notice was given of places where information relating to the work of *Active Service* and the publications of the Crystal Press might be obtained. Fifteen were listed in the United States, four in Australia, two in New Zealand, two in Canada, and one each in South Africa, Argentina, France, and Holland. The outreach of *Active Service* was being extended over the world.

Response was evidently quite favorable to the society, both in Britain and elsewhere. The issue of January 3, 1920, lists English organizations in London, Birmingham, Felixstone, Hastings, Ipswich, Letchworth, Manchester, New Castle on Tyne, Norwich, Edinburgh; American centers at Minneapolis, Pittsburgh, St. Louis, Detroit, New York, Chicago, Milwaukee; and several in Canada, with others in Italy, Spain, Sweden, and Australia. Ethne Tatham seems, next to Rawson, the most important figure in the movement. Effie Hogg's name appears for the first time in a 1918 issue. She is mentioned in the issue of January 30, 1920, as taking Rawson's place on certain occasions at the headquarters in his absence—a responsibility shared with others, among them Miss Tatham.

In 1920 Rawson made an extended tour through the United States and Canada, lecturing and giving class instruction and treatments, with the result that a goodly number of SSKTP centers were established in American and Canadian cities. In general it was through the already established New Thought groups that Rawson was welcomed to the cities he visited. Many of the groups eagerly welcomed him, and aided in the forming of societies. The thoroughly noncreedal, nondogmatic character of the SSKTP made it acceptable to them, as it did also to some of the churches. For example, in San Francisco a prominent Episcopal rector invited Rawson to speak in his church and became the chairman of the SSKTP which was organized in San Francisco. That the rector apparently suffered no disciplinary action from his superiors is evidenced by the fact that he went on to the cathedral church in Fresno, California, where he gave lectures and taught classes and conducted healing activities for a week.

While in America Rawson gave a definite series of class instruction, for which a fee of $25.00 was charged for five lessons. These were so successful that on his return to England he undertook to offer similar classes for a similar fee, five pounds, five shillings for five classes of an hour and a half each, plus treatments and the chance to ask questions. For those who did not

live in centers where the classes were given, he offered a cor-
respondence course, a series of seven lessons for the same fee.
All the financial returns would of course go to the support of
Active Service.

In St. Louis, having given a number of treatments, Rawson
was arrested and indicted for practicing medicine without a
license. The charge was dismissed on his promise that he would
not hold further meetings or perform other healings. Since he
was just at the point of leaving for Chicago anyway, he readily
acquiesced and was set at liberty. Later he made other trips to
the United States, and some of his centers flourished for a time.
So far as I have been able to discover there are only two or three
definite exponents of his doctrines and practices in the United
States today, though his books continue to be sold in considerable
numbers and are studied by individuals in this country.

Although Rawson was distinctly Christian Science in his
basic outlook, once excluded from the church, he co-operated
enthusiastically with the New Thought groups. Many of his
contacts in the organization of SSKTP were made through New
or Higher Thought groups in America or England. *Active Service,*
almost from its first issue, carried articles or extracts from the
writings of recognized New Thought as well as Christian Science
leaders or publications. For example, in the issue of June 12, 1920,
there are extracts from Warren Felt Evans' *Divine Law of Cure.*
In succeeding numbers articles appear from many sources and
on various themes—articles from the *Christian Scientist, Nautilus,
Master Mind, Advanced Thought,* etc. But there were articles also
from Buddhist and Hindu sources, under the general title "Paths
of Truth." Articles by Glen Kratzer appeared frequently, and his
books were advertised in almost every issue for a number of
years, as being distributed by the Crystal Press.

The magazine also frequently chronicled events which were
primarily New Thought in character. The First International
New Thought Congress had been held in Knightsbridge Hall
in 1914. When in 1917 it was proposed that a National New
Thought Congress be held in London, *Active Service* co-operated

in every way in its organization, in giving it publicity, in making arrangements, in its program, and after it was over, in reporting the meetings.

Rawson held the definite idea that the end of the world was imminent, and he addressed the congress on the subject. The exact date had been set, only a few months after the congress was to end. Naturally his predictions were taken with no small degree of skepticism by most of those not identified closely with him. When the end did not come as expected and announced, Rawson had some explaining to do. Why had it not occurred on December 3, 1917? He explains it this way:

This turned out to be the end of one of the recurring periods of the history of the world. It was not correct, as I had relied upon my intellect, which is a broken reed, instead of upon treatment. Still it confirmed a good deal of what I had put forward. If none of us made any mistake we would soon find ourselves in heaven. The man who never made a mistake never made anything.

Great scientist that he was, Rawson entertained a number of ideas that find no acceptance among the majority of scholars. One of these was that the British and the Americans were the *true* Israel—that is, he held and expounded the Anglo-Israel theory, which commended itself to a good many within New Thought and the metaphysical field in general, as for example Mrs. Eddy. He wrote for *Active Service* an extensive series of articles on the subject under the title, "Why the British Are Such Splendid Fighters, or the Anglo-Israel Theory," repeating the familiar reasons usually set forth by the partisans of that belief. It might be alleged that his scientific competence lay in the field of the physical sciences rather than in that of history and philosophy—or, one might add, of biblical interpretation, for it was on this that he chiefly based the prophecies of the imminent destruction of the world. The Anglo-Israel series ran through some forty issues of the magazine, in the first and second volumes.

One of the most valuable features of *Active Service* for an understanding of Rawson's thought was the section in each issue which contained questions that had been addressed to him, together with his answers. No teacher that I have read in the New Thought field was ever so patient and explicit in stating not only his thought on the given questions, but also his method of meeting the problem of the individual sufferer or the one who was attempting to heal another. He deliberately asked that people write in as to the kinds of difficulties they were meeting, and in an extended series of articles he undertook to give specific directions as to the sort of treatment that should be given. In the course of these articles he chronicled experiences of his own which leave one bewildered or incredulous. Few parallels to them are to be found in the whole range of New Thought literature.

The outreach of New Thought beyond the narrow limits of the organized societies is reflected in many articles that appeared in *Active Service*. In the very first issue, that of August 5, 1916 (pp. 11-12), Rawson writes of Archdeacon Wilberforce of Westminster Abbey. Wilberforce, he says,

came every now and then to 90 Regent St., to ask for information in connection chiefly with divine healing. He often sent cases also, usually incurable ones, though Rawson knew of times when he had advocated divine healing for cases that were not incurable by materia medica.

The first time Wilberforce consulted Rawson was in connection with prayers for members of his congregation who were sick or dying. He told Rawson how he "worked" first of all "thinking of God and getting as clear a realization of God as he could, then dropped from the divine to the material and placed the individual right at the center of what he was thinking of as God." This, according to Rawson, was wrong, and he told Wilberforce so, that it was quite enough to "realize God in the way he was first doing." Wilberforce never accepted the Rawson denial of the reality of matter.

On hearing of the intended publication of *Life Understood*, Wilberforce had asked for an advance copy, which was sent to him. Wilberforce then wrote, according to Rawson, saying, "It was the most wonderful, or the most interesting book he had ever read, and I forget which, and that he had been unable to put it down. He wrote later that he was going to read it through twenty times, and then give his opinion in writing for publication." (*Active Service* [I, 12]) "As far as I could tell," he continued, "there was nothing of importance on which we disagreed except with respect to the nature of matter."

In the issue of August 12, he quotes (p. 33) from a volume of Wilberforce, "Why Does not God Stop the War," in which he makes a number of definite New Thought declarations, such as "yourself as one of the vehicles for the self-realization of Infinite Mind," "We humans are Spirit; we are one with God; nothing can hurt us, or our real selves," "God in us is infinite love, and peace, and wisdom." Rawson criticizes this, saying, "We are in God, not God in us." In discussing the method of Wilberforce, (*Active Service* [I, 12]), Rawson disclosed the heart of his own method of healing. "I pointed out to him," he wrote, that in thinking of the person to be healed

he was doing more harm than good, and that it was quite sufficient to realize God in the way he was doing. He argued that unless the healer thought of the patient, the action of God could not take place on him. I pointed out that all that was necessary was the intention to heal the patient and that I never worked in any other way.

He thinks that Wilberforce accepted this and that he said he would pray in the way indicated. But Rawson did not know with what results, as this was the last time he saw Wilberforce.

Rev. L. Watson Fearn, a colleague of Wilberforce at Westminster up to the time of the latter's death, and later founder of the Church of the Mystical Union, of which he was warden, also seems to have been influenced by New Thought. He was one of the speakers at the Second National Congress of New Thought which was held in London in 1918. Another Anglican clergyman, Rev. Stewart Stitt, Rector of Stretham Ely, wrote of *Life Understood* in highly laudatory terms. He characterized it as "the most valuable commentary on the teaching of the Lord and the apostles that has appeared in a very long time." The names of other clergymen appear from time to time in the magazine. Certainly the SSKTP was well received in a number of churches.

Rawson died in 1923, but the SSKTP movement went on and *Active Service* continued publication. Sometime in 1923, the magazine began to carry Daily Readings from the Bible with correlative passages from *Life Understood,* selected by a committee. These have continued until the present day. The magazine appeared weekly until August, 1940, when it became a monthly. The loss of Rawson inevitably had an effect upon both the magazine and the SSKTP. Lacking was his dynamic and authoritative touch which none of his followers, though some of them were very able indeed, could supply.

Miss Effie Hogg assumed the post of director, and continued as such until her passing in 1958. Indeed, she is still listed officially as director, since, I was told, there seemed to be no one who could quite take her place. The actual direction of the society is presently in the hands of a committee rather than an individual. In 1944 there began to appear in the Daily Readings passages from the writings of Miss Hogg as well as from those of Rawson. Since then references have been included from her two books, *Gleams of Truth* and *Right Thinking, Its Rise and Standpoint.*

In the issue of *Active Service* for July 2, 1932, centers were listed in Edinburgh; in Glasgow; in Calgary and Winnipeg, Canada; in Hastings and other cities in England; in Johannesburg; in Malaga, Spain; in New York City; and in Paris. The list of study groups included those in Dundee, Scotland; Durlach, Baden, and Karlsruhe, Germany; Perth, Australia; Peshawar, India; Chicago, Milwaukee, Oakland, Salt Lake City, and San Francisco; and Vancouver, B. C.

An issue of 1938 announces that helpful rules for the practice of True Prayer might be obtained from headquarters (then, as now, at 14a Ecclestone Street, London) in English, French, German, Icelandic, Spanish, and Swedish. Translations of various pamphlets are announced in Italian, French, Norwegian, Russian, Spanish, and Swedish.

An article in a 1960 issue stated that Rawson's *Life Understood* and both of Miss Hogg's books were available in Swedish translation, and the translator of these had himself written and published a book in Swedish in which he said, "The basic attitude I have endeavored to give expression to is that of Mr. Rawson in *Life Understood.*"

Elizabeth Banks, who was long secretary to Effie Hogg, is the present secretary of the society. She and a small staff carry on the work of the society — its public meetings, its healing, its publication activities.

A thorough student but not a slavish follower of Rawson, Miss Hogg was apparently able to organize his rather unsystematic teachings into a more intelligible and viable form. She did not feel, however, that there was any one basic interpretation of Rawson's work which must be accepted.

There seems to be a much greater flexibility in this movement than in Christian Science. Though SSKTP members claim they are really Scientists, and have no disposition to condemn Christian Scientists for their organizational rigidity, they feel no desire to join with Christian Science or indeed with any New Thought group. All the groups, they hold, have their own ways of apprehending the truth, but these ways are not satisfying from the SSKTP standpoint.

SSKTP is in no sense a derivative of New Thought, according to Miss Banks — the two are kindred, but different, attempts to get at truth. Though some New Thought literature is read by SSKTP members, there has been no effort to secure New Thought speakers from America. Miss Banks knows of Arthur Corey, former member of the Christian Science organization and now an important writer and exponent of Christian Science outside the organization, and she has read the works of Ernest Holmes and others.

She says that that now and then SSKTP members are asked to speak to some small groups within the Anglican church, but they have never been able to get one of their spokesmen on the British Broadcasting Company's programs. The Society holds periodical meetings, and each year in June convenes a congress, the proceedings of which are reported in subsequent issues of *Active Service*. This may only be attended by members of the Society. At one time actively affiliated with INTA, SSKTP is no longer related to it.

Only scattered news notes, mostly from the *Bulletin* of INTA, are available as sources of information concerning the movement in England from the 1920's until recent years. In the *Bulletin* of June, 1925, Miss Callow writes of a congress to be held in July. The September issue reported an interest on the part of the British leaders in the reconstitution of the British Section— evidence that it had not been active for some time. Elizabeth Towne visited and spoke in many centers in London and Birmingham that year and Paul Tyner wrote of successful classes in Glasgow and Edinburgh.

Nona Brooks visited England in September and October, 1926, and Elizabeth Towne reports in December, 1926, that the British Section had a representative general committee and council which brought together all the centers of New Thought, psychology, and other groups of allied interests. It met quarterly and was currently preparing for a big assembly in 1927. As a result of visits by Miss Brooks, Divine Science Fellowships were organized in 1927 in various parts of London. Miss Callow wrote that they were preparing for the Tenth Annual Congress, modestly adding: "I think there is some good work being done in England."

A report in the *Bulletin* of August, 1928, says that since the Conference of 1927 the work had "gone forward by leaps and bounds." New headquarters had been secured, membership had increased, a library of some two thousand volumes had been set up, and a periodical had been published. In 1929 W. G. Hooper, field lecturer for the British Section, was reported as having visited Australia, New Zealand, Ceylon, and Egypt, and was about to visit America. A later *Bulletin* reported splendid lectures which he gave in San Francisco, as well as class work, and announced his early sailing for South Africa and New Zealand.

A congress of the British Section was reported in a 1934 *Bulletin*, with Victor Morgan and Julia Seton attending from America.

In 1920 Henry Thomas Hamblin had begun his work, known as the Science of Thought, and in 1921 he began publishing a magazine with the same title, one of the most influential periodicals to appear in the New Thought world, particularly in its impact upon New Thought leaders, both in England and in America. In *My Search for Truth*, Hamblin tells the story of his life. Born into a God-fearing family, grandson of a minister, he lived the life of an ordinary boy, though he was perhaps more sensitive than the average. He reports an occasional mystical experience, but says that he was not wise enough to follow the impulses these gave him. He became, he says, quite worldly, and made a definite financial success, though he was never happy at what he was doing. About 1904 he began to read in the field of New or Higher Thought, and was deeply impressed. In 1914 he retired from his business and moved to the country.

After a tour of military duty he began to write and first produced the book *Within You Is the Power*, which had a wide distribution, eventually selling over 200,000 copies. It was translated into several European languages. He also wrote *Look Within*. A series of articles written for an American magazine were published in England under the title *The Message of a Flower*. His *Art of Living* and *Power of Thought* also enjoyed a good circulation. He was writing, he says, in his search for Truth.

He did little or no public speaking. He seldom appeared on a platform, but through his books and magazine he became one of the most highly regarded New Thought leaders in England. He carried on a large correspondence, and his correspondence courses were widely studied. In his earlier career his principal emphasis was on getting on in life, being successful, and this emphasis may account in part for the ready acceptance of his books. But later a change came in his writing. It was more "spiritual." He had come to a greater appreciation of the place of feeling as well as thought in living. He came to the conclusion, he says, that feeling is greater than thought. It is necessary, he came to believe, that we feel what we think — otherwise there is little power. One knows with the heart as well as with the mind. Thought, he wrote, "can bring us only to the foot of the mountain of Truth after which we have to proceed by intuition and feeling. (*My Search for Truth,* p. 60)

It was a great day, he says, when he discovered that whereas he had been seeking God, the truth was that "God was seeking him, trying to bring every possible good into his life." The object of religion, he came to feel, was "to get behind the material to find the spiritual, to pass from the temporal to the eternal." (p. 65)

At first he had made a specific charge for his lessons, but he had never felt happy about it. So he stopped charging, and allowed people merely to send in "love gifts."

He came to a point, he says, where absolute surrender was the only way, and his teaching became correspondingly more spiritual and less psychological or metaphysical. He felt he could not go on using the earlier materials. He burned up literally tons of booklets, pamphlets as well as lessons he had prepared. This material constituted most of his capital, and it all had to be replaced by other things written by himself. Some of his books he withdrew from circulation and rewrote. As a consequence he lost a great many students, but this did not greatly trouble him. He was finding a new and deeper satisfaction in what he was doing.

Henry Thomas Hamblin was never an organization man. He had very little connection with any organized form of New Thought. When Dr. Bitzer wrote him saying that the INTA *Bulletin* was glad to list his publication without charge, he wrote in answer,

I would rather that you did not do this, as we do not belong to I.N.T.A. and have no intention to joining it. I have never joined anything, as I prefer to be a free-lance, and also we are not a group. All that we do is publish the *Science of Thought,* which goes to the uttermost parts of the earth. (Letter of March 1, 1956)

In another letter of July 25, 1956, he wrote thanking Dr. Bitzer for an invitation to attend the INTA congress.

I thank you, but cannot accept. For one thing my work is a one man show, and I have always to be here to keep things going. It is not only that, but this is also a center and haven of refuge for the poor and needy who come here expecting food and money and clothing, so I never like to be away from the place, because I might disappoint one of these needy ones. Consequently my wife and I have not had a holiday for about twenty-five years.

And so it was until the end. He lived until 1960, dying at the age of ninety. His son succeeded him as editor of the *Science of Thought Review*, but he too died a year later. The magazine continues to be published by some of his devoted followers, and still continues to print either material that the founder had not published or reprints of earlier articles from his pen.

Dr. Bitzer, during his years as president of INTA, has twice visited England, has spoken in a number of centers there and has kept in active correspondence with English leaders. In a letter to one of them in 1956 he wrote of his vision of holding another INTA annual congress in London, but this has not yet been done. He has been instrumental in making possible the attendance of various English New Thought leaders at the INTA congresses. Around 1950 a Council of Truth Centers was formed, having the Countess of Mayo as president and Maie Hitchens as chairman, with the object "of bringing the various Truth groups and kindred movement into close contact one with another." It was proposed to hold a Truth Convention in 1950. Attached to a letter bearing the Council's letterhead was a list of centers represented on the Council or actively connected with it. It included some nineteen or twenty groups in Blackpool, Manchester, St. Anne on the Sea, Childwall, London, Lancashire, Bramhall, Caernarvon, Nottingham, High Cliff, Stanmore, Kensington Park, and several more in London. This organization still exists and is more or less active. Visiting lecturers from America — Joseph Murphy, Harry Gaze, Robert H. Bitzer, Irwin Gregg,

Raymond Charles Barker, and others—have continued to appear on the platforms of England, Scotland, and Ireland, and have had a good hearing.

Conventions, either regional or national, were reported frequently during the fifties. A news note in 1959 indicated that the Council had disbanded, but been reformed. Unity was making big strides in England. Divine Science had grown; Religious Science now had at least two English centers. But the conviction is forced on the objective observer that in Britain the movement is organizationally not strong.

A contemporary expression of New Thought in England is the dynamic World Healing Crusade, founded and led by Brother Mandus, with headquarters in Blackpool, England. It is not, strictly speaking, an organization at all, in the sense of having a definite membership of persons who hold certain beliefs, grouped in local communities, identifiable as belonging to or under the direction of a central agency. It is aptly designated as a crusade, and the leader, Brother Mandus, is the only one who stands out in it. There is a "Sanctuary" at Blackpool, and there are offices which provide for the necessary publicity, the publications of the Crusade, and the arrangements for the wideranging journeyings of Brother Mandus, who in a very real sense covers the world with his message of healing.

He seems to be quite uninterested in the formation of a specific group which might carry on in the fashion of New Thought centers. Rather, he says in a personal letter (February 13, 1961), "the whole of our enterprise is dedicated to helping other churches, whether New Thought or orthodox, to lift their vision and express their love and faith, and to inspire people to come with these spiritual qualities into the church of their choice."

Thus, although "completely at one with the general New Thought vision and concept," he regards his Crusade as wholly interdenominational, but "based entirely on the full expression of positive Christianity." He thinks of the World Healing Crusade as providing something like a bridgehead between New Thought and the orthodox churches. In every aspect of our service we are emphasizing these fundamental principles [I take it he means New Thought principles] in every church of every denomination, without any deviation, seeking to break down the isolation between groups, by revealing the essential unity between them all through the expression of the One Power which, after all, fundamentally unites all humanity. . . . We look for the One Spirit in all, and therefore find the reality of the Divine Love which heals and changes lives. To which purpose, of course, all churches are dedicated. Like New Thought, we insist on the reality of the Divine experience.

He finds, strangely enough, that New Thought does not seem to have had a great impact in England, though there are some active and effective New Thought centers under highly dedicated leaders. But he believes that there is "a tremendous amount of New Thought activity in private," that is, "persons who are reading books and introducing these principles into their lives, even though their allegiance may be focused in the orthodox churches of their own choosing." This judgment he bases on the response in hundreds of meetings held in those churches, where he has "never found difficulty in awakening the positive consciousness in hundreds of thousands of people."

He feels personally that the "real possibility for New Thought lies in introducing their principles in a form which can be adopted and accepted by the whole spiritual community," and for this "there is a tremendous opportunity through literature, tape recordings, radio and television," all of which he himself employs constantly. He is, he says, advocating the quickening of vision to behold the significance of what New Thought has to say when it can be released in some interdenominational way beyond the orbits of their own churches as such, which will provide a New Thought ministry directed to the personal needs of people "who could never be won away from their denominational allegiance."

Brother Mandus was born in an English seaport — Hartlespool, apparently — in 1907, son of a water clerk for a ship's chandler. He recalls vividly a bombardment of his city during World War I, when he was a small boy, and the frantic attempts to escape;

also a later visit from a German Zeppelin which dropped a small and not very destructive bomb on the port. An average mischievous youngster in school, he and a companion, in celebration of Guy Fawkes Day and the Gunpowder Plot to blow up the House of Parliament, had made gunpowder with chemicals bought with their pooled resources, constructed bombs of ink bottles filled with the powder, and nearly succeeded in blowing up the house and neighborhood. Naturally they received a sound thrashing. As an aftermath of this experience, he says, standing one day before a mirror in a gilt frame, somehow he knew that "there was only eternal life and endless security." He says he felt so strongly that he would live forever that he took a nail and scratched on the bottom of the frame, "I will live forever" — a rather odd experience for a growing boy, and one of few that he had, for in his writings he says that on only four occasions did he ever experience what he would call a vision.

His parents belonged to the Established Church of England, and he was baptized and confirmed in that church. At nineteen years of age he went to South America, where he spent seven years. Returning at twenty-six, he visited a friend who had undergone a remarkable change since they had last met, and they talked of things spiritual until the small hours of the night, when, he says, he was filled with a Power from beyond himself and knew he had to respond to it. He had not up to that time even owned a Bible. He got one next morning and opened it first to John 15, "I am the true vine." As he read, he says, "these words burned in my mind like fire . . . it was as though the Voice of Christ was speaking to me." He knew then "that the words were truth and that here was a way of life with infinite possibilities."

At once he knew that he must dedicate his business—what it was is not disclosed—to God, praying that it would prosper and that ultimately it would take care of the financial needs of himself and family, and release him for service in whatever capacity God might direct. And he prospered.

World War II came and went. Meanwhile he had been introduced by a friend to the most important practice he has ever known, how to meditate in the Silence. And in this practice he spent many hours. People came to share their troubles with him and he was able to help them, but it was always to the future that he continued to look for the opportunity of rendering full-time service.

Then came an opportunity, as he thought, to make a great deal of money in a relatively short time. He put all his capital into it, thinking that soon he would have security and sufficient resources to enable him to give himself wholly to God's service. One day while helping dry the dishes after lunch, standing before the drawer of the sideboard, putting away the knives and forks, he was suddenly "flooded with the most intense blue-white light I have ever seen. . . . It was like looking into the face of the sun magnified several times in its light intensity." He seemed to have lost all sense of self "in a total immersion in Light." "An unbearable ecstacy accompanied it. All sense of time or self disappeared." It all occurred in a fraction of a second, he says, but he knew

only a sense of infinite dimension, and that this was the Spirit of God Almighty which was the hidden Light-Life-Love in all men, all life and all creation . . . that nothing existed apart from this Spirit. It was infinite Love, Peace, Law, Power, Creation, and the Ultimate Truth and Perfection.

Suddenly he became himself again, still standing, putting away the cutlery. Though never again repeated, it was, he declares, "the most vital moment of his life." And out of it was born the mission to which for many years he has wholly dedicated his life.

He was sure now that God would prosper the business and that he would thus be released for service. But the business, though at times it seemed to succeed, failed, and he became aware that he had lost all his capital. Strangely enough, instead of being depressed, he found himself experiencing a great peace. He stopped at a little chapel which he had been in the habit of frequenting each day on his way home from work. As he knelt before the altar he heard, he writes, three loud "cracks" above the altar, and a deep inner Voice said,

now my son, your day has come. I want you to open a Sanctuary of Divine Healing by Prayer. Now you possess nothing of the world, and you must have perfect trust in Me, asking no man for material help, but giving your whole life in a service of unconditional love, completely dependent on Me for every thing.

Closing out his business, he found that he was still in debt to the extent of $1,200. Selling his insurance policies, he paid off the debt and had left only enough to keep the family for a short time. But, he writes, "I was a man with a mission and the happiest man in all the world."

Within three weeks he had been provided with a modest two rooms, one for an altar and one for an office in which to carry on his work. His first patient was a woman of some sixty years of age, suffering with arthritis in the legs and badly crippled. She was completely healed, he reports, apparently instantly, after prayer—a wondrous sign to him, he writes, that God had set his seal upon the word that had been given to him. He knew, he says, that "this Love-Power of Christ is the same today as it ever was" and "in this one act of answered prayer was potentially the complete solution to every problem on earth, from personal disease and disaster right through to warfare."

Others came and were healed instantly; some yielded only slowly to cure; and some received no physical healing, but were "lifted up in courage, faith and love."

Daily he discovered the "external evidence of divine guidance, Healing, Supply and steady progression." In amazing fashion his weekly material needs were met, though he solicited help from no one, and "down through the years the Father has never failed to meet the fast multiplying expenses of the Sanctuary." (*How God Called Me*, p. 7. Most of the material concerning Brother Mandus has been taken from this and another pamphlet, *The Faith That Removes Mountains*, in the "Revelation Series.")

At first he only prayed with people who came for help. Then

people began writing for healing intercession, and so the ministry was extended until today hundreds of letters are received daily from all over the world, and Brother Mandus reports that many have been healed and blessed in this way. It soon became evident, he writes, that the Power of the Written Word in letters formulated in prayer is effective without limits of time or space.

A little later he felt that he should take his gospel out into the world. He had had no training in public speaking, but when invited to address a company of people he did so without notes, and as he began speaking all nervousness disappeared and he was given words to say. He has since spoken to crowded halls and churches all over the world, and always, he relates, the words are given to him as he speaks.

One night it came to him that he should publish a free monthly magazine devoted to the principle he was teaching through the Sanctuary and through correspondence. He had no money for such an enterprise, but by the time the printer's bill was presented, provision for its payment had been made, and today something like a quarter of a million copies go out quarterly free of charge to those who ask for them—a million a year. And there is always money to pay the printing and postage bills.

As the first Sanctuary became unavailable, another and larger was offered, and when this was outgrown the present Sanctuary and World Healing Crusade headquarters were acquired. Here a dedicated staff of ever increasing numbers carries on the work of the Crusade.

In an article in the *Crusader* (November, 1959, pp. 5-6), under the title "Pray Without Ceasing," some idea is given of how Brother Mandus' work at the Sanctuary at headquarters is carried on. Letters from all over the world are received daily and placed on the altar, "and the needs of every one are given to the Father for Divine adjustment." Every letter is answered with loving help and encouragement "and with the teaching of spiritual Principles which naturally helps us all to keep in communion with God and with each other."

In addition, says the article, the staff members use a scientific principle only now beginning to be understood and practiced. They have proved that the Love-faith-prayer consciousness when released into the written or spoken word, even in a tape recording or over the radio, releases the same power to those who are receptive to it. In their worldwide work with tape recordings of healing prayer and spiritual teaching they have discovered that they can convey the same "prayer Consciousness to those who listen to them, perhaps ten thousand miles away and months or years later." This is true because "the only reality is Divine Mind, God, and whatever is released in communion with the Lord must be forever real."

Therefore they have, in addition to the daily personal prayer sessions, "a night and day continuous Service of Prayer by Brother Mandus, recorded for this purpose. Twenty-four hours a day, week by week, month by month, this release of Christ-Power is reaching all the world and every individual who comes into attunement with it."

At any moment, Brother Mandus writes, "prayer for your highest well-being is being spoken in our Sanctuary. If you relax and become receptive you will feel and accept the Healing Love of Christ which is there for you. This is also something you can prove scientifically as you observe the rules and the results."

There came a time when Brother Mandus was invited to conduct divine healing services as well as to speak, and for several years much of his time has been taken up in wide journeyings to all parts of the English-speaking world. Often his itineraries are arranged through New Thought centers in the various countries, and he has been widely called upon to lecture by New Thought groups. But his ministry is quite as frequently in the orthodox churches. For example, in South Africa in 1960 the places of his meetings included a Methodist ministers' retreat; Methodist churches in Queenstown, East London, Capetown, Pretoria, and Port Elizabeth; Presbyterian churches in Capetown, Durban, and Johannesburg; Anglican churches in East London, Port Elizabeth, and Durban; and a Congregational church in Capetown—all these besides meetings in various New Thought centers, the whole itinerary set up by a New Thought minister. In Australia and New Zealand it was much the same, and American churches of various denominations as well as New Thought centers heard him, from New York to California.

The *Crusader* (September, 1960, pp. 17 ff.) affords an interesting set of directions as to what to do. The individual is urged to take paper, write down what is his greatest need today, what he requires to make his life perfect, what Christlike quality he would like the Lord to give him so that he could be like Christ himself. This is then to be sealed in an envelope, and all during the month he is to go with the envelope in his hands, but without looking at the paper, into the Silence, into the presence of God. He is to thank God for the perfect answers to the needs and objectives he has released to God in the envelope. He is to accept completely that these needs are now being abundantly met, and that they will reach him with infallible precision at the right time for his highest good. This is repeated again and again during the month.

It is always the paramount duty under the Law of Love to help others who are in need. "The truth you know should be shared with others." The individual is assured that all the Love of Christ is right there where he is now. Every perfect answer to every need is already granted within him. His only need at any time is to abide in this perfection and to believe that all the infinite Love of God for him is in supreme operation to bring the right answers into his experience now and in the right way and the right time according to the will of God for his highest good.

This seems to be very much like Unity technique. Certainly it is New Thought in one of its forms. Brother Mandus always couples with this sense of expectancy the necessity of yielding the self for whatever service may be required of the individual. In receiving he must be always willing and eager to give.

Brother Mandus is not one to discount the function of the physician, and he would have little patience with the general Christian Science refusal to accept treatment at the hands of doctors in particular situations. On the other hand, he believes that the minister and doctor should work hand in hand. In an article in the *Crusader* (September, 1960, p. 12) he writes,

Let the minister and doctor work together with a vigorous faith and great works will follow. It is truly one of God's greatest blessings that through the inspiration and dedication of countless doctors and medical research workers, human skills and knowledge have provided the facilities available today. The next BIG medical step forward will be the acceptance of use of the spiritual principles and prayer as paramount factors in ensuring the total health of mind and body of those who become sick. Hospitals will eventually become Power stations of prayer, and human skills will be linked with Divine Power, Inspiration and Guidance. And a mighty work will be done to prevent disease by teaching and insisting on the use of spiritual principles as a practical and abundant way of life. Prevention is far better than cure.

Where did Brother Mandus get the ideas which are the basis of his labors? Was it pure discovery through personal experience? Had he read or heard the message of New Thought leaders and through them come to the experiences he narrates? Nothing is said as to the religious ideas of the young man with whom he talked into the night, with the result that he gained a new perspective and power. There are few indications of his having read from others. The one most revealing reference is to Henry Thomas Hamblin, of whom he writes in the *Crusader* (May, 1960, p. 6), "He has been a beloved spiritual father to me. Our fellowship in spirit and his constant example of the Christ way of life, forever inspired me to go steadfastly on the course into which the Lord was directing me." Also he speaks appreciatively of various contemporary New Thought leaders for whom he has great respect and for whom he frequently lectures. But these seem rather to be influences which have contributed to his thought and life along the way which he had already begun to travel.

Nevertheless, his ideas and his language are clearly those of New Thought, though he is admittedly much more orthodox in his terminology than most New Thought leaders. Take for example this bit of his basic philosophy (*Crusader*, October, 1960, p. 4):

The one most important realization of all is that there is One Mind of God, and that the human mind conscious and subjective, is the gift of Divine Mind for use in a personal way. In truth the individual mind is like a wave on the surface of the ocean, one of millions of similar waves. Each wave is an individual in itself, but one with every other wave in the deeps of the ocean. The water of the wave is the water of the ocean.

The creative power of mind in man is the same as the creative power of God. He projects universes in Divine imagining; we project our limited creativeness in the tiny self and our civilization, but we use the same power.

This seems to be precisely what Thomas Troward taught.

It is in a pamphlet, *The Kingdom of God,* that the extreme immanentist concept of God so frequently found in New Thought appears. Here God is represented as speaking in person:

I am everything, seen and unseen. I am the power within the trees and birds, I am the song in the heart of the nightingale and a mother. My laughter is in the happy play of children. I share man's joy in the expansion of my Love in spring time. I am in every flower and every mind, for my spirit rejoices in beauty and my Love produces eternal harvest of seed and soul.

Brother Mandus does not exclude happiness and prosperity from his interests. He declares in his pamphlet, *Perfect Prosperity* (p. 10), "The need has always been for us to teach that God-Power is practical, that He will go forth into a failing business, a diseased body, a disrupted home, or a sick soul and produce health, happiness, success and abundance." And again: "When God is allowed to pervade our lives in every activity, our complete success is automatically established." (p. 25)

Perhaps the main difference between Brother Mandus' viewpoint and that of the New Thought movement in general is that he succeeds in clothing essentially New Thought ideas with an emotional warmth often lacking in the more specifically intellectual formulation so frequently found in New Thought speaking and writing. The All, the Omnipresent, the Perfect Law, Mind, Consciousness, is also the loving Father, manifesting his Perfect

Love on a personal level which is, if not more easily understood and explained, at least more attractive to the average person whose concern is not a nicely logical system of thought, but the satisfaction of some deeply felt personal need. It is Brother Mandus' ability so to express the essential New Thought ideas in terms familiar to the orthodox believer which makes him welcome in the pulpits of many orthodox churches.

15

New Thought on the Continent

ORGANIZED NEW THOUGHT in France is not extensive, at least under that name. *New Thought* lists one member group in Southern France and one Affiliated Truth Center in Paris, Unité Universelle. At one time there seems to have been a Unity group in Paris, and a recent Unity publication indicates that Unity literature is available at Astra, a Parisian book publishing house, but lists no organized groups. Most of the information upon which this section is based was obtained from Dr. Mary Sterling (Mrs. Robert Sterling), the dynamic and hardworking English founder and present leader of Unité Universelle.

The historic beginnings of New Thought in France are not clear. Horatio Dresser, in his history of the movement published in 1919, simply states that a Mme Struve was carrying on a work chiefly among soldiers at the time his book was being written. Dr. Sterling writes me that previous to her founding of Unité Universelle, Mme Struve, representing Unity School of Christianity, "did gallant work under most difficult conditions." She and Miss Grace Gassette, an American painter of distinction and a free-lance teacher of metaphysics, "really plowed dry ground." Miss Gassette's work, "which saved hundreds of French soldiers from remaining cripples, through her outstanding orthopedic work," won for her the Cross of the Legion of Honor. And Miss Gassette, she says, always claimed that what she accomplished was really the result of True Prayer.

Dr. Mary Sterling, an Englishwoman who had lived the greater part of her life in France and is bilingual, founded a

Center of Ontology and Psychology in Paris in 1946, to which she gave the name Unité Universelle. It was not in any sense a branch of New Thought. Indeed at the time Dr. Sterling did not even know of the existence of the International New Thought Alliance. She conceived of Unité Universelle as an entirely independent effort "to teach ontology and to present to the French speaking people the works of the great ontologists and metaphysicians regardless of their origins." She has insisted both in writing and in person that Unité Universelle is not a member of INTA, but only one of the Affiliated Truth Centers. Her reasons for this are quite understandable to those who know the cultural backgrounds of the people among whom she works. But she does welcome to her lecture platform outstanding New Thought leaders from America and elsewhere. Such men as the late Harry Gaze, Robert H. Bitzer, Raymond Charles Barker, Joseph Murphy, and others have been delighted at the large and interested hearing they have had in Paris from her platform.

Born and bred in England, Dr. Sterling became convinced at a very early age that the teachings of Jesus of Nazareth are not presented to the world by the orthodox churches as the Master would wish them to be. At the age of sixteen, therefore, she left the church into which she had been born and began her search for absolute truth. A friend presented her with a subscription to Henry Thomas Hamblin's magazine, the *Science of Thought Review,* and a copy of Emilie Cady's *Lessons in Truth.* She worked with these and, many years later, discovered that *Lessons in Truth* was a Unity textbook.

Meanwhile, she was led to help a certain number of people in a friendly, informal way, but after a time their number grew and she found herself on a platform, addressing dozens and presently hundreds of seekers after Truth. Then, for a time, she represented Unity School of Christianity in France. But she was intuitively led to found her own center so as to be in a position to present to the French people the works of the great ontologists regardless of their denomination. She obeyed the leading and Unité Universelle came to life. Its teaching has now spread to other French-speaking countries and groups in Europe, Africa, and Canada.

Dr. Sterling shares the fear and distrust of organization which is felt by many in New Thought and Christian Science, who are afraid of the loss of freedom implied in organization. They fear the eventual loss of the Truth itself, or at least the limitation upon it which they see to have resulted so often historically from the growth of organization. Dr. Sterling, of course, has her own organization, small though it may be, and it is continually extending its influence through teaching, lectures, correspondence, personal consultation, and perhaps most of all through the literature provided and distributed by it.

Unité Universelle has no definite membership. Dr. Sterling thought that perhaps an estimate made by another than herself that some five thousand persons were in some way or another connected with it might not be exaggerated, though she thought that would by no means include all who read the books it circulates, or the periodical, *Unité Universelle,* which it publishes, to which some two thousand persons subscribe.

There is constant emphasis upon literature in her lectures, in the periodical, and in her teaching. And there is a substantial list of New Thought books and pamphlets available in French. Certainly some New Thought books were translated and circulated in France before any presently known New Thought organization appeared there. Ralph Waldo Trine's *In Tune with the Infinite* was translated by Marguerite Coppini under the title *A l'Unison de l'Infini,* and published by Fischbacher in Paris as early as 1902. W. W. Atkinson's *The Power of Thought* appeared under the title *La Force Pensée,* in 1904, published by the Bureau d'Etudes Psychiques in Paris. And a few of O. S. Marden's books, all now out of print, were in circulation rather early in France. Others of Trine's books were later translated and published.

Dr. Sterling herself has been tireless in translating New Thought books and pamphlets, as well as articles which she has published in *Unité Universelle.* These have been mainly from American New Thought writers, though not a few articles in

Unité Universelle were translated from the English magazine of
Henry T. Hamblin, the *Science of Thought Review,* as well as
from the magazines *Ideas of Today* and *Adventures in Ideas.*
Currently distributed by Unité Universelle are twenty-one books
or pamphlets which Dr. Sterling has translated—four by Lillian
de Waters, six by Dr. Joseph Murphy, three by B. Gertrude Hall,
and others by Willa Fogle, Florence C. Shinn, Raymond Charles
Barker, Frederick Bailes, and Edward Kramer. Besides these
there are five pamphlets which she herself wrote, most of which
were first given as lectures in her regular monthly lecture hour.
She also publishes and distributes affirmation or prayer cards,
some of them both in French and English, somewhat after the
fashion of Unity. At the time of my interview with her she had
completed and in the hands of a new publisher another, "Kinship
with All Life," by Allen J. Boone, which she hoped might get a
wider circulation than those usually published by known publishers of metaphysical books. In recognition of her outstanding
work a Doctor's degree was conferred upon her in 1954.

Clearly Dr. Sterling and Unité Universelle are in the best New
Thought tradition. In her "rugged individualism," or her determi-
nation to maintain her freedom from external or central authority,
she is definitely in that tradition. She is certainly far removed
from the tendency in some branches of New Thought toward a
tighter and more centralized sort of organization, and particularly
from the tendency to make of her group a church in any sense.
Except for a meditation at the beginning and end, she has no
worship features in her public lecture hour. It is held in a rented
hall devoid of any and all religious symbolism. Also in her circulation of some books, such as Spaulding's *Life of the Masters* and
The Aquarian Gospel, as well as other books which seem to some
to verge on the occult, she is only following a pattern of liberty
which has been common enough in historic New Thought.

Unité Universelle has comfortably equipped quarters in Paris.
It provides an attractive reception room in which currently
circulated literature is exhibited. There is also a reading room,
somewhat after the manner of a Christian Science reading room,

where students and others may come to read and study. There is a classroom for Dr. Sterling's weekly class session and the monthly advanced class. Here also at an appropriate hour is held an instruction class for children, with a class for parents at the same time.

There is a room where the Silent Service Members counsel and pray with those who come for spiritual guidance or healing. Then there is Dr. Sterling's own cheerful office and consulting room. Altogether the center is a well-furnished, comfortable, and inviting place.

Dr. Sterling keeps up a wide correspondence. She showed me stacks of files of letters from all over France, Belgium, Switzerland, Algeria, Canada, and even the French Congo. Many of the letters contain touching testimonials of healing of physical, mental, and spiritual ailments. Unité Universelle advertises Silent Help for any who may telephone, telegraph, or write, very much after the fashion of Silent Unity.

People from many walks of life make up the classes and attend the lectures—housewives, workmen, secretaries, teachers, lawyers, doctors, engineers, military and government personnel, businessmen and women, students.

Is the movement self-supporting? "Quite," she said. "We operate strictly on a love offering basis, no dues, or specific charges for consultation, treatment, or healing, and we do not lack. Our sales of books and other literature are substantial." But, she added, "like every other service organization we could always use increased funds to advantage."

"And remember," said Dr. Sterling, "neither I nor the Unité Universelle are members of the International New Thought Alliance, though we love it and greatly honor its leaders. We do not want to be beholden to any organization. I want freedom to move in the direction in which I feel led to move. Today, I teach ontology and live it. I do not know what I shall teach next year."

A second New Thought group in France, one which is listed in *New Thought*, the INTA quarterly, is called Institut de Psychosynthèse Spirituelle. Its headquarters is at Roquebrun-Cap Martin, Alpes Maritimes, in the South of France. It was founded by Auguste Joseph Berg and his wife who, while he was employed as interpreter at the United Nations in New York, became acquainted with New Thought in its various American forms, and were taught by Dr. Ervin Seale. Greatly attracted to New Thought, M. Berg, a Frenchman, resolved in his retirement to devote his time to the introduction of New Thought into France, where it was little known, but as he thought much needed. In looking over the New Thought field, it seemed to him that Science of Mind as then taught by Dr. Ernest Holmes and Frederick Bailes would be best suited to the French mentality.

When, therefore, in 1954, after seven years in America, he returned to France, his first task, he thought, was to make available suitable New Thought reading matter in French. He set himself to the translation and publication of Holmes's *Science of Mind*. Later he translated Ervin Seale's *Learn to Live* and other New Thought volumes and wrote books of his own, including his *Cours de Psychosynthèse Spirituelle Pratique*, and *La Guérison par Lavage du Subconscient*. He secured from the Church of Religious Science of Los Angeles the right to translate and publish the main features of their periodical, *Science of Mind*, in the French monthly magazine which he founded under the name *La Science du Mental*. These, including daily meditations for the month, he personally translates, besides writing articles of his own for each issue. Begun in 1957, the magazine, though not yet wholly self-supporting, is slowly but surely gaining in circulation and influence.

It is his aim, Berg writes, to have New Thought teaching as widely known as possible in all French-speaking territories, rather than to have one church in one particular place. He would like to build up groups for meeting and study in all major French-speaking centers of the world. Since he has no financial backing, progress is slow, the chief difficulty being to find teachers of conviction who are willing to carry on without financial assistance. Even so, he reports that there are some little groups that "limp rather than run" in Marseilles, Bordeaux, Paris, and a few other places. Listed in the magazine are other addresses either of meeting places, mostly thus far in private homes, or of persons from whom information concerning the movement or its literature may be obtained, in Beziers, Pau, Toulouse, Lyon, Haute-Savoie, Strasbourg, Le Havre, Perpignan, Nice, in France; and in other lands in Lausanne, Switzerland; Quebec, Canada; Togo; and Martinique. Those in Pau, Perpignan, and Lausanne have at least some meetings.

The entire inside back cover of the magazine is filled with the offer of books in the field of New Thought which may be purchased through headquarters. Among the authors—mostly of books that have been translated into French, though there are some volumes originally in French—are Raymond Charles Barker, Frederick Bailes, Joseph Murphy, Emmet Fox, and others.

Though bearing the name Institut de Psychosynthèse Spirituelle, in the quarterly *New Thought*, the group seems to be advertised in France also as Amour et Lumière, Société des Amis des Sciences Religieuses Appliqués—that, is Love and Light, Society of the Friends of Applied Religious Science. In a bit of promotional literature the society is described as not a Christian sect, nor a theology; indeed, it has no fixed creed or confession which it requires its members to believe. In fact, members have no other spiritual obligations than that of respecting absolutely the freedom of each human to follow the word of St. Paul, to "prove all things and hold to that which is good," and to lend aid everywhere and to all in the spirit of active harmony. There is no church, no clergy, though techniques of a psychospiritual nature are taught, which the members are free to apply or not as they choose, but which applied in good faith will prove to them that it can harmonize all that is unharmonious in their own lives and in those of others. Applied Religious Science is, it states, in harmony with medical science and the faith of all confessions, religious or lay, which are actuated by love of others and absolute respect for their freedom.

Here, as in the case of the Unité Universelle, is seen the

extreme care to avoid all identification with religion as such that is produced by the peculiar situation of religion in France today. Anything which smacks of religious authoritarianism or narrow dogmatism is to be scrupulously avoided. The approach through psychology and philosophy seems to the members of the society to be the only way to reach the mind of contemporary France.

One hears also now and then of the Alliance Universelle (Universal Alliance), which is considered by many as New Thought. Actually it does include much that is New Thought, but it is so much more inclusive than the American New Thought or perhaps even the British that the American and British movements have not seen fit to join it. On the other hand, the German New Thought accepted the proposals of the Alliance Universelle by which the Alliance Universelle would officially represent the Deutscher Neugeist-Bund of Germany in the French-speaking world, and Neugeist the Alliance Universelle in the German world.

It would have been strange if the New Thought Movement had not spread to Germany and other German-speaking lands. For Germany was the home of the great idealistic philosophers, Kant, Fichte, Schelling, and Hegel, as well as the poet Goethe, whose writings, reaching New England largely via British writers, were influential in the rise of Transcendentalism, which we have shown was, in its turn, a major influence in the emergence of New Thought.

Warren Felt Evans, first articulate exponent of New Thought through his writings, made constant reference to these writers, affirming over and over their support for the New Thought ideas as to the nature of reality and of the world, from which he derived his practical ideas of mental healing.

Dresser's *History of the New Thought Movement* (1919) makes no mention of any organization in Germany, but does say that there was a demand for New Thought books. This was confirmed by the present head of the movement, K. O. Schmidt, who says that as early as 1900 Englehorn-Verlag at Stuttgart was publishing translations of books by such writers as Ralph Waldo Trine. Indeed, he reports that as many as 35,000 copies of the translation of *In Tune with the Infinite* had been distributed by 1908, and that as many as 100,000 copies of various Trine books had been sold. Books by O. S. Marden were also widely sold, some 700,000 copies having been circulated between 1900 and 1924. This wide interest comes about because, says Schmidt, "The American New Thought Movement is analogous and congenial to *deutscher Idealismus,* the movement of German idealism, so to speak, on its practical side." Dr. Max Christlieb of Marburg was the translator of most of these books.

The Psychologischer Verlag at Berlin, no longer in existence, published from 1904 to 1907 the periodical *Neue Gedanken (New Thoughts),* with articles chiefly from William Walter Atkinson. They also published some of his books, e.g., *Die Neue Weltanschauung* and *Das Wesen der Neuen Gedanken.* Among other New Thought contributors to the periodical were Ella Wheeler Wilcox, Elizabeth Towne, S. Meacham, Uriel Buchanan, J. A. Edgerton, Sidney Flower, Hannah Moore Kohaus, and Lillie Duncan.

Baum-Verlag, best known and most influential of the New Thought publishers in Germany, was founded in 1912. An article celebrating its fortieth anniversary, published in *Die Weisse Fahne,* furnishes the information on which its story is here chiefly based. Founded in Berlin, it was acquired by Dr. Victor Schweizer. He was the son of a clergyman, born at Lomersheim (Württemberg) on December 9, 1872. He studied in theological seminaries in Schontal and Urach and received the Ph.D. degree at the University of Leipzig. He became a publisher first at Leipzig, later at Berlin, where he took over Baum-Verlag. In 1919 he moved the press to Pfullingen in Württemberg, where the development to its present internationally known position began. Aided in his efforts by such New Thought leaders as Mrs. Alice Hall Simpson and H. T. Hamblin of England, Mme Nicoline d'Hamecourt of Holland, and other English, French, Dutch, and American friends, he began to bring out, as an exponent of the

Neugeist (New Spirit) the monthly periodical *Die Weisse Fahne* (*White Flag*), and added thereto a growing number of living books of the Good Thought of German idealism, the related books of New Thought from America, and other books of kindred interest from the Near and Far East, successfully popularizing them.

Under his direction there appeared more than five hundred works which contributed to the formation of a strong realist-idealist and anti-materialist movement in German-speaking lands, a movement which in 1923 was constituted as the Neugeistbund (New Spirit Society). The publications of Baum-Verlag centered around three major themes:

1. The inner life of the spirit—*Neugeist.* Here stood in the foreground the life-creating element of religion in the sense of an undogmatic Christianity with a practical orientation toward right thoughts, right speech, right actions; more humanitarianism and more love and practical help from man to man, people to people; the encouragement of co-operation in the service of the higher ethical development of mankind. The religious practices and teachings of the Christian mystics were also emphasized, together with those from the non-Christian cultures such as Sufism in Islam, Taoism in China, Yoga, Vedanta, and Buddhism in India, and Zen Buddhism in Japan, as well as the new spiritual principle of religious tolerance and freedom.

2. Fruitful or successful living—*Neuleben.* Here attention was and is given to the new spiritual method of positive living known as Biosophy and the successful mastery of life (*Biokratie*) through the right employment of thought power and faith power, obedience to inner direction, and mobilization of the inner strength at the center. Here too are emphasized practical psychology and psychodynamics, will and character training, concentration and meditation practice, depth psychology and psychotherapy, as well as scientific parapsychology.

3. New wholeness and life renewal—*Neuheil.* To this area of interest belong the modern efforts toward life-reforming and natural wholeness, pursued without sectarianism, fanaticism, or one-sidedness.

In the decade 1922-32, Baum-Verlag developed into a center for all forthright spiritual and religious currents and life renewal efforts. Over 200 societies of the German Spiritual Society were joined together. More than 100,000 people belonged to the New Spirit Movement in 1932. At that time 50 workers co-operated in the Baum-Verlag, and the daily postal receipts ran to as many as 700-1,000 letters or other communications.

From 1922 to 1932 there were published 4,380,000 copies of *Die Weisse Fahne*, 2,019,000 copies of New Thought books and reform writings, and some 25,000,000 copies of New Thought leaflets and pamphlets. The catalogue of Baum-Verlag published in 1936 carried titles from nearly two hundred writers, most of whom were in the broad field in which the German New Thought Movement was interested. But in 1941 every one of these books was prohibited by the Nazi government, and the entire stock was destroyed.

With the rise of the Nazis in Germany, the New Thought Movement began to be subjected to various restrictions and persecutions. From 1933 onward Dr. Schweizer, who, in addition to the opposition to his ideas, had the added handicap of having married a Jewess, was increasingly under suspicion and Party surveillance. In addition he was blackmailed by Party profiteers who threatened him with Party measures, the result being a heavy loss to the publisher of as much as a million Reichsmarks. The Gestapo was continually threatening him with suppression of *Die Weisse Fahne* and his publishing business. Finally, on November 15, 1935, Dr. Schweizer was arrested. He died shortly afterward of a heart attack undoubtedly brought on by the sufferings attendant on his arrest.

If the Nazis thought that this would destroy the New Thought Movement they were quite mistaken. A few days after the death of Dr. Schweizer, Otto Orlowsky, at the request of K. O. Schmidt, who for more than a decade had been associated with Dr. Schweizer and was the editor of *Die Weisse Fahne*, took over the management of the press, and though threatened constantly by the enmity of the Party and the Gestapo, managed through the use of his fortune and personal influence to prevent the complete collapse of the publishing house. Its periodical continued to appear regularly. In a story of those perilous years with the title *The Dark Days,* K. O. Schmidt reveals something of the struggle the publishers went through in trying to keep the work going. Everything they did was watched by their persecutors. It is rather remarkable that they were able to say some of the things they did. For instance, Schmidt writes, "under the very eyes of the Gestapo we pointed out the inevitable consequences of the abuse of force which we absolutely condemned as an unclean method."

In one number (March, 1936) they wrote of the "superiority of the ethically minded over the worshipers of force":

An ethically minded man on his just path is a more redoubtable power than all the money and all the guns of those who are without ethics. For the former is backed up by powers for which property and guns are mere toys, and he is supported by the loftiest tendencies of mankind. Therefore he knows that in the end he will be victorious against all powers opposed to the supreme end. (p. 135)

These and other statements brought renewed attacks on the periodical in the Party press. The publishers were finally compelled to request their friends in the International New Thought Alliance in the United States and Switzerland not to write to them in Germany in order not to endanger their work.

In 1937 an article appeared in *Die Weisse Fahne,* entitled "Growing by Risking." It said in part:

It does not require deep insight into the laws of destiny to realize how inexorably every misdeed will react upon the wrong doer. . . . I know people who caused infinite distress to others by their egotism and brutality, and who enriched themselves by the death of those whom they deceived. To all appearances they are allowed to do as they wish . . . and to succeed in everything they do. *But they do not know the end. . . . They do not guess how quickly fate enforces the bitter compensation.* Those who venture on doing evil encourage powers to grow, powers not of good but of ruin.

And they concluded the warning by saying:

Let the deceivers declare a hundred-fold that their spoil was the result of their own efficiency; let them slander those supporting the deceased; let them obscure the light — *some day they will be suffocated by their prey, some day their way will lead them down into the abyss. Let them win ever so many sham victories, in the end they are beaten.* (p. 604)

The Party press, the *Schwarze Korps,* Ludendorff's monthly, and other papers attacked *Die Weisse Fahne* with increasing bitterness "as pacifist, as being a danger to the state, as being run by international powers." Book after book published by Baum-Verlag was confiscated. It was a difficult time.

Meanwhile, the editor and the publisher were active in working underground against the Nazi domination. In 1937, when opposition groups were organized, they co-operated with them, fighting "in a secret but all the more stubborn manner for the laying of foundations for a new order of things" which they felt "was bound to come about after the downfall of the accursed Hitler regime." It was a risky thing to do, which might cost them their freedom or even life itself.

In 1941 *Die Weisse Fahne* published a warning which seems to have been "the last straw." It read in part as follows:

Wherever the naturally creative will degenerates to vanity, to an extension of power and to an exaggerated perfection, and wherever it is debased to ruthlessness and even to cruelty, to the suppression of individual opinion, nay of the freedom of others, wherever the creative will is loveless and, like a vampire, weighs on others, wherever will is perverted into arbitrariness, consciousness of power into inebriation and abuse of power—there either the resistance of the oppressed or the law of compensation will, sooner or later, lead to the breakdown of the phantom power. This development is often shown in human history. (p. 12)

Shortly after this *Die Weisse Fahne* was prohibited and so the possibility of public expression of its publishers' views was cut off.

One day while at work in the publishing house, Otto Orlowsky and K. O. Schmidt were arrested by the Gestapo, and after a brief confinement in the Gestapo prison in Stuttgart they were transferred to a concentration camp. Baum-Verlag was closed down, the workers were dismissed, all the files and commercial books of the company were confiscated; several thousand books from their own personal libraries and irreplaceable manuscripts were seized; and finally more than 167,000 kilos of books and pamphlets published by Baum-Verlag were seized and destroyed.

A Baum-Verlag catalogue published in 1936 reveals the nature of the books and pamphlets that were destroyed. Nearly two hundred authors were listed among its writers. Among the books destroyed were those dealing with the works of the great Christian mystics Jacob Boehme and Meister Eckhart, and certain of the great idealistic philosophers. Among non-German writers were Kahlil Gibran, Champat Rai Jain, Edward Bulwer-Lytton, and American New Thought writers Orison Swett Marden, Prentice Mulford, and Ralph Waldo Trine. And of course there were the writings of K. O. Schmidt and other contemporary German New Thought leaders. Among books destroyed were such dangerous volumes as *Mankind Is Free* and *Man Without Fear;* a whole group on the mystics of the Middle Ages and of the new age; one on the struggle against materialism; one on health and healing; others on suggestion and hypnosis, Yoga practice in the East, the after life, dreams, and parapsychology.

This partial list reveals the breadth of interest of the German New Thought Movement, and it is confirmed by an examination of the nature of the articles that appear in *Die Weisse Fahne,* the magazine which for most of the period of its existence has represented New Thought at its best in Germany.

The arrest was naturally a heavy blow to Orlowsky and Schmidt. They had no way of knowing how far their activities in the underground opposition were known, whether certain revealing pamphlets had been discovered. They were given no reason for their arrest. No opportunity of consulting a lawyer was offered them. No communication between them was permitted. They could only resolve never to give away any of those who shared their views.

They were taken to one of the incredible concentration camps filled with the victims of Nazi terrorism. Men were continually being taken away to be questioned. Some were beaten and returned. Others did not return. What had happened to these, they were not told. It was rumored that those sent "on transport" went to the ill-famed Welzheim or Dachau camps, whence no one returned.

One day Schmidt was called up and told that he was going "on transport." "If the slightest suspicion of escape arises on the way, fire will be opened at once," he was told. "You are forbidden to talk. Do you understand?"

But they did talk, says Schmidt, and the rumor was soon confirmed that they were being taken to Welzheim, where the commandant had set up a reign of terror. Needless to say this added nothing to their peace of mind.

Schmidt does not describe the horror of the place, other than to say that it well deserved the designation, "homestead of arbitrariness and brutality," the place to which Dante's famous words, "Abandon hope all ye who enter here," were exactly fitted.

But, writes Schmidt, even in this evil time he was consoled by the firm conviction that

if chaos ruled the world, then the cosmos would have ceased to exist millions of years ago. But since the cosmos exists, and since everything in the universe is the manifestation of a living order, of a divine planning and purpose, the chaos that now threatens to ruin Germany, yes, Europe, and even the whole world, will not last; seen in the light of eternity it will only be a *transitory stage,* a mere crisis through which we will have to pass, like the birththroes that of necessity herald the genesis of a new era.

Efforts of friends still free, and the fact that Orlowsky, an 80 per cent disabled ex-serviceman of World War I, was at the point of death led at last to the release of the two men. But, says Schmidt, "by what sacrifices!"

The release, they were told, was only conditional. They must sign a declaration that they would abstain from any kind of editorial and literary work; they could not travel without a Gestapo permit; they had to acquiesce in the closing of the press and were not permitted to have any connection with friends at home or abroad, nor to give any information concerning other prisoners. And they must tell no one where they had been.

Schmidt was told that he must leave the district and break off all connections with the publisher; that he would be under continuous surveillance by the Gestapo; and that he would be returned to the concentration camp if he refused to accept the conditions imposed.

The two were informed that they were still regarded as enemies of the state, and, says Schmidt, "It was this willful discrimination that caused us to close our ranks and to intensify our work for the opposition groups." They were able thus to accomplish some things, including the securing of the release of a prominent antifascist from Dachau and the obtaining of better food and better rations for foreign workers.

When the war ended the indelible traces of its passing were left, but the little New Thought group "kept aloof from any kind of hate and have not lost our trust in destiny which was our inner counsellor and comfort in those dark days of bitterness." Although the spiritual work of moral reconstruction had been violently interrupted and it seemed that an end had been put to their writing and publishing activities, they had secretly continued to write and when the end of the war came there were manuscripts ready to be published as soon as means for their publication could be found. Schmidt wrote:

Today we are confronted with the great task of reconstruction and reorganization of a ruined world. Henceforth we intend to devote our lives to that task, exerting all our forces of the soul, and manifesting the same unerring faith in the power of the good as heretofore. In fulfilling this task, we will harbor no bitter thoughts of the dark and depressing events that lie behind us. In doing so we will be bearing our own share in the construction of a new and more peaceful world, and we will, to the best of our abilities, be helping to realize that new spirit which is about to manifest itself in mankind at the present moment.

On December 8, 1948, Otto Orlowsky died as a result of the concentration camp experience and a war wound. After his death began the rehabilitation of Baum-Verlag, now heavily encumbered. The loss suffered had been about a million marks, the compensation nothing. In January, 1950, *Die Weisse Fahne* appeared again, and in the fortieth year of Baum-Verlag the chief textbook of the German New Thought Movement, Schmidt's two-volume *Neue Lebensschule,* was published in a single popular-priced volume, as a visible evidence that the movement was once again, of its own strength, alive and able to circulate its works through Baum-Verlag. Many other New Thought books followed and took their places in the wide spread of New Thought for which the Baum-Verlag and the leaders of German New Thought had made such sacrifices in life, health, and money.

Scarcely any press in Germany has had results equal to those of Baum-Verlag, which has reflected and expressed the spirit of the religious currents of our time. To its work, in large measure, is due such interest as has been awakened in religious-spiritual questions such as are considered in New Thought. The article celebrating the fortieth anniversary of Baum-Verlag ends with this summary and expression of hope:

In the first decade of its existence Baum-Verlag laid the distribution basis for its coming work; in the second there was an astonishing expansion of the Press and of the New Thought Movement. The third decade, 1933-1942, was a decade of war and testing of the Movement's capacity to endure. The fourth decade was that of gathering new strength of renewal for the second wave of deepening and broadening which, in the fifth decade, it hopes may be carried to complete fulfillment. All friends of Baum-Verlag wish them in the interest of a wider spread and forthgoing of the New Thought Movement, with a whole heart, a wider and more and more blessed work in a united Europe of peace and freedom.

Schmidt is a prolific writer. His books have had an amazing circulation in German-speaking countries and have been translated into other languages.

An advertising sheet listing more than fifty titles from his pen says that over a million and a half copies of his writings have been circulated. His textbook, *Neue Lebensschule,* which provides a year's plan of study, is in its third edition with 36,000 copies sold. His *Art of Living* has sold 159,000 copies; *The Religion of the Sermon on the Mount,* 22,000; *Self and Life Mastery Through the Power of Thought,* 250,000; *The Wisdom of the Soul,* 22,000; *New Thought, the Movement of Modern Times,* 30,000.

An article published in *Die Weisse Fahne* on the occasion of his fiftieth birthday provides the following information concerning Schmidt. Born January 26, 1904, he comes from Flensburg. He has served as a lecturer for the Theosophical Society and other spiritual circles. His interests include oriental and occidental mysticism and philosophy, practical psychology, as well as Vedanta and Yoga. He wrote his first article for *Die Weisse Fahne* on "Success Psychology," and eventually joined its staff, having been attracted by its interest in the oneness of all religions. At the same time he began to make contacts with heads of the New Thought organizations in other countries. This was easily possible because of his knowledge of English and Esperanto. His first book after associating himself with Dr. Schweizer was *Self and Life Mastery* which, as we have said, has had a remarkable circulation. A whole series of booklets followed. He translated a number of American New Thought authors, among them Prentice Mulford, Ralph Waldo Trine, and O. S. Marden.

After the postwar re-establishment of Baum-Verlag and *Die Wiesse Fahne,* new books by Schmidt were issued in rapid succession—*The Art of Living, Life Without Fear,* and on his fiftieth birthday a ground-laying book in dynamic psychology, *Der geheimnisvolle Helfer in Dir.* He has written a series of articles on Meister Eckhart for *Die Weisse Fahne,* and has in preparation a number of other studies which will eventually constitute a ten-volume work on meditation and contemplation as a way to cosmic consciousness.

Schmidt, who, in addition to being a prolific New Thought writer, is also a professional librarian, serves as district president of INTA for Germany; he is a member of the French Alliance de

Croyants as well as of many other organizations. A number of his books have been translated into other languages including Japanese, French, and Dutch.

The New Thought Society, which had existed from 1923 to 1935, was reorganized and properly registered on January 1, 1953. The society is a public, nonsectarian, working organization of individuals, groups, and societies which strives for:

1. The renewal of life of its members on the basis of New Thought.

2. The deepening and soul-perfection of its members by means of depth psychology and soul culture.

3. The training for successful life-mastery through the methods of modern success psychology.

4. The realization of the thought of mutual help as a prerequisite of healthy community living.

By New Thought the society does not mean a new religion, but a renewal of the religious life from within. New Thought becomes in this sense an art of shaping life harmoniously and significantly. In the narrower sense, New Thought is the practice of spiritual consciousness, rooted in living religiousness and the successful mastering of life and fate which brings the individual into harmony and peace with himself, his neighbor, and those farthest from him.

In its work program the society promotes the study of religions, sciences, and philosophies with the purpose of developing in the members a workable world-view or philosophy and the progressive realization of their personality and life.

The society serves these ends through providing lectures; through personal counseling and publication; through society newssheets, as well as books and pamphlets; through organization and development of local New Thought circles; and through co-operation with other life-renewal movements both within the country and abroad.

Today, New Thought in Germany lays little stress upon recruiting and enlistment of members or upon forming groups.

Before World War II, Neugeist (New Spirit) had laid great emphasis upon the organization of thousands of groups and circles. But having seen that this work leads to a constant "externalization" of the endeavors and tendencies of the New Thought work, it now lays emphasis on "internalization"—that is, the inner work and the inwardness of the individual—and not on forming groups. The best recommendation of good thoughts, the New Thought followers think, is to *live* them now. The German New Thought literature therefore chiefly stresses the realization of New Thought in daily life. The German "New Thoughters" now work silently and are concerned for inward growth and improvement—a silent evolution and revolution.

Work of this nature is possible in East Germany and is done there, though the forming of New Thought groups is not permitted and literature cannot be spread publicly. Communication between those in East and West Germany is difficult and dangerous because of communist censorship of all letters and communications.

In Austria New Thought works very much as in Germany. The total number of members in these German-speaking countries is not known. No statistics are available even as to the number of centers or circles. Among German New Thought followers it is not held to be necessary to break with their traditional religious groups. Most, therefore, retain their membership in the churches at the same time that they are following and living New Thought principles. New Thought in Germany has no interest in forming a new religion, but desires to help every one in living his religion better and in realizing its demands.

16

New Thought in Africa, Australia, and Japan

THE OUTREACH of New Thought into Africa has been limited chiefly to the Union of South Africa and to the English-speaking population. But not entirely. Unity lists one center in Nigeria and reports a circulation of considerable quantities of its literature among some of the black tribes. Also some New Thought books and periodicals in French reach French-speaking African folk, according to reports.

Visiting lecturers from England and America have spent longer or shorter periods lecturing and teaching in the principal cities of South Africa. A number of those who ministered in Australia and New Zealand went also to South Africa, and some organizations were founded and flourished for a time. A Unity center was reported in Johannesburg in 1919.

In 1930 William G. Hooper of the British Section of INTA was in South Africa, lecturing and teaching. Mrs. Phoebe Holmes had organized various Radiant Health Clubs in South African cities, as she had earlier in Australia and New Zealand. In 1932 Edna Lister, onetime president of INTA, was in South Africa on behalf of INTA, lecturing and teaching. In 1934 Harry Gaze was there representing the British Section of the INTA, and a South African Section of INTA was formed with Mrs. Masterson as president. She, with Miss Alice Burney, covered most of the provinces and formed groups in new places that had not formerly known of the existence of the Alliance.

In 1948 Dr. Hester Brunt, who had been a most successful worker, head of a center in Montreal, lectured in Capetown and

Johannesburg. While there she met Nicol Campbell and recommended him and his group for membership in INTA, a relationship which has remained constant. Indeed, Campbell became a life member of the Alliance. Dr. Brunt, recently deceased, served as district president for the Union of South Africa. Her work locally is related to the International Association of Religious Science Churches, and there are other centers as well.

Recent New Thought visitors to South Africa from the United States have included President Robert H. Bitzer of INTA, who was there in 1958. Dr. Joseph Murphy of Los Angeles has also been there, and Joel Goldsmith is reported to have formed a group of the Infinite Way on the occasion of a recent visit. Brother Mandus of the World Healing Crusade has made repeated visits, ministering not only through the various metaphysical groups but in a number of the orthodox churches also.

One of the very active groups of New Thought in South Africa is the School of Truth, with headquarters in Johannesburg. Established as the School of Practical Christianity in 1937, it later changed its name. It has centers in several cities of South Africa —Pretoria, Durban, Cape Town, Port Elizabeth, East London, Salisbury, and Bulawayo—and quite recently one has been opened in Los Angeles. In all of these centers lectures are given at stated times, and the centers are open for prayer and meditation as well as consultation. Besides the centers, there are other places outside these cities where lectures are given, some seventy-five a month, and a total of seventy paid workers carry on the work of the movement. An extensive correspondence is carried on with inquirers—thousands of letters each month, they report—seeking help in every sort of problem that the human individual faces. Prayers are continuous throughout the day, and three prayer sessions are held daily in the Johannesburg Chapel, attended by most of the staff.

In the earlier day there was a textbook for study, but this has been discontinued and each member is given, without charge, a copy of the monthly periodical, the *Path of Truth*, which serves the purpose of instruction. This is a pocket-sized magazine of about sixty-four pages, and enclosed with it goes a copy of *Young Ideas,* for young students of Truth, which usually runs to about thirty-two pages.

The adult magazine carries regularly a list of all centers and meeting places, the schedule of lectures for the month, and some twenty pages or more of articles on a variety of subjects. A typical issue has several pages of extracts from letters to the centers, many of them testimonies to the physical, moral, and economic benefits that have been received from the ministry of the movement. There are articles with such titles as "I Asked You to Pray" and "Doing God's Will." Then comes what is a regular feature of the magazine, a page of "Inspiring Thoughts for Each New Day"—each beginning with a verse of scripture, followed by appropriate comment, and ending with an affirmation. The affirmation generally picks up the thought of the scriptural passage.

Young Ideas announces that it is presented by the School of Truth for the younger members of the family that they too may walk in the path of truth and find there Love, Happiness, Health, and True Prosperity. It is filled with poetry, stories, and illustrations; and a brief meditation theme is supplied for each week of the month.

In one issue of the *Path of Truth* lectures were announced in thirty-eight different centers or halls in thirty-one different towns or cities. In some of the cities there are two or three different local halls where lectures are given. Apparently there is as yet no such thing as a church building. Notices say that the lectures are to be held in memorial halls, town halls, city halls, Masonic halls, one in a banqueting hall, and one in Dale Carnegie Auditorium in Pretoria. Eight different lecturers are announced in one number of the magazine. The founder and president, Nicol Campbell, is to lecture weekly in Johannesburg, monthly in Pretoria, and occasionally in other places.

Some thirty years ago Nicol Campbell was, according to the story of his life written by one of his followers (a student in the School of Truth), a lonely, confused, and quite fearful young man, living at home in Cape Town. His parents were Presbyterian.

His grandfather was a Presbyterian minister, so he was brought up in a Christian home. He was a student of the Bible. He believed in God and according to ordinary standards would have been judged a good average Christian young man. But he longed to prove the beliefs he held, and in his sheltered home there seemed no way to do this. Nor did he know any religious leader to whom he could go who had proved these beliefs.

Campbell had no money, but he felt impelled to strike out on his own and put to proof the gospel that he had been taught. He left home with only a few pounds in his pocket and went to another city a thousand miles away. Here he gave away all his remaining cash to a spiritual agency and found himself quite alone and utterly dependent on God for all his physical needs. He got a job, but refused to name a salary. As a result advantage was taken of him by his employer, who paid him nothing. He was often hungry, living chiefly on "office tea," which in that country it is the custom to serve twice daily. He told no one about his financial straits, but extolled the love of God and his unfailing care.

Once he was reduced to the point where he had not even a postage stamp with which to mail a letter which it seemed to him he must write and post. He set off for the post office not knowing how he would succeed in mailing it. But on the way out of the building the caretaker asked him to carry some letters and mail them. He waited a moment, his own letter in hand, while the stamps were being affixed to the letters. "Here, let me put a stamp on that for you," said the caretaker, taking it from him. So the letter got mailed. It was a turning point in his life. This demonstration, small though it seemed, was really the beginning of a career of practical service which was to be blessed richly in the spreading of the Truth message. This small coin became, as it were: "the seed which when planted in the soil of service had to multiply." It had proven to him that his trust had not been misplaced, and from that day to this he has conducted his entire enterprise on the basis of this faith. It was not always easy—there were difficult days through which he and his movement had to pass—but he never ceased to preach utter reliance upon

God as the source of supply, and his movement, he says, stands as proof of the gospel he preached.

Asked by the writer what it was that first turned him in the direction of New Thought, he replied that it was the reading of a poem by Linda Buntyn Willie, "The Law."

Thou criest out that thou didst ask
And yet didst not receive,
And now thou sayest in thy heart
There is no law of good.
But hadst thou kept the law of good,
  Or didst thou, asking, doubt?
Nay, nay, 'twas not the law that failed
  'Twas thou who trustedst not.
Is law for Me alone to keep?
  Nay, thou must do thy part.
Thou art to ask for naught but good
  And asking, never doubt.
That is the law that thou must keep—
  Seek good, and e'er believe.
When thou hast kept this law of good,
  Then ask; thou wilt receive.

This, he said, sent him to a deeper study of the New Testament, and when the light broke through he began to put the Master's teaching of the Law of Love into everyday practical living. His own teaching, he continued, has always been based upon what he has proved for himself in working with this Law of Love.

The support of the work he carries on is purely on the basis of voluntary gifts. There is no charge for any of the services of any of its ministers. Even its literature is distributed freely. His book, *My Path of Truth,* is given away, not sold. Over seven thousand copies of it have been freely distributed. The magazines, of which some fifty thousand are circulated each month, have no subscription price.

At first Campbell worked only as an individual with individuals whom he met. Then a small group of people, made up, he thinks, of persons who had had their interest aroused by hearing Edna Lister and Harry Gaze lecture, and which met weekly, seeking something on which to depend and to which they might give themselves, asked him to talk to them and explain his belief, revolutionary though age-old, that God was man's sufficiency in everything. Lacking in self-confidence, he could at first only read to them. Many found help through his ministry. Finally he was persuaded to devote his entire time to helping those in trouble. Among those helped were many who were ill, though he never claimed to be a healer, but only a teacher. For, says his student, "it is his contention that in God's expressions there can never be anything that requires healing."

Telling his own story of the finding of the way through contact with Nicol Campbell, this student says that one thing which greatly impressed him was that Campbell always took his own medicine. It was never a question of do as I say, not as I do.

If he asked me to pardon, he pardoned the many who mocked him, went out of their way to hurt him and tried by any and every means to discredit him; if he advocated giving, he gave away his all; and if he assured me that God was my supply, he depended on no other source whatever; and when he insisted that Love was the fulfillment of the law, he radiated it daily. So eventually—not without heart ache, hardships, delays, and disappointments—he succeeded in overcoming evil with good.

But Nicol Campbell was always a seeker and an investigator. Meditating on the words of the Master, "I and my Father are one," he reached a new stage in his religious growth. And when he announced his new discovery, it came as a shock to many of his followers and nearly ten thousand of them fell away, feeling that he had gone beyond the bounds of all reason, when he declared that there is no separation between man and his maker, for man is God expressed. But opposition did not deter him. From that day on he has taught "that there is no such thing as God-and anything else, God-and-man, God-and-sickness, God-and-poverty, misery, frustration, fear, and failure—but only God become visible as phenomena."

Prayer became for him no longer a petitioning God for that which he did not have. He took the words, "Son, thou art ever with me, and all that I have is thine," seriously. They signified to him that man and his maker are indivisibly one, and man "as a component part of God" must participate in all that he is and does.

God is Spirit, Life, Love, Wisdom, Intelligence, All-power, All-knowledge, and Omnipresence. Since he is all, he can lack nothing, in him there can be no imperfection, and since man is a component part of God, there can be no imperfection in man; he can lack nothing, is not subject to sickness, poverty, unhappiness, frustration, failure. Man need not, therefore, pray for the removal of these things or the granting of their opposites. What he must do is to discern spiritually the Truth about himself, and in the consciousness of his essential unity with God, claim God's attributes and use them in his service and that of his brethren. "He must deliberately accept his Good and in gratitude give thanks for it, live in the consciousness of it and act in connection with it wisely and well."

The student sums up briefly the teachings of Nicol Campbell, which are of course the teachings of the School of Truth. Their main points are:

1. Man is God in manifestation, not a forlorn entity fighting a losing battle against adverse situations and events.

2. Love is the fulfilment of the law of progress in all good, and only as he loves all things—great and small—does the individual truly live.

3. God was from the beginning, and is, and ever shall be the supply of man's every need, the consummation of his every right desire, his all-sufficiency in all things, his guarantee of complete well-being here on earth, so that in the entire universe he has nothing to fear, nothing to ask for, nothing in which to seek change.

4. His one duty on this and every other plane of consciousness is to love, first God, and then his neighbor—who is himself—as himself.

As one reads the book, *My Path of Truth*, and the other pub-

lications of the movement, he gets the impression that while this
is definitely New Thought in its general outlook and in the emphasis on health, prosperity, and happiness, and on affirmation as
a technique, it seems to be much more identified with the orthodox Christian faith than some of the American branches. There
seems to be a more constant use of the Bible. It is constantly
quoted and almost all the lectures and addresses as well as
articles start from a biblical text. While there are occasional
references to Buddha or some oriental religious concept, these
seem to be much less frequent than in other New Thought writings. Indeed, Campbell is at pains, it seems, to discount the karmic
theory and that of reincarnation, which is taught even in Unity.

Nor does he make constant use of such terms as "Christ consciousness" or "the Christ within." There seems to be a much
more frequent reference to Jesus than in most New Thought
writing, and without the distinction usually made between Jesus
and the Christ. The average non-theologically-trained Christian
might read Nicol Campbell's writings without suspecting that he
stood outside the regularly accepted churches. He is much more
likely to speak in terms of prayer than of affirmation, though he
does employ affirmation.

He often remarks about the inadequacy of an anthropomorphic
God, and again and again speaks of personality in God as a limitation. In a lecture on "Prosperity Is Yours" he uses the text, "Commit thy way unto the Lord, trust also in Him, and he shall bring
it to pass." But, he asks, what does committing mean and who is
the Lord? How does one commit his way unto Him? "If," he
writes, "you think of Him as a personality, the whole message is
lost, but if you read it this way, 'Commit thy way unto the Law,
trust also in It, and It shall bring your good to pass,' then you
have found the secret of the inner meaning of the promise." Apparently for him Law is something abstract, not subject to
change, while God as person might be changed. Yet all through
his writings he speaks in the warmest personal terms of God. God
is All-good, All-loving, All-knowing, All-understanding, etc. Every
one of the modifying adjectives implies personality.

That, I suspect, is one of the major sources of Campbell's appeal to persons who come out of the evangelical tradition—that he uses much of the old familiar vocabulary, but imports a new meaning into it that they have not always found in their churches. In this respect he reminds one of Brother Mandus of the World Healing Crusade.

Regarding the course of the New Thought Movement in Australia and New Zealand, there are only scattered notes in various American periodicals, plus a page or two in Dresser's *History of the New Thought Movement*. However, Grace Aguilar, one of the "down under" leaders for many years and INTA district president of her area in Australia, is engaged in preparing a detailed history of New Thought in that part of the world which may run to two volumes. Dresser states that Sister Veni Cooper-Mathieson began the work there in 1903, under the name of the Woman's White Cross Moral Reform Crusade. Miss Aguilar writes that it started with Dr. and Mrs. James Porter Mills and Veni Cooper-Mathieson, but without mentioning any date. She says that the Millses finished the first edition of *Practical Metaphysics* in her parents' home. Miss Aguilar states, again without mentioning the date, that she took up active work after completing her studies with Willoughby Connor of the Hobart Society in Tasmania. Dresser mentions Veni Cooper-Mathieson, but speaks of neither the Millses nor Willoughby Connor.

The stimulus to organize and develop New Thought in Australia seems to have come chiefly from America and England. Several American leaders have lectured there, among them Annie Rix Militz, who was there for some time in 1913-14. Her magazine, *Master Mind*, carried occasional news from that area. For example, in the September issue of 1913 it was reported in a letter from the pastor of a New Thought church in Sydney that the work was going famously. Again in October it was reported that there was a very active center in Adelaide, "full of life and interest," with many branches of work, including a woman's auxiliary and a Metaphysical Society. The arrival of Dr. Julia Seton in Sidney was reported in the April issue of 1916. She was welcomed enthusiastically by that "splendid New Thought pioneer Sister Veni Cooper-Mathieson." In October, 1916, mention was made of a conference organized by Miss Grace Aguilar in Brisbane, where she had established a New Thought center.

Three times Dr. Julia Seton visited Australia and spoke to large crowds in most of the centers, bringing encouragement and enthusiasm to the pitifully small number of workers on whom fell the burden of carrying the New Thought message to the widely scattered people of Australia and New Zealand. Distances between the centers were great; resources were meager. It was difficult to get a general continent-wide association of New Thought followers. The result was that while various groups started or reawakened enthusiastically, they were unable, for lack of workers and adequate support, to maintain a vigorous follow-up, and hence many interested persons fell away.

But the work continued in most principal centers. In 1926 P. H. Nichols, leader of a group in Adelaide, was being heard fortnightly over Australian radio. The INTA *Bulletin* for December, 1926, reports that the work was proceeding steadily in Hobart, which had had visits from various New Thought leaders, including Grace Aguilar. In 1927 Sister Veni Cooper-Mathieson reopened, under the name of the Church Universal and Metaphysical College, work which she had begun in Sydney in 1903, but which had apparently ceased operation.

The November, 1927, *Bulletin* gave notes from the *Australian New Thought Review* concerning centers in Perth and Adelaide, a New Thought and a Divine Science center in Melbourne, and a Truth center in North Sydney. This magazine had been founded in April, 1926, "to be a unifying medium for all New Thought Centers." It prospered, and in 1928 was reported as "still making good."

W. G. Hooper, field secretary of the British Section of INTA, visited Australia in 1927 and the Australian New Thought Alliance was formed. It was reported in 1928 that it was firmly established and that "a wonderful spirit of unity pervades all the Centers."

There were no debts in connection with either the *Review* or the Alliance. The organization stated that it would welcome visiting lecturers from abroad and do everything possible to help them in arranging tours, but was not in financial condition to help pay the expense of travel or hotel, advertising, or hall rentals. It had no desire, however, to share in any profit which a visiting lecturer might make who came at his own expense. Australia, it said, offered a wide field of opportunity for teachers and lecturers, especially in the smaller cities where hundreds were ready for the New Thought message. Visiting lecturers and teachers should be able to do much better than merely pay expenses. Evidently most of those who came went chiefly to the larger cities.

The second conference of the Australian New Thought Alliance met in January, 1928, and it was now launched as an independent organization, able to pay its own way and have a modest surplus. But at the same time it was noted that no delegates were present from other states, though some friends in Adelaide were asked by others to represent them. Evidently the Alliance was not widely representative, and I have seen no reference to it or the periodical in any subsequent reports, save an announcement of a convocation in Adelaide in 1929. At a business meeting of INTA in 1930 it was reported that the Alliance was "now disbanded," though the president believed that it was not really disbanded and that the work would go forward.

In 1930 Miss Nona Brooks lectured and held classes in a number of cities of Australia. In 1932 the *Bulletin* notes that Dr. Herbert Suttcliffe, D.P., of Melbourne had spent two years in America and conducted very successful campaigns in Providence. He had a School of Radiant Living there as well as one in New Bedford. He had been lecturing in various New England and Canadian centers and later on the West Coast, on his way back to Australia. Dr. Joseph Murphy visited Australia and New Zealand in 1955 and spoke at Perth, Adelaide, Sydney, and Auckland, as well as in South Africa, Japan, and Hawaii.

A. S. Webb of Perth, leader of the Seekers Center in Western Australia, writes that Dr. and Mrs. Mills visited Australia about

1903, touching Sydney, Melbourne, Adelaide, and Perth, besides
Hobart in Tasmania. In Perth, he says, Mrs. Veni Cooper-Mathieson, a local teacher and something of a mystic, was practicing
at the time. Later she retired to Tasmania, withdrawing from
the movement.

Webb's own movement, the Seekers Christian Fellowship, he
founded in 1930, with a few associates. He had been a minister
for a dozen years, was an officer and combatant in World War I,
then studied some three years in London. On his return to Perth
he decided to form a fellowship that would practice "the complete
ministry of healing on New Testament lines." He has published
a magazine, *The Seeker,* for more than a quarter of a century.
For the past decade it has maintained a circulation of three
thousand or more. There is no formal membership in the Fellowship, but Webb estimates that it has served between ten and
fifteen thousand people during his ministry. His movement is
not linked definitely with the New Thought Movement, but
does distribute Unity literature, and Webb feels that it "does
help people who are seeking to find their way through orthodoxy
into some practical useful way of faith." Three times Joel Goldsmith has visited Webb's center and has been helpful to its students. The center is situated in the middle of the city of Perth,
with a lecture hall, a library, and lunching and counseling rooms,
in addition to the Blue Room, which is used for meditation. Very
few lecturers have come from New Thought, except Dr. Joseph
Murphy. Webb has urged Dr. Bitzer to come out for a visit to
Australia, but he has been unable to arrange it. Also, Webb had
suggested to other New Thought leaders the value of some conference which would bring representatives of the various Australian centers together, but nothing has come of this.

Charles Randall, minister and director of Science of Mind
Church and College, also of Perth, reports that a center established in Perth by Dr. Julia Seton had had as many as 250 members at one time. By 1940 perhaps a dozen remained. Mrs. Marie
Phoebe Holmes had established a Radiant Health Center, now no
longer in existence. Randall suggested as the reason for its demise

a change of emphasis from "thinking to eating." His own group, which he prefers to call Religious Science or Science of Mind, was founded in 1940. It functions just as such a New Thought center does in the United States. It is the only one of its kind in Australia. Most of the literature used by the group comes from America. Randall reports that Religious Science, Divine Science, and Unity seem to be the New Thought groups best known in Australia, and in that order. There may, he thinks, be two or three or more New Thought centers in each capital city. But he knows of no overall association or alliance that brings them together. The movement, he writes, is in its infancy.

Miss Aguilar, who has served as leader longer than any other in the movement in Australia, and in various centers, mentions a number of periodicals that have appeared from time to time. Longest lived of all these has been *The Seeker*. Miss Aguilar herself issues a small periodical which is called *The Affirmer*.

Apparently World War II took heavy toll of New Thought in Australia. George Paul of Sydney writes that "Our combined Australia and New Zealand picture was far more colorful before those world wars. The second World War has reduced many of the brilliant workers and time has prevented others from taking their places. Besides, the population is not large enough to promise adequate support."

New Thought seems to have progressed from Australia to New Zealand, at least to Auckland. So far as he could discover, writes Charles Silcock, head of the Auckland Center, work in his own city began with the coming of a Matthew Walker, who was interested in the Progressive Thought Center in Australia. He came to Auckland in his professional capacity as a health specialist and gave lectures along health and Progressive Thought lines. But whatever was done had apparently lapsed with the coming of World War I. When Silcock arrived in 1920 a few friends began meeting in their homes to study New Thought. In 1922 Julia Seton gave a series of lectures and classes, and as a result of this a center was formed under the name of the Church of the New Civilization. This was changed in 1926 to

Higher Thought Center. That year it was decided to build a temple, and the foundation was laid in 1927. On Easter, 1928, it was dedicated. The work then flourished until the coming of World War II, from which the group has never fully recovered. Silcock, a busy businessman, has been the organizer and leader across the years. But the strain of business and lack of leisure for the cause, as he says, together with the failure of younger leadership to develop, has made it impossible to carry on the aggressive kind of a program which is needed. He says that so far as he knows his is the only center operating in New Zealand at present.

But in the past others have been active. A report in the *Bulletin* in July, 1928, states that Mrs. Phoebe Holmes of Los Angeles had recently visited Wellington; that hundreds had registered for her classes and large crowds attended her lectures, and that a Radiant Health Club of some three hundred members had been formed. Even in Christ Church, the most conservative center of New Zealand, she drew capacity audiences while hundreds took her classes and many joined her Radiant Health Club. If they still exist, Silcock does not know about them. He estimates that there are perhaps not more than two hundred persons in the whole Dominion who are interested today. No publication is at present appearing. Dependence for literature is upon American and English sources. Unity literature is circulated and is apparently used to some extent by his own group.

Although New Thought in one form or another has its largest following in the Western world, there is no other single organized branch of the movement which can claim as large a following as one in Japan—an organization so recently established that its founder is still living and active. It is called Seichono Iye, and was founded by Dr. Masaharu Taniguchi. It is explained that the word-sign for the name in Japanese is made up of elements meaning "life," "Eternal Word," "in," and "house." When these are put together the combination is said to mean, "The life of the soul (or man) is housed in the Universal Word or Truth."

(Fenwicke L. Holmes and Masaharu Taniguchi, *The Science of Faith*, p. 99. Seichono Iye is written variously in English.)

This recalls a statement attributed to the Buddha in the *Hannyo Shinko*: "Once we come to understand that all complicated phenomena of human life are, after all, shadows, we shall be clear of all doubt," which means, say the authors of *The Science of Faith*, "that we shall not judge the world by what it appears to be, but by what it really is, God's world." This, they feel, runs parallel to the opening of John's Gospel, "In the beginning was the Word," and to what Dr. Holmes thinks is implied in the first chapter of Genesis, "that God thought, that is, made the world by thought, so that all we see in the visible world is God's thought."

The rise of this vigorous new religion in Japan is an interesting example of the interrelatedness of our world. Who, seeing Seichono Iye in operation in Japan, would ever think of it as having any connection with a Western writer, and one in no sense thought of as related to religion in any form? Indeed, with a man who, while admired for his artistry and literary creativity, was regarded in his own time as morally corrupt? But in *The Science of Faith*, which the founder, Dr. Taniguchi, wrote in collaboration with Fenwicke Holmes, brother of Ernest Holmes, of Religious Science, the story is told.

Dr. Taniguchi was a student at Waseda University. There he became acquainted with the writings of Oscar Wilde, who came to be one of his favorite authors. Wilde's earlier writings, dramas such as *Salome* and *Lady Windermere's Fan*, were what Fenwicke Holmes called "worldly estheticism." But Wilde's bitter experiences of suffering and serving time in prison brought a new note into his work. As a convict, he had one day seen an old man carrying a heavy cask of water, staggering under its weight. He suddenly felt pity for the man and undertook to help him. It was his very first experience of "losing his own life." To his surprise it filled him with delight.

The Ballad of Reading Gaol revealed a different Wilde, one who saw in Jesus' life "the most beautiful of all dramas," for he "lived as other men lived, but he did it with such a faith, such interest in others, such identity with the *devotion* of Mary, the *toil* of Martha, the *hunger* of the multitudes, the *temptation* of Peter, the *love* of Mary his mother, that we are tempted to be like Him." This, continues Holmes, "was what Oscar Wilde felt and expressed so clearly that Dr. Taniguchi was inspired by him." He was deeply moved by Wilde's idea and made to think what he himself could do to carry into effect that inspiration. Then it was that he formulated the principles of Seichono Iye, and began to put them into definite form both in his life and in his writings. Dr. Taniguchi writes that "in those days I came to understand for the first time that man's real joy cannot be realized through the five senses. I needed a sixth sense which included and at the same time outreached them all." (p. 183) It was in 1921 that his first book was published.

Since that time he has attracted more than a million followers all over Japan, and from his pen have streamed books and pamphlets which are widely read not only by members of Seichono Iye, but by the general public. Some of his writings are now regarded as the scriptures of the movement.

Seichono Iye has published a number of magazines which seem to parallel closely those published by Unity School of Christianity. Sometimes, indeed, Seichono Iye has been called the "Japanese Unity." But it seems to have even closer ties with Religious Science than with Unity or any other New Thought group. This is indicated by the book, *The Science of Faith*, referred to earlier, on which Dr. Taniguchi and Fenwicke Holmes collaborated. There is in the book no indication of which author was responsible for any specific section, though internal evidence will sometimes indicate rather clearly the authorship. Curiously enough, Fenwicke Holmes had never been in Japan and had never met Dr. Taniguchi in person, but Seichono Iye had published Dr. Holmes's *Law of Mind in Action* and others of his books, so it was natural enough that they should have joined in writing *The Science of Faith*. Dr. Holmes's *Calm Yourself* has had a wide distribution in Japan. He was invited at one time to visit

Japan; indeed, a $5,000 guarantee had been deposited in a bank to assure reimbursement for the expenses of the trip. But he was unable to make the journey and another went in his stead. He sent a personal message to be read at a great convocation of Seichono Iye at which some fifty thousand persons were present, and it was broadcast as well. Later, Dr. Ernest Holmes, Fenwicke, and Dr. William H. D. Hornaday made a recording in which they discussed the Religious Science teachings. This was translated into Japanese and made into a recording in that tongue, which has been widely circulated in Japan.

It would not do, of course, to say that Seichono Iye is identical with any Western New Thought system. It is clearly oriental in many respects. There appear in it, as would be most natural, elements which came from the founder's Buddhist background or are expressed in terms that those of such background—as most Japanese are to some extent—would understand. But the characteristic ideas and techniques of New Thought are there.

In *Konro-no-Hou*, a scripture of Seichono Iye, it is said, "With God appears Goodness, Righteousness, Charitable Love, and naturally, Harmony is brought forth." From this is deduced the belief that "pain is not a positive existence." It is "another name for God's absence, and so when God appears, pain is destined to vanish away." (p. 164)

Dr. Taniguchi's books are full of accounts of healings of every kind of disease. The methods are not always those of Western New Thought, though prayer and affirmation are familiar elements. The teaching is clearly "metaphysical," and there is no dependence on materia medica.

Does Seichono Iye follow the New Thought pattern of belief concerning supply? Evidently yes, for early in his work Dr. Taniguchi very much wanted and needed a desk. "I was so poor," he writes,

that I could not afford a desk of my own, though I desired it earnestly. I therefore entered into a state of higher spiritual consciousness and released my desire in the form of a demand on Universal Mind. I accepted and acted upon the teachings of Jesus, "When you pray believe ye have received and ye shall receive." This I accepted with all my heart.

A young carpenter in another city (Osaka), a Christian, skilful in mosaic work, wrote that as he sat in his shop an idea came to him "and seemed to float there." He wrote to ask Dr. Taniguchi if he would like a desk and if so to specify exactly what style he would like. And the desk came. "It seems to me," writes Dr. Taniguchi,

that it showed that the Bible teaches "for all we are one body." The whole universe is a living organism and so though unseen, the network of what may be called the nerve tissue spreads everywhere, so that when a man wants something that desire is transmitted to the organ whose function it is to gratify it. That is what in Seichono Iye we call the "Boundless Supply" or "Everything granted at will." (p. 209)

There is in Buddhism a parable to the effect that God is a Boundlessly Rich Man, and man is his child and heir, and another represents man as having a priceless diamond sewn into the collar of his kimono, but ignorant of that fact. He is rich, but does not know it. If man were only aware of it he would be rich indeed. Seichono Iye seeks to make man aware of the abundant supply which is his.

Mrs. Dan Custer, who lived many years in Japan, herself now a Mental Science practitioner, says of Dr. Taniguchi in the preface to *The Science of Faith*:

Gentle, unassuming, even retiring, one feels the powerful strength of his great soul who knows his identity with the vast spiritual forces. The light of heaven is in his eyes. He is loved devotedly by a multitude of people in Japan. His penetrating understanding of the human problems coupled with his broad sympathy, makes him a great teacher and leader. Thousands of lives have been rehabilitated through his influence, and health, hope, success, and happiness have come to them under his guidance.

The organizational activities of Seichono Iye are carried on in centers in various cities. Large mass meetings are frequent. A note in a recent periodical says that they seldom have less than four hundred persons in attendance at their meetings, and often they attract three to four thousand. They have a beautiful temple in Tokyo, and not far from that city they maintain a Conference Center, using what was during the war years a hospital with extensive grounds, where there are frequent conferences of various sorts, particularly of youth.

Seichono Iye has followed Japanese emigrants, especially to southern Brazil, where in recent years leaders have found an enthusiastic response. And in America, Stella Mann writes of speaking to a group in Los Angeles, to which Robert Bitzer has also spoken. Dr. Taniguchi's books are now appearing in English translation, chiefly for Japanese who no longer speak their native tongue. Ernest Holmes, Robert H. Bitzer, and others have written forewords of commendation for some of these editions. And several leaders from America have lectured under the auspices of Seichono Iye.

So, New Thought makes its way abroad as it has in America. Slowly to be sure, but steadily. Many of those at the heart of the movement are quite convinced that in their faith lies the answer to mankind's deepest needs. Not a few are quite content that the movement continue as it always has been, a relatively small minority group keeping alive and making effective ideas which are finally taken over, whether consciously or not, by the larger religious bodies, and thus reach an ever increasing number of the world's people. Others are not satisfied with this role, and aspire to be a constantly growing and increasingly effective movement ministering to an ever widening circle at home and abroad. But thus far they have developed no missionary passion such as that, for example, of the Mormons, who, though until quite lately a comparatively small minority, are experiencing an extraordinary rate of numerical growth and a remarkable extension of their faith across the world.

What the future may bring forth, no one may certainly know, but he may be sure that the essential truth for which New Thought stands will ultimately make its way, in one form or another, to those who stand in need of it.

Appendix

Appendix

Appendix

CONGRESSES AND PRESIDENTS OF INTA

Date	Place Congress Was Held	President Elected
1915	San Francisco	James A. Edgerton
1916	Chicago	James A. Edgerton
1917	St. Louis	James A. Edgerton
1918	Boston	James A. Edgerton
1919	Cincinnati	James A. Edgerton
1920	Kansas City, Mo.	James A. Edgerton
1921	Denver	James A. Edgerton
1922	Atlanta	James A. Edgerton
1923	Washington, D.C.	James A. Edgerton[1]
1924	Buffalo	Elizabeth Towne
1925	Los Angeles	G. Rupert Leach
1926	New York	Mary T. Chapin
1927	Indianapolis	Harry Granison Hill
1928	Cincinnati	Mrs. Murrel G. Powell
1929	Philadelphia	Lorenzo B. Elliott
1930	San Francisco	Thomas Parker Boyd
1931	Cleveland	Thomas Parker Boyd
1932	Louisville	Mrs. Murrel G. Powell
1933	New York	Edna Lister
1934	Buffalo	James A. Edgerton
1935	Cincinnati	James A. Edgerton
1936	Boston	James A. Edgerton
1937	New York	James A. Edgerton
1938	Washington, D.C.	Erma Wells
1939	Minneapolis	Erma Wells
1940	San Francisco	Erma Wells
1941	Nashville	John S. Garns

Date	Place Congress Was Held	President Elected
1942	*No Congress*	John S. Garns
1943	Chicago	Raymond Charles Barker
1944	Louisville	Raymond Charles Barker
1945	*No Congress*	Raymond Charles Barker
1946	**Milwaukee**	Ervin Seale
1947	Rochester, N.Y.	Ervin Seale
1948	Sacramento	Ernest C. Wilson
1949	Los Angeles	Robert H. Bitzer
1950	Washington, D.C.	Robert H. Bitzer
1951	Detroit	Robert H. Bitzer
1952	Chicago	Robert H. Bitzer
1953	New York	Robert H. Bitzer
1954	Los Angeles	Robert H. Bitzer
1955	Cincinnati	Robert H. Bitzer
1956	Washington, D.C.	Robert H. Bitzer
1957	Los Angeles	Robert H. Bitzer
1958	New York	Robert H. Bitzer
1959	San Diego	Robert H. Bitzer
1960	Denver	Robert H. Bitzer
1961	Miami	Robert H. Bitzer
1962	Los Angeles	Robert H. Bitzer
1963	New York	. . . .[2]

[1]James A. Edgerton was elected president by the 1923 Congress. He resigned February 25, 1924. Mrs. Elizabeth Towne was chosen by the Executive Board to succeed him.

[2]1963 Congress had not yet convened at the time this book went to press.

Bibliography

Bibliography

THIS IS A selective bibliography: listing of a work does not necessarily mean that it has been used in connection with this study, though most of the more important works have been examined, if not read entire. Materials included are chiefly these:

1. All the important original source materials, primarily the writings of the major figures in the early rise of the New Thought Movement. Besides these published sources there are the archives of the INTA, the earliest records largely to be found in the New Thought Collection at Bridwell Library, Southern Methodist University, the later at the office of the INTA, 7677 Sunset Boulevard, Hollywood. The writer has had full access to all the archives.

2. Books reflecting the New England milieu out of which New Thought grew.

3. Books regarding the rise of mental healing through nonreligious but psychological means.

4. Books about the movement as a whole or about particular segments of it.

5. Books by or about the founders of the major New Thought groups.

6. Books by presidents of the movement, and by distinguished New Thought leaders who have influenced substantial numbers of people in their own time.

7. Books which show the penetration of New Thought into the churches.

8. Books illustrative of the secular outreach of the movement.

9. Books dealing with the general spiritual healing field.

10. Periodicals of the movement, past and present.

As the bibliographical items are grouped according to category, it should be mentioned that most authors will be readily located by reference to the index.

The most basic original item in any study of the New Thought Movement in America is *The Quimby Manuscripts.* The papers comprising this work were deposited in manuscript form in the Library of Congress by Horatio W. Dresser, who had received them from the son of Phineas P. Quimby, George Quimby, his father's secretary for many years. After the death of George Quimby they were edited by Horatio W. Dresser and in 1921 were published, along with a selection of letters of Mary Baker Eddy and a brief biography of Dr. Quimby, under the title *The Quimby Manuscripts* (New York: Thomas Y. Crowell Co.) Later editions omit the Eddy letters.

In recent years the complete original Quimby Manuscripts, including portions omitted in the Dresser edition, have been put on microfilm and are now available at Bridwell Library, Southern Methodist University, and the Pacific School of Religion Library, Berkeley. Harvard's Rare Books collection contains handwritten copies of parts of the Manuscripts, given by Horatio Dresser's family.

Another version of the Quimby material, *Quimby Manuscripts,* was edited in part by the late W. Frederic Keeler and was formerly obtainable at Lakeside Unity Center in Oakland, California, but is no longer available.

"The Science of Health and Happiness" (the unpublished writings of Phineas P. Quimby) was copied from the original in the Library of Congress by E. S. Collier (New York, 1939); a reproduction which is made from typewritten copy is available at the New York Public Library.

In 1961 the Julian Press of New York republished the second edition of Dresser's book, long out of print, with an excellent introduction and editorial notes by Dr. Ervin Seale of the Church of the Truth, New York.

Dr. Seale was instrumental in securing a microfilm of the unpublished "Diary of Lucius Burkmar," Dr. Quimby's hypnotic subject, written during the period when Burkmar was traveling with Dr. Quimby and assisting in his lectures on and demonstration of hypnotism. This is available at Bridwell Library. The owner of the "Diary" has indicated that it will eventually be deposited in the Library of Congress.

Other major early works include those listed below by Warren Felt Evans, Annetta G. and Julius A. Dresser, Mrs. Ursula Newell Gestefeld, Mrs. Emma Curtis Hopkins, and Frances Lord.

Evans, Warren Felt. *The Divine Law of Cure.* Boston: H. H. Carter & Co., 1881.

————. *Esoteric Christianity and Mental Therapeutics.* Boston: H. H. Carter & Karrick, 1886.

————. *The Mental Cure: Illustrating the Influence of the Mind on the Body both in Health and Disease and the Psychological Method of Treatment.* Boston: Colby & Rich, 1869; 8th ed., 1886.

————. *Mental Medicine: A Treatise on Medical Psychology.* Boston, 1873; 15th ed., Boston: H. H. Carter & Co., 1885.

————. *The Primitive Mind Cure: The Nature and Power of Faith, or Elementary Lessons in Christian Philosophy and Transcendental Medicine.* Boston: H. H. Carter & Karrick, 5th ed., 1886.

————. *Soul and Body: The Spiritual Science of Health and Disease.* Boston: Colby & Rich, 1876.

DRESSER, ANNETTA GERTRUDE. *The Philosophy of P. P. Quimby, with Selections from His Manuscripts and a Sketch of His Life.* Boston: George H. Ellis, 1895. Reprinted, New York: Builders Press, Church of the Truth.

DRESSER, JULIUS A. *The True History of Mental Science: A Lecture Delivered at the Church of the Divine Unity, Boston, February 6, 1887.* Revised with additions, Boston: Alfred Budge & Sons, 1887.

GESTEFELD, URSULA NEWELL. *The Breath of Life: A Series of Self-Treatments.* New York: Gestefeld Publishing Co., 1897.

————. *The Builder and the Plan: A Textbook of the Science of Being.* Pelham, N.Y.: Gestefeld Publishing Co., 1901.

————. *A Chicago Bible Class.* New York: U.S. Book Co., 1891.

————. *And God Said: An Interpretation of the Book of Genesis.* Chicago: Exodus Publishing Co., 1905.

————. *How We Master Our Fate.* New York: Gestefeld Publishing Co., 1897.

————. *The Master of the Man.* Chicago: Exodus Publishing Co., 1907.

————. *A Modern Catechism: For the Use of Those Who Are Outgrowing Their Swaddling Clothes.* New York: Lovell, Gestefeld & Co., 1892.

————. *Reincarnation or Immortality.* New York: Alliance Publishing Co., 1899.

————. *Statement of Christian Science.* Chicago: Privately printed, 1888.

————. *What Is Mental Medicine?* Chicago: Magill & McClure, 1887.

HOPKINS, EMMA CURTIS. *Bible Interpretations Series.* First, Second, and Third Series. Cornwall Bridge, Conn.: High Watch Fellowship, n.d.

——. *Esoteric Philosophy in Spiritual Science.* Cornwall Bridge, Conn.: High Watch Fellowship, n.d.

——. *High Mysticism: A Series of Twelve Studies in the Wisdom of the Sages of the Ages.* Cornwall Bridge, Conn.: High Watch Fellowship, n.d. Originally published separately, Philadelphia: Harper Printing Co., 1920-22.

——. *Judgment Series in Spiritual Science.* Cornwall Bridge, Conn.: High Watch Fellowship, n.d.

LORD, FRANCES. *Christian Science Healing, Its Principles and Practices.* Chicago: Lily Publishing House, 1888.

NEW ENGLAND BACKGROUND

DILLAWAY, NEWTON. *The Gospel of Emerson.* Reading, Mass.: Dillaway Books, 1939; 6th ed., Wakefield, Mass.: Montrose Press, 1949.

EMERSON, RALPH WALDO. *Essays.* Boston: James Munroe & Co., 1841.

——. *Essays: Second Series.* Boston: James Munroe & Co., 1844.

FROTHINGHAM, OCTAVIUS BROOKS. *Transcendentalism in New England: A History.* New York: G. P. Putnam's Sons, 1876; New York: Harper Torchbooks, 1959.

MILLER, PERRY (ed.). *The Transcendentalists: An Anthology.* Cambridge: Harvard University Press, 1950. Contains significant material from the great Transcendentalists Bronson Alcott, Orestes A. Brownson, James Freeman Clarke, William Ellery Channing, Ralph Waldo Emerson, Margaret Fuller, Frederic H. Hedge, Theodore Parker and others, with bibliographical notes on their writings.

SWEDENBORG, EMANUEL. *The Divine Love and the Divine Wisdom.* New York: Swedenborg Foundation, 1946.

MENTAL HEALING OUTSIDE THE NEW THOUGHT MOVEMENT

BROMBERG, WALTER. *Man Above Humanity: A History of Psychotherapy.* Philadelphia: J. B. Lippincott, 1954.

DUBOIS, PAUL. *The Psychic Treatment of Nervous Disorders.* New York: Funk & Wagnalls, 1905.

GREGORY, MARCUS. *Psychotherapy, Scientific and Religious.* London: Macmillan Co., 1939.

GUNTRIP, HENRY JAMES SAMUEL. *Psychotherapy and Religion.* New York: Harper & Bros., 1957.

HILTNER, SEWARD. *Preface to Pastoral Theology.* Nashville: Abingdon Press, 1958.

——. *Religion and Health.* New York: Macmillan Co., 1943.

McCANN, RICHARD V. *The Churches and Mental Health.* New York: Basic Books, 1962.

Pastoral Psychology. Edited by Simon Doniger. Manhasset, N.Y.: Pastoral Psychology Press. A periodical issued monthly except July and August, 1950 — .

SADLER, WILLIAM SAMUEL. *The Physiology of Faith and Fear: The Mind in Health and Disease.* Chicago: A. C. McClurg & Co., 1912.

SEABURY, DAVID. *The Art of Living Without Tension.* New York: Harper & Bros., 1958.

———. *Help Yourself to Happiness.* Garden City, N.Y.: Halcyon House, 1947.

——— and UHLER, ALFRED. *How to Get Things Done.* New York: Julian Messner, 1938.

———. *How Jesus Heals Our Minds Today.* Boston: Little, Brown & Co., 1940.

———. *How to Worry Successfully.* Boston: Little, Brown & Co., 1940.

WACHTEL, CURT S. *The Idea of Psycho-somatic Medicine: Scientific Foundation, Spirit and Scope.* New York: Froben Press, 1951.

———. *Your Mind Can Make You Sick or Well.* New York: Prentice-Hall, 1959.

WORCESTER, ELWOOD, McCOMB, SAMUEL, and CORIAT, ISADOR H. *Body, Mind and Spirit.* Boston: Marshall Jones Co., 1931.

———. *The Christian Religion as a Healing Power.* New York: Moffatt, Yard & Co., 1909.

———. *Religion and Medicine.* New York: Moffatt, Yard & Co., 1908.

BOOKS BY PRESIDENTS OF INTA

BARKER, RAYMOND CHARLES. *Miscellaneous Writings of Raymond Charles Barker.* New York: First Church of Religious Science, 1958.

——— and HOLMES, ERNEST. *Richer Living: How to Use Your Mind Power for More Successful Living.* New York: Dodd, Mead & Co., 1953.

———. *The Science of Successful Living.* New York: Dodd, Mead & Co., 1957.

———. *Treat Yourself to Life.* New York: Dodd, Mead & Co., 1954.

BITZER, ROBERT H. *All Power to You.* Los Angeles: Scrivener & Co., 1940.

———. *The Bellevue Meditations.* Boston, 1927.

———. *The Creative Word.* Los Angeles: Scrivener & Co., 1957.

———. *How to Make Your Mental Computer Work for You.* Los Angeles: Scrivener & Co., 1963.

————. *Ye Shall Be Comforted*. Los Angeles: Scrivener & Co., 1951.

BOYD, THOMAS PARKER. *The Finger of God*. San Francisco: California Press, 1934.

————. *The How and Why of the Emmanuel Movement: A Handbook on Psycho-Therapeutics*. San Francisco: Emmanuel Institute of Health, 1914.

————. *The Principles of the Spiritual Life*. San Francisco: California Press, 1934.

————. *The Voice Eternal: A Spiritual Philosophy of the Fine Art of Being Well*. Berkeley: Emmanuel Press, 1912.

CHAPIN, MARY ETHERIDGE THOMPSON. *The Way Out*. With an Introduction by FRANK CRANE. New York: Chapin Press, 1926.

EDGERTON, JAMES A. *Glimpses of the Real*. Denver: Reed Publishing Co., 1903.

————. *Invading the Invisible*. Washington, D.C.: New Age Press, 1931.

————. *The Philosophy of Jesus: The Basis of a New Reformation*. Boston: Christopher Publishing House, 1928.

GARNS, JOHN SEAMAN. *Prosperity Plus: Brief, Informal Chapters Showing a Simple and Scientific Way to Prosperity, Harmony and True Happiness*. Minneapolis: School of Psychology and Divine Science, 1938.

————. *There's a Thrill in Business*. Los Angeles: DeVorss & Co., n.d.

HILL, HARRY GRANISON. *Paradox and Principle*. Cincinnati: Ruter Press, 1938.

————. *Rational Religion*. Cincinnati: Caxton Press, 1931.

LISTER, EDNA. *Faith the Challenger*. Cleveland, 1954.

————. *I Am Joy*. San Gabriel, Calif., 1958.

————. *Time the Adjuster of Life*. Cleveland, 1954.

SEALE, ERVIN. *The Great Prayer: An Interpretation of the Lord's Prayer*. New York: Delhi Publishing Co., 1946.

————. *Learn to Live: The Meaning of the Parables*. New York: William Morrow & Co., 1955.

————. *Success Is You*. New York: William Morrow & Co., 1957.

————. *Ten Words That Will Change Your Life*. New York: William Morrow & Co., 1954.

TOWNE, ELIZABETH (JONES). *Elizabeth Towne's Experiences in Self-Healing*. Holyoke, Mass.: E. Towne Co., 1905.

————. *How to Use New Thought in Home Life*. Holyoke, Mass.: E. Towne Co., 1915.

————. *Joy Philosophy*. Chicago: Psychic Research Co., 1903.

————. *Just How to Wake the Solar Plexus*. Holyoke: E. Towne, 1912.

———. *Lessons in Living.* Holyoke, Mass.: E. Towne Co., 1910.

———. *The Life Power and How to Use It.* Holyoke, Mass.: E. Towne Co., 1906.

———. *Making Money: How to Grow Success.* Holyoke, Mass.: E. Towne Co., 1929.

———. *Practical Methods for Self-Development.* Holyoke, Mass.: E. Towne Co., 1904.

———. *You and Your Forces: Or the Constitution of Man.* Holyoke, Mass.: E. Towne Co., 1905.

WELLS, ERMA WILEY. *Every Good Desire.* Los Angeles: Unity Classics, 1948.

———. *Have We Lived Before?* Kansas City, Mo.: Unity School of Christianity, 1936.

———. *Master Class Lessons: First Series.* Kansas City, Mo.: Unity School of Christianity, 1935.

———. *The Protecting Presence: An Interpretation of the 91st Psalm.* Kansas City, Mo.: Unity School of Christianity, 1937.

———. *The Shining Heart: A Book of Verse.* Spokane: Fountain Publishers, 1947.

———. *The Song of Life: An Interpretation of the 23rd Psalm.* Kansas City, Mo.: Unity School of Christianity.

———. *Think on These Things.* San Gabriel, Calif.: Willing Publishing Co., 1946.

BOOKS BY FOUNDERS OF NEW THOUGHT GROUPS,
OR REPRESENTATIVE OF THESE GROUPS

1. CHURCH OF THE TRUTH

GRIER, ALBERT C. *The Spirit of the Truth.* New York: Theo. Gans' Sons, 1930.

——— and LAWSON, AGNES M. *Truth and Life.* New York: E. P. Dutton & Co., 1921.

———. *The Truth Way.* New York: Theo. Gans' Sons, 1930.

2. DIVINE SCIENCE

BROOKS, NONA L. *Basic Truths.* Denver: College of Divine Science, 1921.

———. *Mysteries.* Denver, 1923.

———. *The Prayer That Never Fails.* Denver: Divine Science Church and College, 1935; 6th ed., 1959.

————. *Short Lessons in Divine Science.* Denver, third edition, 1928.

————. *Studies in Health.* Denver: Divine Science Church and College, 3rd ed., 1953.

CRAMER, MALINDA E. *Basic Statements and Health Treatment of Truth.* San Francisco, 1893; 9th ed. revised, Denver: College of Divine Science, 1916.

————. *Divine Science and Healing: A Textbook for the Study of Divine Science and Its Application in Healing.* San Francisco, 1905.

————. *Lessons in the Science of Infinite Spirit and the Christ Method of Healing.* San Francisco: Privately printed, 1890.

DEANE, HAZEL. *Powerful Is the Light: The Story of Nona Brooks.* Denver: Divine Science College, 1945.

GREGG, IRWIN. *What Divine Science Offers You.* Denver: Divine Science Church and College, n.d.

JAMES, FANNIE. *Truth and Health: Science of the Perfect Mind and Its Law of Its Expression, the College Text Book.* Denver: College of Divine Science, 4th ed., 1911; 7th ed., 1922. *Divine Science, Its Principles and Practice: A New Textbook* is made up of selections from this book and *Divine Science and Healing,* by MALINDA E. CRAMER. It is also published by the College of Divine Science.

3. HOME OF TRUTH

MILITZ, ANNIE RIX. *Concentration.* Los Angeles: Master Mind Publishing Co., 1918.

————. *Primary Lessons in Christian Living and Healing.* New York: The Absolute Press, 1906.

————. *Prosperity through Knowledge and Power of Mind: Lectures and Mental Treatments 1900-1913.* Los Angeles: Master Mind Publishing Co., 1913; 8th ed. revised, Los Angeles: DeVorss Co., 1937. Republished under the title *Both Riches and Honor,* Kansas City, Mo.: Unity School of Christianity, 1945.

————. *The Renewal of the Body.* Holyoke, Mass.: Elizabeth Towne Co., 1913.

————. *The Sermon on the Mount.* Chicago: F. M. Harley Publishing Co., 1899.

————. *Spiritual Housekeeping: A Study in Concentration in the Busy Life.* Los Angeles: Master Mind Publishing Co., 1910.

4. PSYCHIANA

ROBINSON, FRANK B. *The Strange Autobiography of Frank B. Robinson.* Moscow, Idaho: Psychiana, 1941.

————. *Your God Power: With 20 Lessons on How to Find and Use It*. Moscow, Idaho: Psychiana, 1943.

5. RELIGIOUS SCIENCE

ARMOR, REGINALD C. *Mind Does It*. San Gabriel, Calif.: Willing Publishing Co., 1939.

————. *Thought Is Power*. Los Angeles: Scrivener & Co., 1945.

————. *Very Present Help*. Los Angeles: Scrivener & Co.; 1941.

HOLMES, ERNEST. *Alcoholism: Its Cause and Cure*. Los Angeles: Institute of Religious Science, 1941.

————. *The Basic Ideas of Science of Mind*. Los Angeles: Church of Religious Science, 1957.

————. *The Bible in the Light of Religious Science*. New York: Robert M. McBride Co., 1929.

————. *Creative Mind*. New York: Robert M. McBride Co., 1919; second edition revised and enlarged, New York: Dodd, Mead & Co., 1957.

————. *Creative Mind and Success*. New York: Dodd, Mead & Co., 1919; revised ed., 19th printing, 1957.

————. *Ebell Lectures on Spiritual Science*. Los Angeles: DeVorss & Co., 1934.

————. *Ernest Holmes Seminar Lectures*, ed. GEORGIA C. MAXWELL. San Gabriel, Calif.: Willing Publishing Co., 1955.

————. *Give Us This Day: An Interpretation of the Lord's Prayer*. Los Angeles: Scrivener & Co., 1959.

———— and HORNADAY, WILLIAM H. D. *Help for Today: How to Achieve Security by Using the Power Within You*. New York: Dodd, Mead & Co., 1958.

————. *How to Use the Science of Mind*. New York: Dodd, Mead & Co., 1948.

———— and LATHEM, MAUDE ALLISON. *It's Up to You*. Los Angeles: Institute of Religious Science, 1936.

————. *Lessons in Spiritual Mind Healing*. Los Angeles: Church of Religious Science, 1943.

———— (ed. with LATHEM, MAUDE ALLISON). *Mind Remakes Your World*. New York: Dodd, Mead & Co., 1941.

———— and KINNEAR, WILLIS H. *A New Design for Living*. New York: Prentice-Hall, 1959.

————. *New Thought Terms and Their Meaning: A Dictionary of the Terms and Phrases Commonly Used in Metaphysical and Psychological Study*. New York: Dodd, Mead & Co., 1942.

————. *Pray and Prosper.* Los Angeles: Church of Religious Science, 1944.

———— and SMITH, ALBERTA. *Questions and Answers.* Los Angeles: Institute of Religious Science; new enlarged ed., New York: Dodd, Mead & Co., 1935.

————. *Religious Science.* Los Angeles: Institute of Religious Science, 1932.

———— and BARKER, RAYMOND CHARLES. *Richer Living: How to Use Your Mind Power for More Successful Living.* New York: Dodd, Mead & Co., 1953.

————. *Science of Mind: A Complete Course of Lessons in the Science of Mind and Spirit.* New York: Robert M. McBride Co., 1926. Completely revised and enlarged in editorial collaboration with MAUDE ALLISON LATHEM, New York: Dodd, Mead & Co., 1938; 25th printing, 1957.

————. *This Thing Called Life.* New York: Dodd, Mead & Co., 1943.

————. *This Thing Called You.* New York: Dodd, Mead & Co., 1948.

———— and SELLS, MILTON. *Values: A Philosophy of Human Need.* Chicago: University of Chicago Press, 1932.

———— and HOLMES, FENWICKE L. *The Voice Celestial: An Epic Poem.* New York: Dodd, Mead & Co., 1960.

————. *What Religious Science Teaches.* Los Angeles: Institute of Religious Science, 1944.

————. *Words That Heal Today.* New York: Dodd, Mead & Co., 1949.

————. *You Will Live Forever.* New York: Dodd, Mead & Co., 1960.

————. *Your Invisible Power.* Los Angeles: Church of Religious Science, 1940.

HOLMES, FENWICKE L. *Being and Becoming: Lessons in Science of Mind.* New York: Robert M. McBride Co., 1920.

————. *Calm Yourself: A Key to Serenity.* New York: Dodd, Mead & Co., 1949.

————. *How to Develop a Faith That Heals.* Los Angeles: J. F. Rowny Press, 1920.

————. *The Law of Mind in Action: Daily Lessons and Treatments in Mental and Spiritual Science.* New York: Robert M. McBride Co., 1919.

————. *Love and the Law.* New York: Robert M. McBride Co., 1928.

————. *Lyrics of Life and Love.* New York: Robert M. McBride Co., 1930.

———— (ed). *Mental Science Poems.* Contains poems by Angela Morgan, Sidney Lanier, Richard Watson Gilder, Edwin Markham, and Fenwicke Holmes.

———. *My Book of Treatments*. New York: Robert M. McBride, 1930.

———. *Religion and Mental Science*. New York: Robert M. McBride Co., 1929.

———and TANIGUCHI, MASAHARU. *The Science of Faith: How to Make Yourself Believe*. New York: Dodd, Mead & Co., 1953.

———. *Songs of Silence and Other Poems*. New York: Robert M. McBride Co., 1923.

———. *Textbook in the Science of Mind: Psychology and Metaphysics Applied to Everyday Living*. Chicago, 1925.

———. *The Truth About Matter*. Los Angeles: DeVorss & Co., 1944.

———. *The Twenty Secrets of Success*. New York: Robert M. McBride Co., 1927.

———. *Visualization and Concentration, and How to Choose a Career*. New York: Robert M. McBride Co., 1927.

——— and HOLMES, ERNEST S. *The Voice Celestial: An Epic Poem*. New York: Dodd, Mead & Co., 1960.

HORNADAY, WILLIAM H. D. and HOLMES, ERNEST. *Help for Today: How to Achieve Security by Using the Power Within You*. New York: Dodd, Mead & Co., 1958.

HORNADAY, WILLIAM H. D. *Life Everlasting*. Los Angeles: DeVorss & Co., n.d.

———. *Success Unlimited*. Los Angeles: Scrivener & Co., n.d.

KINNEAR, WILLIS H. (ed.). *The Creative Power of Mind: The Scientific Use of Your Thought for Abundant Living*. New York: Prentice-Hall, 1957. Contains discussion by scientists and philosophers as well as religious leaders and various prominent personalities of the nature of thought and how it can be used creatively.

6. UNITY

BACH, MARCUS. *The Unity Way of Life*. New York: Prentice-Hall, 1962.

CADY, H. EMILIE. *God a Present Help*. New York: Rogers Bros., 1908; revised ed., New York: R. F. Fenno & Co., 1912; presently published Lee's Summit, Mo.: Unity School of Christianity.

———. *How I Used Truth*. Lee's Summit, Mo.: Unity School of Christianity. Formerly *Miscellaneous Writings*, revised ed. Kansas City, Mo.: Unity School of Christianity, 1916.

———. *Lessons in Truth*. Lee's Summit, Mo.: Unity School of Christianity.

DECKER, JAMES A. (ed.). *The Good Business Treasure Chest*. New York: Hawthorn Books, 1958.

—— (ed.). *Unity's Seventy Years of Faith and Works*. Lee's Summit, Mo.: Unity School of Christianity, 1959.

FILLMORE, CHARLES. *Atom-Smashing Power of Mind*. Kansas City, Mo.: Unity School of Christianity, 1949.

——. *Christ Enthroned in Man*. Kansas City, Mo.: Unity School of Christianity, n.d.

——. *Christian Healing*. Kansas City, Mo.: Unity School of Christianity, 1909.

——. *Jesus Christ Heals*. Kansas City, Mo.: Unity School of Christianity, 2nd ed., 1940.

——. *Metaphysical Bible Dictionary*. Kansas City, Mo.: Unity School of Christianity, 1931.

——. *Mysteries of Genesis*. Kansas City, Mo.: Unity School of Christianity, 1936; revised and enlarged ed., 1944.

——. *Mysteries of John*. Kansas City, Mo.: Unity School of Christianity, 1946.

——. *Prosperity*. Kansas City, Mo.: Unity School of Christianity, 1936.

——. *Talks on Truth*. Kansas City, Mo.: Unity School of Christianity; 4th ed. revised and enlarged, 1943.

——. *Teach Us to Pray*. Kansas City, Mo.: Unity School of Christianity, 1941.

—— and FILLMORE, CORA. *Twelve Powers of Man*. Kansas City, Mo.: Unity School of Christianity; 7th ed., 1943.

FILLMORE, LOWELL. *New Ways to Solve Old Problems*. Kansas City, Mo.: Unity School of Christianity, 1938.

——. *Things to Be Remembered*. Lee's Summit, Mo.: Unity School of Christianity, 1952.

—— (ed.). *Unity Treasure Chest*. New York: Hawthorn, 1956.

FILLMORE, MYRTLE. *How to Let God Help You*. Lee's Summit, Mo.: Unity School of Christianity, 1956.

——. *Letters of Myrtle Fillmore*, ed. FRANCES FAULKNER. Kansas City, Mo.: Unity School of Christianity, 1936. Republished as *Myrtle Fillmore's Healing Letters*. Lee's Summit, Mo.: Unity School of Christianity, 9th printing, 1956.

FREEMAN, JAMES DILLET. *The Household of Faith: The Story of Unity*. Lee's Summit, Mo.: Unity School of Christianity, 1951.

GATLIN, DANA (ed.). *Unity's Fifty Golden Years: A History of the Unity Movement, 1889-1939*. Kansas City, Mo.: Unity School of Christianity, 1939.

TEENER, JOHN W. "Unity School of Christianity." Unpublished Doctoral dissertation, University of Chicago, 1942.

OUTREACH OF NEW THOUGHT IDEAS AND PRACTICES THROUGH
WRITERS OUTSIDE THE MOVEMENT

ALLEN, CHARLES L. *Healing Words*. Westwood, N.J.: Fleming H.
Revell Co., 1958.

BEARD, REBECCA. *Everyman's Adventure*. New York: Harper & Bros.,
1955.

———. *Everyman's Goal*. New York: Harper & Bros., 1951.

———. *Everyman's Mission*. New York: Harper & Bros., 1952.

———. *Everyman's Search*. New York: Harper & Bros., 1950.

CARNEGIE, DALE. *How to Win Friends and Influence People*. New
York: Simon & Schuster, 1936.

CLARK, GLENN. *How to Find Health through Prayer*. New York:
Harper & Bros., 1940.

———. *I Will Lift Up Mine Eyes*. New York: Harper & Bros., 1937.

———. *A Man's Reach*. New York: Harper & Bros., 1940.

———. *The Soul's Sincere Desire*. Boston: Atlantic Monthly Press,
1925; Silver Anniversary ed., Boston: Little, Brown & Co., 1950.

———. *On Wings of Prayer*. St. Paul, Minn.: Macalester Publishing
Co., 1951.

COLLIER, ROBERT J. *The Secret of the Ages*, formerly *The Book of Life*.
7 vols. New York: R. Collier, 1926.

DOUGLAS, LLOYD. *Magnificent Obsession*. Chicago: Willett Clark &
Co., 1929. 33rd printing, 1933.

DUNNINGTON, LEWIS L. *Handles of Power*. Nashville: Abingdon-
Cokesbury, 1942.

———. *The Inner Splendor*. New York: Macmillan Co., 1954.

———. *Power to Become*. New York: Macmillan Co., 1956.

PEALE, NORMAN VINCENT. *The Art of Living*. New York: Doubleday
& Co., 1938.

——— and BLANTON, SMILEY. *The Art of Real Happiness*. Nashville:
Abingdon-Cokesbury, 1940; enlarged and revised ed., New York:
Prentice-Hall, 1955.

——— and BLANTON, SMILEY. *Faith Is the Answer*. Nashville: Abingdon-Cokesbury, 1940; enlarged and revised ed., New York:
Prentice-Hall, 1955.

———. *Guide to Confident Living*. New York: Prentice-Hall, 1948.

———. *Power of Positive Thinking*. New York: Prentice-Hall, 1952.

———. *The Tough-Minded Optimist*. New York: Prentice-Hall, 1961.

RUSSELL, ROBERT ALFRED. *The Creative Silence*. Denver, 1935.

———. *God's Workshop*. Denver, 1935.

———. *Victory over Fear and Worry*. Denver, 1952.

——. *Vital Points in Demonstration*. Denver, 1949.
——. *You Can Get What You Want, If —*. Denver, 1948.
——. *You Too Can Be Prosperous*. Denver, 1950.
SANFORD, AGNES. *Behold Your God*. St. Paul, Minn.: Macalester
Publishing Co., 1958.
——. *The Healing Light*. St. Paul, Minn.: Macalester Publishing
Co., 1947.

SPIRITUAL HEALING WITHIN THE CHURCHES

CABOT, RICHARD, and DICKS, RUSSELL. *The Art of Ministering to the
Sick*. New York: Macmillan Co., 1936.
CRANSTON, RUTH. *The Miracle of Lourdes*. New York: McGraw-Hill
Book Co., 1955.
HAMILTON, MARY. *Incubation: Or the Cure of Disease in Pagan
Temples*. London, 1906.
IKIN, A. GRAHAM. *New Concepts of Healing*. New York: Association
Press, 1956.
McDONALD, ROBERT. *Mind, Religion and Health*. New York: Funk
& Wagnalls, 1908.
OURSLER, WILL. *The Healing Power of Faith*. New York: Hawthorn
Books, 1957.
POWELL, LYMAN P. *The Emmanuel Movement in a New England
Town*. New York: G. P. Putnam's Sons, 1909.
ROBERTS, ORAL. *If You Need Healing, Do These Things*. Tulsa, Okla.:
Healing Waters, Inc., 1954.
STEINER, LEE. *A Practical Guide for Troubled People*. New York:
Greenberg: Publishers, 1952.
——. *Where Do People Take Their Troubles*. New York: Interna-
tional Universities Press, 1945
WEATHERHEAD, LESLIE D. *Psychology, Religion and Healing*. Nash-
ville: Abingdon Press, 1951.
WISE, CARROLL A. *Religion in Illness and Health*. New York: Harper
& Bros., 1942.
WORCESTER, ELWOOD, McCOMB, SAMUEL, and CORIAT, ISADOR H.
Body, Mind and Spirit. Boston: Marshall Jones Co., 1931.
——. *Religion and Medicine*. New York: Moffatt, Yard & Co., 1908.

THE MORE SECULAR ASPECTS OF NEW THOUGHT

BRISTOL, CLAUDE M. *The Magic of Believing*. New York: Prentice-
Hall, 1948.

――. *TNT: The Power within You — How to Release It and Get What You Want,* ed. HAROLD SHERMAN. New York: Prentice-Hall, 1954.

HADDOCK, FRANK CHANNING. *Business Power: A Practical Manual in Financial Ability.* Auburndale, Mass.: Powerbook Library. 32nd ed., Meriden, Conn.: Pelton Publishing Co., 1910.

――. *The Culture of Courage: A Practical Companion-book for Unfoldment of Fearless Personality through the White Life of Reason and Harmony.* 16th ed., Meriden, Conn.: Pelton Publishing Co., 1915.

――. *Power for Success through Culture of Vibrant Magnetism.* Auburndale, Mass.: Powerbook Library, 2nd ed., 1910; 18th ed., 1917.

――. *The Power of Will: A Practical Companion-book for Unfoldment of Selfhood through Direct Personal Culture.* Auburndale, Mass.: Powerbook Library, 2nd ed., 1907; 75th ed., Meriden, Conn.: Pelton Publishing Co., 1915; 216th ed., 1918-20. Later issued as *Haddock's System for Success.*

HILL, NAPOLEON. *How to Sell Your Way through Life.* Meriden, Conn.: Ralston University Press, 1939.

――. *Law of Success in Sixteen Lessons.* Meriden, Conn.: Ralston University Press, 1928.

――. *Think and Grow Rich.* Meriden, Conn.: Ralston University Press, 1937.

MARDEN, ORISON SWETT and HOLMES, E. R. *Every Man a King.* New York: Thomas Y. Crowell Co., 1906.

MARDEN, ORISON SWETT. *Getting On.* New York: Thomas Y. Crowell Co., 1910.

――. *He Can Who Thinks He Can.* New York: Thomas Y. Crowell Co., 1908.

――. *How to Get What You Want.* New York: Thomas Y. Crowell Co., 1917.

――. *The Miracle of Right Thought.* New York: Thomas Y. Crowell Co., 1910.

――. *Peace, Power and Plenty.* New York: Thomas Y. Crowell Co., 1909.

――. *Prosperity and How to Attract It.* New York: Success Magazine Corp., 1922.

――. *Pushing to the Front.* New York: Thomas Y. Crowell Co., 1894.

――. *The Secret of Achievement.* New York: Thomas Y. Crowell Co., 1898.

NEW THOUGHT PERIODICALS

The following makes no pretense of being a complete list of New Thought periodicals. The total number would run into the hundreds. Many of them were very short lived, and are seldom to be found in libraries. For many of those listed it has been impossible to give the dates of publication, where they were published, or by whom edited. The author will welcome information concerning any here mentioned or others, and Bridwell Library at Southern Methodist University would welcome single issues or complete files of any of them for its New Thought Collection. The periodicals are listed alphabetically, rather than chronologically or in order of their importance; those known to be currently issued are starred.

*Active Service. London, SSKTP, founded and edited by Frank L. Rawson, 1916. Monthly since 1940.

Advanced Thought. Edited by W. W. Atkinson. "A monthly journal of Mental Science, practical psychology, instructive occultism, metaphysical healing." Chicago, 1916-24.

*The Affirmer. Edited and published by Miss Grace Aguilar. New Thought Center, Marimoo, N.S.W., Australia.

Arena. For a short period, 1897-1904, while published by the Alliance Publishing Co., New York, this was a New Thought oriented magazine.

*Aspire to Better Living. College of Divine Science, Denver, 1916. Appeared in 1916 as Daily Studies in Divine Science, later as Divine Science Monthly.

Australian New Thought Magazine. Founded 1926, discontinued apparently about 1930.

Builders. "A magazine devoted to the study of Thomas Troward's philosophy of Mental Science." Founded and edited by Genevieve Behrend. Brooklyn, 1918 — ?

Christian Metaphysician. Edited by George B. Charles, Chicago, 1887-97. "A guide to health and happiness." Illinois Metaphysical College, bi-monthly.

Christian Science. Edited by Joseph Adams, Chicago, 1888-92. A mental healing monthly. Later the Chicago Truth Gleaner.

Christian Victory. Edited by W. Frederic Keeler, San Francisco, 1930 — ? Metaphysics, etc.

The Column. Founded and edited by Dr. Julia Seton Sears, 1911-12, first in Denver, later in New York.

The Comforter. Edited by Florence Crawford, Portland, Ore., 1911 — ?

The Coming Light. San Francisco, 1896-99. Merged with *Arena.*

Constructive Thinker. "A periodical of unitive higher thought." Edited by W. Frederic Keeler, Baldwin, New York, 1913-16.

Cosmic World. Edited by Christian D. Larson, Chicago, 1908 – ?

Crusader. A monthly founded and edited by Brother Mandus, Blackpool, England, 1954 – .

Daily Word. Unity School of Christianity, Lee's Summit, Mo., 1924–.

Das Wort. A periodical devoted to mental healing, for German-Americans. St. Louis, 1893 – ?

The Dawn. Edited by John Ball, 1910 – ?

Die Weisse Fahne (The White Flag). Monthly bulletin of Neugeist (New Spirit) for German-speaking countries. Baum-Verlag, Pfullingen, Württemberg, Germany, 1927 – .

Eleanor Kirk's Idea. "From the ideal to the actual." Edited by Mrs. Ames, New York, Vols. I-XVII. Ceased publication 1905.

The Essene. Edited by Grace Brown, Denver.

Eternal Progress. Edited by Christian D. Larson. Chicago, 1912-21.

Exodus. Monthly, edited by Ursula Gestefeld, Chicago, 1896-1904.

Floyd's Self-Mastery. Edited by Andrew Floyd, Union, N.J., 1910-22, earliest numbers as *Self-Mastery.*

The Fountain. Edited by Erma Wells, Spokane, Wash.

Free Man. Bangor, Me., 1897-1907.

The Gleaner. Edited by W. John Murray, New York, 1909 – ?

Good Business. Formerly *The Christian Business Man,* Kansas City, Mo., Unity School of Christianity, 1922; later *Christian Business.* Currently published at Lee's Summit, Mo.

Good News. "Health, Life, etc." Columbus, Kans., 1901-4.

Harmony. Edited by Mrs. M. E. Cramer, San Francisco, 1888-1906.

The Higher Law. Published by the Metaphysical Club of Boston, 1899-1902, edited by Horatio W. Dresser.

Ideal American. Yonkers, N.Y., 1897-1907.

Immortality. A quarterly edited by J. F. C. Grumbine, Chicago, 1894-1901. Merged with *Universal Religion,* Chicago, 1901.

Independent Thinker. New York, 1900-1902.

The Inner Life. "Herald of the New Age." Monthly, Akron, Ohio, 1933-38.

Journal of Practical Metaphysics. Boston, 1896-98, edited by Horatio W. Dresser. Merged with *Arena,* 1898.

Keeler's Comments. Edited and published by W. Frederic Keeler, San Diego.

Library of Health. Monthly, edited by C. B. Patterson, Alliance Publishing Co., New York, 1897-1900.

The Life. Monthly, edited by A. P. Barton, Kansas City, Mo., 1897-1908.

Man. New York, Metaphysical Publishing Co., 1895-1912.

The Master Christian. Edited by Henry Victor Morgan, Tacoma, Wash.

Master Mind. Monthly, edited by Annie Rix Militz, Los Angeles, 1911-31. Changed to *The Christ Mind,* edited by Harriet Hale Rix, 1931 — ?

Mental Healing Monthly. Said to be the first mental science magazine published in Boston, 1886-88.

Mental Science Magazine. Edited by A. J. Swartz, Chicago, 1884-89.

Mental Science Magazine. Monthly, Denver, 1939 — ?

Mente. Institute of Mental Science, Santiago, Chile. Spanish language magazine. 1920 — ?

Mind. Alliance Publishing Co., New York, 1897-1906.

Mind Digest. "The magazine of self-discovery." Monthly, Paradise, Pa., 1945-47.

Mind Magazine. Monthly, edited by James E. Dodds, Los Angeles, 1931-35.

Modern Thought. Founded and edited by Charles Fillmore, Kansas City, Mo., 1889. Later *Christian Science Thought,* then *Thought.* Merged in 1892 with *Unity.*

The Moment's View. Edited by Sarah Crosse, Boston, 1901-2.

Nautilus. Founded and edited by Elizabeth Towne. Portland, Ore., 1898-1900; Holyoke, Mass., 1900-1953.

New Ideal. Boston, 1888-90.

New Man. Beloit, Kan., 1895-1901. Continued as *Self-Culture,* Omaha, 1902 — ?

New Thought. "A magazine devoted to mental healing." Melrose, Mass., 1894 — ? First publication to use the name *New Thought.*

New Thought. Founded and edited by Sidney Flower. Originally the *Hypnotic Magazine,* which in 1898 became *Suggestive Therapeutics.* In 1902 it was merged with the *Journal of Magnetism,* taking the name *New Thought,* which it bore until 1910. Merged with *Health and Success Magazine,* Plymouth, Ill., and ceased publication in 1917.

°New Thought. London, 1929 —. Official organ of the British Section of INTA. Formerly *International New Thought Alliance Record,* 1927.

°New Thought. "A quarterly devoted to right thinking." Founded in 1915 as the *New Thought Bulletin.* Has appeared under various names and at varying intervals; a quarterly since 1941. The official organ of the INTA, edited by the president of the Alliance.

New Thought Companion. Plymouth, Ill., 1910-17.

New Thought Index. "A cultural review and metaphysical guide." Irregular, 1927-38.

New Thought Truth. St. Louis, 1915-17.

The New Way. "A magazine devoted to unfoldment of the higher life." Washington, D.C., 1905-6.

Now. "A journal of affirmation." Founded and edited by Henry Harrison Brown, San Francisco, 1902 — ? Later published in San Jose, Calif.

O Pensamento. Published by the Esoteric Circle, São Paulo, Brazil, 1907 — ? Reported as still appearing in the early 1920's.

Optimist. Metaphysical School of Healing, Boston, New York, 1906-9.

*The Path of Truth. Edited by Nicol Campbell. Official organ of the School of Truth. Published monthly, Johannesburg, South Africa. Carries a supplement, *Young Ideas,* for young Truth students.

Power. Monthly, edited by Charles E. Prather, Denver, 1911 — ?

Practical Ideals. Monthly, edited by J. W. Winkley, Boston, 1900-1912.

*Progress. Originally published by Unity School of Christianity, Kansas City, Mo., as *Youth,* 1924; then *Progress;* later *You;* and finally *Progress,* published at Lee's Summit, Mo.

Radiant Center. Washington, D.C., 1900-1903.

The Rally. Official organ of the New Thought Extension Work in England, London.

Realization. Monthly, organ of the Realization League, H. Edward Mills, Washington, D.C., 1900 — ?

Reason. "A monthly journal devoted to psychic science, education, healing, success and social reform." Los Angeles, 1905 — ?

*Religious Science. Monthly, published by the International Association of Religious Science Churches, Carmel, Calif., 1949 — .

*La Science du Mental. Monthly, edited by A. J. Berg, Roquebrun-Cap-Martin, France.

Science of Life & Health. Boston, New York, 1912-15.

*Science of Mind. Monthly, Institute of Religious Science, Los Angeles, 1927 — .

*Science of Thought Review. Founded and edited by H. T. Hamblin, Chichester, England, 1921 — .

Scientific Christian. Edited by T. J. Shelton, Little Rock, Ark., Denver, 1894-1921.

*The Seeker. Published by the Seekers Christian Fellowship at Perth, Australia. Reported in 1962 as appearing "for more than a quarter of a century."

Success Magazine. Edited by Napoleon Hill.

Success Magazine. Edited by O. S. Marden, 1897-1911. Followed by *New Success Magazine,* 1918-24.

The Temple. "A monthly magazine devoted to the fuller unfoldment of the Divinity of Humanity." Edited by Paul Tyner, Denver, 1897-98; merged with *Arena,* 1898.

Triumphant Living. Official journal of the Canadian Metaphysical Alliance.

Truth. London, 1891-1926.

Truth Magazine. Edited by Albert C. Grier, 1912-31.

Truth Messenger. Monthly, edited by Mary Butterworth, 1923 – ?

The Truth Seeker. Australia, 1905; combined with *The Healer,* 1915, as *The Revealer.*

Unité Universelle. "Revue mensuelle d'Ontologie, et de psychologie," founded and edited by Mary Sterling. Paris, 1956 – .

Unity. Kansas City, Mo.; later Lee's Summit, Mo. 1893 – .

Universal Truth Monthly. Edited by Fannie M. Harley, Chicago, 1888-98.

Washington Newsletter. Washington, D.C., 1897-1921.

Wayside Lights. Edited by L. C. Graham, Hartford, Conn.

Wee Wisdom. Children's magazine. Unity School of Christianity, Kansas City, Mo., 1893; later Lee's Summit, Mo.

Weekly Unity. Unity School of Christianity, Kansas City, Mo., 1909; later Lee's Summit, Mo.

Weltmer's Magazine of Suggestive Therapeutics. Nevada, Mo., 1901-9.

Wilmans' Express. Edited by Helen Wilmans, Sea Breeze, Fla.

Wise Man. Edited by Alexander Wilder and L. E. Whipple, New York, 1903-11.

World's Advanced Thought. Edited and published by Mrs. Lucy A. Mallory, Portland, Ore., 1886-1918.

New Thought Abroad

1. africa

Campbell, Nicol C. *My Path of Truth.* Johannesburg: School of Truth, 1953.

2. england

Early History of the Higher Thought Movement in England. Booklet, n.d.

Gaze, Harry. *My Personal Recollections of Thomas Troward.* San Gabriel, Calif.: Willing Publishing Co., 1958.

TROWARD, THOMAS. *Bible Mystery and Bible Meaning.* London: Stead & Dauby; New York: Goodyear Book Concern, 1913.

———. *The Creative Process in the Individual.* London, 1909; new and revised ed., New York: Robert M. McBride Co., 1917.

———. *The Doré Lectures on Mental Science.* London, 1909; New York: Dodd, Mead & Co., 20th printing, 1955.

———. *The Edinburgh Lectures on Mental Science.* London, 1904; New York: Dodd, Mead & Co., 1904.

———. *The Hidden Power, and Other Papers on Mental Science.* New York: Robert M. McBride Co., 1921.

———. *The Law and the Word.* London; New York: Dodd, Mead & Co., 1917; 19th printing, 1958.

———. *Troward's Comments on the Psalms.* New York: Robert M. McBride Co., 1929.

The Healing Crusade

BROTHER MANDUS. *The Grain of Mustard Seed.* London: L. N. Fowler & Co., 1959. 4th printing, 1960.

———. *This Wondrous Way of Life.* London: L. N. Fowler & Co., 1956; 6th printing, 1960.

World Healing Crusade Booklets. Three series: "The Revelation Series" (7), "Lecture Series" (8), and an untitled series (7). Blackpool: World Healing Crusade, n.d.

Science of Thought

HAMBLIN, HENRY THOMAS. *Divine Adjustment: How Divine Law Works in Our Life.* Chichester: Science of Thought Press, 1937.

———. *Life of the Spirit.* Chichester: Science of Thought Press.

———. *Life Without Strain.* San Gabriel, Calif.: Willing Publishing Co., 1951.

———. *The Message of a Flower: Or the Divine Immanence.* Chichester: Science of Thought Press, 1921.

———. *Within You Is the Power.* Chichester: Science of Thought Press, 4th ed., 46th thousand, n.d.

The Society for Spreading the Knowledge of True Prayer — SSKTP

HOGG, EFFIE. *Gleams of Truth Through the Lamp of Right Thinking.* London: Crystal Press, n.d.

————. *Right Thinking, Its Rise and Standpoint.* London: SSKTP Publishing Dept., n.d.

RAWSON, FREDERIC L. *Life Understood: From a Scientific and Religious Point of View, and the Practical Method of Destroying Sin, Disease, and Death.* London: Crystal Press, 1912; 7th ed., London: SSKTP, 1947.

————. *Man's Powers and Work, with Biographical Sketch and Portrait of the Author.* London: Crystal Press, 4th ed., n.d.

————. *The Nature of True Prayer.* London: Crystal Press, 6th ed., 1930.

————. *Plea for the Open Door: The Evolution of the Knowledge of Truth and the Organization of the Mother Church of Christ, Scientist, Boston.* London: Crystal Press. n.d.

————. *Right Thinking the Basis of True Prayer.* London: Crystal Press, n.d.

————. *Treatment or Healing by True Prayer.* New York: J. J. Little & Ives Co., 1922.

3. FRANCE

Most New Thought books in French are translations of books that appeared first in English, including one or more by such writers as Ralph Wado Trine, Thomas Troward, Thomas Hamblin, Emmet Fox, Ernest Holmes, Joseph Murphy, Raymond Charles Barker, and Frederick W. Bailes, and several by K. O. Schmidt of Germany. Mme Robert Sterling, founder of Unité Universelle, has published various pamphlets and booklets including *La Vraie Prière, Les Morts sont vivants,* and a book, *Meditations.* A. J. Berg, in the South of France, editor of *La Science du Mental,* has also written some books including *La Guérison par Lavage du Subconscient* and *Dirigez Votre Pensée,* and has translated others from English.

4. GERMANY

SCHMIDT, K. O. *Neue Lebensschule.* Pfullingen, Württemberg. Schmidt is the author or translator of some thirty or more volumes in German, a number of which have been translated into other languages, including Japanese.

5. JAPAN

TANIGUCHI, MASAHARU. *Divine Education and Spiritual Training of*

Mankind. Tokyo: Seichono Iye Foundation, Divine Publication Dept., 1956.

———— and HOLMES, FENWICKE L. *The Science of Faith: How to Make Yourself Believe.* New York: Dodd, Mead & Co., 1953.

————. *You Can Heal Yourself.* Tokyo: Nippon Kyobunsha Co., 1960.

GENERAL

ALLEN, JAMES. *As a Man Thinketh.* Chicago: Sheldon Press, 4th ed., 1908.

————. *Eight Pillars of Prosperity.* New York: Thomas Y. Crowell Co., 1911.

————. *Foundation Stones to Happiness and Success.* New York: Thomas Y. Crowell Co., 1913.

————. *From Poverty to Power.* Chicago: Science Press, 1916.

————. *Man, King of Mind, Body and Circumstance.* London: Ryder, 1911.

ATKINSON, W. W. *History and Principles of New Thought.* Holyoke, Mass.: Elizabeth Towne Co., n.d.

————. *The Inner Consciousness.* Chicago: Advanced Thought Publishing Co., 1908.

————. *The Law of New Thought: A Study of Fundamental Principles and Their Application.* Chicago: Psychic Research Company, 1902.

————. *The Secret of Success: A Course of Nine Lessons.* Chicago: Advanced Thought Publishing Co., 1908.

————. *Thought Forces in Business and Everyday Life.* Chicago: New Thought Publishing Co., 1902.

————. *Thought Vibration: Or the Law of the Thought World.* Chicago: New Thought Publishing Co., 1906.

————. *Your Mind and How to Use It.* Holyoke, Mass.: Elizabeth Towne Co., 1912.

BAILES, FREDERICK W. *Healing Power of Balanced Emotions.* Los Angeles: Logos Press, 1952.

————. *Hidden Power for Human Problems.* New York: Prentice-Hall, rev. ed., 1957.

————. *Peace in a Changing World.* 2 vols. Los Angeles: DeVorss & Co., 1952.

————. *Your Mind Can Heal You.* New York: Dodd, Mead & Co., 1941.

BALLOU, JENNIE. *Period Piece: Ella Wheeler Wilcox and Her Times.* Boston: Houghton Mifflin Co., 1940.

BARROWS, CHARLES M. *Facts and Fictions of Mental Healing*. Boston: H. H. Carter & Co., 1887.

BLANDING, DON. *Joy Is an Inside Job*. New York: Dodd, Mead & Co., 1953.

———. *Today Is Here*. New York: Dodd, Mead & Co., 1947.

COLLIER, ROBERT GORDON. *Make Your Own World*. 2 vols. Tarrytown, N. Y.: Book of Destiny, 1954.

COLVILLE, W. J. *The Peoples Handbook of Spiritual Science*. Boston: Banner of Light Publishing Co., 1902.

———. *The Spiritual Science of Health and Healing*. Chicago: Educator Publishing Co., 1888; 5th ed., 1894.

COOK, JAY W. *Absolute Science*. San Francisco: California Press, 1927.

CRANE, AARON MARTIN. *Knowing the Master through John*. Boston: Lothrop, Lee & Shepard Co., 1926.

———. *Right and Wrong Thinking and Their Results*. Boston: Lothrop, Lee & Shepard Co., 1908.

CURTIS, DONALD. *Human Problems and How to Solve Them*. New York: Prentice-Hall, 1962.

———. *Your Thoughts Can Change Your Life*. New York: Prentice-Hall, 1961.

CUSTER, DAN. *The Miracle of Mind Power*. New York: Prentice-Hall, 1960.

DEL MAR, EUGENE. *The Conquest of Disease*. London: L. N. Fowler & Co., 1902.

———. *Man the Master*. London: L. N. Fowler & Co., 1925.

DE WATERS, LILLIAN. *The Christ Within: A Study in the Absolute*. Stamford, Conn., 1925.

———. *The Finished Kingdom*. Stamford, Conn., 1926.

———. *In His Name*. Stamford, Conn., 1926.

———. *Thinking Heavenward*. Boston, 1908.

———. *The Voice of Revelation*. Stamford, Conn., 1926.

DODDS, JAMES E. *Conscious Immortality: A New Approach to Creative Thinking*. Santa Barbara, Calif.: J. F. Rowny Press, 1942.

———. *Six Lessons on the Silence*. Los Angeles: College of Practical Metaphysics, 1921.

DREIER, THOMAS, *et al. The Story of Elizabeth Towne and the Nautilus Magazine*. Holyoke, Mass.: E. Towne Co., 1911.

DRESSER, HORATIO W. *A Book of Secrets*. New York: G. P. Putnam's Sons, 1902.

———. *The Christ Ideal*. New York: G. P. Putnam's Sons, 1901.

———. *Education and the Philosophic Ideal*. New York: G. P. Putnam's Sons, 1900.

——. *Ethics in Theory and Application.* New York: Thomas Y. Crowell Co., 1925.

——. *The Greatest Truth.* New York: Progressive Literature Co., 1907.

——. *Handbook of New Thought.* New York: G. P. Putnam's Sons, 1917.

——. *Health and the Inner Life: An Account of the Life and Teachings of P. P. Quimby.* New York: G. P. Putnam's Sons., 1906.

——. *A History of Ancient and Medieval Philosophy.* New York: Thomas Y. Crowell Co., 1926.

——. *A History of Modern Philosophy.* New York: Thomas Y. Crowell Co., 1928.

——. *History of the New Thought Movement.* New York: Thomas Y. Crowell Co., 1919.

——. *Human Efficiency.* New York: G. P. Putnam's Sons, 1912.

——. *The Immanent God.* Boston: Privately printed, 1894.

——. *In Search of a Soul.* Boston: G. H. Ellis, 1897.

——. *Knowing and Helping People.* Boston: Beacon Press, 1933.

——. *Living by the Spirit.* New York: G. P. Putnam's Sons, 1900.

——. *Man and the Divine Order.* New York: G. P. Putnam's Sons, 1903.

——. *A Message to the Well.* New York: G. P. Putnam's Sons, 1910.

——. *Methods and Problems of Spiritual Healing.* New York: G. P. Putnam's Sons, 1899.

——. *On the Threshold of the Spiritual World: A Study of Life and Death Over There.* New York: G. Sully, 1919.

——. *The Open Vision: Psychic Phenomena.* New York: Thomas Y. Crowell Co., 1920.

——. *Outlines of a Psychology of Religion.* New York: Thomas Y. Crowell Co., 1929.

——. *The Perfect Whole.* Boston: G. H. Ellis, 1897.

——. *The Philosophy of the Spirit.* New York: G. P. Putnam's Sons, 1908.

——. *A Physician to the Soul.* New York: G. P. Putnam's Sons, 1908.

——. *The Power of Silence.* Boston: G. H. Ellis, 1895.

——. *Psychology in Theory and Application.* New York: Thomas Y. Crowell Co., 1924.

—— (ed.). *The Quimby Manuscripts.* New York: Crowell, 1921.

——. *The Religion of the Spirit in Modern Life.* New York: G. P. Putnam's Sons, 1914.

——. *The Spirit of New Thought.* New York: Thomas Y. Crowell Co., 1917.

————. *Spiritual Health and Healing*. New York: Thomas Y. Crowell Co., 1922.

————. *The Victorious Faith: Ideals in War Time*. New York: Harper & Bros., 1917.

————. *Voices of Freedom*. New York: G. P. Putnam's Sons, 1899.

————. *Voices of Hope: Essays on the Problem of Life, Optimism and the Christ*. Boston: G. H. Ellis, 1898.

EDDY, MARY BAKER. *Science and Health with Key to the Scriptures: Authorized Edition*. Christian Science Publishing Society, 1906. Close to 400 editions or printings have been made by various publishers, but the text has been almost entirely unchanged since the author's death in 1910.

FLETCHER, HORACE. *Menticulture: Or the ABC of True Living*. New York: Herbert S. Stone & Co., 1899.

————. *The New Menticulture: Or the ABC of True Living*. New York: Frederick A. Stokes Co., 46th thousand, 1906.

FOX, EMMET. *Alter Your Life*. New York: Harper & Bros., 1950.

————. *Around the Year with Emmet Fox*. New York: Harper & Bros., 1958.

————. *Find and Use Your Inner Power*. New York: Harper & Bros., 1940.

————. *Power through Constructive Thinking*. New York: Harper & Bros., 1940.

————. *Make Your Life Worth While*. New York: Harper & Bros., 1946.

————. *The Sermon on the Mount*. New York: Church of the Healing Christ, 1934; New York: Harper & Bros., 1935; French ed., 1934; Spanish ed., 1945.

————. *Stake Your Claim*. New York: Harper & Bros., 1952.

————. *The Ten Commandments: The Master-key to Life*. New York: Harper & Bros., 1953.

GAZE, HARRY. *Emmet Fox: The Man and His Work*. New York: Harper & Bros., 1952.

————. *How to Live Forever*. New York: Prentice-Hall, 1954.

————. *My Personal Recollections of Thomas Troward*. San Gabriel, Calif.: Willing Publishing Co., 1958.

GOLDSMITH, JOEL S. *The Art of Meditation*. New York: Harper & Bros., 1956.

————. *The Infinite Way*. San Gabriel, Calif.: Willing Publishing Co., 1947.

JEFFERY, H. B. *Coordination of Spirit Soul and Body*. Cambridge, Mass.: Ruth Laighton, 1948.

———. *The Fruit of the Spirit*. Cambridge, Mass.: Ruth Laighton, 1939; 5th printing, Fort Worth: Christ Truth League, 1940.

———. *Mystical Teachings*. Fort Worth: Christ Truth League, 1954.

———. *The Principles of Healing*. Cambridge: Ruth Laighton, 1939.

———. *The Spirit of Prayer*. Cambridge, Mass.: Ruth Laighton, 1938. 5th printing, Fort Worth: Christ Truth League, 1938.

LANDONE, BROWN. *The ABC of Truth: 55 Lessons for Beginners in New Thought Study*. London: L. N. Fowler & Co., 1926.

———. *How to Turn Your Desires and Ideals into Realities*. Holyoke, Mass.: E. Towne Co., 1927.

———. *The Methods of Truth Which I Use*. Holyoke, Mass.: E. Towne Co., 1928.

———. *Powers That Turn Failure into Success*. Holyoke, Mass.: E. Towne Co., 1933.

LANYON, WALTER C. *Demonstration*. Carthage, Mo.: Privately printed, 1921.

———. *The Eyes of the Blind*. London: L. N. Fowler & Co., 1938.

———. *I Came*. New York: Snellgrove Publications, 1940.

———. *Life More Abundant*. New York: Snellgrove Publications, 1940.

———. *That Ye Might Have*. New York: Snellgrove Publications, 1940.

———. *Treatment*. Carthage, Mo.: Privately printed, 1921.

LARSON, CHRISTIAN D. *The Creative Power of Mind*. Los Angeles: Privately printed, 1930.

———. *How the Mind Works*. Los Angeles: New Literature Publishing Co., 1912.

———. *How to Stay Well*. Los Angeles: New Literature Publishing Co., 1912.

———. *The Pathway of Roses*. Los Angeles: New Literature Publishing Co., 1912.

———. *Practical Self-Help*. New York: Thomas Y. Crowell Co., 1922.

———. *Your Forces and How to Use Them*. Los Angeles: New Literature Publishing Co., 1912.

LE GALYON, CAROLYN BARBOUR. *All Things New*. 4 vols. Los Angeles: Scrivener & Co., n.d.

LYNCH, RICHARD. *Health and Spiritual Healing*. New York: Unity Press, 1924.

———. *Man and His Powers*. New York: Dodd, Mead & Co., 1928.

———. *Mind Makes Men Giants*. New York: Dodd, Mead & Co., 1926.

MANN, STELLA TERRILL. *Change Your Life through Faith and Work*. New York: Dodd, Mead & Co., 1953.

———. *Change Your Life through Love*. New York: Dodd, Mead & Co., 1949.

————. *Change Your Life through Prayer*. New York: Dodd, Mead & Co., 1945.

————. *How to Use the Power of Your Word*. New York: Dodd, Mead & Co., 1955.

MARTIN, EVA. *Prentice Mulford, New Thought Pioneer*. 1921.

MILLS, JAMES PORTER. *From Existence to Life: The Science of Self-Consciousness*. New York: Edward J. Clode, 1916.

————. *Health: Omnipresence, Omniscience, Infinite, Abstract, and Concrete*. Washington, D.C.: B. S. Adams, 1908.

————. *Mind's Silent Partner: The High Counsellor Within*. New York: Brentanos Publishers, 1922.

————. *A New Order of Meditation*. New York: Brentanos Publishers, 1915.

MORGAN, ANGELA. *Gold on Your Pillow*. Los Angeles: DeVorss & Co., 3rd printing, 1952.

————. *The Imprisoned Splendor*. New York: Baker, Taylor, 1915.

————. *Selected Poems*. New York: Dodd, Mead & Co., 1927.

MORGAN, HENRY VICTOR. *The Healing Christ: Studies in the Science of Jesus*. Tacoma: Master Christian Publishing Co., 1917.

————. *Hymns of Health and Gladness: New Words to Old Tunes*. Tacoma: Master Christian Publishing Co., 1917.

————. *Songs of Victory*. Chicago: The Library Shelf, 1911.

————. *The Spirit Singing and Other Poems*. Tacoma: Master Christian Publishing Co., 1921.

MULFORD, PRENTICE. *Your Forces and How to Use Them*. ("White Cross Library.") 6 vols. New York: F. J. Needham, 1888-92.

MURPHY, JOSEPH. *How to Use Your Healing Power*. San Gabriel, Calif.: Willing Publishing Co., 1957.

————. *Love Is Freedom*. San Gabriel, Calif.: Willing Publishing Co., 2nd ed., revised and enlarged, 1952.

————. *The Magic of Faith*. San Gabriel, Calif.: Willing Publishing Co., 1954.

————. *The Meaning of Reincarnation*. San Gabriel, Calif.: Willing Publishing Co., 1954.

————. *The Miracles of Your Mind*. San Gabriel, Calif.: Willing Publishing Co., 1953; rev. ed., 1955.

————. *Peace within Yourself*. San Gabriel, Calif.: Willing Publishing Co., 1956.

————. *Pray Your Way through It*. San Gabriel, Calif.: Willing Publishing Co., 1958.

————. *Prayer Is the Answer*. San Gabriel, Calif.: Willing Publishing Co., 1956.

————. *Techniques in Prayer Therapy*. San Gabriel, Calif.: Willing Publishing Co., 1960.

————. *Traveling with God*. San Gabriel: Willing Publishing Co., 1956.

MURRAY, W. JOHN. *The Astor Lectures*. New York: Divine Science Publishing Association, 1917.

————. *Mental Medicine*. New York: Divine Science Publishing Association, 1923.

————. *The Necessity of Law*. New York: Divine Science Publishing Association, 1924.

————. *New Thoughts on Old Doctrines*. New York: Divine Science Publishing Association, 1918.

————. *The Realm of Reality*. New York: Divine Science Publishing Association, 1922.

————. *The Sanity of Optimism*. New York: Divine Science Publishing Association, 1918.

NEVILLE (GODDARD, NEVILLE LANCELOT). *Awakened Imagination*. Los Angeles: G. & J. Publishing Co., 1954.

————. *The Power of Awareness*. Los Angeles: G. & J. Publishing Co., 1952.

————. *Your Faith Is Your Fortune*. New York: Goddard Publications, 1946.

RIX, HARRIET HALE. *Christian Mind Healing*. Los Angeles: Master Mind Publishing Co., 1914.

ST. JOHNS, ADELA ROGERS. *Affirmative Prayer in Action*. New York: Dodd, Mead & Co., 1957.

SCOTT, CLARA H. (ed.). *Truth in Song*. New York: R. F. Fenno & Co., 1896.

SEARS, F. W. *How to Attract Success*. New York: New Thought Publishers, 1914.

————. *The Law of Cause and Effect*. New York: New Thought Publishers, 1912.

————. *New Thought Lectures*. 2 vols. New York: New Thought Publishers, 1913

SETON, JULIA. *Concentration, the Secret of Success*. New York: E. J. Clode, 1912.

————. *Destiny, a New Thought Novel*. New York: E. J. Clode, 1917.

————. *Freedom Talks*. New York: E. J. Clode, No. 1, 1906; No. 2, 1914.

————. *Fundamental Principles of the New Civilization*. New York: E. J. Clode, 1914.

————. *The Key to Health, Wealth and Love*. New York: E. J. Clode, 1917.

536   SPIRITS IN REBELLION

———. *The Science of Success*. New York: E. J. Clode, 1914.

Songs for the New Day. New Day Hymnal Association. Hollywood: House-Warven Publishers, 1953.

TRINE, RALPH WALDO. *The Best of Ralph Waldo Trine*. Indianapolis: Bobbs-Merrill Co., 1957.

———. *In Tune with the Infinite*. New York: Thomas Y. Crowell Co., 1897; Dodd, Mead & Co., 535th thousand, 1897; 625th thousand, 1921. Since 1933 published by Bobbs-Merrill, Indianapolis. Reprinted entire in *The Best of Ralph Waldo Trine*.

———. *The Higher Powers of Mind and Spirit*. New York: Dodge Publishing Co., 1913.

———. *The Power That Wins*. Indianapolis: Bobbs-Merrill Co., 1929.

———. *This Mystical Life of Ours*. New York: Thomas Y. Crowell Co., 1907.

———. *The Winning of the Best*. New York: Dodge, 1912.

Unity Song Selections. Lee's Summit, Mo.: Unity School of Christianity. Rev. ed., 1935; 7th printing, 1962.

WELTMER, ERNEST. *Realization: The Story of a Climber*. Nevada, Mo.: Weltmer Institute of Suggestive Therapeutics Co., 1912.

———. *Relaxation, Health and Happiness: How to Live Efficiently, Healthily, Abundantly*. Nevada, Mo.: Weltmer Institute of Suggestive Therapeutics Co., 1928.

———. *The Secret of Power*. Nevada, Mo.: Weltmer Institute of Suggestive Therapeutics Co., 1928.

WELTMER, S. A. *The Healing Hand: Teaching the Principles of Healing through Suggestion*. Nevada, Mo.: Weltmer Institute of Suggestive Therapeutics Co., 1922.

———. *The Real Man*. Nevada, Mo.: Weltmer Institute of Suggestive Therapeutics Co., 1901.

———. *Suggestion Simplified*. Nevada, Mo.: Weltmer Institute of Suggestive Therapeutics Co., 1900.

———. *The Weltmer Brief Course in Practical Psychology: A Key to Success, Health and Happiness*. Nevada, Mo.: Weltmer Institute of Suggestive Therapeutics Co., 1924.

WHIPPLE, LEANDER EDMUND. *A Manual of Mental Science*. New York: American School of Metaphysics, 1911.

———. *Mental Healing*. New York: Metaphysics Publishing Co., 5th rev. ed., 1905.

———. *The Philosophy of Mental Healing*. New York: Metaphysics Publishing Co., 1893; 3rd ed., 1901.

———. *Practical Health*. New York: Metaphysics Publishing Co., 1907.

WILCOX, ELLA WHEELER. *The Art of Being Alive: Success through Thought.* New York: Harper & Bros., 1914.

——. *The Heart of New Thought.* Chicago: Psychic Research Co., 1902; 17th ed., Chicago: New Thought Book Publishing Co., 1904; London: L. N. Fowler & Co.

——. *New Thought and Common Sense: What Life Means to Me.* Chicago: W. B. Conkey, 1908.

——. *Poems of Power.* Chicago: W. B. Conkey, 1903.

——. *The World and I: An Autobiography.* New York: George H. Doran Co., 1915.

WILMANS, HELEN (POST). *The Conquest of Death.* Sea Breeze, Fla.: International Scientific Association, 1899.

——. *A Conquest of Poverty.* Sea Breeze, Fla.: International Scientific Association, 1899.

——. *Home Course of Instruction in Mental Healing.* Douglasville, Ga.: Privately printed, 1890.

——. *A Search for Freedom.* Sea Breeze, Fla.: International Scientific Association, 1898.

WILSON, ERNEST C. *Have You Lived Other Lives?* New York: Prentice-Hall, 1956.

WILSON, MARGERY. *Believe in Yourself.* Philadelphia: J. B. Lippincott Co., 1948.

WOOD, HENRY. *Edward Burton: An Idealistic Metaphysical Novel.* Boston: Lee & Shepard Co., 1890; 8th ed., 1901.

——. *God's Image in Man.* Boston: Lee & Shepard Co., 1892.

——. *Has Mental Healing a Valid Scientific and Religious Basis?* Boston: Lee & Shepard Co., 1895.

——. *Ideal Suggestion through Mental Photography.* Boston: Lee & Shepard Co., 1893.

——. *The New Old Healing.* Boston: Lothrop, Lee & Shepard Co., 1908.

——. *The New Thought Simplified: How to Gain Harmony and Health.* Boston: Lothrop, Lee & Shepard Co., 1908.

——. *Studies in the Thought World: Or Practical Mind Art.* Boston: Lee & Shepard Co., 1896.

——. *The Symphony of Life.* Boston: Lee & Shepard Co., 1901.

——. *Victor Serenus: A Story of the Pauline Era.* Boston: Lee & Shepard Co., 1898.

ZAGAT, HELEN. *Faith and Works.* New York: Divine Unity Press, 1955.

ZWEIG, STEFAN. *Mental Healers: Anton Mesmer, Mary Baker Eddy, Sigmund Freud.* Garden City, N.Y.: Garden City Publishing Co., 1932.

Books about New Thought or Its Constituent Groups

ATKINS, GAIUS GLENN. *Modern Cults and Religious Movements.* Westwood, N. J.: Fleming H. Revell Co., 1923.

BACH, MARCUS. *They Have Found a Faith.* Indianapolis: Bobbs-Merrill Co., 1946.

BRADEN, CHARLES S. *These Also Believe.* New York: Macmillan Co., 1949.

————. *Varieties of American Religion.* Chicago: Willett, Clark & Co., 1936.

JAMES, WILLIAM. *Varieties of Religious Experience.* New York: Longmans, Green & Co., 1902.

RANDALL, J. H. *A New Philosophy of Life.* New York: Dodge Publishing Co., 1909.

REGARDIE, ISRAEL R. *The Romance of Metaphysics: An Introduction to the History, Theory, and Psychology of Modern Metaphysics.* Chicago: Aries Press, 1946.

ROSTEN, LEO (ed.). *Guide to the Religions of America.* New York: Simon & Schuster, 1955.

SPENCE, HARTZELL. *The Story of America's Religions.* New York: Holt, Rinehart & Winston, 1960.

Index

Index